Africa and the Disruptions of the Twenty-first Century

For Skip
In admiration and
appreciation for your
extraordinary contributions
to scholarship and
the emancipation of
the African diaspora
and Africa.

Paul Tiyambe Zeleza
Nairobi, February 24, 2021

This book is part of the CODESRIA Book Series.

Africa and the Disruptions of the Twenty-first Century

Paul Tiyambe Zeleza

CODESRIA

Council for the Development of Social Science Research in Africa
DAKAR

Council for the Development of Social Science Research in Africa
Avenue Cheikh Anta Diop, Angle Canal IV
BP 3304 Dakar, 18524, Senegal
Website: www.codesria.org

ISBN: 978-2-86978-997-5

Typesetting: Alpha Ousmane DIA
Cover Design: Genevieve Simpson

Distributed in Africa by CODESRIA
Distributed elsewhere by African Books Collective, Oxford, UK
Website: www.africanbookscollective.com

The Council for the Development of Social Science Research in Africa (CODESRIA) is an independent organisation whose principal objectives are to facilitate research, promote research-based publishing and create multiple forums for critical thinking and exchange of views among African researchers. All these are aimed at reducing the fragmentation of research in the continent through the creation of thematic research networks that cut across linguistic and regional boundaries.

CODESRIA publishes *Africa Development*, the longest standing Africa based social science journal; Afrika Zamani, a journal of history; the *African Sociological Review*; *Africa Review of Books* and the *Journal of Higher Education in Africa*. The Council also co-publishes *Identity, Culture and Politics: An Afro-Asian Dialogue; and the Afro-Arab Selections for Social Sciences*. The results of its research and other activities are also disseminated through its Working Paper Series, Book Series, Policy Briefs and the CODESRIA Bulletin. All CODESRIA publications are accessible online at www.codesria.org.

CODESRIA would like to express its gratitude to the Swedish International Development Cooperation Agency (SIDA), the Carnegie Corporation of New York (CCNY), Andrew W. Mellon Foundation, the Open Society Foundations (OSFs), UNESCO, Oumou Dilly Foundation, Ford Foundation and the Government of Senegal for supporting its research, training and publication programmes.

Contents

IV
Africa's Persistent Mythologisation

V
Disruptions in Higher Education

Epilogue
In Memory of Two Intellectual Icons

Preface

I write this preface in the midst of the coronavirus pandemic and lockdowns in many countries around the world, including Kenya where I currently live. A major crisis is not only hugely disruptive, it always holds a giant mirror to society and in this case to the world at large, exposing its underlying structural deformities and dysfunctions.

The coronavirus pandemic offers a stark reflection of national and global political economies in disarray and the colossal underinvestments in the economic and social well-being of the masses of working people. Engendering the multiple crises brutally pried open by the pandemic were the austerities, inequalities and ideological inanities of neoliberal globalisation, retrogressive populisms and wanton assaults on nature and the environment.

The essays in this volume seek to make sense of the various disruptions and dysfunctions of the early twenty-first century for Africa, of which the coronavirus pandemic is sadly symptomatic. They were written from two locations, namely, the United States where I lived for more than two decades and Kenya where I moved to take up a new position in January 2016.

Thus, they reflect discourses from mutually reinforcing spatiotemporal positions, in North America and Africa, the global North and the global South, the African continent and the diaspora. As such, the essays combine observations and analyses of developments in these spaces that particularly intrigued me or struck me as significant. In short, they represent my personal meditations as an engaged Pan-African scholar and global citizen on key developments during the second decade and beginning of the third decade of the twenty-first century.

The essays first appeared in various outlets. Some were presented as keynote addresses. Others were published in the traditional media. Many more were posted as blogs on social media. Several were transposed from one medium to another. But they all retain, with minor adjustments, their original content and flavour. For each essay, I have indicated the date on which it was written or delivered. This opens a window into both the framing of public debates and my own perspectives at the time the different essays were written.

As always, my writings benefit from numerous engagements with my extensive network of intellectual friends, collaborators and critics in various parts of the world, especially the transatlantic Pan-African world. I would like to thank all of them for the intellectual sustenance I derive from them. I trust they will understand that I have refrained from naming them individually to avoid making this preface too long and for fear of missing out anyone.

But I trust it is in order to mention Cassandra Rachel Veney, my life partner, best friend and intellectual interlocutor who is always the first person to read anything I write before it leaves our intimate and exclusive conversations and enters the public realm. She is incredibly incisive in her comments and critiques, thorough in picking up poor writing and awkward expressions and generous in her prodding for greater clarity in my arguments and backup evidence.

As I get older, I become more preoccupied, counterintuitively, with the future of my beloved continent, our global diaspora and the world at large. I am keener than ever about the quality of education we give our young people and the mentoring that the members of my generation provide to younger scholars. I am worried about the world we have created for future generations. But I am also more hopeful as I watch and witness the amazing energy, imagination, creativity, agency and fearlessness of young people.

I dedicate this book to the young people in my personal and professional life, including my students at USIU-Africa and other universities at which I taught in recent years, and to the young members of my transnational extended family. I hope they will continue striving to create a better world than the one recorded in this book.

Nairobi, 25 July 2020

List of Abbreviations

AAU	African Association of Universities
ACB	Anti-Corruption Bureau
ADB	Asian Development Bank
AFL-CIO	American Federation of Labor
ANC	African National Congress
ASA	African Studies Association
AU	African Union
BRICS	Brazil, Russia, India, China and South Africa
CADFP	Carnegie African Diaspora Fellowship Program
CARES	Coronavirus Aid, Relief, and Economic Security
CARICOM	Caribbean Community
CBC	Congressional Black Caucus
CCNY	Carnegie Corporation of New York
CIA	Central Intelligence Agency
CNN	Cable News Network
CODESRIA	Council for the Development of Social Science Research in Africa
COSATU	Congress of South African Trade Unions
DMC	Developing Member Countries
DPP	Democratic People's Party
ECOWAS	Economic Community of West African States
EEQ	Essential employability qualities
EFF	Economic Freedom Fighters
EMDEs	Emerging Market and Developing Economies
EU	European Union
FAO	Food and Agriculture Organization

FBI	Federal Bureau of Investigation
FDI	Foreign Direct Investment
FKE	Federation of Kenya Employers
FTSE	Financial Times Stock Exchange Group
GDP	Gross Domestic Product
GDPR	General Data Protection Regulation
GNU	Government of National Unity
HBCUs	Historically Black Colleges and Universities
HELB	Higher Education Loans Board
HNWI	High Net Worth Individuals
HPC	High-performance Computing
HRDC	Human Rights Defenders Coalition
HWCUs	Historically White Colleges and Universities
IBM	International Business Machines Corporation
ICT	Information and Communication Technology
IEBC	Independent Electoral and Boundaries Commission
ILO	International Labour Organization
IMF	International Monetary Fund
IPCC	Intergovernmental Panel on Climate Change
IUCEA	Inter-University Council of East Africa
KCSE	Kenya Certificate of Secondary Education
KENET	Kenya Educational Network
MCP	Malawi Congress Party
MDC	Movement for Democratic Change
MEC	Malawi Electoral Commission
MERCUSOR	Southern Common Market
MINT	Mexico, Indonesia, Nigeria, Turkey
MOOC	Massive Open Online Course
NAACP	National Association for the Advancement of Colored People
NAFTA	North American Free Trade Agreement
NASCAR	National Association for Stock Car Auto Racing
NATO	North Atlantic Treaty Organization
NFL	National Football League
NGO	Non-governmental Organisations
NHIF	National Hospital Insurance Fund
NPO	Non-profit Organisations

NSSF	National Social Security Fund
OAU	Organisation of African Unity
OAU	Organisation of African Unity
ODA	Official Development Assistance
OECD	Organisation for Economic Co-operation and Development
OPEC	Organization of the Petroleum Exporting Countries
PAC	Public Affairs Committee
PBO	Public Benefit Organisations
PPP	Purchasing Power Parity
PPPs	Public–private Partnerships
R&D	Research and Development
SADC	Southern African Development Community
SAP	Structural Adjustment Programmes
SAPs	Structural Adjustment Programmes
SARUA	Southern African Regional Universities Association
SEL	Social and Emotional Learning
STEM	Science, technology, engineering, and mathematics
TFT	Targeted Free Tuition
TTTI	Testing, Tracking, Tracing and Isolation
UDF	United Democratic Front
UK	United Kingdom
UN	United States
UNDP	United Nations Development Programme
UNESCO	United Nations Educational, Scientific and Cultural Organization
UNRISD	United Nations Research Institute for Social Development
US	United States
USA	United Stated of America
USIU-Africa	United States International University Africa
USSR	Union of Soviet Socialist Republics
UTM	United Transformation Movement
WEO	World Economic Outlook
WHO	World Health Organization
ZANU-PF	Zimbabwe African National Union – Patriotic Front

About the Author

Paul Tiyambe Zeleza, has been at a dozen universities in six countries on three continents and the Caribbean region. He held distinguished academic and senior administrative positions in Canada and the United States for 25 years before taking the position of Vice Chancellor (President) and Professor of the Humanities and Social Sciences at the United States International University-Africa in January 2016. He has published more than 300 journal articles, book chapters, reviews, short stories and online essays and authored or edited 28 books, several of which have won international awards. He has presented about 250 keynote addresses, papers, and public lectures at leading universities and international conferences in 32 countries and served on the editorial boards of more than two dozen journals and book series. He presently serves as Editor-in-Chief of the Oxford Bibliographies Online in African Studies. He is currently a member of the Administrative Board of the International Association of Universities, the Advisory Board of the Alliance for African Partnership, as well as Chair of the Advisory Council of the Carnegie African Diaspora Fellowship Program that he helped establish, Chair of the Board of Trustees of the Kenya Education Network, and is a member of the University of Ghana Council.

Introduction

This collection of essays contains reflections on some critical issues that have preoccupied me since I published my last two books, namely, *Africa's Resurgence: Domestic, Global and Diaspora Transformations*[1] (2014) and *The Transformation of a Global Higher Education, 1945–2015*[2] (2016). In many ways, the essays represent continued analyses of issues discussed in those two books and my earlier work. They centre on my interest in African and global political economies, social and intellectual history, especially how Africa is studied and constructed, and the histories and roles of African diasporas in the pasts, present and futures of their ancestral continent.

We live in exceptionally turbulent times marked by challenges that require urgent redress. There is the rise of dangerous populism fuelled by deepening inequalities and political and social alienation. For the Pan-African world, this is reflected in the resurgence of racism against Africans and the diaspora, as evident in the United States under the unhinged presidency of Donald Trump. There are recessions of development and democracy in many parts of the world. Global hegemonic rivalries are intensifying with dangerous consequences for world peace and security. Moreover, the sustainability of human life on this fragile, vulnerable and increasingly devastated planet is clearly under threat.

Moments like this require sustained research and reflection and strategic policy initiatives and interventions. As a scholar, I find it disconcerting that universities, which should serve as factories and marketplaces of generative ideas, are not doing so adequately. Higher education institutions have become more self-referential than ever, divorced from the unstable and unsustainable worlds around them. Academics in many institutions and societies have largely abandoned aspirations for public intellectual engagements. Universities seem to wallow in the narcissism of institutional competitiveness and rankings as their academics indulge in theoretical and disciplinary navel-gazing, oblivious to the great questions facing humanity.

The poverty of thinking is particularly evident in African universities. Since returning to the continent in 2016, I have been struck by how little intellectual debate takes place on our university campuses compared to the 1970s and even the lost decade of the 1980s when I was a student and a young lecturer. The consultancy syndrome that took root during the 1980s, which grossly undermined research cultures and productivity in African universities, is now reinforced by adjuncting. The latter is a product of the rapid increase of universities without the commensurate growth in faculty.

The paltry remuneration of faculty, a legacy of the assault on higher education that began in the 1980s, further facilitates adjuncting. The wobbly edifice of African higher education rests on the pervasive and perverse anti-intellectualism of contemporary African states and societies. For many, going to university is not about getting educated, immersing oneself in the infinitely fascinating, enlightening and empowering world of ideas, but about acquiring credentials. No wonder academic fraud, manifest in contract cheating, sex for grades and other corrupt practices, is running rampant in many higher education institutions across the continent.

In short, the quality of intellectual discourse has declined precipitously. Increasingly, half-baked, hurriedly written and often angry exchanges on social media are replacing reasoned argument and public engagement. The quality of teaching and learning is also lower than it was in the 1960s and 1970s when my generation went to college. This is not simply nostalgia for an ageing generation but is evident to faculty who believe in academic rigour and to employers looking for skilled graduates.

To be sure, there are far more universities enrolling much larger numbers of students than ever before, which is a good thing. However, many African universities are no better than glorified high schools, dominated by unqualified academics and poorly administered. The result is masses of unemployable graduates and insignificant contributions to the knowledge production needed to solve pressing national, regional and global challenges.

These are some of the issues I discuss at length in this book. The book is divided into five parts. Part I is on America's Racial Dysfunctions. I start with the United States intentionally. It partly reflects the fact that I spent the longest period of my personal and professional life in that country, whose citizenship I also carry. In addition, Pan-Africanism and the diaspora condition are integral to my political, professional and personal identities.

The existence of the diaspora reminds us about the globality of Africa, that the histories of the continent and its peoples are an essential part of world history – what happens in the world affects Africa and vice versa. This is an antidote against isolationist views of Africa, about its assumed eternal marginality. Both outside observers and Africans themselves often articulate these views, although from different vantage points.

Specifically, in this section, I explore the enduring legacies of America's foundational matrix – slavery and its persistence and mutation over generations. I discuss the racial violence that ravages African-American communities, through policing and the racist underbelly of the Republican Party that is evident in the party's austere and reactionary ideology and policies, which fostered the election of an openly bigoted President Trump.

Also examined is the meaning of the 400th commemoration of the arrival of the first enslaved Africans in what is today the United States, in 1619. At stake is how the United States, the diaspora and Africa remember and reckon with the monumental history of the Atlantic slave trade, which ushered in the modern capitalist system in all its dimensions and dynamics, complexities and contradictions.

Part I closes with a reflection on the brutal murder by police of George Floyd in Minneapolis on 25 May 2020, which provoked the largest protests in American history and which spread to many parts of the world. The Floyd protests forced the US and many other countries around the world to confront the enduring legacies of anti-black racism, white supremacy and racial capitalism.

Continuing with the rationale of Part I, Part II focuses on Navigating Global Turbulence. In it, I discuss various dimensions and manifestations of the worldwide disorders of the 2010s and their possible legacies for the 2020s. These range from the imperial nostalgia and fantasies of Brexit, which rocked Europe, to the new superpower hegemonic rivalries between the United States and China, which will likely dominate the world political economy during the first half of the twenty-first century.

In one chapter I summarise and examine the six key trends that characterised the 2010s, namely: how tribalism went global; worldwide democratic recessions and resistance; rising economic disequilibrium; shifting global hierarchies and hegemonies; the emergence of surveillance capitalism; and what I call the rebellion of nature. The turbulence was evident everywhere, although it was mediated by a particular constellation of national and regional forces and geopolitical locations.

The decade closed with the outbreak of the coronavirus pandemic, the devastations of which on global health, economies, societies, governments and institutions are still unfolding at the time of writing. This is the subject of another chapter in this section. It is hard to predict the kind of world that will emerge from the pandemic. Some current studies and reports variously suggest or wish for profound transformations or a return to the recent normal. But the pandemic has already made history in the massive disruptions and devastation it has caused and in the dysfunctions it has revealed.

The section ends with a chapter on diaspora engagements and contributions to Africa. The diaspora mediates the continent's capacities to navigate the global order and division of labour. The chapter underscores the pivotal role the historic diaspora played in the development of Pan-Africanism, out of which the territorial nationalisms that led to independence were incubated. It also analyses the economic, social and intellectual contributions of the new diaspora. I briefly examine a project I played a role in establishing, the Carnegie African Diaspora Fellowship Program, which seeks to promote what I call 'intellectual remittances' from the diaspora to the continent.

Part III dwells on Africa's Political Dramas. Anchoring the discussion are momentous political events the continent has experienced since it embarked on the bumpy road to democracy, following the onset of struggles for the 'second independence' in the 1980s and 1990s. At the juncture of the struggles for the 'first independence' – decolonisation in the 1950s and 1960s – and the 'second independence' – democratisation in the 1980s and 1990s – are South Africa and the iconic Nelson Mandela.

Thus, the section opens with a chapter on Mandela's Long Walk with African History, which places the stories of South Africa and Mandela in the mainstream of African nationalist struggles and historiography. President Zuma's kleptocratic regime, discussed in another chapter, squandered the promises of Mandela's rainbow nation. In 2017, South Africa's northern neighbour, Zimbabwe, overthrew its octogenarian and autocratic leader, President Mugabe. Zimbabwe tragically embodies the complicated and failed transition from national liberation to the construction of a viable, developmental democracy that is true of many postcolonial states. In contrast, the nullification of elections in two older and equally troubled postcolonial states – Kenya, in September 2017, and Malawi, in February 2020 – show the possibilities of building democratic cultures and systems. These divergent trajectories within and among countries underscore the complexities and contradictions of African political economies and unfolding political cultures that transcend the unilineal progression and predictability beloved by positivist social science or the unrelieved Afro-pessimism peddled by Africa's detractors.

In Part IV, Africa's Persistent Mythologisation, I return to my perennial preoccupation with the construction of negative images and knowledge of Africa. I begin by discussing how the 2014 Ebola outbreak was portrayed. Through the trafficking of old, sterile stereotypes, the continent and African bodies were viciously denigrated. The pernicious disparagement, diminution, dehumanisation and homogenisation of Africa reached an apogee when President Trump lampooned its 'shithole' countries. So deep is the miseducation and misinformation on Africa that even self-avowedly progressive commentators and cultural producers find it hard to escape the tropes of Eurocentrism. This is evident in the widely acclaimed movie, Black Panther, a homage to Afro-futurism that unwittingly reprises the colonial gaze.

In other chapters in this section, I analyse more directly the questions of decolonising and constructing more accurate and empowering African knowledges. As I argue in one of the chapters, it is critical for African scholars and students to understand Africa's divergent libraries, of which the colonial library is only one. We need to continue the project of constructing a synthesis of these libraries and creating epistemologies that enable us to understand Africa and its peoples, societies, economies, polities and ecologies, and their bewildering complexities, contradictions and continuous transformations.

In the last chapter in this section, I revisit the trajectories of African studies especially in the United States, whose model influenced African studies in other world regions notwithstanding their differences and specificities. I discuss the fierce contestations between the three Africas of African studies – of European-American Africanists, African-American scholar-activists and African migrant academics. I propose ways forward including the integration of African and diaspora studies and the revitalisation of African universities, especially in terms of their research capacities.

The issue of universities is the subject of Part V, Disruptions in Higher Education. I begin by summarising what I see as the six capacity challenges of African universities. They are institutional supply, resource deficits, faculty shortages and research underperformance, as well as the low quality of graduate outputs and weak governance and leadership. Subsequent chapters elaborate on these issues.

One looks at the value proposition of higher education as reflected in the persistent challenges of employability for university graduates. This problem is of course not confined to Africa, as it is evident among developed countries, which suggests the limits of pervasive academic capitalism. Another reflects on the unequal and uneven patterns of internationalisation in African universities and the perennial struggles between internationalisation and indigenisation in African higher education institutions.

A key challenge facing universities around the world centres on the Fourth Industrial Revolution. I review the conceptual debates in and the likely impact of this revolution on higher education given changes in the future of work. The trends spawned by the revolution for universities include digital disruptions in all aspects of the higher education enterprise, meeting rising demands for public service and engagement, unbundling of the degree and escalating imperatives for lifelong learning. The section concludes with a chapter pondering the financial crises facing universities from the United States to Kenya and some of the possible solutions.

I close the book with an epilogue in which I pay tribute to two extraordinary African public intellectuals, Ali Mazrui and Thandika Mkandawire, who left us in October 2014 and March 2020, respectively. These two iconic giants, whom I had the privilege of knowing personally in different ways, represented the essence of a meaningful and transformative intellectual life that I believe we should all try to emulate in our own ways. They were committed Pan-Africanists and global citizens, driven by a passion for ideas, an abiding conviction that ideas matter, and that deep, critical and engaged thinking is indispensable for the progressive transformation of Africa, the diaspora and the world at large.

As always, the inscriptions of my social biography inspire my writing and reflections. They are part of my deep-seated curiosity and enduring efforts to engage in prevailing debates in the African, diaspora and global intellectual circles in which I am immersed. I hope to contribute to those debates and provoke further debate.

I believe, as public intellectuals, we have a responsibility to enlighten ourselves as individuals, each other as communities and our societies about some of the pressing epistemic and existential challenges we face in our highly unequal and insecure world. This is my modest contribution reflecting my thoughts over the last several years since the publication of my last two books.

Notes

1. Paul Tiyambe Zeleza, Africa's *Resurgence: Domestic, Global and Diaspora Transformations*, Los Angeles: TSEHAI Publishers, 2014.
2. Paul Tiyambe Zeleza, *The Transformation of Global Higher Education, 1945–2015*, New York: Palgrave Macmillan, 2016.

I

America's Racial Dysfunctions

1

America's Enduring Racial Sin

The names are added to the long hall of infamy with sickening, stultifying regularity. In the early 2010s they included Trayvon Martin, Michael Brown, Eric Garner, Tamir Rice and all those black boys and men sacrificed at the altar of America's racism, the country's enduring original sin. This primordial transgression, its staying power, its infinite capacities to make a mockery of the country's vain self-congratulation as the land of freedom, democracy and the rule of law, confronts each generation of Americans. Their nation's claim falls on deaf ears for its minority citizens and the outside world, who experience and see the hypocrisies, contradictions and inconsistencies spawned by the destructive deformities of racism.

The degeneracy of American racism runs deep, rooted in more than two centuries of slavery, the foundational matrix of American society, economy and politics. It was renewed and recast during a century of Jim Crow laws. It survived and mutated over the next half century of civil rights. It persisted in the Obama era, confounding misplaced expectations of a postracial society that the election of the country's first black president was magically supposed to usher in.

Each generation of African Americans faces eruptions of this racial degeneracy, most tragically captured in deadly assaults by police on unarmed black males, which predictably provoke widespread local and national protests. Each moment acquires its symbols and slogans. In 2014, it was Ferguson and the battle cry 'Hands Up Don't Shoot', and New York and Eric Garner's plaintive cry for life, 'I Can't Breathe'. Both became rallying anthems of protest across the nation following the grand jury decisions not to indict the police officers who killed the two men.

Outrage often centres on altercations between the law enforcement agencies and African-American communities because of the racial disproportionalities in surveillance, profiling, arrests and sentencing. Mountains of data show that African Americans are subject to forms of policing that are far more excessive, abusive and disrespectful than European Americans are. This has resulted in the creation of an American gulag of black imprisonment, a prison pipeline especially for black males from the schools, streets and sidewalks of America.

The broken relations between African-American communities and law enforcement agencies represent the contemporary forms of America's age-old racial structures, hierarchies and ideologies. The exponential growth of a black prison industrial complex in the era following the Civil Rights struggles constitutes the country's new Jim Crow regime of existential, economic and epistemic violence against black lives, black well-being and black citizenship.

Police brutality and unaccountability for violence against African Americans is facilitated by and a manifestation of the wider society's values, expectations and interests. The challenge is not simply to provide the police with better training or technologies, although that would help. Lest we forget, video footage captured Eric Garner's death and yet the grand jury still refused to indict the police officer. In a bygone era, public lynchings were spectacles of morbid public entertainment. The real issue is the value placed on black lives, black bodies and black humanity by American society.

The discourse by the police and their supporters often taps into persistent racial codes: the bodies of the black victims are full of brawn, not brains, depicted as embodiments of some fearsome bestial power that threatens their police interlocutors, which can be tamed only by superior weapons and intelligence. The police officer who killed Michael Brown described him as an overpowering Hulk Hogan 'demon' who 'grunted' and charged at him like a mindless animal. A Republican Congressman blamed Eric Garner for his own death, saying, 'If he had not had asthma and a heart condition and was so obese, he would not have died from this.' In another instance, twelve-year-old Tamir Rice was mistaken for a twenty-year-old, a homage to the black man-child stereotype of racial discourse in white supremacist America – and colonial Africa.

Each generation of Americans is forced to reckon with the journey it has travelled towards racial equality. It discovers that while progress has been made, the distance it has travelled from the past, from the original sin of slavery, is much shorter than the road ahead. Each generation of African Americans is given no choice but to renew the struggles of previous generations against America's racial degeneracy.

The complicity of the wider society in its perpetuation, the cognitive inability to take race and racism seriously, the political refusal to address it systematically, the obliviousness of too many people to its destructiveness for not only its victims but also its perpetrators and beneficiaries – these all mark America's racial backwardness and sustain its cowardice. Racism diminishes the entire society, robbing it of its citizens' full human potential; it leaves in its trail a horrendous wastage of human resources and lives.

America's failure to have a concerted conversation on race and racism is not surprising, for too much is at stake for too many people, interests and institutions. However, racism will not disappear by ignoring it, dismissing it or wishing it away through fanciful invocations of a postracial society or misguided censure against political correctness. Failure to address it will continue to erode the nation's moral, political and constitutional fibre and make it a global laughing stock by underscoring the glaring mismatch between what it preaches abroad and practises at home.

At the height of the Cold War and decolonisation, the United States lost hearts and minds in Africa, Asia and Latin America because of the racist treatment of its black citizens. In today's era of changing global hegemonies marked by 'the rise of the rest' in Asia, Africa and Latin America, the ancestral homelands of America's minorities, images of police violence against people of colour beamed from American cities diminish the country's global soft power that it so badly needs as its hard power erodes. Neighbours aware of abuse cannot respect a serial domestic abuser, as is the case for America in today's world of hyper-connectivity.

In so far as we are all raced, race and racism is our collective problem. It is not a black problem. It is an American and a global problem. We must find the courage and the honest language to address it with the seriousness it deserves in all aspects of our lives at individual, interpersonal, institutional, community, national and global levels. Only then will the colour bar of previous centuries be erased and future generations can begin to realise the possibilities that lie in the indivisible and interconnected nature of our collective humanity to build truly democratic, inclusive and humane societies.

This is what the lives, tragic deaths and memories of Trayvon Martin, Michael Brown, Eric Garner and Tamir Rice and countless others before and since mean to me. The struggle for racial justice remains a historical and humanistic imperative. As we say in southern Africa, the struggle for liberation continues—for our liberation as peoples of African descent from centuries of Euro-American racism, and for the humanisation and democratisation of our countries in the diaspora and the world at large.

First written 6 December 2014

2

Republicans, Racists and the Obama Derangement Syndrome

Watching the Trump phenomenon from outside the United Sates during the presidential election campaign in 2016 was a strange phenomenon. I was often asked to explain by puzzled observers how such a bombastic, obnoxious, moronic, misogynistic, chauvinistic, racist and hustler businessman with a record of serial bankruptcies could ever be a serious candidate, indeed a frontrunner in the Republican Party primaries, who seemed poised to win the nomination and might be within striking distance of capturing the presidency. Many were often surprised that I was not surprised.

Trump is a Republican creation, notwithstanding the ferocious civil war his candidacy, appeal and electoral victories unleashed in the party, the incredulity and panic he initially provoked among the party establishment. Trump articulates and represents with frightening clarity the Republican underbelly that same establishment has nurtured for generations, the party's enduring values – incurable racism, bigotry and intolerance, reflexive jingoism, nativism and imperial aggression. In Trump, the chickens of age-old white supremacy and modern neoconservatism came home to roost.

Trump is the ultimate embodiment of white racist rage in the Republican Party and American society triggered by the Obama Derangement Syndrome. Obama's historic presidential victory in 2008 turned up the heat of racist paranoia as it symbolically upended the stubborn racist order established by America's original sin, slavery; it subverted the abiding hierarchies and hypocrisies of white supremacy and black inferiority. Trump became the prophet of birtherism, the insane notion that Obama was not American-born, was not a real American, did not love the country and was a dangerous Muslim radical bent on the destruction of the United States.

The Republican Party shamelessly cultivated, courted, cuddled, celebrated and cheered on the birthers and other white supremacists. The party adopted unyielding opposition to President Obama's policies, even those borrowed from the Republicans, such as the Affordable Care Act, otherwise known as Obamacare, his signature achievement. They treated him with utmost personal disrespect and vowed to make him a one-term president. When their efforts spectacularly crashed in 2012, they sought to turn him into a failed president. In 2016, in an unprecedented break with tradition, the Republicans refused to hear the president's budget and flatly declined to consider his nomination to the Supreme Court to replace the deceased racist, Justice Antonin Scalia.

Republican obstructionism and intransigence, their contempt for government and governing, and their racist disdain for Obama paved the way for Trump, the hypocritical outsider and celebrity neofascist. Trump's bloated ego and desperate rhetoric to 'Make America Great Again' tapped into and inflamed the dark forces of white supremacy threatened by vast disruptive forces at home and abroad. Domestically, these included America's changing demographics and the rekindled struggles for equality, most powerfully represented by the Black Lives Matter movement spawned by police brutality. Globally, American power is in decline, sapped in part by the very historic geopolitical strategic blunders of the neoconservative wars in Afghanistan and Iraq, and the rise of new powers, especially China.

The Obama phenomenon connects these disparate developments in the collective mind of Republicans and white racists. This syndrome derives part of its power from the fact that Obama's election simultaneously underscored changes in American society and stoked fears of those changes by many whites, whose historical claim to privilege was embodied in the colour of their skin, not the content of their talents. No wonder there was a widely reported rise in self-destructiveness by so-called white Middle America, through suicide, alcoholism and an epidemic of substance abuse. These angry whites constitute the bedrock of Trump's campaign and followers. Thus, the Obama and Trump phenomena underscore both the erosion of racism by generations of civil rights struggles and its resurrection from the battered closets of white supremacy.

The Obama Derangement Syndrome offered a potential historic turning point in American politics on the scale of the realignments of the 1930s–1940s and the 1960s–1970s. The Roosevelt New Deal created a new coalition of the Democratic Party, which included African Americans who had drifted from the Republican Party, the Party of Lincoln. In the immediate aftermath of the successes of the Civil Rights movement, the Republican Party launched its Southern Strategy, which turned the support of the South from the Democrats to the Republicans.

The transformation was accelerated by the defection of the Reagan Democrats, voters who had been discomfited by the growing presence of minorities and women and their agendas in the party, and who found succour in the predominantly white and masculinist Republican Party. The Clinton administration had largely conceded to Republican hegemony with its New Democratic Coalition and Third

Way rightward centrism. Under President Obama, the Democratic Party not only recovered and flexed its long muted liberal voice, the Republicans lost the cultural wars and began spiralling into the tailspin of the Obama Derangement Syndrome. This was evident in the rise of the fundamentalist zealotry of the Tea Party and Washington's descent into shameless incivility and ungovernability.

Then, we witnessed the fracturing of the Republican Party under its incurable infection by the Obama Derangement Syndrome. This is one reason Obama was a historic president, notwithstanding all the limitations of his administration, both self-imposed and those inflicted by Republican obduracy. His era will be remembered for ushering in a possible realignment of American politics reminiscent of the interwar and post-civil rights eras. It seemed likely the future would be played, at least for a while, on terms his presidency had set in so far as a Trump presidency promised to undo Obama's legacy.

The Obama Derangement Syndrome is not confined, of course, to electoral politics, to the flirtations and fixations with Trump's dangerous buffoonery. It is apparent in other institutional contexts, from corporate boardrooms to college campuses and in the often-deadly encounters of black communities with police, in the backlash against diversity and inclusion, in the perverted discourses of white victimisation. The Obama Derangement Syndrome gave rise to the Tea Party and Trump phenomenon, which spawned new struggles for equality and inclusion spearheaded by the Black Lives Matter movement.

In the academy, the institutional context I am most familiar with, the Obama era initially seemed to open new possibilities for minority faculty, students and administrators but gradually gave way to the corrosive reversals of micro-aggression and the persistence, even reincarnations, of structural exclusions. For example, after I and another black administrator left a university in New England, far from the allegedly more racist South, the senior administration reverted to being blissfully all white. This would make Trump and his fervent supporters proud and at home there.

No wonder Trump is making electoral waves across the proverbial divides of the North and South. He is the Frankenstein created by Republicans and racists, inflamed and unhinged by the Obama Derangement Syndrome. He offers America an ugly mirror to its past, present and future in its failure to slay the beast of racism, bigotry and intolerance.

First written 28 March 2016

3

The Tragedy and Farce that is Trump's America

The world and many Americans reeled in shock and anxiety at the election of Donald Trump as the next president of this mighty, but deeply disunited and disoriented country. All but a handful of opinion polls had pointed to the victory of the incomparably experienced Hillary Clinton, to the historic possibility of electing America's first female president. However, they were utterly, unforgiveably, embarrassingly wrong. They couldn't pick up Trump's 'silent majority' of ordinary white voters, not just the unapologetic Alt-Right that had quietly cheered on the boisterous candidate who openly said in public what Republicans and racist whites said in private.

The postmortems on the polls and other failures of America's collective imagination that resulted in this stunning election result were brutal – on the rapacious role of the media in selling Trump for ratings and earnings; on the shortfalls of the candidacy and campaign of Hillary Clinton; on the relative turnout rates of the Trump and Clinton supporters; on the perfidious role of Russia, Wikileaks and the FBI. In this popular American political sport of endless punditry and second-guessing, few would take real responsibility for having enabled Trump, few in polite circles would own up to having voted for Trump, much as many whites in South Africa denied ever having been ardent supporters of apartheid as the noxiousness of the system attracted international opprobrium.

Americans chose Donald Trump, a dangerous buffoon, ill prepared and ill tempered for any serious job, let alone the presidency of a superpower, even one in decline. It would be no prediction to expect that America's slide into global ignominy would accelerate under Trump's predictably inept leadership and the country's apparently irreconcilable tribal polarisations. What does it say about a country that could elect such an unsavoury character and would hand all three branches of government to the stewardship of the Republican Party, a party that should have forfeited its right to rule for its glaring political sins of bigotry, obstructionism, myopia and incompetence?

Countries get the leaders they deserve. Only a racist electorate could vote for such an unabashed racist candidate. Only misogynists could find such an irredeemable misogynist appealing. Only xenophobes could go for such a dangerous xenophobe. Only those who do not realise American citizenship is premised on allegiance to an idea, not common bloodlines, could vouch for a proponent of racialised notions of citizenship. Only enraged and deranged white nationalists could pick such a frighteningly enraged and deranged white nationalist. Only nativist bigots and bullies could endorse such an insecure nativist bigot and bully. Only narcissists could show preference for a tax-dodging conman with no history of public service. Only unethical people could be attracted to a pathological liar and serial philanderer. Only those who do not believe in the rule of law could support such a lawless man. Only deplorables could elect such a deplorable leader.

Clearly, Trump's victory was a horrible reflection, to the country itself and the world at large, of the tragedy and farce that is America; the tragedy that such an unfit man could succeed America's first black president, a man of such remarkable talent and uncommon integrity, decency and commitment to public service. In a revolting twist of fate, President Obama had been replaced by the godfather of birtherism, the racist lie that Obama was not American-born, not a real American. His nemesis would dismantle Obama's legacy.

The tragedy would also be evident in the country's inability, and in the Euro-American world more generally as illustrated recently most graphically with Brexit, to deal effectively with inclusion, integration and inequality – to manage the inclusion of racial, ethnic and religious minorities and the integration of nations under rapid social change, to redress the inequalities engendered by the economic injustices and inanities of neoliberalism, that dangerous dogma that has reigned supreme since the turn of the 1980s and robbed tens of millions of people of decent livelihoods and even their lives, of opportunities and the promises of democratic society.

Therefore, in many parts of the world, the increasingly pauperised and neglected social classes left behind by the draconian injunctions and destructive interventions of neoliberalism turn to demagogues adept at riding on the misguided fantasies of the common person; demagogues who rail against the establishment and old or new marginal 'others'; demagogues cut from the same cloth of neoliberal zealotry that has wrecked the lives of working people and the middle classes; demagogues who are least able to resolve the crises of well-being of their fellow citizens.

This is to suggest that some of the biggest losers from the dangerous infatuation with Trump were his most ardent followers. African Americans have never been major beneficiaries of America's largesse, not even under President Obama, nor have the millions of Latino immigrants who toil in the underbelly of the American agricultural and service economy. Trump would not 'Make America Great Again', but would make it hate again with impunity. He would not bring back factory jobs that assured high-school-educated white men middle-class lifestyles. He would not restore their racist supremacy and deformed masculinities in a world so transformed by civil rights, feminist and gay rights struggles and victories in popular culture and imagination. Indeed, the antediluvian values, attitudes and policies of the Trump coalition in the White House, Congress and the judiciary would give these struggles a new lease of life.

For the world at large, Trump's election elicited different fears, perspectives and expectations. There were fears that postwar internationalism would be upended by isolationism, as the United States – its champion – wallowed in rabid white nationalism in a world where the 'coloured nations' were on an inexorable rise. International trade agreements, the structural face of neoliberal globalisation, were under threat from a potentially protectionist administration. The recent global compact on climate change, upon which the very future of humanity and our fragile little planet rests, would face renewed obstacles from one of the world's greatest polluters. Some predicted apocalypse, that the Trump presidency would lead to the demise of the west, as we have known it. Some even doubted the future of the NATO alliance under President Trump with his 'America First' doctrine.

Right-wing populist forces would be emboldened, especially in European democracies already rocked by Brexit. Dictatorships would cheer the triumph of Trump, the admirer of dictators and an aspiring autocrat. Putin's Russia, which had done its best to influence the US elections through cyber destabilisation, would be especially enchanted. The shambolic and invective-ridden US elections would be a godsend to Chinese propagandists who proclaimed the bankruptcy of American democracy and the superiority of the Chinese system.

The same sentiments would find expression in African and other democracies and dictatorships around the world. The structural and ideological underpinnings of US–Africa policy would not change much from the swings of the humanitarian and security paradigms that had been dominant over the past half-century. However, the developmental and democratic inflections that sanitised these policies in the previous Clinton, Bush and Obama administrations were likely to lose their currency.

Overall, the loss of the US democratic model may be a good thing for democrats and democracies in other parts of the world especially in the global South, including Africa. The Trump presidency separated out democratic theory and governance from the intertwined tyrannies of American universalism and exceptionalism. It demonstrated the hollowness of the idea of 'mature' democracies that African countries should import as turnkey projects. It opened up space for a serious and creative construction of African modes and modalities of inclusive, integrated, innovative democratic developmental states and societies. With Trump's election, everyone now knows, if they did not before, the American democratic emperor has no clothes. Let us proceed to make our own democratic clothes befitting our histories, struggles and desired futures.

On a more personal note, I found the election of Trump shocking but not entirely surprising. Shocking because like many people I had believed the polls. Unsurprising because having lived in the US for two decades I had come to realise how deeply racism, sexism and xenophobia are entrenched in American society and imagination. That is why I was so relieved to relocate to Kenya when I was fortunate enough to get a university leadership position. There, I could do my job and live without the debilitating psychic costs of always defending my humanity and professionalism as a black person. However, when I lived in the United States, whose citizenship I carry, I also came to value and will always do, the traditions of struggles for a more inclusive union by the marginalised minorities and women. The retrogressive and historically renegade Trump presidency is likely to rekindle and re-energise these struggles.

History is indeed a house of many mansions, where tragedies open new avenues of struggle and possibility. The Trump presidency will not be an exception.

First written 9 November 2016

4

Reckoning with 400 Years

Some 400 years ago, in late August 1619, a slave ship named *White Lion* landed on the shores of Point Comfort, in what is today Hampton, Virginia. On board were more than twenty African women and men. They had been seized from a Portuguese ship, *São João Bautista,* on its way from Angola to Veracruz in Mexico. Virginia, the first English colony in North America, had been formed only twelve years earlier, in 1607.

Thus, the two original sins of the country that would become the United States of America – the forcible seizure of the lands of the indigenous people and the deployment of forced labour from captive and later enslaved Africans – began almost simultaneously. The Africans were stolen people brought to build stolen lands, as I noted in the lead short story in my collection, *The Joys of Exile,*[1] published in 1994.

Remembrance and Resilience

I attended the First Landing Commemorative Weekend in Hampton, Virginia on 23 and 24 August, 2019. I did so partly for professional reasons as a historian who has done extensive work on African diasporas, and partly in homage to my acquired diaspora affiliations and the diaspora identities of some key members of my immediate family, including my wife and daughter.

In the events in which I participated, the stories and songs and performances of remembrance enraptured me. The powerful invocations of resilience, the unyielding demands for responsibility and reparations, and the yearnings for redemption and recovery from what some call Post Traumatic Slave Syndrome, inspired me.

The multitudinous, multiracial and multigenerational audiences bristled with anger, bitterness and bewilderment at the indescribable cruelties of slavery, segregation and persistent marginalisation of African Americans. However, there was also rejoicing at the abundant contributions, creativity and the sheer spirit of indomitability, survival and struggle over the generations. 'We still stand!', one speaker proclaimed with proud defiance, at which the audience beamed and chanted, 'Yes, we do!'

The scholars exercised their academic prowess as they methodically peeled away the layers of falsehoods, distortions and silences in the study of American history and society. They unravelled the legacies of slavery in every aspect of American life, from the structure and destructive inequities of American capitalism to what one called the criminal injustice system rooted in the slave patrols of the plantations, as well as the history of struggles for democracy, freedom and equality that progressively formed America's initially vacuous democratic ideals.

The artists and media practitioners assailed and celebrated the 400 years of pain and triumphs. They exhorted African Americans to tell and own their stories. A renowned CNN pundit reminded the audience that there are four centres of power in the United States, namely, Washington (politics), Wall Street (finance), Silicon Valley (digital technology) and Hollywood (media), and that African American activists have to target all of them, not just the first.

The politicians implored the nation to confront the difficult truths of American history with honesty and commitment. Two former governors and the current governor of Virginia paid tribute to the centrality of African Americans in US history and their role in bridging the yawning contradiction between the claims of representative democracy and the heinous original sin and exclusions of slavery. They proceeded to promise various policy remediations. Black members of Congress bemoaned the incomplete progress made in the march to freedom and inclusion and denounced the resurgence of hate, racism and white supremacy. An eleven-year-old orator electrified the crowd with his passionate plea for fostering a community of care and kindness that would make the ancestors proud.

Two hundred and forty-one years after the arrival of the first Africans in Hampton in the summer of 1860, the last ship that brought African captives to the shores of the United States landed north of Mobile, Alabama. The *Clotilda* brought 110 women, men and children. The Senegalese historian, Sylviane Diouf, has told their story with her characteristic care, compassion and eloquence in her book, *Dreams of Africa in Alabama.*[2]

The following year, in April 1860, the American Civil War broke out primarily over the institution of slavery. The abolition of slavery finally came in 1865. By then, hundreds of ships had plied the Atlantic and brought nearly half a million African captives to the United States. They and their descendants endured 246 years of servitude and slavery, a century of Jim Crow segregation and another half a century of an incomplete and contested civil rights settlement.

The African men and women who landed as captives in Hampton arrived out of two confluences of pillage: from Angola and in the Atlantic. They were pawns in the imperial rivalries and internecine wars engendered by the burgeoning slave-based Atlantic economy enveloping what became the insidious triangle of western Africa, western Europe and the Americas that emerged from the early 1500s.

Nevertheless, even in their subjugation they were history-makers. They became indispensable players in the construction of Atlantic economies and societies. In short, their history of servitude, which before long calcified into slavery, is the history of the United States of America, of the making of the modern world in all its complexities and contradictions, tragedies and triumphs, perils and possibilities.

By the time the first captive Africans arrived in Virginia, more than half a million Africans had already crossed the horrendous Middle Passage to the incipient Portuguese, Spanish and English colonies of South America and the Caribbean. In fact, Africans who came with the conquistadors from the Iberian Peninsula in both servitude and freedom had preceded them in other parts of North America. For example, the first recorded person of African descent to reach Port Royal – now, Nova Scotia, Canada – in 1604 was Mathieu Da Costa, a sailor and translator for French settlers from Portugal.

It is citical to remember that north-western Africans (often referred to as Moors, Muslims or Arabs in Eurocentric textbooks) had conquered the Iberian Peninsula in 711 and ruled parts of the Iberian Peninsula for eight centuries. Later, the descendants of Africans sometimes referred to as Afro-Iberians, having been brought as captives to Spain and Portugal from the 1440s, plied the Atlantic world as sailors, conquistadors and labourers in the conquest and colonisation of the Americas. In what is today South Carolina in the United States, it appears that in 1526 enslaved Africans rebelled against a Spanish expedition and settlement.

This is to underscore the importance of placing the arrival of Africans in Virginia in 1619 in a broader historical context. Their horrendous journey, repeated by 36,000 slave ships over the centuries, was part of a much larger story. It became embedded in the emergence of the modern world system that has dominated global history for the last 500 years, a system characterised by shifting hierarchies and hegemonies, by enduring structures and logics of capitalist greed, exploitation and inequality. I found the broader transatlantic and global contexts somewhat missing from the commemorations in Hampton.

Capitalist modernity and barbarism defined the new world system that emerged out of the inhuman depredations of the Atlantic slave trade, slavery and the economic revolutions it spawned. This new world involved multiple players, comprising political and economic actors in Europe, Africa and the expanding settler societies of the Americas. Scaffolding it was the ideology of racism, the stubborn original fake news of eternal African inferiority, undergirded by physiological myths about African bodies. Other insidious constructs of difference over gender and sexuality, religion and culture often supplemented racism.

Much of what I heard at the Commemorative Weekend and read in the American media, including the searing and sobering series of essays under The 1619 Project in *The New York Times Magazine*, powerfully echoed the academic literature that I am familiar with as a professional historian. Befitting the nation's most prestigious paper, The 1619 Project is ambitious: 'It aims to reframe the country's history, understanding 1619 as our true founding and placing the consequences of slavery and the contributions of black Americans at the very center of the story we tell ourselves about who we are.'[3]

The essays paint a complex and disturbing picture of American history. One traces the shift from forced labour, which was common in the Old World, to the rise of commercialised, racialised and inherited slavery in the Americas. It describes how this ruthless system generated enormous wealth and power for nation-states in Europe and the colonies, institutions including the church, and individuals. As the plantation economy expanded, the codification of slavery intensified into a rigid system of unmitigated exploitation and oppression.

Another essay underscores how the backbreaking labour of the enslaved Africans built the foundations of the American economy, how cotton became America's most profitable commodity, accounting for more than half of the nation's exports and world supply and generating vast fortunes. Yet, the enslaved Africans had no legal rights to marry or to justice in the courts. They could not own or inherit anything, not even their bodies or offspring, for they were chattel – property that could be sold, mortgaged, violated, raped and even killed at will. And they had no rights to education and literacy.

One contributor to the series stated categorically: 'In order to understand the brutality of American capitalism, you have to start on the plantation.' Incubated on the plantation were key institutions and models that have come to characterise the American economy. They included the relentless pursuit of measurement and scientific accounting, workplace supervision, the development of the mortgage and collateralised debt obligations as financial instruments and the creation of large corporations. Slavery made Wall Street, America's financial capital. In short, slavery is at the heart of what one author calls the country's 'low-road capitalism' of ruthless accumulation and glaring inequalities.

However, the contributions of African Americans went beyond the economic and material. Several essays discuss and applaud their cultural contributions. Music is particularly noteworthy. Much of the quintessential American music exported and consumed ravenously across the world is African American, from jazz to blues, rock and roll to gospel to hip-hop. Forged in bondage and racial oppression, it is a tribute to the creativity and creolisation of diaspora cultures and communities, the soulful and exuberant soundtrack of an irrepressible people.

One could also mention the indelible imprints of African-American cuisine, fashion and even the aesthetics of cool. We also know now, through the work of African-American historians and scholar-activists and others, such as Craig Steven Wilder in his groundbreaking book, *Ebony & Ivy: Race, Slavery and the Troubled History of America's Universities*,[4] that the growth of leading universities from Harvard to Yale to Georgetown was inextricably linked to the proceeds of slavery. So are some of the dominant intellectual traditions and ideologies.

No less critical have been the massive contributions by African Americans to defining the very idea of freedom and expanding the cherished, but initially rhetorical and largely specious, ideals of American democracy. Juxtaposed against the barbarities of plantation economies was the heroism of slave resistances, including rebellions. It is the generations of African-American struggles that turned the United States from a slavocracy (ten of the twelve first presidents were slave owners) to a democracy. It is they who turned the ideal and lie of democracy into reality, paving way for other struggles, including those for women's, gay, immigrant and disability rights that engulfed twentieth-century America and still persist. The struggles were both overt and covert, militant and prosaic, episodic and quotidian. They started among the captives en route to the slaveholding dungeons on the coasts of western Africa, through the Middle Passage, to the plantations and the mushrooming towns and cities of colonial America.

The African-American struggles for human rights peaked during Reconstruction as electoral offices opened to them. The 13th, 14th and 15th amendments were passed outlawing slavery, guaranteeing birthright citizenship and the right to vote, respectively. However, these advances soon triggered a backlash that gave rise to the racial terror of Jim Crow, which reinstated the caste system of American racism for nearly a century.

After the Second World War, the long crusade for civil rights that resulted in the Civil Rights and Voting Rights Acts of 1964 and 1965, respectively, convulsed the country. However, as with every victory in America's treacherous racial quagmire, a racist counter-offensive soon erupted, which intensified during and after the historic Obama presidency. And the struggle continues today in myriad ways and venues.

Making of the Modern World

The Atlantic slave trade and slavery in the Americas have generated some of the most heated debates in the historiographies of modern Africa, the Americas, Europe and the world at large. A trading and labour system in which the commodities and producers were enslaved human beings cannot but be highly emotive and raise troubling intellectual and moral questions.

The controversies centre on several issues, five of which stand out. First, there are fierce debates about the total number of Africans exported. Second, is the demographic, economic and social impact of the slave trade on Africa. Third, the impact of Africans and slavery on the development of economies, societies, cultures and polities in the Americas. Fourth, the role of the Atlantic slave trade and slavery in the development of industrial capitalism in the western world generally. Finally, the contentious demands for reparations for the slave trade and slavery that have persisted since abolition.

The Atlantic slave trade remains the foundation of the modern world capitalist system and the ultimate moral measure of the relationship between Africa, Europe and the Americas, between Africans and Europeans and their descendants in modern times. Consequently, the amount of intellectual and ideological capital and heat the subject has engendered for the past half millennium should not be surprising. Predictably, also, all too often many scholars and ideologues hide their motives and biases behind methodological sophistry, rhetorical deflections and outright lies.

Many of the contemporary disputes are as old as the Atlantic slave trade itself. Two approaches are dominant in the debates, although there are considerable overlaps. Some academics, especially those of European descent, tend to minimise the adverse impact that the slave trade had on Africa and Africans on the continent and on the enslaved Africans in the diaspora. Others, mostly of African descent, tend to emphasise the role of the slave trade in the underdevelopment of Africa, development of the Americas and western Europe and the marginalisation and reconstruction of African diaspora cultures and communities in the Americas.

The Atlantic slave trade began slowly in the fifteenth century and then grew dramatically in the subsequent centuries, reaching a peak in the eighteenth and nineteenth centuries. Dominating the trade were first the Portuguese in the fifteenth and sixteenth centuries, then the Dutch in the seventeenth century, the British in the eighteenth century and the Europeans settled in the Americas (USA, Cuba, Brazil, etc.) in the nineteenth century.

The bulk of the enslaved Africans came from the western coast of Africa covering the vast regions of Senegambia, Upper Guinea Coast, Gold Coast, Bight of Benin, Bight of Biafra, Congo and Angola. In short, West and Central Africa were the two major streams of enslavement that flowed into the horrific Middle Passage to the Americas.

Triggering the Atlantic slave trade was the demand for cheap and productive labour in the Americas. Attempts to use the indigenous peoples had floundered because they were familiar with the terrain and could escape. In addition, exposure to strange new European diseases and the ruthless brutalities and terror of conquest increasingly killed them. It was not possible to bring labourers from Europe in the quantities required. In the sixteenth and seventeenth centuries, Europe was still recovering from the Black Death of the mid-fourteenth century, which had wiped out between a third and half of its population.

Therefore, attention turned to western Africa. Why this region, not other parts of Africa or Asia for that matter, one may wonder. Western Africa was relatively close to the Americas. If geography dictated the positioning of western Africa in the evolving and heinous Atlantic slave trade, economics sealed its fate.

The African captives were highly skilled farmers, artisans, miners and productive workers in other activities for which labour was in great demand in the Americas. In addition, unlike the indigenous peoples of the Americas, they were more resistant to European diseases since the disease environments of the Old World of Europe, Africa and Asia overlapped.

Furthermore, the captives were stolen. Slavery entailed coerced, unpaid labour, which made both the acquisition of captives and use of slave labour relatively cheap. The captives were acquired in several ways, predominantly by force in the form of warfare, raids and kidnapping. Judicial and administrative corruption also played a role by sentencing into servitude people accused, often capriciously, of violating the rules of society and of conducting witchcraft. Some were seized as a form of tribute and taxation.

Thus, the process of enslavement essentially involved the violent robbery of human beings. The families of the captives who disappeared never saw them again. Unlike voluntary European migrants to the Americas and contemporary migrants from Africa, the families of the captives never got anything for the loss of their relatives. There were no remittances.

Few of the enslaved ever saw Africa or the wider world again, except for the sailors who plied the Atlantic. The exceptions include individuals like Olaudah Equiano, who left us his remarkable memoir, *The Interesting Narrative of the Life of Olaudah Equiano.*[5] There are also the striking stories of return to Africa among some of those whose memoirs are recorded in Allan D. Austin's pioneering compendium, *African Muslims in Antebellum America.*[6]

For their part, the slave dealers – from the local merchants and rulers in Africa to the European merchants at the hideous fortresses that dot the coasts of western Africa – and slave owners in the Americas, shared all the ill-gotten gains of captivity, servitude and enslavement. One of the difficult truths we have to face is the role of Africans in the Atlantic slave trade, a subject that casts a pall between continental Africans and their historic diaspora in the Americas.

African merchants and ruling elites were actively involved in the slave trade, not because their societies had surplus population or underutilised labour, as some historians have maintained, but for profit. They sought to benefit from trading a 'commodity' they had not 'produced', except for organising transport to the coast. The notion that they did not know what they were doing, that they were 'bamboozled' by the European merchants, is just as untenable as the view that they generated, controlled or monopolised the trade.

To assume that African merchants did not profit because their societies paid a heavy price is just as ahistorical as to equate their gains with those of their societies. In other words, African slave traders pursued narrow interests and short-term economic calculations to the long-term detriment of their societies. It can be argued that they had little way of knowing that their activities were depopulating and underdeveloping 'Africa', a configuration that hardly existed in their consciousness or entered into their reckoning.

However, Europe and European merchants bear ultimate responsibility for the Atlantic slave trade. The Europeans controlled and organised the trade. African merchants and rulers did not march to Europe to ask for the enslavement of their people; in fact, some actively resisted it. It was the Europeans who came to buy the captives, transported them in their ships to the Americas and sold them to European settlers who used them to work on mines and plantations and to build the economic infrastructure of the so-called New World.

Clearly, the consequences of the Atlantic slave trade varied significantly for Africa on the one hand and Europe and the Americas on the other. While much of the historiography focuses on the economic underdevelopment of Africa and the economic development of the Americas and Europe, the uneven and unequal demographic impact of slavery needs to preface it.

As noted earlier, there is no agreement on the numbers of captive and enslaved Africans. The late American historian, Philip Curtin, in his 1969 book, *The Atlantic Slave Trade: A Census*,[7] estimated that 9,566,100 African captives were imported into the Americas between 1451 and 1870. His successors proposed a slight adjustment upwards as more data became available. In much of the western media, including *The New York Times Magazine's* The 1619 Project, the figure quoted is 12.5 million.

In a series of articles and monographs, Joseph Inikori, the Nigerian economic historian, questioned the computation methods of Curtin and his followers and the quality of the data they employed, particularly in underestimating the slave imports to Spanish, Portuguese and French America. He suggested a 40 per cent upward adjustment of Curtin's figures, which brings the Atlantic slave exports to 15.4 million, of whom about 8.5 million were from West Africa and the rest from Central Africa.

The exact number of African captives exported to the Americas may never be known, for there may be extant sources not yet known to historians or others that have been lost. Moreover, it is difficult to establish the number of captives who arrived through clandestine or 'illegal' trade and those who died between the time of embarkation and arrival in the New World in both 'legitimate' and clandestine trade. Even harder to discern is the number of captives who died during transit to, or while at, the coast awaiting embarkation and of those who were killed during slave wars and raids.

As I argued in my 1993 book, *A Modern Economic History of Africa*,[8] the 'numbers game' is really less about statistical exactitude than the degree of moral censure. It is as if, by raising or lowering the numbers, the impact of the Atlantic slave trade on the societies from which the captives came and on the enslaved people themselves can be increased or decreased accordingly. There is a long tradition in western scholarship of minimising the demographic impact of the slave trade on Africa. It began with the pro-slavery propagandists during the time of the Atlantic slave trade itself.

There is now considerable literature that shows the Atlantic slave trade severely affected the demographic processes of mortality, fertility and migration in western African. The regions affected by the slave trade lost people directly through slave exports and deaths incurred during slave wars and raids. Indirectly, epidemics caused by increased movement and famines brought about by the disruption of agricultural work and flight to safer but less fertile lands, also induced population losses.

All the available global estimates seem to agree that by 1900 Africa had a lower share of the world's population than in 1500. Africans made up 8 per cent of the world's population in 1900, down from 13 per cent in 1750. It took another 250 years for Africa's population to return to this figure; it reached 13.7 per cent of the world's population in 2004. Inikori has argued that there would have been 112 million additional people in Africa had there been no Atlantic slave trade. This is because the slave trade also altered the age and gender structures of the remaining populations, and the patterns of marriage, all of which served to depress fertility rates. The exported people were largely between the ages of sixteen and thirty, that is, in the prime of their reproductive lives, so that their forced migration depressed future population growth. Moreover, they were lost at an age when their parents could not easily replace them owing to their own declining fertility.

The age structure of the population left behind became progressively older, further reinforcing the trend towards lower population growth. Thus, population losses could not easily be offset by natural increases, certainly not within a generation or two. The gender ratio was generally 60 per cent for men and 40 per cent for women. This affected marriage structures and fertility patterns. The proportion of polygynous marriage increased, which, since it may have meant less sexual contact for women than in monogamous marriages, probably served to depress fertility as well.

The spread of venereal diseases and other diseases from Europe also adversely affected fertility in the coastal areas. Syphilis and smallpox, both brought by European slave traders, ravaged the Mpongwe of Gabon, for instance. Smallpox epidemics killed many people, including those at the peak of their reproductive years, which, coupled with the disruption of local marriage customs and the expansion of polygyny, served to reduce fertility.

Thus, for Africa the Atlantic slave trade led to depopulation, depleted the stock of skills and shrank the size of markets and pressures for technical innovation. At the same time, violence associated with the trade devastated economic activities. It has been argued that the Atlantic slave trade aborted West Africa's industrial take-off.

The slave trade not only distorted demographic and economic structures, it also affected social and political institutions and values. Consequently, even after the abolition of slavery in the Americas, the infrastructures developed to supply captives for enslavement remained. They were used to expand local labour supplies to produce commodities demanded by industrialising European economies. As the great radical Guyanese historian, Walter Rodney, argued in the late 1960s the slave trade contributed to the expansion of slavery within Africa itself, rather than the other way round, as propagated by Eurocentric historians.

The sheer scale and longevity of the Atlantic slave trade generated a culture of violence and led to the collapse of many ancient African states and the rise of predatory slave states. Thus, the slave trade was one of the main sources of corruption and political violence in modern Africa. The political economy of enslavement tore the moral economy of many African societies. Contemporary Africa's crass and corrupt elites who mortgage their country's development prospects are the ignominious descendants of the slave trading elites of the horrific days of the Atlantic slave trade.

In contrast to Africa, the Atlantic slave trade and slavery in the Americas became the basis of the Atlantic economy from the sixteenth century until the mid-nineteenth century. It was the world's largest and most lucrative industry. The crops and minerals produced by the labour of enslaved Africans, such as sugar, cotton, tobacco, gold and silver, were individually and collectively more profitable than anything the world had ever seen. This laid the economic foundations of the Americas and the economic development of western Europe more broadly. As Walter Rodney showed in his 1972 provocative classic, *How Europe Underdeveloped Africa*,[9] trade in produce by slave labour provided the basis for the rise of manufacturing, banking, shipping and insurance companies, as well as the formation of the modern corporation and transformative developments in technology, including the manufacture of machinery. This book became the intellectual bible for my generation of undergraduates hungry to understand why Africa remained so desperately poor despite its proverbial abundant natural resources

Inikori argues persuasively in his award-winning book, *Africans and the Industrial Revolution in England*,[10] that Africans on the continent and in the diaspora were central to the growth of the international trade in the Atlantic world between the sixteenth and nineteenth centuries that spawned Britain's industrialisation. Britain, which became the world's first industrial nation, was the leading slave-trading nation of the eighteenth century. As Europe became more industrialised, it acquired the physical capacity, as well as the insatiable economic appetite and the ideological armour of racism, to conquer Africa.

Thus, the colonial conquests of the late nineteenth century were a direct outcome of the Atlantic slave trade. Instead of exporting captive labour, the continent was now expected to produce the commodities demanded by an industrialising Europe and to serve as a market for European products and an investment outlet for its surplus capital.

There can be little doubt that the Atlantic slave trade and enslaved Africans laid the economic, cultural and demographic foundations of the Americas. Often, it is not well appreciated that it was only with the end of the slave trade that European immigrants, whose descendants now predominate in the populations of the Americas, came to outnumber forced African immigrants to the Americas.

For the United States the median arrival date of African Americans – the date by which half had arrived and half were still to come – is remarkably early, about 1780. The similar median date for European Americans was remarkably late – about 1890. In short, the average African American has far older roots in the United States than the average European American.

The contributions of captive and enslaved Africans are greater still. African music, dance, religious beliefs and many other aspects of culture became key ingredients of the new creole cultures in the Americas. This makes the notion of the Americas as an autogenic European construct devoid of African influences laughable. The renowned Ghanaian-American philosopher, Kwame Anthony Appiah, correctly urges us in his book, *The Lies That Bind: Rethinking Identity*, to give up the idea of the west and the attendant vacuous notions of western civilisation and western culture, which are nothing but coded racial euphemisms for whiteness.

The Americas, including the United States, have never been and will never be an exclusive extension of white Europe, itself a historical fiction, notwithstanding the deranged fantasies of white supremacists. Brazil, the great power of South America, tried a whitening project following the belated abolition of slavery in 1888, by importing millions of migrants from Europe, but failed miserably. Today, Afro-Brazilians are in the majority, although their evident demographic and cultural presence pales in comparison to their high levels of socioeconomic and political marginalisation.

The Atlantic slave trade, the largest forced migration in world history, had another pernicious and persistent legacy. It may not have created European racism against Africans in the global imaginary, but it certainly bred it. As Orlando Patterson demonstrated in his magisterial 1982 study, *Slavery and Social Death: A Comparative Study*,[12] before the Atlantic slave trade began slavery existed in many parts of the world and was not confined to Africa. Indeed, studies show that in 1500 Africans were a minority of the world's slaves.

The tragedy for Africa is that the enslavement of Africans expanded as the enslavement of other peoples was receding. By the nineteenth century, slavery had become almost synonymous with Africa, so that the continent and its peoples carried the historical burden of prejudice and contempt accorded to slaves and despised social castes and classes. In short, because of the very modernity of

African slavery, Africans became the most despised people on the planet, relegated to the bottom in regional and local racial, ethnic and colour hierarchies. Slavery left a scourge of superiority complexes among the peoples of Europe and Asia against Africans and inferiority complexes among Africans and peoples of African descent in the diaspora. This sometimes manifests itself in obsessive colourism, which can degenerate into mutilations of the black body through skin lightening and other perverted aspirations for whiteness.

The prejudices born out of slavery are also evident in inter- and intragroup antagonisms in diaspora locations, between the new and historic African diasporas, between recent continental African migrants and African Americans, so painfully and poignantly captured in the documentary film by Peres Owino, a Kenyan-American film-maker, *Bound: Africans vs African Americans.*[13] The documentary attributes the antipathies, antagonisms and anxieties that shape relations between the two groups to the lack of recognition of the collective traumas of each other's respective histories of slavery and colonialism.

Reparations and Redemption

The Atlantic slave trade and slavery left legacies of underdevelopment, marginalisation, inequality and trauma for Africans and African diasporas. This has engendered various demands for restitution and redemption. Demands for compensation to the descendants of the enslaved Africans in the Americas and Europe have been made from the time of the abolition of slavery in the Americas, captured in the United States in the prosaic claim for 'forty acres and a mule'.

In the United States, Democrat Representative John Conyers started the reparations campaign in Congress in 1989. Every year he introduced a bill calling for the creation of a Commission to Study Reparation Proposals for African Americans. By the time he retired in 2017, not much had been achieved. Nevertheless, in the interim, seven states proceeded to issue apologies for their involvement in slavery (Alabama, Delaware, Florida, Maryland, New Jersey, North Carolina and Virginia). Some private institutions followed suit, such as JP Morgan Chase and Wachovia, and so did a growing number of universities, such as Georgetown.

Claims for reparations found a powerful voice among some influential African-American intellectuals and activists. One was Randall Robinson, the founder of the lobbying organisation, Trans-Africa, who made a compelling case in his book, *The Debt: What America Owes to Blacks.*[14] In 2017, the incisive commentator, Ta-Nehisi Coates, reignited the national debate with a celebrated essay in *The Atlantic* magazine, 'The Case for Reparations'.[15]

In 2009, shortly after President Obama assumed office, the US Senate unanimously passed a resolution apologising for slavery. The United Nations Working Group of Experts on People of African Descent encouraged the United

States Congress to look into the issue of reparations. However, opposition to reparations remained among the majority of Americans. In a 2014 survey[16] only 37 per cent of the respondents supported reparations.

In the charged political season of 2019, and with presidential elections due in 2020, reparations rose up the national agenda as never before. Several leading Democratic Party presidential candidates (Elizabeth Warren, Cory Booker, Tulsi Gabbard, Bernie Sanders, Kamala Harris and Beto O'Rourke) openly embraced the reparations cause. At the same time, the reparations debate seemed to gather momentum in private institutions, including universities, buoyed by the unveiling of some universities' links to slavery, the radicalising energies of the #BlackLivesMatter movement and mounting resistance to resurgent white supremacy.

The Caribbean region boasts one of the most vibrant reparations movements in the Americas. The fact that the demands are not directed at national governments, as in the United States, but to Britain as the former leading slave-trading nation and later colonial power over some of the Caribbean islands, partly explains it. In addition, the Caribbean enjoys a long tradition of Pan-African activism. The call by Caribbean leaders for European countries to pay reparations became official in 2007. Various heads of state in several forums, including the United Nations, subsequently repeated it. Hilary McD Beckles became the leading figure of the Caribbean reparations movement (he is a former colleague of mine at the University of West Indies where we both joined the History Department in 1982 and where he currently serves as vice chancellor). In 2013, he published his influential book, *Britain's Black Debt: Reparations for Caribbean Slavery and Native Genocide.*[17] In 2013, the CARICOM (Caribbean Community) Reparations Commission was created.

In Europe, the reparations movement has been growing. Black British campaigns intensified and reached a climax in 2008 during the 200th anniversary of the British abolition of the slave trade. In 2007, Prime Minister Tony Blair and London Mayor Ken Livingstone offered apologies for Britain's participation in the Atlantic slave trade. In 2017, the Danish government followed suit and apologised to Ghana for the Atlantic slave trade. However, apologies have not found favour in countries such as Portugal, Spain and France, which participated actively in this monumental business of human trafficking. Even for Britain and Denmark, reparations have not made much headway.

African states have exhibited a conflicted attitude towards reparations. On the one hand, they have shown eagerness to call on the Atlantic slave-trading nations of Europe and slave-holding societies of the Americas to pay reparations to Africa. The African World Reparations and Repatriation Truth Commission established in 1999 put the figure at a staggering US$77 trillion. At the global level, the issue of reparations was a major subject at the 2001 UN World Conference against Racism, Racial Discrimination, Xenophobia and Related Intolerance held in

Durban, South Africa. Then, in 2010, the renowned Harvard scholar, Henry Louis Gates, published an essay in *The New York Times* in which he raised the thorny question of whether Africans who were involved in the Atlantic slave trade should pay reparations.[18] Few African leaders have been prepared to apologise for their societies' complicity in the slave trade. In 1999, the President of Benin was among the first to apologise to African Americans. Ghana followed suit with an apology to African Americans in 2006. In January 2019, Ghana's President Nana Akufo-Addo declared 2019 'The Year of Return' to mark the 400th anniversary of the arrival of the first captive Africans in Hampton, Virginia.

The responsibility for the Atlantic slave trade falls on the shoulders of many state and elite actors in Africa, Europe and the Americas. The major benefits of slavery in the Americas accrued to the elites and states in the Americas and Europe. This suggests differentiated levels of responsibility for reparations and redemption. African governments in the regions involved in the Atlantic slave trade must seek the redemption of apology to the historic African diasporas in the Americas through the regional economic communities and the African Union. Only then can the process of healing and reconciliation for the sons and daughters of Africa on both sides of the Atlantic begin in earnest. The transformative power of education should sustain the acknowledgement and mutual recognition between Africa and its diasporas. The curriculum at every level across the continent should incorporate teaching the history of the Atlantic slave trade, slavery in the Americas and the contributions of the historic African diasporas.

African governments and institutions must also make deliberate efforts to facilitate and promote multidimensional engagements with the historic diaspora. The African Union's designation of the diaspora as Africa's sixth region must be given teeth in terms of political, economic, social and cultural rights. The charge goes beyond governments. The private sector and civil societies in African nations and the diaspora must also establish mutually beneficial and empowering modalities of engagement.

There are encouraging signs of new intellectual and artistic bridges being built by members of the new African diaspora, who straddle in their upbringing, identities, experiences and sensibilities the sociocultural geographies and political ecologies of continental Africa and diaspora America. A few examples will suffice. There is no better accounting of the divergent yet intimately connected histories of Africa and America from the eighteenth century to the present than Yaa Gyasi's sprawling and exquisite first novel, *Homegoing*.[19] It tells the story of two sisters, one sent into slavery and the other who remained in West Africa, and the parallel lives of their descendants. Another skilful exploration and painful reckoning with slavery is Ayesha Harruna Attah's *The Hundred Wells of Salaga*,[20] set in a bustling trading market for the Atlantic slave trade. Recounting the travails of an enslaved African traversing the expanse of the black Atlantic is Esi Edugyan's soaring story in her novel *Washington Black*.[21] Among contemporary African migrants, there is Imbolo Mbue's *Behold the Dreamers*,[22] set in New York, which captures the aspirations, anxieties, agonies, assaults and awakening by the new diaspora to the routine hypocrisies, hardships, harassments and opportunities of American life.

For me, my commitments to the project of reconnecting Africa and its global diasporas in truly transformative and mutually beneficial ways provide the inspiration behind my research work on diaspora histories that I've been engaged in for the past two decades. This work led to the establishment of the Carnegie African Diaspora Fellowships Program, which facilitates the engagement of African-born academics in Canada and the United States with universities in six countries (Ghana, Nigeria, Kenya, Tanzania, Uganda and South Africa). The programme is being expanded into the Consortium of African Diaspora Scholars Programs, which seeks to promote flows between scholars from both the historic and new diasporas from anywhere in the world to anywhere in Africa.

As I left the Commemorative Weekend in Hampton to fly back to Kenya, I felt deep sadness at what our brothers and sisters have had to endure over the last 400 years of their sojourn in the United States, but also immense pride at what they have been able to achieve against all odds. Let me put it graphically, as I did at a training seminar recently for African diplomats: in 2017, the forty-odd million African Americans had a purchasing power of US$1.2 trillion compared to US$2.2 trillion for the 1.2 billion Africans on the continent. If African Americans were a country they would be the seventeenth richest country in the world, richer than Nigeria, South Africa and Egypt combined.

Surely, this continent with its abundant human and natural resources can do better, much better. Africa and its diaspora owe each other principled, not transactional, solidarity if we are to navigate the complex and unsettling demands and disruptions of the twenty-first century better than we fared during the last half millennium, a period characterised by the disabling histories of slavery, Jim Crow segregation and white supremacy backlashes in the United States and colonialism, neocolonialism and postcolonial authoritarianism in Africa. To echo Kwame Nkrumah's mid-twentieth-century dream, let us strive to make the twenty-first century truly ours!

Notes

1. Paul Tiyambe Zeleza, *The Joys of Exile*, Toronto: House of Anansi Press, 1994.
2. Sylviane Diouf, *Dreams of Africa in Alabama: The Slave Ship Clotilda and the Story of the Last Africans Brought to America*, Oxford University Press, 2007.
3. *The New York Times Magazine*, 'Why we Published The 1619 Project', 20 December 2019. https://www.nytimes.com/interactive/2019/12/20/magazine/1619-intro.html
4. Craig Steven Wilder, *Ebony & Ivy: Race, Slavery and the Troubled History of America's Universities*, New York: Bloomsbury Publishing, 2013.

5. Olaudah Equiano, *The Interesting Narrative of the Life of Olaudah Equiano, or Gustavus Vassa, The African: Written by Himself,* Mineola, New York: Dover Publications, 1999 [1789].
6. Allan D. Austin, *African Muslims in Antebellum America: Transatlantic stories and Spiritual Studies,* New York: Garland Publishing, 1984.
7. Philip Curtin, *The Atlantic Slave Trade: A Census,* Madison, Wisc: University of Wisconsin Press, 1969.
8. Paul Tiyambe Zeleza, *A Modern Economic History of Africa,* Dakar: CODESRIA Books, 1993.
9. *Walter Rodney, How Europe Underdeveloped Africa*, Washington, DC: Howard University, 1981 [1972].
10. Joseph Inikori, *Africans and the Industrial Revolution in England: A Study in International Trade and Economic Development,* Cambridge, UK: Cambridge University Press, 2002.
11. Kwame Anthony Appiah, *The Lies That Bind: Rethinking Identity,* New York: Liveright Publishing, 2018.
12. Orlando Patterson, *Slavery and Social Death: A Comparative Study,* Cambridge, MA: Harvard University Press, 2018.
13. Peres Owino (director), Bound: Africans vs African Americans (motion picture), Los Angeles: Quiver, 2015.
14. Randall Robinson, *The Debt: What America Owes to Blacks,* New York: Dutton, 2001.
15. Ta-Nehisi Coates, 'The Case for Reparations', *The Atlantic,* June 2014. https://www.theatlantic.com/magazine/archive/2014/06/the-case-for-reparations/361631/
16. Peter Moore, 'Overwhelming opposition to reparations for slavery and Jim Crow', 2 June 2014. https://today.yougov.com/topics/politics/articles-reports/2014/06/02/reparations
17. Hilary McD Beckles, *Britain's Black Debt: Reparations for Caribbean Slavery and Native Genocide,* Kingston, Jamaica: University Press of the West Indies, 2013.
18. Henry Louis Gates, Jr, 'Ending the Slavery Blame-Game', *The New York Times,* 22 April 2010. https://www.nytimes.com/2010/04/23/opinion/23gates.html
19. Yaa Gyasi, *Homegoing,* New York: Knopf Doubleday Publishing, 2016.
20. Ayesha Harruna Attah, *The Hundred Wells of Salaga,* New York: Other Press, 2019.
21. Esi Edugyan, *Washington Black,* New York: Knopf Doubleday Publishing, 2018.
22. Imbolo Mbue, *Behold the Dreamers,* New York: Penguin Random House, 2016.

First written 24–25 August 2019

5

The American Uprising of 2020: Black Lives Matter Gains Traction

History occasionally accelerates with unexpected speed as its slow, subterranean motions suddenly erupt into surges of change, sparked by an event whose ordinariness acquires an extraordinary potency out of a unique confluence of forces. The triggers vary, of course, but there is a particular poignancy that comes with the incendiary intimacy of individual murders. Such killings strike a powerful emotional and cognitive chord in the human imagination in a way that mass murders might not because their sheer scale congeals into a mind-numbing abstraction.

The public execution of George Floyd on 25 May 2020, with its casual performance of suffocating and snuffing out the life of that black body, became a frightful spectral presence in the minds of tens of millions of people in the United States and around the world. It captured with terrifying clarity the utter depravity of the police officers involved and their degradation of a black life, and validated the humanistic and historic demands of the Black Lives Matter movement.

The spontaneous demonstrations that erupted across every state and hundreds of cities and towns in the United States, including some with small black populations and even those infamous for harbouring white supremacy movements and militias, quickly turned into the nation's largest and most widespread protest movement against systemic racism since the 1960s and, some claim, in American history.[1] It brought both the country and the shambolic Trump presidency to an inflection point.

The uprising over Floyd's murder derived its fiery multiracial and multigenerational rage from the coronavirus pandemic that was disproportionately devastating the lives and livelihoods of black and poor people. It tapped into the surplus time and energies of people seeking release from the isolating suffocations of COVID-19 lockdowns. It also benefitted from the inept and provocative responses of racist politicians and police forces. Further, it was catalysed by the persistent struggles of longstanding activists and social movements.

Assassinations as Historical Inflections

Assassinations have served to trigger major events throughout history. Think of the assassination of the Archduke Ferdinand of Austria, heir to the throne of the Austro-Hungarian Empire, on 28 June 1914 in Sarajevo. This event helped ignite World War I by prying open long-simmering nationalist and imperialist rivalries in Europe. The conflicts were engendered by and coalesced around rival alliances that catapulted the world into an unprecedented conflagration.

Think of the brutal lynching of 14-year-old Emmett Till in Mississippi on 28 August 1955, for allegedly whistling at a white woman. The photographs of his mutilated body served to galvanise the American Civil Rights movement by inflaming age-old grievances and agitation against systemic racism, white supremacy and the country's North-South divides, overlaid by the global reverberations of Cold War superpower rivalries and the decolonisation struggles in Africa and Asia.

Think of the self-immolation of Mohamed Bouazizi, a young street vendor, on 17 December 2010, in protest against Tunisia's state repression and the economic distress of young people. It provoked the Tunisian Revolution and the Arab Spring uprisings against autocratic and corrupt ruling coalitions in North Africa, other parts of Africa, Asia and South America, adding fuel to the democratic wave unleashed by the end of the Cold War. Elsewhere, in North America and Europe, the Arab Spring inspired the Occupy movement.

However, the Arab Spring soon turned into the Arab Winter, pushed back by counter-revolutions comprising resurgent Islamism, the reinstatement of military rule in Egypt, descent into autocracy in Turkey and ferocious civil wars in Libya, Syria and Yemen. As for the victories of the Civil Rights movement in the US in the 1960s, they remained limited and provoked a racist backlash. The Republican Party embarked on the Southern Strategy of courting white racists, and systemic racism and white supremacy were strengthened by new structural and ideological scaffolding. For its part, World War I led to the consolidation of colonialism in Africa and Asia, reaped the whirlwinds of fascism and Stalinism in Europe and unleashed the spectre of economic devastation that culminated in the Great Depression.

In short, revolutionary moments generate complex and contradictory futures in which progress is often checkmated by reversals, underscoring the fact that history is a dialectical process. The racist backlash against Obama that led to Trump's election seemed to have succeeded in creating an anti-racist backlash.

The Floyd moment in which the Black Lives Matter movement gained traction in the US and around the world would not be an exception. Progress would be made in chipping away at some of the practices, symbols and performances of anti-black racism, but the fundamental structures of white supremacy were likely to survive and mutate.

In the Shadows of 1968

The American uprising of 2020 shared some parallels and connections with the uprising of 1968 that followed the assassination of the Rev. Martin Luther King. The script of 1968 remained, notwithstanding some progress, in so far as the 2020 protests sprang from the deep well of institutionalised racism, economic inequality, social despair, political disenfranchisement and the dehumanising terrors of police brutality and constant denigration of blackness in the national imaginary.

The road to 2020 was paved with the legacies of 1968. As Peniel Joseph, a renowned African-American historian, wrote in *The Washington Post*:

> The flames that engulfed large portions of America during the 1960s helped to extinguish the promise of the Great Society by turning the War on Poverty into a dehumanizing war against poor black communities. America has, in the ensuing five decades, deployed state of the art technology to criminalize, surveil, arrest, incarcerate, segregate and punish black communities. Floyd's death represents the culmination of these political and policy decisions to choose punishment over empathy, to fund prisons over education and housing and to promote fear of black bodies over racial justice.[2]

The America of King's dream of racial equality and social justice not only remained deferred, but was actively sabotaged by the courts, politicians and business. The landmark legislative achievements of the Civil Rights movement – the Civil Rights Act of 1964 and the Voting Rights Act of 1965 – wilted as the prison industrial complex burgeoned, and socioeconomic inequalities and social despair among the poor, both black and white, deepened.

Since 1968, there had been periodic eruptions of protests, most memorably the 1992 Los Angeles uprising that followed the acquittal of four police officers charged with the widely publicised beating of Rodney King, and the 2014 uprising that began after the fatal shooting of Michael Brown in Ferguson, Missouri, by a police officer. After each uprising, police, judicial and other reforms were announced, but they largely gathered dust as the protests faded into memory until the next eruption elsewhere. Only time will tell if the 2020 uprising was different, a transformative watershed in a long history of protests against systemic racism and police brutality. Some commentators were doubtful, others more hopeful. A sample of the divergent opinions can be seen among two dozen experts convened by *POLITICO Magazine*.[3]

Those who doubted that the Floyd protests represented an inflection point worried about the challenges of sustaining the momentum of protest, dynamic grassroots organisation and cohesive leadership and unity around a clear set of goals, as well as the powers of state suppression and repression in the reactionary name of 'law and order'. Further, hyperpartisanship was more glaring than ever, facilitated by the political polarisation and media fragmentation that make reconciliation difficult.

Those who were more hopeful about the positive impact of the uprising pointed to the nationwide scale of the protests, the ubiquity of video images of police brutality and the fact that the protests were occurring in the face of a pandemic and mass unemployment that disproportionately ravaged black people and other people of colour. Moreover, the presence of an outrageously racist, divisive and authoritarian-minded president increasingly alienated moderate whites.

Many believed that the expansive geography of the protests portended the historical significance of the moment. In the 1960s, 'most protests were held in major cities and on college campuses – and most Americans saw them on the television news'. The 2020 uprising was different. 'National media focuses on the big demonstrations and protest policing in major cities, but they have not picked up on a different phenomenon that may have major long-term consequences for politics. Protests over racism and #BlackLivesMatter are spreading across the country – including in small towns with deeply conservative politics.'[4] Altogether, according to some counts, the Floyd protests occurred in 1,280 places.[5]

If polls were to be believed, as harbingers of the future possibilities for transformation, according to *The New York Times* 'support for Black Lives Matter increased by nearly as much as it had over the previous two years, according to data from Civiqs, an online survey research firm. By a 28-point margin, Civiqs finds that a majority of American voters support the movement, up from a 17-point margin before the most recent wave of protests began.'

The paper continued:

> A Monmouth University poll found that 76 percent of Americans consider racism and discrimination a "big problem," up 26 points from 2015. The poll found that 57 percent of voters thought the anger behind the demonstrations was fully justified, while a further 21 percent called it somewhat justified. Polls show that a majority of Americans believe that the police are more likely to use deadly force against African Americans and that there's a lot of discrimination against black Americans in society. Back in 2013, when Black Lives Matter began, a majority of voters disagreed with all of these statements.'[6]

In short, the 2020 uprising seemed to represent progress over 1968 in the scale of its multiracial composition and breadth of demands for racial justice. It suggested white America and other Americans of colour were coming to understand the depth and scope of unrelenting black pain under institutional racism and white supremacy. In the words of Alex Thompson in POLITICO, 'The killing of George Floyd has prompted a reckoning with racism not only for Joe Biden, but for a wide swath of white America', which, he argued, could reshape the 2020 elections.[7]

However, given the history of the United States, doubts remained whether this moment represented a defining turning point. The road towards racial equality and justice would continue to be bumpy because what was at stake was the entire system of racial capitalism that reproduced white supremacy, not just its manifestations evident in heinous practices such as police brutality.

What was certain was that the terrain of American race relations was shifting. Floyd's death spearheaded the country's largest and broadest anti-racist movement and made Black Lives Matter an acceptable slogan, not the dreaded and derided radical idea it once was. Behind the movement's newfound traction lay six long years of tireless work by its activists.

The Trails of Slavery

The modern world was created by the triangular slave trade between Africa, Europe and the Americas. These continents have been linked ever since by the historical geographies and political economies of exploitation and struggle. The US uprising inspired worldwide protests. This reflected the ubiquity of America, a superpower with an outsize presence in the global imagination, and the almost universal anti-black racism born out of the Atlantic slave trade that created the modern world.

The protests tapped into the growing recognition in many western countries that racism is a problem. According to *The Economist:*

> The share of Americans who see racial discrimination in their country as a big problem has risen from 51 per cent in January 2015 to 76 per cent now. A YouGov poll last week found that 52 per cent of Britons think British society is fairly or very racist, a big rise from similar polls in the past. In 2018, 77 per cent of the French thought France needed to fight racism, up from 59 per cent in 2002. Pew Research found last year in most countries healthy majorities welcome racial diversity.[8]

The unprecedented scale of the protests in the US provoked confrontations between the obdurate and callous Trump administration and city mayors and state governors around the country. It produced iconic moments and images. Most graphically, in an act of political pornography and vandalism, there was the picture of Trump awkwardly holding a Bible in front of a church after the National Guard had forcibly cleared peaceful demonstrators from Lafayette Square using teargas and rubber bullets. The mayor of Washington responded by painting and ceremonially naming two blocks of the street leading to the White House, Black Lives Matter Plaza. The newly extended perimeter from the White House was turned into an exuberant makeshift exhibition of resistance art, posters and graffiti.

Trump's overreaction triggered a powerful backlash. Widely condemned for accompanying the president to his ill-fated photo-op, the Defence Secretary and Chief of Staff apologised. Several former military leaders expressed disgust and alarm. John Allen, former commander of the NATO International Security Assistance Force and US forces in Afghanistan, warned: 'The slide of the United States into illiberalism may well have begun on June 1, 2020. Remember the date. It may well signal the beginning of the end of the American experiment.'[9]

Other retired military leaders sought to distance their beloved Pentagon from the clutches of the aspiring autocrat and renowned draft-dodger. They included John Mattis, who had served as Trump's own defence secretary, and Colin Powell, a former Chief of Staff and Secretary of State who accused Trump of unprecedented divisiveness. The Pentagon promised to review the conduct of the National Guard against the protests. Former presidents Clinton, Bush and Obama expressed their misgivings and some Republican politicians nervously tried to distance themselves from a president who increasingly looked like a deranged dictator in the mould of the despots he clearly admired and envied.

Before long, anti-racist struggles and protests spread to countries with their own troubled histories of anti-black racism, from Canada to Brazil in the Americas, the former colonial powers of Europe, and the outposts of European settler colonialism in Australasia. Electrifying images were beamed on televisions and downloaded on social media around the world. A sample appeared in *The Atlantic*, 'Images from a Worldwide Protest Movement'.[10]

In each country and city where the Floyd protests took place, parallels were drawn with local histories of anti-black racism, social injustice, exclusion and marginalisation. The demonstrations and marches were organised by local groups of the Black Lives Matter movement, political and civil society activists and local groups that had long fought against all forms of exclusion and discrimination. The protests often took place in front of US embassies, national parliaments, public squares, as well as in front of detested statues and monuments to slavery, imperialism and colonialism and along major thoroughfares.

As the specious cocoon of democratic exceptionalism spectacularly burst, American diplomats found it galling that the US had become the target of human rights protests around the world. *The New York Times* observed, in 'U.S. Diplomats Struggle to Defend Democracy Abroad Amid Crises at Home', that:

> In private conversations and social media posts … [they] expressed outrage after the killing of George Floyd and President Trump's push to send the military to quell demonstrations. Diplomats say that the violence has undercut their criticisms of foreign autocrats and called into question the moral authority the United States tries to project as it promotes democracy and demands civil liberties and freedoms across the world.[11]

The Americas harbour the largest population of the African diaspora, mostly descended from enslaved Africans. While there have been some national differences in the constructions of racial identities, since the sixteenth century the black experience across the region has been uniformly that of being exploited and oppressed, characterised by slavery, institutionalised racism, exclusion and police brutality. Canada, which likes to see itself as the gentler face of North America, is no exception. The country has an ugly history of anti-black racism and genocidal brutality against its indigenous people. Not surprisingly, the uprising in the US resonated in all that country's provinces and major cities, from Halifax, Sydney and Yarmouth in Nova Scotia, where the black loyalists from the American War of Independence settled, to Fredericton, Moncton and Sackville in New Brunswick, St. John's in Newfoundland and several cities in Quebec, including Montreal, Quebec City and Sherbrooke. Huge protests also took place across Ontario in such cities as Barrie, Hamilton, Kingston, Kitchener, London, Ottawa, Thunder Bay, Toronto and Windsor, and in the western provinces of Alberta (Calgary, Edmonton and Lethridge), British Columbia (Vancouver and Victoria and other cities), Manitoba (Winnipeg) and Saskatchewan (Saskatoon and Regina).

Unknown to many people is the fact that Mexico has an African diaspora population and that racism is deeply entrenched there despite the myths of *mestizaje*, or racial mixing. White Mexicans have dominated the country and marginalised its indigenous people and African descendants for centuries. Protests and vigils occurred in Guadalajara, Mexico City and Xalapa. They spread to South America from Argentina (Buenos Aires), which whitened itself in the nineteenth century through a campaign of black extermination, to Brazil (Curitiba, Rio de Janeiro, São Paulo), the country with the largest African diaspora in the world and a horrible history of systemic racism despite the cruel myth of racial democracy, as well as Ecuador (Quito) and Colombia (Bogotá), another country with a massive African diaspora presence.

In the Caribbean, most of the islands have majority African-descended populations. Historically, the region's intellectual activists played a crucial role in the development of Pan-Africanism. Migrations from the region in the nineteenth and twentieth centuries to South and North America and Europe have given its inhabitants intricate global connections, which means that developments in these regions reverberate locally immediately. Protests took place in Bermuda, Kingston in Jamaica and Port of Spain in Trinidad and Tobago.

The protests particularly resonated in Europe, with its colonial histories and failures to integrate recent waves of migrants and refugees from its imperial outposts in Africa and Asia. The black British journalist and academic, Gary Younge, brilliantly dissected the resonance of the American uprising. 'Europe's identification with black America, particularly during times of crisis, resistance and trauma, has a long and complex history. It is fuelled in no small part by traditions of internationalism and anti-racism on the European left, where the likes of Paul Robeson, Richard Wright and Audre Lorde would find an ideological – and, at times, literal – home.'[12]

However, he continued:

> this tradition of political identification with black America also leaves significant space for the European continent's inferiority complex, as it seeks to shroud its relative military and economic weakness in relation to America with a moral confidence that conveniently ignores both its colonial past and its own racist present. From the vantage point of a continent that both resents and covets

> American power and is in no position to do anything about it, African Americans represent to many Europeans a redemptive force: the living proof that the US is not all it claims to be and that it could be so much greater than it is.

Britain and France, the former colonial superpowers, became the epicentres of large protests in solidarity with the Black Lives Matter movement and in pursuit of local anti-racism and social justice struggles. Predictably, right-wing politicians and the punditocracy dismissed the solidarity protests, claiming, as British black historian, David Olusoga, noted, 'The US situation is unique in both its depth and ferocity, they say, so that no parallels can be drawn with the situation in Britain. The smoke-and-mirrors aspect of this argument is that it attempts to focus attention solely on police violence, rather than the racism that inspired it.'[13]

Olusoga also noted that this argument has an old history going back to 1807, 'with the abolition of the slave trade and picked up steam three decades later with the end of British slavery, twin events that marked the beginning of 200 years of moral posturing and historical amnesia'. In Britain, demonstrations broke out from 28 May and for the next two weeks roiled all the major cities, from Brighton to Edinburgh. Some believed this marked a turning point in the UK as, in the words of the *Guardian*, 'demands for racial justice now have a new and unstoppable urgency'.[14]

France suffers from a pernicious tradition of colonial denial and amnesia, clothed in facetious fidelity to universal values, which it rationalised at the height of empire with the myth of assimilation. But the country has its own history of police brutality and killings of black people. It was rocked by unrest in Paris, Bordeaux, Lille, Lyon, Marseille and Toulouse in which protesters invoked George Floyd and their own black martyrs to French racism.

The cities of other former colonial powers were not spared. In Belgium there were widespread protests. Germany was another country that saw demonstrations by thousands of people in more than two dozen cities, including Berlin, Dresden, Düsseldorf, Munich, Nuremberg and Stuttgart. Italy, too, was engulfed by protests in many cities. In Portugal, the last imperial power to be booted out of Africa, thousands of people marched in Lisbon and Porto. Spain, whose African colonial empire had been the smallest, witnessed protests in a dozen cities, including Barcelona and Madrid.

Protests spread to other European countries that had been involved in establishing slave-trading forts or colonial settlements across the western seaboard of the African continent. In Denmark, whose slave forts dot the coastline of modern Ghana, hundreds and thousands of people gathered and marched in Aalborg, Aarhus, Copenhagen and Odense. In the Netherlands, the country that gave South Africa its Afrikaner architects of apartheid, solidarity vigils and protests took place from 1 June for the next fortnight in several cities. In Norway, a country that was unified with Denmark during the era of the slave trade, protesters marched in Bergen, Kristiansand, Oslo and Tromsø.

Such has been the global reach of the uprising against racism and police brutality that yet other European countries were caught in the turbulence. In Vienna, Austria, more than 50,000 people marched on 4 June. Large protests also took place in Sweden and Switzerland. Smaller protest marches also took place in Sofia in Bulgaria, Zagreb in Croatia, Nicosia in Cyprus, Prague in the Czech Republic, Helsinki in Finland, Athens and Thessaloniki in Greece, Budapest in Hungary, Reykjavík in Iceland, Cord, Dublin and Limerick in Ireland, Pristina in Kosovo, Vilnius in Lithuania, Luxembourg, Valletta in Malta, Podgorica in Montenegro, Kraków, Poznań, Warsaw in Poland, Bucharest in Romania, Belgrade in Serbia and Bratislava in Slovakia.

Asia became another theatre of Floyd protests, although not on the scale of the Atlantic world except for Australia, a settler colony with a notorious history of systemic racism and police brutality against the indigenous people and Asian and African immigrants. The protests in Brisbane and Sydney attracted tens of thousands of people and sizeable numbers took part in other Australian cities, too.

Hundreds and in some cases thousands of people protested in Japan (Tokyo and Osaka), Taiwan, Hong Kong, South Korea (Seoul), India (Kolkata), Pakistan (Karachi), Sri Lanka (Colombo), the Philippines (Quezon City), Thailand (Bangkok), Kazakhstan (Almaty and other cities), Armenia (Yerevan), Georgia (Tbilisi), Iran (Tehran), Israel (Tel Aviv, Jerusalem and Haifa) – led by Israelis of African origin who face racism and disproportionate police arrests – Lebanon (Beirut) and Palestine (Bethlehem).

The protests in the United States and around the world focused on a broadly similar range of targets. First, law enforcement agencies that uphold the system of racial capitalism that marginalises and disempowers black people. Second, the symbols of white supremacy embodied in public commemorations that honour the perpetrators of enslavement, colonisation and plunder. Third, private institutions, organisations and corporations that tolerate and reproduce racial inequality.

Ironically, it was in Africa that protests over Floyd's death were relatively muted. To be sure, there were some demonstrations often involving dozens or hundreds of people in several countries, such as Ghana (Accra), Kenya (Nairobi), Liberia (Monrovia), Nigeria (Abuja), Senegal (Dakar), South Africa (Cape Town, Johannesburg and Pretoria), Tunisia (Tunis) and Uganda (Kampala). More extensive and powerful expressions of solidarity were vented in petitions by activists, intellectuals and artists (I participated in one called 'We Cannot Remain Silent') and especially on social media, according to Nana Osei-Opare, writing in *The Washington Post.*[15] This intriguing phenomenon reflects three complex factors.

First, in spite of Pan-Africanist rhetoric among African leaders and intellectuals there is an enduring disconnect between Africans on the continent and the African-descended people in the diaspora. It is borne out of limited engagements that ordinarily would emanate through the educational system and other forms of positive mutual exposure. Instead, there is an overexposure to negative stereotypes in the media that often traffic Eurocentric constructs and tropes on both sides of the other's 'civilisational' lack. More deeply, the unknowing of the diaspora, the willful ignorance of its tribulations, elides Africa's complicity in the very creation of the Atlantic diasporas through the slave trade.

Second, is the ambivalent postcolonial mindset rooted in the colonial denial of African humanity and historicity. It is a miscognition that simultaneously breeds resentment of the empire and craving of its prowess. This generates a strange desire among the colonised to be embraced and absorbed into the empire's imagined superiority and advancement, enveloped in whiteness. But, like Sisyphus, it is destined never to achieve this, thereby inducing a state of perpetual self-doubt and self-denial. This fosters both envy of the diaspora ensconced in the heart of empire and blindness to its plight, a slippery disposition that engenders a deficit of sympathy and often slides into blaming the victim.

Third, there is what I would call the shortage of surplus political capital for solidarity, the dispositions to accommodate transnational diaspora struggles. Surplus capital can be externalised for better or ill, as is evident in the impetus for the new imperialism of the late nineteenth and early twentieth centuries, one of whose drivers was the export of surplus financial capital. But, save for their elites, many African communities in their plebeian daily lives, now made infinitely worse by the coronavirus pandemic, are fettered by debilitating economic, political and social conditions and perpetual struggles against often autocratic regimes or illiberal democracies whose law enforcement agencies have retained the deformities of colonial state violence and repression. There is thus little surplus capital in Africa.

Reclaiming Public Memory

The monuments that became the focus of public protests, accompanied by demands for more accurate, holistic and inclusive historical representations, were part of the struggles for liberating highly sanitised and racialised public spaces and memories. The protesters in Euro-America were seeking to insert African-descended peoples, their presence and invaluable contributions into their national and regional histories.

The removal and desecration of racist monuments was a powerful rebuke of their brazen glorification of imperial and colonial conquests, exploitation and oppression. These acts of iconographic liberation struck at the willful production of ignorance and limited understanding of the unsavoury histories that made Euro-America, which are routinely reproduced through the educational system, popular histories and films and television. The monuments had been targeted for decades as offensive symbols and reminders of slavery and racial oppression.

The conversations forced by the assault on racist monuments provoked much-needed historical reckoning and accounting for the persistent racial inequalities, injustices and hierarchies bequeathed by enslavement, colonialism and empire. They helped dismember contemporary constructions of belonging and citizenship, of who constitutes and can enjoy the rights of the social and political community of the nation-state in Europe and the settler societies of the Americas and Australasia.

In the US, the removal of the statues and symbols of the renegade losers of the Civil War who fought to retain slavery intensified and reached the hallowed halls of Congress. House Speaker Nancy Pelosi urged the removal of eleven statues representing Confederate leaders and soldiers, noting that the 'statues pay homage to hate, not heritage'. The Pentagon announced its willingness to rename military bases associated with Confederate figures, a move that was endorsed by the Republican-controlled Senate despite Trump's expressed opposition.

The scale of the task was huge as there are about 1,800 Confederate symbols across the US (776 of which are monuments). At the time of writing, only 141 (61 monuments) had been removed and seven were pending removal.[16] For their part, 'the Navy and Marine Corps announced that they will ban the display of the Confederate flag at their facilities and events'.[17] Church symbols were not exempt. The president of the Southern Baptist Convention 'called for the retirement of a gavel that carries the name of a 19th-century Southern Baptist leader who was a slaveholder and led the convention in support of the Confederacy'. He proceeded to say 'black lives matter' six times in his presidential address.[18]

In Britain, protesters toppled the statues of slave traders, including Edward Colston in Bristol and Robert Milligan in London. City councils under the Labour Party, led by the capital, London, announced their intention to set up commissions to review sculptures, buildings and street names associated with slavers, while Conservative councils came under increased pressure to do the same. Activists hoped the toppling of the public memorialisations of the symbols of slavery and colonialism would force the country to confront the sordid historical injustices that had shaped it.

Several institutions, including hospitals and universities, also began the process or conversations to remove historical figures associated with the slave trade. Calls intensified for the disposal of the notorious imperialist Cecil Rhodes, a campaign that had begun in 2016 on the heels of the #RhodesMustFall campaign at the University of Cape Town, and racist icons of the British establishment such as Winston Churchill and Baden-Powell, founder of the Scouts movement. But as journalist Catherine Bennett observed cynically, 'As statues of slave traders are torn down, their heirs sit untouched in the Lords.'[19]

In Antwerp, the statue of King Leopold II of Belgium, the architect of one of the worst genocides of the twentieth century, which wiped out 10 million people in the Congo, was removed. In Barcelona, debate was rekindled for the removal of the statue of Christopher Columbus, which glorified the conquest of the Americas. Some councillors had voted for its toppling in 2016 and for its replacement by a memorial to those who had resisted imperialism and the oppression and segregation of the indigenous people and enslaved Africans and their descendants.

The removal of the statues of slave traders and imperialists in Europe was a homage to the unfinished project of decolonisation that began after World War II. The struggle over historical memory, constructions and emblems was about the legacies of the past that disfigured the present and threatened to burden the future if reckoning and resolution continued to be postponed. The refusal to deal with the past and its stifling shadows on contemporary society was infantile and an ingrained part of the repertoire of anti-black racism in the Americas, Europe and elsewhere. Removing statues is of course a symbolic act, but symbols matter. As the South African commentator, Eusebius McKaiser, reminded us, 'We know from South Africa that toppling statues is no silver bullet – but it's a start.'[20]

Thus, at stake in the political and discursive struggles over the statues was a collective public denial or willingness to reckon honestly with the complicated and messy histories and persistent legacies of slavery and empire, to dismantle false national mythologies and self-righteous delusions that breed shameless hypocrisies and perpetuate human rights abuses. Many of the contested statues were created decades or even centuries after the individuals or events their creators sought to glorify (in the US the Confederate monuments were created in the early 1900s as part of the revisionist romanticisation of the 'Lost Cause'). This underscores the fact that they had been built to augment the arsenal of selective political constructs in the ignominious service of white supremacy.

Performative Activism

The struggles to reclaim public spaces and historical memory from the accretion of generations of racist practices and ideologies led powerful institutions and individuals to embrace performative anti-racist activism that would not cost them much but served to burnish their brands. The growing traction of the Black Lives Matter movement in public opinion raised the opportunity costs of casual anti-black racism, as a majority of Americans increasingly came to believe that racism is a problem in the US.

This moment was ironically facilitated by Trump's presidency, characterised by unabashed racism, dizzying incompetence, authoritarian impulses and perpetual chaos. Trump succeeded in accelerating the erosion of the conservatism he was elected to protect from the country's changing demographics and liberal drift. Thus, the Trump administration, which emerged out of a racist backlash against the Obama presidency, helped to both reinforce and upend systemic racism and white supremacy.

Trump simultaneously brought racism out of the post-Civil Rights closet and made racism increasingly embarrassing to the moderate whites of so-called Middle America and unacceptable to younger white Americans more exposed to multiracial experiences and expectations, not least because of the symbolic possibilities of the Obama presidency, notwithstanding all its limitations. The national uprising was remarkably multiracial, far more than the Civil Rights struggles of the 1950s and 1960s were. It was dominated by young people, as revolutionary moments and moments tend to be.

Trump's victory in 2016 often obscures the fact that the shifts in racial attitudes had begun earlier. One observer contended: 'For all the attention paid to the politics of the far right in the Trump era, the biggest shift in American politics is happening somewhere else entirely', namely, in the move to the left of white liberals on questions of race, racism and other priorities of the Democratic coalition, such as immigration reform. He called it the 'Great Awokening', which had begun with the 2014 protests in Ferguson. 'Opinion leaders often miss the scale and recency of these changes because progressive elites have espoused racial liberalism for a long time.'[21]

A poll published on 9 June 2020 found that 'nearly two-thirds of Americans, including 57 per cent of whites, are "very" or "extremely" concerned about systemic racism'. It was this shift in public opinion that made performative support for anti-racism more imperative for more constituencies and actors in the public and private sphere, from corporations to the media, sports and academe. *The New York Times* put it pithily: 'From Cosmetics to NASCAR, Calls for Racial Justice Are Spreading. What started as a renewed push for police reform has now touched seemingly every aspect of American life.'[22]

As the opprobrium for anti-black racism rose, racist behaviour and statements that previously would have been ignored increasingly threatened the careers and social standing of their perpetrators. It became a season of apologies from media personalities, sports figures, university professors, publishers and film directors for offensive statements they had made in the past or following Floyd's horrific killing.

Public imagination was especially captured by the apologies and affirmations of Black Lives Matter by sports figures. The NFL Commissioner Roger Goodell stated, 'We, the National Football League, condemn racism and the systematic oppression of black people.' He went on to stress, 'We, the National Football League, admit we were wrong for not listening to NFL players earlier and encourage all to speak out and peacefully protest.'[23] Confronted by criticism that he did not mention Colin Kaepernick, a quarterback who had popularised kneeling during the national anthem as a form of protest against police brutality, he later did so and appealed for Kaepernick's reinstatement into the NFL. Nascar, the speed-racing event especially popular among Southern whites, announced the banning at its events of Confederate flags, a despised symbol among African Americans, which it had discouraged since 2015 to no avail.

Apologies and protests spread to the rarefied white-dominated world of fashion, as the editor-in-chief of *American Vogue*, Anna Wintour, apologised for publishing hurtful or intolerant stories and not hiring enough people of colour.[24] The editor of *The Philadelphia Inquirer* resigned 'after an article with the headline "Buildings Matter, Too," on the effects of civil unrest on the city's buildings, led to a walkout by dozens of staff members'.[25]

For their part, 'more than 300 leading stage artists signed a letter decrying racial inequality in the world of "White American theater"'.[26] Some musicians converted to the new anti-racist tune. 'Lady Antebellum, the Grammy-winning country music trio behind one of the highest-selling country songs of all time, is dropping the "antebellum" from its name.'[27] The cinematic arts also saw the light. Television shows such as *Cops* and films such as *Gone with the Wind*, which glorify police violence and elide the brutalities of slavery respectively, were terminated or removed from streaming. However, critics maintained that censoring old films and TV shows was not enough; what mattered was employing more people of colour in the industry.[28]

Restiveness among technology companies also became evident. The announcement by IBM and Amazon, that they were withdrawing their face-recognition technology from being used by police forces in racial profiling and mass surveillance, was widely hailed in some quarters. In the meantime, more

> than 200 Microsoft employees have signed a letter calling on the company to stop supplying software to law enforcement agencies; to support efforts to defund the Seattle Police Department; and to join a call for the mayor of Seattle, Jenny Durkan, to resign. The signers are a tiny fraction of Microsoft's more than 140,000 employees. But the letter is another sign of increasing activism by employees at major technology companies on a range of political issues, which executives have been forced to address – if only to explain why they would not comply with workers' requests.[29]

Performative anti-racist solidarity was also expressed in other countries, although to a more limited extent. In Britain, the tea-obsessed nation paid attention when 'Top U.K. Tea Brands Urge #Solidaritea With Anti-Racism Protests', to quote a headline from a story in *The New York Times*.[30] The story noted that a series of tea companies had doubled down after right-wing complaints about businesses' support for Black Lives Matter.

Clearly, as silence on race increasingly ceased to be an option, American companies and institutions fell over each over to proclaim their support for Black Lives Matter. Anti-racism suddenly became a badge of honour for companies eager to burnish their brands under America's emerging new normal. Corporate America proudly wore its newly acquired conscience on its malleable sleeves.

The bandwagon expanded by the day and encompassed every sector, as noted in the following partial list. Automobile industry: BMW AG, General Motors, Toyota Motor Corp., Daimler AG and Volkswagen AG. Banking and finance:

American Express, Barclays Bank, Bank of America, Goldman Sachs, MasterCard. Delivery services: FedEx and Deutsche Post DHL. Film and television: Academy Films, Warner Media, The Walt Disney Company, Paramount Pictures Corp., Fox Corp. Gaming: Logitech (Astro Gaming), CBS Interactive (GameSpot), Nintendo of America, Inc, Sony Interactive Entertainment (PlayStation), The Pokémon Company.

Health and insurance: MetLife Inc, New York Life Insurance Co., UnitedHealth Group. Food and Beverages: Unilever (Ben & Jerry's), Restaurant Brands International (Burger King, Popeyes), Chipotle Mexican Grill, Chick-fil-A, The Coca-Cola Company, PepsiCo (Pepsi, Doritos), McDonald's, the Kellogg Company. Music and performance: Warner Music Group, Prometheus Global Media (Billboard), Universal Music Group (Capitol Records, Virgin Records), the Metropolitan Opera. Oil and gas: BP plc. Pharmaceuticals and pharmacies: Bayer AG, CVS Health, Merck Group and Pfizer Inc. Publishing: Advance Publications (Condé Nast).

Retail and grocery: adidas AG, Giorgio Armani S.p.A., Gap, Inc., Home Depot, Inc., IKEA, Proctor & Gamble, Tesco plc. Sports: Nascar and NFL. Technology and e-commerce: Apple Inc, Cisco Systems, Facebook, Alphabet, Inc. (Google), Microsoft Corp. Telecommunications: AT&T Inc, Verizon Wireless, Deutsche Telekom AG (T-Mobile). Transport: Alaska Airlines, American Airlines, Inc., Lyft, Inc. and Uber Technologies, Inc.

The flood of corporate anti-racist statements was often accompanied by donations to venerable civil rights organisations, such as the NAACP, Urban League and National Action Network, and other groups fighting racial inequality. Businesses also included vague promises to promote diversity and inclusion in their own companies without spelling out meaningful enforcement mechanisms. The donations tended to be largely token, but some were sizeable. For example, SoftBank Group Corp. allocated US$100 million to invest in minority entrepreneurs, while 'PayPal, Apple and YouTube collectively pledged $730 million to racial justice and equity efforts'.[31] Estée Lauder, the cosmetics giant, raised its donation from US$1 million to US$5 million after its initial offer was derided by employees who compared it unfavourably to Ronald Lauder's far more generous donations to Trump.

Many corporate executives saw the anti-racism cause as part of their corporate social responsibility, which for some amounted to political corporate social responsibility. In 2019, 181 US corporations signed a revised statement on the purpose of a corporation issued by Business Roundtable. The corporate executives committed to lead their companies for the benefit of all stakeholders by 'Delivering value to our customers', 'Investing in our employees', 'Dealing fairly and ethically with our suppliers', 'Supporting the communities in which we work' and 'Generating long-term value for shareholders'.[32]

While welcoming pledges by corporations to engage in anti-discrimination efforts and programmes to support black businesses and communities, many black corporate leaders and civil rights activists remained sceptical, as noted in a long article in *The New York Times*, entitled 'Corporate America Has Failed Black America'. The newspaper stressed the need to tie executive pay to diversity metrics, which a few companies, such as Microsoft Corp., Intel and Johnson & Johnson, had embraced.[33]

By and large, critics of corporate America were not impressed by this performative anti-racism. They highlighted the glaring gap between the fluffy anti-racist rhetoric and the reality of entrenched racist practices in most American companies. Some of the advice given to companies by their cheerleaders exacted little cost. One corporate sympathiser urged them to expand their relationships with historically black colleges and universities, advertise more openly, create diverse interview panels at all levels, provide extensive sensitive training for all employees and set the tone for inclusion at the top.[34]

The Economist contended:

> Good intentions of bosses aside, untangling the problem of race and corporate America requires addressing four questions. First, what is the evidence that blacks are disadvantaged in the workplace? Second, how much is business to blame rather than society as a whole? Third, do any such disadvantages impact how businesses perform? And finally, what if anything can business do to improve matters?

Its answer to all four questions underscored the prevalence of systemic racism and black under-representation throughout American business. It concluded, 'Experts recommend creating a diversity strategy specifically for black employees, implementing clear and consistent standards for promotion and securing a firm commitment from the top to overcome bias among middle managers … that points to the importance of metrics and measurement.'[35]

The anti-racist rhetoric grew with a breathtaking speed that confounded many people. Unhinged white conservatives bemoaned the trend and redoubled their virulent attacks on the Black Lives Matter movement and denounced the protesters as rioters and even domestic terrorists. Anguished white liberals shed their silence and commiserated with each other about racism and inundated their black colleagues with outpourings of sympathy, support and queries, which some blacks welcomed and others disdained. The latter resented the added burden of cleansing white consciences.

For their part, African Americans seized this rare opportunity to be heard by the wider society with an avalanche of painful and often harrowing experiences with racism in their daily lives, which they had previously hidden from their white colleagues. New social media tags were created, such as #BlackInTheIvory, which was deluged by stories of marginalisation, isolation, devaluation, frustration and hostility experienced by black academics. Sales of books on race and racism, many by black authors, skyrocketed. The uprising also inspired thousands of people in the US and around the world to create powerful art. From 'street murals near the White House to editorial comics created near where Floyd died, artists are delivering political messages through often stark imagery'.[36]

The battles over racism and the protests raged on social media, the public square of the digital age. They engulfed platforms often not in the public eye. For example, as reported by *The New York Times*, 'Upper East Side Mom Group Implodes Over Accusations of Racism and Censorship. A large Facebook parenting group temporarily shut down after silencing black members. Now new groups for parents are forming that are explicitly anti-racist.'[37]

Trouble in the Ivory Tower

Colleges and universities were embroiled in the sprawling national crisis, although closures of campuses in response to the coronavirus pandemic saved them from protests on their own campuses and in university towns. Linda Ellis warned in *The Chronicle of Higher Education*, 'For Colleges, Protests Over Racism May Put Everything On the Line'.[38] She predicted that the reckoning would come once colleges and universities reopened and as students returned to campuses, already energised by the national uprising triggered by Floyd's horrific killing.

Many universities issued statements that expressed sympathy, pain, even support for Black Lives Matter. Predictably, the statements varied in length, depth and breadth. Many were formulaic and fluffy, written by communication departments afraid of antagonising powerful donors, state law-makers and alumni. They invoked the role of the university as a positive force in society, forgetting the fact that American universities and education in general have been integral to the production and reproduction of the structures and ideologies of systemic racism.

As numerous studies have shown, building on Craig Steven Wilder's groundbreaking *Ebony & Ivy: Race, Slavery and the Troubled History of America's Universities*,[39] many of the renowned Ivy League universities were founded by or with resources from slave-owners and slave-traders. Over the generations, the ideologies and practices of anti-black racism have been concocted, refined and sanctified in the academy. Black history, contributions, concerns, interests and experiences are routinely excluded and devalourised in the American academy.

The constant assault and surveillance of racism by the white academy on black students and faculty is draining and exhausting. Some academics succumb to the stresses of racial battle fatigue and become less productive and alienated from a vocation they had chosen with passion and expectation. They seemingly retire on the job in that they psychologically check out and simply go through the motions. Others persist and become adept at concealing the pain, humiliation and hostility they often face. However, professional progress offers no immunity. In fact, the higher one rises, the more one is surveilled in the fishbowl of systemic racism that permeates American academic cultures and institutions.

African-American students and academics are grossly underrepresented in prestigious universities, programmes and fellowships, while black-centred knowledge is often filtered out from the holy grail of academic publications, journals, grants and conferences. There are of course differences according to discipline and field. The situation in the sciences is particularly egregious.

On 10 June 2020 almost 6,000 scientists and academicians participated in a one-day strike. The event was organised under various hashtags, including #Strike4BlackLives, #ShutDownStem and #ShutDownAcademia, by scientists who complained about perversive racism in science. Besides classes, several leading scientific journals, such as *Nature, Science, Physical Review Letters* and *arXiv*, cancelled activities that day.[40] Protests spread to other academic journals. For example, after Harald Uhlig, the editor of *Political Economy Review,* wrote a tone-deaf tweet criticising the Black Lives Matter supporters as 'flat earthers', an array of economists, which included the former chair of the Federal Reserve, Janet Yellen, and Paul Krugman, a Nobel prize winner, called for his resignation. In the US, economics as a field is white-male dominated, which has led to the devaluation of research and publications by women and blacks and on gender and race.[41]

I can relate to the challenges faced by African Americans in the academy. As a college dean and an academic vice president at predominantly white universities in California and Connecticut, respectively, I was subject to doubt and disrespect that none of my colleagues in similar positions experienced. As is all too common, I was the first black person to occupy those positions. Earlier in my career, when I served as director of one of the largest centres for African Studies at a Research 1 university in the Midwest, I witnessed the exclusion of Africans and African Americans in the study of their own ancestral continent, Africa.

It became too much for me. Fortunately, I was able to flee to Kenya. I often commiserate with friends and colleagues I left behind, some of whom have risen to higher positions as deans, provosts and presidents. They continue to walk the fine line of racial discrimination and exclusion in the American academy. In the aftermath of the uprising, many of them have courageously stepped up to denounce systemic racism and call for honest dialogue and real change on their own campuses and share their pernicious experiences with racism as black men and women. I salute them.

Taming Law Enforcement

A key demand of the protesters was the urgent need to address systemic police brutality, racial bias, misconduct and unaccountability. The evidence of racism in the criminal justice system was overwhelming, as an exhaustive list of studies in *The Washington Post* showed.[42] As if to prove the objections of the Black Lives Matter movement right, the police reacted to the demonstrators with excessive force and brutality that resulted in eleven deaths and nearly 10,000 arrests within a fortnight. This galvanised the protest movement even further. The public and elected leaders could no longer ignore police behaving as an invading army, and the armour of police untouchability began to crack.

To be sure, there were occasional scenes of police officers kneeling in solidarity with the protesters. Some African-American police chiefs, caught between their racial identity and police fraternity, shared their agonies, dilemmas, challenges and frustrations of trying to change their departments from within and reconcile their personal and professional, private and public lives.[43]

Police departments across the country came under pressure to review their policies and practices as public agitation for comprehensive police reform mounted. City councils, state assemblies and Congress were forced to begin enacting long-standing demands and legislation banning grievous repressive practices and promoting police reform. For some, more radical measures were needed and they adopted the slogan, 'Defund the Police'. The Center for Community Change Action framed the much-needed restructuring in terms of redistribution for reconstruction, taking funds from law enforcement to improve health care, education and other social services and opportunities in communities of colour.

In the House of Representatives, Democrats unveiled the Justice in Policing Act of 2020, the provisions of which included requiring police to use body and dashboard cameras, restricting the transfer of military equipment to police, prohibiting chokeholds and unannounced raids through the issuance of no-knock warrants, and enhancing police accountability by restricting the application of the qualified immunity doctrine that made it difficult to prosecute law enforcement personnel. It encompassed establishing a federal registry of police misconduct complaints and disciplinary actions, granting power to the Justice Department's Civil Rights Division to issue subpoenas to police departments with a pattern and practice of bias or misconduct, and requiring state and local law enforcement agencies that received federal funding to adopt anti-discrimination policies and training programmes.

Republicans were caught flat-footed. *The New York Times* noted, 'Having long fashioned themselves as the party of law and order, Republicans have been startled by the speed and extent to which public opinion has shifted under their feet in recent days after the killings of unarmed black Americans by the police and the protests that have followed. The abrupt turn has placed them on the defensive.'[44] The party charged the only black Republican Senator, Tim Scott, to draft its own bill on police reform.

On 17 June, 2020, the Republicans:

> unveiled a policing reform bill that would discourage, but not ban, tactics such as chokeholds and no-knock warrants, offering a competing approach to legislation being advanced by House Democrats that includes more directives from Washington. The Republican proposal, which Senate leaders said would be considered on the floor next week, veers away from mandating certain policing practices, as the Democratic plan does. … Prospects for reaching common ground in the coming weeks remain unclear.[45]

The stage was set for a legislative brawl between the two parties, the outcome of which was unpredictable.

Under mounting pressure, the previous day President Trump had issued an executive order. He offered tepid 'support for curtailing police abuses while reiterating a hard line on law and order', reported *The Wall Street Journal.* The order:

> has three main components: establishing an independent credentialing process to spur departments to adopt the most modern use-of-force practices; creation of a database to track abusive officers that can be shared among different departments; and placing social service workers to accompany officers on nonviolent response calls to deal with issues such as drug addiction and homelessness. Chokeholds would be banned under the recommended standards, Mr. Trump said, unless an officer's life is at risk.[46]

Within two weeks of the national uprising following Floyd's death, several states and cities had enacted legislation to reform the police services along some of the lines of the Democratic bill in Congress. The New York State Assembly passed a bill allowing felony charges to be brought against police using the chokehold or similar restraint, and for the release of disciplinary records for individual police officers, firefighters or corrections officers without their written consent. The governor ordered all police departments to develop and get approvals for reform plans by 1 April 2021 if they were to remain eligible for state funding, while the mayor of New York City announced plans to shift some funds from the police department's US$6 billion budget to other services.

Los Angeles cut funding by US$150 million from its police department. In Seattle, the mayor promised to invest US$100 million in the Seattle Black Commission for community-driven programmes for black youths and adults. The Minneapolis City Council voted overwhelmingly to abolish the police department. In Louisville, Kentucky, the City Council unanimously passed 'Breonna's Law', which banned the use of 'no-knock' warrants, named after Breonna Taylor who had been killed in her own home by police who had forced their way in with a battering ram. In Washington DC the City Council also banned the use of tear gas, pepper spray, rubber bullets and stun grenades to disperse protesters.

Some critics maintained that focusing on the police was not enough. In the words of *The New York Times* columnist, Charles Blow:

> But, these bills, if they pass as conceived, would basically punish the system's soldiers without altering the system itself. These bills would make the officers the fall guy for their bad behavior while doing little to condemn or even address the savagery and voraciousness of the system that required their service. This country has established a system of supreme inequity, with racial inequity being a primary form and used the police to protect the wealth that the system generated for some and to control the outrages and outbursts of those opposed to it and oppressed by it. We need more than performative symbols of solidarity. We need more than narrow, chaste legislation.[47]

'Defund the Police' turned into a battle cry for the supporters and opponents of comprehensive police reform. For its proponents it was a demand for a fundamental reimagining and restructuring of American law enforcement, which was rooted in the systemic racism and white supremacy of slave patrols that evolved into the gendarmes of Jim Crow and subsequent crackdowns on black protests and the highly racialised War on Drugs.

The critics argued that the nearly US$100 billion spent on law enforcement could be used, to quote Paige Fernandez, the Policing Policy Advisor of the American Civil Liberties Union, writing in *Cosmopolitan*, to fund 'more helpful services like job training, counseling and violence-prevention programs. … Funneling so many resources into law enforcement instead of education, affordable housing and accessible health care has caused significant harm to communities.'

The author reminded her readers:

> Much of the work police do is merely engage in the daily harassment of Black communities for minor crimes or crimes of poverty that shouldn't be criminalized in the first place. Consider this: Out of the 10.3 million arrests made per year, only 5 percent are for the most serious offenses, including murder, rape and aggravated assault. These are the ones that truly threaten public safety. … That means that police spend the most resources going after minor incidents that actually don't threaten everyday life but do lead to mass criminalization and incarceration.[48]

The brutality of the police forces escalated with their militarisation, a process that accelerated, wrote Simon Tisdall in the *Guardian,* in response to:

> … the 9/11 attacks, when George W Bush plunged the country into a state of perpetual war. Paradoxically, his 'global war on terror' intensified international and domestic insecurity. It sparked a huge, parallel expansion in the powers and reach of the homeland security apparatus. As Pentagon spending grew to a whopping $738bn this year, total police and prison budgets have also soared, reaching $194bn in 2017. About 18,000 law enforcement agencies employ 800,000 officers nationwide. Many are armed to the teeth.[49]

In short, the crisis of policing in the US flowed from the devil's brew of entrenched racism, excessive militarism, xenophobic nationalism and imperial decline.

Transforming Racial Capitalism

Many leaders and opinion-makers in political, business, media and academic circles promote legislative and policy solutions as antidotes to systemic racism. However, anti-black racism has persisted despite the enactment of a myriad laws and policies since the 1960s. White supremacy and its pathological disdain for black people, black bodies and black humanity emanates from deep cultural and cognitive spaces that lie beyond the reach of well-crafted legislation and policy pronouncements.

In short, the struggle to eradicate systemic racism and white supremacy has to transcend police reform and electoral politics. After all, racial bias, violence and inequality persisted under Republican and Democratic administrations alike, including Obama's own and under black leaders in state assemblies and black mayors in cities. Thus, for young African Americans who have grown up in cities and a country with thousands of black elected officials compared to the 1960s, the promises of electoral politics do not carry the same transformative appeal. As in Africa following decolonisation, achieving political representation, a worthy goal in itself, is inadequate for the herculean task of fundamentally changing the structures of economic and political power and systemic racism in the United States. The younger generations demand, and are seeking to build, a new black and national politics of accountability and transformation.

The complicity of Democratic presidents, senators and congressmen and congresswomen in the construction of the prison-industrial complex since the 1980s is all too well known. President Clinton's crime and welfare reform legislation fuelled mass black incarceration and impoverishment. For his part, President Obama failed to meet the radical expectations placed on his administration in terms of reforming the criminal justice system, reducing economic inequalities and curtailing the corporate power that engendered the Great Recession. Just as Clinton had passed draconian immigration laws, Obama's deportation of undocumented immigrants reached record levels.

Fundamental change requires a much broader and bolder vision and an expansive and inclusive politics. It has to transcend the paralysing dogmas of neoliberalism and encompass transforming the multiple structural pillars and cultural dynamics of racial capitalism, as well as building new multiracial and class coalitions and alliances. There is no shortage of blueprints for a different future from America's radical thinkers and activists committed to building a future envisaged in Martin Luther King's dream of a 'beloved community', based on the pillars of economic and social justice free from poverty, discrimination and violence.

The Harvard political scientist, Danielle Allen, suggested creating a new national compact that encompassed some of the following elements: expanding the House of Representatives; adopting ranked-choice voting; instituting universal voting and instant voter registration for all eligible Americans; establishing an expectation of national service by all Americans; limiting Supreme Court justices to 18-year terms; building civic media to counteract the challenges introduced by social media; finding honest ways to tell the nation's story; and increasing 'resources and resolve for community leadership, civic education and an American culture of shared commitment to constitutional democracy and one another'.[50]

In the magazine, *The Harvard Gazette*, a group of six of the university's faculty members discussed 'how best to convert the energy of this moment into meaningful and lasting change'. Some explicitly supported or echoed the demands of the Black Lives Matter movement. More specifically, they variously proposed: a serious reckoning of the foundational exclusions of African Americans and Native Americans; the pursuit of economic democracy; the need for a new Voting Rights act; and a fundamental reconsideration of the Constitution for a Third Reconstruction involving 'a fundamental reconsideration of our Constitution, systems, institutions and practices to uphold human rights and ensure equal opportunity for all'. Centring black women in the struggle for collective liberation is imperative and for the university itself 'to move beyond the rhetoric of "diversity and inclusion" and become anti-racist'.[51]

Michelle Alexander, the author of the influential book, *The New Jim Crow: Mass Incarceration in the Age of Colorblindness*,[52] admonished the nation in *The New York Times:* 'America, This is Your Chance. We must get it right this time or risk losing our democracy forever.' She implored the country's diverse citizens, 'We must face our racial history and our racial present', 'We must reimagine justice' beyond tinkering with token or unsustainable fixes, 'We must fight for economic justice' by transforming the economic system and embracing one based on economic justice.[53]

For some, economic justice also entailed reparations, an issue that gained some traction. The reparations movement has a long history, but it has remained on the fringes of American intellectual and political discourse. An influential essay by Ta-Nehisi Coates, the African-American writer who some regard as a successor to the great James Baldwin, 'The Case for Reparations' published in *The Atlantic* in June 2014, brought the issue to the mainstream media. He argued powerfully, 'Two hundred fifty years of slavery. Ninety years of Jim Crow. Sixty years of separate but equal. Thirty-five years of racist housing policy. Until we reckon with our compounding moral debts, America will never be whole.'[54]

The data on what America owes African Americans is damning. In her book, *The Color of Money,* Mehrsa Baradaran offers a bleak assessment of the racial wealth gap and the limits of community self-help. She shows that in 1863 when the Emancipation Proclamation was signed, the black community owned 0.5 per cent of the country's wealth. More than 150 years later this rose to a paltry 1 per cent! In a recent interview, she argued that America has repeatedly violated its promises of equal protection and equality to African Americans:

> I teach contract law ... When you break a contract, you pay damages. We've broken the contract with Black America. ... We embedded racism into policy. And how do you get that out. How do you fix that? I think reparations is the only answer ... And I think a process of reparations should involve truth and reconciliation. We have the funds. We saw this with the coronavirus. Over a weekend, the Fed infused trillions of dollars into the repo markets and into the economy. We don't have limits of resources. We have limits of empathy and imagination.[55]

The need for white involvement in the anti-racist movement is well understood. No less critical is building strong multiracial alliances among America's racial minorities who, collectively, will in a couple of decades become the county's majority. Each minority group has its own complex history and positioning in the country's racial hierarchy and political economy. Particularly divisive has been the model minority myth applied to Asians, which some Asian Americans have embraced and internalised. It was constructed and served to distance them from African Americans and Hispanic Americans. 'Many Latinos arrive in the United States,' observed a commentator in The *Washington Post*, 'with their own anti-black beliefs rooted in the histories of white European colonialism and slavery in their native countries. ... As they try to assimilate, they often adopt anti-black attitudes "that come from the white majority".'[56]

Differentiation and distanciation from African Americans is the ritual of passage to Americanisation for every migrant group in the United States. Successive waves of Europeans from Irish, Italian, Slavic and Jewish backgrounds were initially not considered white, but were eventually absorbed into whiteness, a process that often entailed socialisation into American racism. Asians whose migration to the United States increased following changes in migration laws due to the Civil Rights movement have revelled in being called a model minority. Even immigrant Latin Americans and Africans have sought dubious solace in their foreignness, in not being African American, until they are brutalised by systemic racism and white supremacy. The 2020 uprising brought a lot of soul-searching for every racial group in the United States in terms of where they stood in the country's enduring racial quagmire.

The national uprising emboldened Asian-American activists to call for solidarity with African Americans in their struggles against systemic racism and white supremacy. Marina Fang, a reporter at HuffPost, noted, 'George Floyd's death has galvanized some Asian Americans to try to start conversations with their families about anti-Black racism' and build solidarity with black communities. 'Anti-Black racism in Asian communities is tied to the "model minority" myth, which white political leaders, particularly in response to the civil rights movement in the 1960s, wielded in order to drive a wedge between Asian Americans and other people of color.'[57]

Writing in The *Washington Post,* Nepalese-American fashion designer, Prabal Gurung, echoed the same sentiments:

> It's time for Asian Americans to shed the 'model minority' myth and stand for George Floyd. … Beyond simple divestment and rejection of our own trope, we must also actively combat anti-blackness – especially within the Asian community. … To break from this cycle, we must begin by asking: Who benefits when minority groups fight each other or are apathetic to one another's struggles?… It is time for us to stand in solidarity with black communities whose sacrifices led to the civil rights and privileges we benefit from.[58]

The Washington Post reported during the protests, 'Many Asian Americans say they feel a need to show solidarity with black protesters. … Asians have their own history of American discrimination from the Chinese Exclusion Act of 1882 to the internment of Japanese Americans during World War II to the slurs and boycotts Asian American restaurant and business owners have faced during the coronavirus pandemic.' One Asian-American protestor 'said his generation is well aware that the success Asians have achieved in the United States is owed directly to black protesters in the 1950s and 1960s and is built "on the backs of those black leaders of the civil rights movement".'[59]

The uprising also forced many whites to accept that silence is complicity and to confess their ignorance about the depths of American racism. David Axelrod, the chief strategist for President Obama's campaigns and senior advisor in the Obama White House, put it poignantly in *The Washington Post*:

> I thought I understood issues of race. I was wrong. … Despite my work, I was too often oblivious – or at least inattentive – to the everyday mistreatment of people of color, including friends and colleagues, in ways large and small. Although I was reporting on the issues of police brutality and unequal justice as a journalist, I didn't experience it. My kids didn't experience it. And I never really engaged my black friends and colleagues about their own experiences. I never asked, so far as I can remember, about their own interactions with police or their fears for their children.

It is worth quoting Axelrod's conclusion:

> A lot of white Americans thought they understood. But the underlying legacy of racism still remains. The laws that were passed were hard-won and important, but they didn't eliminate deeply ingrained biases and layers of discriminatory practices and policies that mock the ideal of equality. The election of a black president was a watershed event in our history that struck at the heart of the racist creed. But it didn't end racism. In fact, it provoked a backlash that empowered a racist demagogue and new policies meant to further embed structural barriers to full citizenship for black Americans.[60]

This is an example of what the philosopher, Charles W. Mills, my former colleague at the University of Illinois at Chicago, called 'white ignorance'. He defined it as a historically constructed group-based cognitive tendency and moral disposition of non-knowing, of motivated irrationality. It is a perversely deforming outlook causally linked to white normativity and white privilege, in which white perception and categorisation, social memory and social amnesia are privileged and non-white experiences and racial group interests are derogated.

White ignorance, Mills insisted, is not confined to whites and is global in so far as the modern world was created by European imperialism and colonialism. It is a foundational miscognition that permeates perceptions, conceptions and theorisations in descriptive, popular and scholarly discourses. In his book, *States of Denial*,[61] Stanley Cohen called it 'denial', the willful act of not wanting to know, wearing blinders, turning a blind eye, blocking out and of evading and avoiding unpleasant realities and horrific atrocities by the perpetrators and by bystanders of repression.

An often-ignored site of the anti-racist struggle is organised labour. In the US trade unions had declined in number precipitously. In the previous four decades union membership had fallen by half, from 20.1 per cent of workers in 1983 (17.7 million) to 10.3 per cent in 2019 (14.6 million). This helped reduce the capacity of the working class to organise against capital in the first instance and to build multiracial coalitions and mobilise against the economic, political and social system of racial capitalism. Deprived or divorced from collective class organisation and struggle, working people had been demobilised by capital and the political class. To be sure, in the United States the configurations of capital, labour and politics had always been fractionalised, not least by the demographics and ideologies of race.

As I noted in my earlier studies on labour movements after World War II, American trade unions at home and abroad were notoriously racist. However, the assault against organised labour accelerated in the post-Civil Rights era, as race was weaponised to camouflage the devaluation of labour under neoliberalism. The Southern Strategy started peeling away white workers from the Democratic coalition. The rise of the Reagan Democrats culminated in the capture, by Trump's unabashedly racist insurgency, of demoralised and deradicalised white workers.

In short, the anti-racist movement must find a way of mobilising the white working class, of aligning class, race and gender for progressive change. More immediately, the labour movement, as reporter Dave Jamieson noted, 'faces a reckoning over police unions'. He commented that 'police unions make a small slice of the AFL-CIO, but progressive members are increasingly uncomfortable associating with them'. Angered by police brutality, some labour leaders called for cutting ties with police unions, increasing their transparency and accountability, and curtailing their funding and political power over both the Republican and Democratic parties.[62]

The importance of transracial solidarity for working people is essential because the struggle is not just against racism, or just against capitalism, each living in splendid isolation from each other, but against both in their articulation as racial capitalism. Race, class, gender and other social inscriptions are not competitive but complementary categories of social and political identity and practice. They constitute interlocking structural, political and representational processes that under racial capitalism reflect and reproduce deformed institutions and pathological social relations. The African-American scholar and public intellectual, Kimberlé Crenshaw, called this 'intersectionality';[63] it offers more nuanced and complex analyses of systemic racism and white supremacy than the binaries of race and class and the isolated categories of race, class and gender.

The concept of racial capitalism captures the interlocking nature of the capitalist system, patriarchy and white supremacy. As academic, Michael Dawson, succinctly argued, each of these three systems of domination not only have 'their own internal logics, which include sources of resistance'. This means 'victories against one system of domination have the potential, too often unrealised, to undermine the other'.[64] In its development, racial capitalism undergoes historical shifts as the regimes of articulation of its constituent parts change. The question that arose with the 2020 national uprising is the extent to which it pried open the contradictions between the three systems of domination.

The modern world system was created in the transatlantic world, including the United States, by racial capitalism, through the genocide of the native peoples, enslavement of Africans and settler colonialism. Racism and patriarchy were integral to the extraction of value by white capitalists from both black and white workers, whose class solidarity was always undercut by white supremacy. Since the onset of neoliberalism following the end of the long postwar boom in the 1970s, the wages of whiteness had precipitously declined, as evident in stagnant incomes, a shrinking middle class and rising inequalities. The prolonged crises of accumulation and legitimacy, exacerbated by the Great Recession, facilitated the mobilisation of disaffected white working and middle classes by the insurgencies of the right-wing populism embodied by Trump in 2016 and by the forces for social justice represented by the 2020 national uprising.

Thus, what was at stake went beyond the reform of America's law enforcement agencies and performative anti-racism. It was about the transformation of racial capitalism. Given the enormous stakes involved and the depth and breadth of the economic, political, social and racial structures of domination the struggle would be long and hard indeed. But the 2020 uprising opened new doors of possibility.

Notes

1. Lara Putnam, Erica Chenoweth and Jeremy Pressman, 'The Floyd protests are the broadest in U.S. history – and are spreading to white, small-town America', *The Washington Post*, 6 June 2020. https://www.washingtonpost.com/politics/2020/06/06/floyd-protests-are-broadest-us-history-are-spreading-white-small-town-america/
2. Peniel E. Joseph, 'Protests in the wake of MLK's assassination and George Floyd's death show what hasn't – and has – changed since 1968', *The Washington Post,* 6 June 2020. https://www.washingtonpost.com/nation/2020/06/06/protests-wake-mlks-assassination-george-floyds-death-show-what-hasnt-has-changed-since-1968
3. *POLITICO Magazine*, 'It Really Is Different This Time. Two dozen experts explain why', 4 June 2020. https://www.politico.com/news/magazine/2020/06/04/protest-different-299050
4. Lara Putnam, Erica Chenoweth and Jeremy Pressman, 'The Floyd protests are the broadest in U.S. history – and are spreading to white, small-town America', *The Washington Post*, 6 June 2020. https://www.washingtonpost.com/politics/2020/06/06/floyd-protests-are-broadest-us-history-are-spreading-white-small-town-america
5. *The Economist,* 'America's Protests Turn Jubilant', 11 June 2020. https://www.economist.com/united-states/2020/06/11/americas-protests-turn-jubilant
6. Nate Cohn and Kevin Qealy, 'How Public Opinion Has Moved on Black Lives Matter', *The New York Times,* 10 June 2020. https://www.nytimes.com/interactive/2020/06/10/upshot/black-lives-matter-attitudes.html
7. Alex Thompson, 'White America is reckoning with racism. It could reshape 2020', *POLITICO Magazine,* 9 June 2020. https://www.politico.com/news/2020/06/09/white-voters-2020-biden-304804
8. *The Economist,* 'The Power of Protest and the Legacy of George Floyd', 13 June 2020. https://www.economist.com/weeklyedition/2020-06-13
9. John Allen, 'A Moment of National Shame and Peril – and Hope', *Foreign Affairs*, 3 June 2020. https://foreignpolicy.com/2020/06/03/trump-military-george-floyd-protests/
10. Alan Taylor, 'Images From a Worldwide Protest Movement', *The Atlantic,* 8 June 2020. https://www.theatlantic.com/photo/2020/06/images-worldwide-protest-movement/612811/
11. Lara Jakes and Edward Wong, 'U.S. Diplomats Struggle to Defend Democracy Abroad Amid Crises at Home', *The New York Times*, 8 June 2020. https://www.nytimes.com/2020/06/06/us/politics/protests-diplomats-coronavirus.html?referringSource=articleShare
12. Gary Younge, 'What black America means to Europe', *Guardian,* 11 June 2020. https://www.theguardian.com/world/2020/jun/11/what-black-america-means-to-europe-protests-racism-george-floyd?CMP=Share_iOSApp_Other
13. David Olusoga, 'Britain is not America. But we too are disfigured by deep and pervasive racism', *Guardian,* 7 June 2020. https://www.theguardian.com/commentisfree/2020/jun/07/britain-is-not-america-but-we-too-are-disfigured-by-deep-and-pervasive-racism

14. Tim Adams, '"Now is the time': London's Black Lives Matter rally looks like a turning point', *Guardian,* 7 June 2020. https://www.theguardian.com/us-news/2020/jun/06/now-is-the-time-londons-black-lives-matter-rally-looks-like-a-turning-point
15. Nana Osei-Opare, 'Around the world, the U.S. has long been a symbol of anti-black racism', *The Washington Post,* 5 June 2020. https://www.washingtonpost.com/outlook/2020/06/05/around-world-us-has-long-been-symbol-anti-black-racism/
16. Naja Sayej, '"It's a big turning point': Is this the end of racist monuments in America?' *Guardian,* 9 June 2020. https://www.theguardian.com/artanddesign/2020/jun/09/america-racist-monuments-civil-war-confederate?CMP=Share_iOSApp_Other
17. Paul Walkman, 'Why Donald Trump is standing up for the Confederacy', *The Washington Post,* 11 June 2020. https://www.washingtonpost.com/opinions/2020/06/11/why-donald-trump-is-standing-up-confederacy/
18. Sarah Pullman Bailey, 'Southern Baptist president wants to retire famed gavel named for slave owner', *The Washington Post,* 11 June 2020. https://www.washingtonpost.com/religion/2020/06/10/southern-baptist-gavel-greear/
19. Catherine Bennett, 'As statues of slave traders are torn down, their heirs sit untouched in the Lords', *Guardian,* 14 June 2020. https://www.theguardian.com/commentisfree/2020/jun/14/as-statues-of-slave-traders-are-torn-down-their-heirs-sit-untouched-in-the-lords
20. Eusebius McKaiser, 'We know from South Africa that toppling statues is no silver bullet, but it's a start', *Guardian,* 9 June 2020. https://www.theguardian.com/commentisfree/2020/jun/09/south-africa-toppling-statues-racist-cecil-rhodes-cape-town?CMP=Share_iOSApp_Other
21. Mathew Yglesias, 'The Great Awokening', Vox, 1 April 2020. https://www.vox.com/2019/3/22/18259865/great-awokening-white-liberals-race-polling-trump-2020?referringSource=articleShare
22. Amy Harmon, et al., 'From Cosmetics to NASCAR, Calls For Racial Justice Are Spreading', *The New York Times,* 16 June 2020. https://www.nytimes.com/2020/06/13/us/george-floyd-racism-america.html?referringSource=articleShare
23. Mark Maske and Adam Kilgore, 'What made Roger Goodell Say "Black Lives Matter" and where it leaves the NFL', *The Washington Post,* 7 June 2020. https://www.washingtonpost.com/sports/2020/06/06/roger-goodell-black-lives-matter/
24. Edward Helmore, 'Can Anna Wintour survive fashion's reckoning with racism?', *Guardian,* 13 June, 2020. https://www.theguardian.com/fashion/2020/jun/13/anna-wintour-vogue-diversity-racism-debate
25. Marc Tracy, 'Top Editor of Philadelphia Inquirer Resigns after "Buildings Matter" Headline', *The New York Times,* 9 June 2020. https://www.nytimes.com/2020/06/06/business/media/editor-philadephia-inquirer-resigns.htm
26. Benjamin Lee, '"This ends today": over 300 stage figures call out "anti-blackness" of US theatre', *Guardian,* 9 June 2020. https://www.theguardian.com/stage/2020/jun/09/us-theater-racism-called-out-open-letter?CMP=Share_iOSApp_Other
27. Emily Yahr, 'Lady Antebellum changes to Lady A, is "regretful and embarrassed" about the name's association with slavery era', *The Washington Post,* 11 June 2020. https://www.washingtonpost.com/arts-entertainment/2020/06/11/lady-antebellum-change-name-lady-a/

28. Vanessa Thorpe, 'Censoring old films and TV shows misses the point, say BAME leaders', *Guardian*, 13 June 2020. https://www.theguardian.com/world/2020/jun/13/censoring-old-films-and-tv-shows-misses-the-point-say-bame-leaders
29. *The New York Times*, 'Sharpton Delivers Eulogy', 10 June 2020. https://www.nytimes.com/2020/06/09/us/george-floyd-funeral-protests.html?referringSource=articleShare
30. Megan Specia, 'Top U.K Brands Urge #Solidaritea With Anti-Racism Protests', *The New York Times*, 18 June 2020. https://www.nytimes.com/2020/06/09/world/europe/yorkshire-tea-pg-tips-black-lives-matter.html
31. Amy Harmon, et al., 'From Cosmetics to NASCAR, Calls for Racial Justice Are Spreading', *The New York Times*, 9 June 2020. https://www.nytimes.com/2020/06/13/us/george-floyd-racism-america.html?referringSource=articleShare
32. *Business Roundtable*, 'Business Roundtable Redefines the Purpose of a Corporation to "Promote an economy that Serves all Americans"', 19 August 2019. https://www.businessroundtable.org/business-roundtable-redefines-the-purpose-of-a-corporation-to-promote-an-economy-that-serves-all-americans
33. David Gelles, 'Corporate America Has Failed Black America', *The New York Times*, 6 June 2020. https://www.nytimes.com/2020/06/06/business/corporate-america-has-failed-black-america.html?referringSource=articleShare
34. Sandra Leung, 'It's finally time for business to address racism. Here's how.' *The Washington Post*, 10 June 2020. https://www.washingtonpost.com/opinions/2020/06/10/its-time-businesses-finally-address-racism-heres-how/
35. *The Economist*, 'Bosses say they want to tackle racial injustice', 11 June 2020. https://www.economist.com/business/2020/06/11/bosses-say-they-want-to-tackle-racial-injustice
36. Michael Cavna, 'George Floyd's death has inspired powerful protest art: "I needed to have another way of seeing him"', *The Washington Post*, 11 June 2020. https://www.washingtonpost.com/arts-entertainment/2020/06/11/protest-art-black-lives-matter/
37. Taylor Lorenz, 'Upper East Side Mom Group Implodes Over Accusations of Racism and Censorship', *The New York Times*, 9 June 2020.
38. Lindsay Ellis, 'For Colleges Protests over Racism May Put Everything on the Line', *The Chronicle of Higher Education*, 12 June 2020. https://www.chronicle.com/article/For-Colleges-Protests-Over/248979
39. Craig Steven Wilder, *Ebony & Ivy: Race, Slavery and the Troubled History of America's Universities*, New York: Bloomsbury Publishing, 2013.
40. Dennis Overbye, 'For a Day, Scientists Pause Science to Confront Racism', *The New York Times*, 10 June 2020. https://www.nytimes.com/2020/06/10/science/science-diversity-racism-protests.html?referringSource=articleShare
41. Ben Casselman and Jim Tankersley, 'Economics, Dominated by White Men, is Roiled by Black Lives Matter', *The New York Times*, 10 June 2020. https://www.nytimes.com/2020/06/10/business/economy/white-economists-black-lives-matter.html?referringSource=articleShare
42. Radley Balko, 'There's overwhelming evidence that the criminal justice system is racist. Here's the proof', *The Washington Post*, 10 June 2020. https://www.washingtonpost.com/graphics/2020/opinions/systemic-racism-police-evidence-criminal-justice-system/?no_nav=true&p9w22b2p=b2p22p9w00098&tid=a_classic-iphone

43. Arelis R. Hernandez and Scott Wilson, 'Black police chiefs express anger and dismay as they try to change their departments from within', *The Washington Post,* 7 June 2020. https://www.washingtonpost.com/national/protests-black-police-chiefs/2020/06/06/120770dc-a738-11ea-b473-04905b1af82b_story.html
44. Katie Edmondson and Nicholas Fandos, 'G.O.P. Scrambles to Respond to Demands for Police Overhaul', *The New York Times,* 9 June 2020. https://www.nytimes.com/2020/06/09/us/politics/republicans-police-reform.html?referringSource=arti-cleShare
45. Seun Min Kim and John Wagner, 'Senate GOP unveils the bill that would discourage, but not ban, tactics such as chokeholds and no-knock warrants', *The Washington Post,* 17 June 2020. https://www.washingtonpost.com/powerpost/senate-republicans-to-unveil-competing-police-reform-bill/2020/06/17/39ae8304-b085-11ea-856d-5054296735e5_story.html
46. Alex Leary and Kristina Peterson, 'Trump Prods Police with Executive Order', *The Wall Street Journal,* 16 June 2020. https://www.wsj.com/articles/trump-signs-policing-executive-order-11592325988
47. Charles M. Blow, 'The Civil Rights Act of 2020', *The New York Times,* 10 June 2020. https://www.nytimes.com/2020/06/10/opinion/police-brutality-protests-legislation.html?referringSource=articleShare
48. Paige Fernandez, 'Defunding the Police Isn't Punishment – It Will Actually Make Us Safer', *Cosmopolitan,* 4 June 2020. https://www.cosmopolitan.com/politics/a32757152/defund-police-black-lives-matter/
49. Simon Tisdall, 'Trump uses force as a first resort. And now the firepower is aimed at his own people', *Guardian,* 7 June 2020. https://www.theguardian.com/commentisfree/2020/jun/07/trump-firepower-aimed-at-own-people-george-floyd?CMP=Share_iOSApp_Other
50. Danielle Allen, 'We seek reforms to policing. But something even deeper needs repair', *The Washington Post,* 11 June 2020. https://www.washingtonpost.com/opinions/2020/06/11/we-seek-reforms-policing-something-even-deeper-needs-repair/
51. Christina Pazzanese, 'After the protest … what next? Harvard experts talk about to turn the moment's energy into lasting change', *The Harvard Gazette,* 11 June 2020. https://news.harvard.edu/gazette/story/2020/06/harvard-experts-discuss-how-to-effect-lasting-change/
52. Michelle Alexander, *The New Jim Crow: Mass Incarceration in the Age of Colorblindness*, New York: The New Press, 2020.
53. Michelle Alexander, 'America, This is Your Chance', *The New York Times,* 8 June 2020. https://www.nytimes.com/2020/06/08/opinion/george-floyd-protests-race.html?referringSource=articleShare
54. Ta-Nehisi Coates, 'The Case for Reparations', *The Atlantic,* June 2014. https://www.theatlantic.com/magazine/archive/2014/06/the-case-for-reparations/361631/
55. Emily Peck, 'Why the US Needs to Do Reparations Now', *HuffPost,* 8 June 2020. https://www.huffpost.com/entry/us-needs-reparations-black-americans_n_5ede5dfbc5b6fb8854dd8d00
56. Sydney Trent, 'Young Asians and Latinos push their parents to acknowledge racism amid protests', *The Washington Post,* 22 June 2020. https://www.washingtonpost.com/local/young-asians-and-latinos-push-their-parents-to-acknowledge-racism-amid-protests

57. Marina Fang, 'How Asian Americans Are Reckoning with Anti-Blackness In Their Families', *HuffPost,* 6 June 2020. https://www.huffpost.com/entry/anti-blackness-asian-americans_n_5ed87ca8c5b6ea15610b5774
58. Prabal Gurung, 'It's time for Asian Americans to shed the "model minority" myth and stand for George Floyd', *The Washington Post,* 5 June 2020. https://www.washingtonpost.com/nation/2020/06/05/prabal-gurung-its-time-asian-americans-shed-model-minority-myth-stand-george-floyd/
59. Patricia Sullivan, 'Thousands gathered across city to protest death of George Floyd', *The Washington Post,* 7 June 2020. https://www.washingtonpost.com/dc-md-va/2020/06/06/dc-protests-saturday-george-floyd/
60. David Axelrod, 'I thought I understood issues of race. I was wrong', *The Washington Post,* 12 June 2020. https://www.washingtonpost.com/opinions/i-thought-i-understood-issues-of-race-i-was-wrong/2020/06/12/a18d18ae-ac0d-11ea-9063-e69bd6520940_story.html
61. Stanley Cohen, *States of Denial: Knowing about Atrocities and Suffering,* Cambridge, UK: Polity Press, 2001.
62. Dave Jamieson, 'The Labor Movement Faces Reckoning Over Police Unions', *HuffPost,* 6 June 2020. https://www.huffpost.com/entry/the-labor-movement-faces-a-reckoning-over-police-unions_n_5eda9958c5b640424ef70cd2
63. Kimberlé Crenshaw, 'The Urgency of Intersectionality', TedWomen 2016. https://www.ted.com/talks/kimberle_crenshaw_the_urgency_of_intersectionality/discussion
64. Michael C. Dawson, 'Racial Capitalism and Democratic Crisis', *Items Insights from the Social Sciences,* 4 December 2018. https://items.ssrc.org/race-capitalism/racial-capitalism-and-democratic-crisis/

First written 13–15 June 2020

II

Navigating Global Turbulence

6

Brexit: From Empire via Europe to Little England

Brexit came as a shock to many people and shook global financial markets. However, both the exit vote and the market convulsions were predictable given Britain's troubled history with the European Union, the psychology of nationalism that can be impervious to economic reality and rationality, and the turbulence of the global economy at the time. Explanations abounded that Brexit reflected the populist repudiation of corrupt political elites and compromised expert opinion, the consequences of austerity and deepening inequality spawned by neoliberalism, the outrage of the masses disenfranchised and disempowered by globalisation, not to mention the reckless gamble of a cocky, lacklustre prime minister.

There can be little doubt that Mr Cameron foolishly gambled the future of his country to save his job over an internal party squabble. Instead of boldly confronting the Eurosceptics who had goaded his predecessors, and the rising right-wing extremists, he called for a referendum, with the characteristic confidence and cluelessness of scions of great privilege. In the end, he lost his job, further fuelled the regional, social and generational polarisations of his already fractious country, and won the dubious distinction of having led it out of the European Union. It was reduced to a small, insular island wedded to a sense of exceptionalism from a bygone era.

Equally evident is the fact that Brexit left the political and corporate establishments that had campaigned vigorously against it, in the United Kingdom, European Union and United States, as shellshocked as the xenophobic nativists who had championed it were ecstatic. The beleaguered European leaders tried desperately to figure out the next steps, to limit the damage, to avoid sinking into their own treacherous domestic quicksands of angry populism. Jubilant Eurosceptics in France, Netherlands, Sweden and elsewhere did not waste time to call for referendums, for their own Frexit, Nexit, Swexit and other awkwardly named exits.

However, some analysis is needed here. Prominent members of the Conservative Party led the Leave campaign in the United Kingdom. Even Nigel Farage, the leader of the UK Independence Party that had energised the campaign, was a former member of the Conservative Party and commodity broker. Factions of the same political class led Eurosceptics elsewhere in Europe. Thus, while the foot soldiers of populist movements are often the disenchanted masses, their leaders are disgruntled members of the same political class they rail against. This is one reason such movements fail to offer real redress.

Clearly, Brexit reflected the chickens of globalisation coming home to roost. The fundamentalist gospel of free-market capitalism and austerity had unleashed grotesque and destructive inequalities that transformed the nature of political struggles, systems and citizenship. Not surprisingly, rising disaffection and anti-establishment rage were upending traditional politics and faith in political elites almost everywhere. However, Brexit was a pyrrhic victory for its supporters among the millions of workers marginalised and alienated by globalisation. Some reportedly woke up from their hangover, shaken by the economic shockwaves it unleashed on the British economy and its prospects, and expressed regret, or Regrexit.

A backlash against the peddlers of Brexit was inevitable as the homegrown ruthless regime of British neoliberalism lost Brussels as its bogeyman. After all, Conservative Party Prime Minister Margaret Thatcher had been one of the key architects of neoliberalism, while Labour Prime Minister Tony Blair had deodorised it with 'Third Way' aroma. The country and future that the Brexit supporters were promised they were taking back would not materialise.

During the rancorous Brexit campaign, the EU became the embodiment of the assorted ills of globalisation, from runaway immigration to deepening inequality, rampant corruption to loss of local control. Globalisation is of course easy to invoke and blame for all manner of national and world problems. There is a need to distinguish between globalisation as a contemporary project and as a historical process. The latter refers to complex age-old processes of inter- and transregional interconnectedness and flows. As a project, contemporary globalisation embodies neoliberalism, a restructuring of global capitalism that emerged at the turn of the 1980s. It wreaked immeasurable damage on the well-being of working people around the world. Historically, the weaker countries and lower social classes have always paid the earliest and heaviest price for capitalist restructuring.

The global South first experienced the high social and structural costs of contemporary globalisation. In Africa, the Structural Adjustment Programmes (SAPs) that were imposed by western countries and international financial institutions with uncompromising missionary zeal led to the 'lost decades' of the 1980s and 1990s. Out of the devastations and dislocations of SAPs emerged new social movements and struggles for the 'second independence', for democratisation, which made unsteady progress across the continent. The angry populist politics witnessed in developed countries represented the revolt of the victims of globalisation there, those who had lost control over their lives and livelihoods.

Instead of the expansion of democratic spaces and governance, xenophobic nationalism and nativism spread. Populist politics was highjacked, as in the Brexit campaign and Trump's xenophobic crusade in the United States, by factions of the same discredited elite least capable or even interested in resolving the multiple crises of contemporary globalisation. Thus, while elements of the old guard lost control they traded places with even more retrogressive elements riding the ferocious beast of populism unleashed by the project of neoliberal globalisation. Lest we forget, Prime Minister Cameron – and Boris Johnson, his fiercest opponent in the Brexit campaign and aspiring successor – were old friends and competitors from elite families and schools.

Anti-establishment rage including Euroscepticism spread widely across Europe. In fact, there were countries such as Greece that could lay greater claim to having been given short shrift by the rigid bureaucratic demands of European Union membership than the United Kingdom. Yet, in 2015, even when faced by the most draconian and humiliating conditionalities for a bailout (similar to what African countries were subjected to under SAPs), Grexit failed. This suggests there was more to Brexit than Euroscepticism or hostility to globalisation by its frustrated losers.

Propelling Britain to its momentous rendezvous with history was the powerful force of nationalism. During the heyday of decolonisation and its aftermath in Africa and Asia, it had become fashionable among British and other western scholars to vilify nationalism as an atavistic political pathology of backward societies. Never mind that nationalism had once been valourised for its emancipatory possibilities in the context of the bloody history of European nation-state formation. The proponents of postmodernism and globalisation who viewed it as historically outdated, a relic of discredited geographies and histories, incapable of shaping the trajectory of contemporary politics, economy and culture, reinforced the dismissal of nationalism.

Needless to say, nationalisms around the world have their own distinctive moments, motivations and meanings, as well as projects, possibilities, perils and even perversions rooted in their specific histories. Brexit reflects the complex dynamics of nationalism in the United Kingdom, rooted in the history of empire and its messy and troubled aftermath. The ethnic identities and nationalisms within Britain were subsumed within the United Kingdom.

It is widely recognised that the colonial superpowers of Europe, Britain and France emerged from the Second World War greatly weakened and destined to play second fiddle to the new superpowers, the United States and the Soviet Union. Decolonisation, the most important political development of the twentieth century, also played a pivotal role in the diminution of British power on the postwar global stage. While France increasingly hitched its fate to the project of European integration to rescue Europe from centuries of destructive wars and promote economic development, Britain ignored Europe and clung to the Commonwealth and fantasies of a great power based on its 'special relationship' with the US.

It was not until 1973 that Britain finally joined the European Economic Community, the predecessor of the EU. However, two years later, a referendum was held to decide the country's continued membership. Sixty-seven per cent approved. Conceived in convenience, not passionate commitment to the European integration project, the marriage limped along. Euroscepticism remained popular, although its support waxed and waned among the dominant Labour and Conservative parties. In 1992, when the euro was introduced into the EU, Britain opted out. Successive British governments sought to limit what they regarded as Brussels' overreach as the EU integration efforts broadened and deepened.

Britain's postwar struggle with its Europeanness reflected and reproduced its difficulties in forging a national identity and new place in the world as a postimperial power and society. Decolonisation and its aftermath, and its wrenching effects on British politics, society and psyche, should not be underestimated. The collapse of empires tends to dissolve the glue of supranationalism into the fissiparous tendencies of ethnic nationalisms in both the imperial metropole and colonial outposts. Britain itself has been subject to the rise of ethnic nationalisms no less destabilising than in some of its former colonies in Asia and Africa. The acrimonious Brexit campaign, characterised by blatant lies, fear-mongering and gratuitous incivility, revealed the deep chasms between the four regional 'tribes' that make up the United Kingdom (to use the term British and other western commentators routinely use in describing politics in African countries): the English, Welsh, Scottish and Irish. The first two voted overwhelmingly to leave (England ranging from 51.8 per cent in the south east to 59.3 per cent in the West Midlands, and Wales 52.5 per cent) and the last two to stay (Scotland 62.0 per cent and Northern Ireland 55.8 per cent).

The electorate also divided along spatial, social and intergenerational lines. Majorities in the cities voted in favour of remaining, while in the countryside and small towns they preferred leaving. Cosmopolitan and multicultural London voted 59.9 per cent to remain. Similarly, people in higher income brackets and those under the age of 45 voted to remain, while those in lower income brackets and over 45 voted to leave. Millennials felt robbed of their future.

The English essentially decided Brexit. It was an expression of English nationalism, a reflection of the country's long descent from its glory days of empire to the anguished and angry nationalism of modern Little Englanders. In the nineteenth century, the Little Englanders were opposed to the expansion of empire; in the early twenty-first century, their offspring were dejected by its end. Two centuries earlier they had gloried in England's exceptionalism as the first industrial nation; now they sulked behind the jingoistic memories of past imperial glory.

The regional divide in the Brexit referendum would have far-reaching implications long after the economic and financial convulsions settled and the global economy moved on to new crises. Brexit would profoundly redefine Britain's position and power as a European nation and its continued existence as a united nation. The disintegration of the UK entered the academic debate in earnest after the Scottish scholar, Tom Nairn, published his book, *The Break-up of Britain*, in 1977.[1] When I first read it as a graduate student in London, its provocative thesis was intriguing, but the critique of nationalism by the eminent historian, Eric Hobsbawm, seemed more persuasive.[2]

The Scottish referendum of 2014 brought Nairn's prediction awfully close to realisation. A second Scottish referendum in the aftermath of the Brexit vote buoyed by the seductions of glocalisation – achieving Scottish nationalism in the bosom of a Pan-European identity and integration – may yet prove him right. In the meantime, Northern Ireland may latch its future as a European country to its southern neighbour, fulfilling the dreams of Irish nationalists. Who is to say, with the triumph of English, Scottish and Irish nationalisms, that Wales would not follow suit?

The future is of course unpredictable. Many people feared that, in the short term, the post-Brexit British economy would be battered into recession and the wobbly European and global economies would be further weakened, perhaps also sliding into recession. After the referendum, the volume of chatter in the financial press, about Britain becoming a less desirable beachhead for global capital seeking European business, increased. There was trepidation that Brexit might present an existential peril for the EU and presage the inexorable demise of the European project.

Even if the worst economic predictions for the United Kingdom, trotted out with increasing desperation by the Remain campaign and their legion of global fellow travellers, did not come to pass, Brexit would show that the United Kingdom had already travelled the predictable road from empire, via regional integration, to Little England. Thus, Brexit went beyond the country's divorce from a loveless marriage with the Europe Union; it represented its historic reckoning as a postimperial nation in the era of neoliberal globalisation.

For a country that once strode a world empire on which the sun never set, the forces and purveyors of global, regional and national integration and disintegration entered a new phase of contestation. The same forces, in varied incarnations and reverberations, would be fighting for the soul of Europe for years to come.

Notes

1. Tom Nairn, *The Breakup of Britain: Crisis and Neo-nationalism*, London: Verso, 1977.
2. Eric Hobsbawm, *Nations and Nationalism since 1780: Programme, Myth, Reality*, Cambridge UK: Cambridge University Press, 1990.

First written 25 June 2016

7

The Western Alliance in Disarray and the Political Economy of Hegemonic Shifts

In June 2018, two images that would have been unthinkable until then transfixed the world media: an American president at war with his G7 allies, and the same president basking in a delirious bromance with a ruthless North Korean dictator. What could one make of these images, of the deluge of daily news about global developments that were so overwhelming that it was often hard to keep up, let alone understand?

Besides the twittering outbursts and theatrics of the unpredictable President Trump, and the great power rivalries within the teetering western alliance and with a towering China, which seemed to be slipping into fierce trade conflicts, world news headlines were dominated by a relentless cascade of catastrophes in various world regions. These included the endless wars, migration crises and human rights abuses and atrocities committed by intolerant governments, terrorist organisations and fundamentalist civil society zealots.

There were of course other powerful stories and forces, slow, subterranean and structural, which were upending the current global order with profound consequences for national, regional and world political economies. These included the rise of dangerous populisms, the recessions of democracy, the generation of unprecedented wealth and deepening inequalities. In addition, there were the development of planetary consciousness, growth of political tribalisms and the contradictory trajectories of the digital revolution that was simultaneously unleashing remarkable economic productivity and social connectivity and threatening to overwhelm humanity with the transformative powers of artificial intelligence, robotics and the Internet of Things.

I would like to suggest that some of the global developments of the time that flooded the media, especially the growing tensions among and within the major global and regional powers and their respective alliances, could fruitfully be understood in the context of hegemonic shifts and contestations that occur periodically in world history. Hegemony comprises both hard power (military and economic dominance) and soft power (cultural and ideological supremacy). During moments of hegemonic transitions, intrahegemonic rivalries and struggles between the declining and rising hegemons tend to intensify, often leading to regional and global wars, both hot and cold.

As a historian, I am very aware that history does not repeat itself in exact or predictable patterns, but neither is any moment including ours immune from the familiar rhythms of historical change. This is to suggest the need to go beyond the pronouncements or shenanigans of particular leaders, or momentary trends that may seem consequential but end up sinking in the shifting sands of history without much trace. Students of world history and the world system have identified various conjunctures in the constructions, contestations and transitions of regional and global hegemonies going back millennia.

Economic and structural crises and escalating political and ideological competition and conflict often trigger or accompany moments of hegemonic shifts. In the field of economic history, which is my specialty, there are fascinating historical accounts going back hundreds of years, of economic crises and some of the hegemonic upheavals they engendered, reflected and reinforced. A few recent examples will suffice.

In the late nineteenth century, there was the shift in economic and military power in Europe, then the centre of the world system, from Britain as the world's first industrial power to Germany following the latter's unification in 1871. This shift occurred during the long global depression of 1873–1896. At the same time, the world drifted towards the New Imperialism, expressed geographically in the colonial conquest of Africa and parts of Asia and geopolitically in the outbreak of World War I.

Western Europe emerged from World War I devastated and exhausted, paving the way for the rise of two new hegemonic powers, the United States and the former Soviet Union. The Great Depression of 1929–1939 and World War II accelerated those two countries' march to superpower status, notwithstanding the economic hardships the Depression had in the USA and the trail of destruction left by World War II in the USSR. The decolonisation of Africa and Asia occurred in the maelstrom of the new global order and the emergence of the Cold War between American-led and Soviet-led geopolitical alliances.

This underscores the fact that moments of hegemonic transitions create both dangers and opportunities for the peripheries. The hegemonic shift of the late nineteenth century among the European powers brought Africa and Asia the historic disaster of colonisation. The shifts in power of the mid-twentieth century, to the huge subcontinental states of the USA and USSR, brought them the momentous promises of decolonisation. What would the latest reconfiguration in global hegemonies portend for Africa?

At the heart of the current conjuncture was the emergence of a multipolar world, following the demise of the Soviet Union and the erosion of US hegemony as the sole superpower since the early 2000s. It seems almost quaint to recall Fukuyama's triumphalist thesis on the 'End of History' – the conceit that the great ideological struggles of history had been vanquished by western liberal democracy – which was proclaimed in the midst of American euphoria following the collapse of 'actually existing socialism'.[1]

The aftermath of 9/11 and the rise of politicised religious fundamentalisms seriously dented this hollow ideological gloating. The rise of China, and other emerging economies that claimed a growing share of the unevenly developed and highly unequal global economy, put more nails in the coffin of American and western supremacy.

On the day that President Obama was inaugurated in January 2009, I wrote an essay on my blog – *The Zeleza Post* (closed in 2012) – which was subsequently included in the collection of essays, *Barack Obama and African Diasporas* (2009),[2] in which I noted the immensity of the challenges facing the new administration. They included 'ending two foreign wars in Iraq and Afghanistan that have depleted the nation of treasure and trust', and 'managing the economic crisis and administering an effective stimulus package that will halt the economic recession and restore growth'.

Furthermore, there were questions of:

> … expanding access to health care and improving the quality of education and overcoming the inequities of the prison industrial complex that have devastated African American and other minority communities; pursuing sound and sustainable domestic and global environmental policies; and promoting smart foreign policies and allegiance to multilateralism. The biggest challenge facing President Obama is how to manage the relative decline of American global supremacy in a world of new and emerging powers.

The Obama Administration tried to manage this challenge through existing multilateral institutions by roping in the emerging economies. It also championed important global causes, such as climate change, by signing the Paris Climate Agreement in April 2016, and containing nuclear proliferation, by signing in July 2015 the 5+1 Iran nuclear deal (officially known as the Joint Comprehensive Plan of Action between Iran and the permanent members of the UN + Germany). It tried to contain rising China by creating the Trans-Pacific Partnership, signed in February 2016.

The Trump Administration tried to undo all this and other domestic and international policies and achievements of the Obama Administration. This should not have come as a surprise. As I wrote on the day after the 2016 election, and which appears as Chapter 3 of this book:

> It is no prediction to expect that America's slide into global ignominy will accelerate under Trump's predictably inept leadership and the country's apparently irreconcilable tribal polarizations … Obama's legacy will be dismantled by his nemesis. … For the world at large, Trump's looming presidency elicits different fears, perspectives and expectations. There are fears that postwar internationalism will be upended by isolationism … .

Unfortunately, some of the worst predictions about the Trump presidency happened – domestic institutions and the aura of the presidency itself were undermined through wanton corruption, ineptitude and perverse narcissism, and international institutions and diplomatic niceties were weakened through insufferable bluster, bombast and boorishness. The proverbial stereotype of the 'Ugly American' became a veritable monstrosity in an American leader who despised allies and adored dictators who had historically threatened American interests or self-image.

However, the challenges went beyond Trump. He channelled the pre-existing ideological impulses and interests of his constituents among the electorate and the establishment, however misguided: the racism, tribalism, chauvinism, xenophobia, jingoism and protectionism of the 'America First' assault on the world. Traditional liberals, conservatives and nationalists wedded to the rules of the crumbling order were deeply alarmed, even apocalyptic in their views about what was happening and what it portended for the future. Some hailed from the global South, including Africa. The western order under assault from the Trump Administration was not constructed to benefit the global South, so it was rather rich for the wealthy countries of western Europe to expect support or solidarity from the emerging economies of the global South in the intrahegemonic battles of Euro-America.

The Trump Administration's contempt for America's allies was on full display at the 2018 G7 Summit and the Summit with the North Korean leader, Kim Jong-un. Annoyed by the statement by the Prime Minister of the host country, Canada, that he would impose retaliatory tariffs on the US and would not allow his country to be pushed around, Trump refused to sign the final agreement, to the indignation of the six leaders of the G7. The cause of disagreement in President Trump's political and economic tantrums was ostensibly about trade – the misguided belief that the major trading partners of the US had exploited it and that it could easily win any subsequent trade war.

In reality, at stake was the viability of the post-World War II order that the USA itself had created and from which it has disproportionately benefitted. It is now a beleaguered hegemon unable to control the world it bestrode for seventy years as a superpower and then as an undisputed colossus after the demise of the Soviet Union. That world has been vanishing. As often happens in such moments of declining hegemony, the padded ideological gloves of soft power give way to the bare-knuckled fists of hard power, which only succeeds in accelerating hegemonic decline.

The challenges and ills confronting the world evident in the current intrahegemonic rivalries and conflicts in the western alliance, in the face of rising new hegemons, especially China, were of course not an isolated American phenomenon. Nativism, nationalism and distrust of the elites, experts and the establishment had gone global, giving succour, in many countries, to populists and dictators and growing preference for strongmen, even in many so-called democracies.

Overarching the intrahegemonic tensions in the Western Alliance was the escalating interhegemonic rivalry between the West and China. As the Trump presidency tarnished the sheen of American democracy, China's meritocratic model of 'selection plus election' for the leadership acquired a new and competing ideological gloss. One Chinese scholar boasted that because of this model and 'despite its many deficiencies, the Chinese polity has delivered the world's fastest growing economy and has vastly improved the living standards for most Chinese'.[3] The Chinese model of governance and selecting leaders, he continued, 'makes it inconceivable that anyone as weak as George W. Bush or Donald Trump could ever come close to the position of the top leadership'.

Some African commentators were attracted to the Chinese model, which had recently resulted in the removal of term limits, arguing that Africa could beneficially borrow from some of its elements, such as the fight against corruption,[4] while others regarded it with alarm as 'an unwelcome gift for African despots who can now point to China as justification for their authoritarian tendencies'.[5]

Of course, the two dynamics of intra- and interhegemonic struggles were only a part of much wider transformations underway in the contemporary world. Other megatrends reflected and reinforced the hegemonic shifts addressed in this chapter. An avalanche of popular and scholarly studies have provided fascinating, although not always accurate or compelling, diagnoses and prognoses of the global condition, bringing hope to some and fear to others. The trends included some already mentioned, such as the apparent erosion of democracy and rise of populisms and the growth of global inequalities that fed into the politics of anger and political tribalism. Others not mentioned thus far included the unfolding economic, social, cultural and political disruptions of technology and profound demographic changes.

Among the books I have particularly enjoyed reading to make sense of our infinitely complex, contradictory and rapidly changing present, notwithstanding my disagreement with some of their premises, methodologies or analyses, the following have stood out. On the rising recession of democracy, Dambisa Moyo, the renowned Zambian economist, gives us her customary trenchant analysis in her book, *Edge of Chaos: Why Democracy is failing to Deliver Economic Growth – and How to Fix It* (2018).[6] Other intriguing reflections on the growing global democratic deficits and the destabilising effects of populism, political tribalism and anger include Yascha Mounk, *The People vs. Democracy: Why Our Freedom is in Danger and How to Save It* (2018).[7] There is also Steven Levitsky and Daniel Ziblatt's *How Democracies Die (2018)*,[8] the riveting *Political Tribes: Group Instinct and the Fate of Nations* (2018)[9] by Amy Chua and the philosophically sophisticated *Age of Anger: A History of the Present* (2017)[10] by Pankaj Mishra.

On wealth and inequality there's Thomas Piketty's brilliant 2013 bestseller, *Capital in the Twenty-First Century*,[11] which spans the past 250 years, while Walter Scheidel's 2017 tome, *The Great Leveler: Violence and the History of Inequality from the Stone Age to the Twenty-First Century*,[12] attempts an even more ambitious treatise. On the impact of technology and the future of humanity, there are the incisive and provocative reflections by Yuval Noah Harari, *Homo Deus: A Brief History of Tomorrow* (2017)[13] and Rachel Botsman's *Who Can You Trust? How Technology Brought Us Together and Why It Might Drive Us Apart* (2017).[14] Gideon Rose has given us *The Fourth Industrial Revolution: A Davos Reader* (2016)[15] and focusing on my own sector, there is Joseph E. Aoun's *Robot-Proof: Higher Education in the Era of Artificial Intelligence* (2017).[16]

The changing dynamics of the world population are marked by ageing populations in some regions, especially the global North and even China, and a youth bulge in others, most dramatically in Africa. There are also the shifting patterns of global migrations, most graphically captured in the death traps across the Mediterranean. While demography is not destiny and the ameliorative powers of technology to rescue ageing societies from economic stagnation should not be underestimated, Africa's demographic explosion could be a developmental and geopolitical asset. The continent is expected to have more than two billion people by 2050, 25 per cent of the world's population and over four billion in 2100, 40 per cent of the world's population. For this boon to materialise, massive investments need to be made in the development of the human capital of the youth – as a matter of urgency, *now* – otherwise the continent's potential demographic dividend will turn into a demographic disaster as uneducated, unskilled and unemployed youth terrorise their societies into a downward spiral of impoverishment, insecurity and instability.

We live, to use an old cliché, in the best of times and the worst of times. One thing for certain is that massive changes will continue to confront the multiple and intersected worlds of the twenty-first century, which will be marked, as all historical processes are, by the structures of historical geography and political economy and the social inscriptions of class, race, ethnicity, gender and religion.

In this most complex and demanding of times, Pan-Africanism ceases to be an affective good for African countries and peoples and becomes, as its founders and purveyors, from W.E.B. Dubois to Kwame Nkrumah to Thabo Mbeki always understood, a historical and geopolitical imperative in an era of shifting global hegemonies. African governments, business, civil society, intergovernmental agencies, think tanks and academia must mobilise the continent's geopolitical thought leaders to properly decipher the implications of this most challenging of global moments in order to minimise its perils and seize its opportunities.

Notes

1. Francis Fukuyama, *The End of History and the Last Man,* New York: Free Press, 2006.
2. Paul Tiyambe Zeleza, *Barack Obama and African Diasporas: Dialogues and Dissensions,* Athens OH and Oxford UK: Ohio University Press and Ayebia, 2009.
3. Zhang Weiwei, 'How China Elects their political Leaders', *Vanguard,* 7 April 2018. https://www.vanguardngr.com/2018/04/china-elects-political-leaders-prof-zhang-weiwei/
4. Peter Kagwanja, 'New revolutionary Xi expands Africa's strategic ties with China', *Daily Nation,* 24 March 2018. https://www.nation.co.ke/oped/opinion/Xi-Jinping-expands-Africa-s-strategic-ties-with-China/440808-4356182-bpbcgpz/index.html
5. David Kiwuwa, 'Why China's removal of term limits is a gift to African despots', *The Conversation,* 8 March 2018. https://theconversation.com/why-chinas-removal-of-term-limits-is-a-gift-to-african-despots-92746
6. Dambisa Moyo, *Edge of Chaos: Why Democracy is failing to Deliver Economic Growth – and How to Fix It,* New York: Basic Books, 2018.
7. Yascha Mounk, *The People vs. Democracy: Why Our Freedom is in Danger and How to Save It,* Cambridge, Mass.: Harvard University Press, 2018.
8. Steven Levitsky and Daniel Ziblatt, *How Democracies Die,* New York: Broadway Books, 2018.
9. Amy Chua, *Political Tribes: Group Instinct and the Fate of Nations,* New York: Penguin Books, 2018.
10. Pankaj Mishra, *Age of Anger: A History of the Present,* New York: Farrah, Straus and Giroux, 2017.
11. Thomas Piketty, *Capital in the Twenty-First Century,* Cambridge, MA: Harvard University Press, 2014.
12. Walter Scheidel, *The Great Leveler: Violence and the History of Inequality from the Stone Age to the Twenty-First Century,* Princeton, NJ: Princeton University Press, 2017.
13. Yuval Noah Harari, *Homo Deus: A Brief History of Tomorrow,* New York: HarperCollins, 2017.
14. Rachel Botsman, *Who Can You Trust?: How Technology Brought Us Together and Why It Might Drive Us Apart,* New York: Public Affairs, 2017.
15. Gideon Rose, *The Fourth Industrial Revolution: A Davos Reader,* Council on Foreign Relations, 2016.
16. Joseph E. Aoun, *Robot-Proof: Higher Education in the Era of Artificial Intelligence,* Cambridge, MA: MIT Press, 2017.

First written 17 June 2018

8

The Turbulent 2010s: A Historical Draft

As 2019 ended and 2020 began, there was a deluge of diagnoses of the trends of the 2010s, sometimes accompanied by prognoses for the 2020s. Such retrospectives and reflections, infinitely varied in both sagacity and silliness, are ritualised cognitive efforts by modern societies to make sense of the messy complexities, overwhelming contradictions and massive changes of the various historical conjunctures of modernity.

Periodisation is of course central to the historian's craft and the historical imagination in general. Decades, like centuries and millennia, provide a convenient and concentrated packaging of otherwise bewildering events and transformations over the unwieldy flows of time. As historians know all too well, interpretations of the past are as much reconstructions of the past as they are constructions of the present and projections of anxieties and aspirations for the future.

Thus, they are always provisional, always subject to re-interpretations by future generations imbued with their own perspectives, preoccupations, problems and possibilities. However, historical reconstructions go beyond temporal dynamics. Historical geography, the location of scholars and commentators in specific times and spaces, as well as the epistemic demands of the enterprise of knowledge production in its multifaceted institutional, intellectual, ideological and individual contexts and intersectionalities, condition them.

This is another way of saying that my reflections on the 2010s reflect my multiple locations and positionings as an African diaspora scholar. I was based in the United States during the first six years of the 2010s and in Kenya during the last four. For me the tens were a turbulent decade characterised by several major trends. Whether or not these trends would prove lasting and determine the unfolding trajectories of the twenty-first century is anyone's guess.

Crystal gazing is not my professional forte as a historian. Indeed, the record of predictions by eminent people in academia, business and media, and other forecasting experts, such as soothsayers and intelligence agencies, is quite dismal. However, the future does not will itself blithely into being; it unfolds from a past that becomes ever clearer with the passage of time.

Some of the developments and events to which we accord significance now may pale into irrelevance in the future, and others that are barely discernible from the noisy clutter of the present may prove more enduring and transformational. Hence, the title of this chapter: it is a historical draft subject to foreseeable and unforeseen revisions. In my view, six key trends characterised the 2010s: first, the globalisation of tribalism; second, democratic recessions and resistance; third, rising economic disequilibrium; fourth, shifting global hierarchies and hegemonies; fifth, the emergence of surveillance capitalism; and finally, the rebellion of nature.

Tribalism Goes Global

During the 2010s, the spectre of tribalism – ethnocultural nationalism, xenophobic racism, religious fundamentalism and jingoistic populism – arose from massive technological and socioeconomic disruptions, undergirded by the devastations of the once-celebrated sprawl of neoliberal globalisation, which suffocated liberal democracies and the promises of diversity and inclusion in many of the world's increasingly multicultural societies. Neoliberal globalisation met its comeuppance in the Great Recession of 2008–2009, which bequeathed to the 2010s widespread economic desolation, deepening inequality, the decline of the middle classes, a rising sense of powerlessness and hopelessness among ordinary people and raging popular distrust of elites and establishments.

The stock of populist demagogues grew, while that of traditional politicians and technocrats fell. As I wrote elsewhere,[1] 'Increasingly perceived as corrupt and ineffective to deliver growth and overcome the roaring headwinds of entrenched poverty, unemployment, declining living standards, social instability, unsustainable indebtedness, technological disruptions and other intractable challenges, liberal democracy retreated as the allure of the fiercely intolerant ideologies of populism, protectionism and partisanship rose.' Several surveys show that, in the 2010s, vast majorities around the world expressed growing distrust of elite-led public and private institutions, including governments, business, media and universities, just to mention a few.

Out of the toxic inheritance of the 2000s emerged the intoxicating and intolerant allure and illusions of identity politics, which seemed to overwhelm older political affiliations framed around the traditional ideologies of the right and the left. Long prevalent, even if always contested, conceptions and solidarities of nationhood and citizenship that valourised difference and inclusion were increasingly upended by more people embracing the perilous and pernicious comforts of sameness, self-referentiality and ethnocultural purity. In short, the ascriptive and often aspirational solidarities of class, community and country gave way to the dangerous essentialist and exclusionary conceits and attachments of culture, creed and colour.

Identity politics was fuelled by the politics of fear and resentment, powerlessness and panic, as well as desperate yearnings for dignity and control of their lives by growing numbers of people. The palpable anxieties and nostalgia for the rapidly vanishing and often imagined certainties of the old normal arose out of deepening social inequalities and marginalisation of masses of people who, encouraged and emboldened by nativist demagogues and ideologues, increasingly blamed their misfortunes on internal and external 'others'.

Minorities and migrants bore the brunt of this aggressive 'othering', of political and social opprobrium for the disappearing or frozen opportunities of social mobility. Seizures of moral panic about undesirable migrants and undeserving minorities, often fanned by unscrupulous politicians and bigoted zealots, gripped rich countries in the global North and subregional powers in the emerging economies.

Thus, political tribalism spread in mature and nascent democracies alike – from the world's largest democracy, India, under Narendra Modi's virulently Hindu nationalist government that came to power in 2014, to the world's wealthiest democracy, the United States, under Donald Trump's unabashedly racist administration that assumed power in 2017, to one of the world's oldest democracies, Britain, under a succession of Conservative Party prime ministers since 2010, which descended into the imperial and provincial fantasies of Brexit.

Intolerant nationalisms also engulfed many newer democracies as well, from South Africa with its periodic convulsions of xenophobic violence, to Brazil under Jair Bolsonaro's unflinchingly right-wing regime that won the 2018 elections, to the fragile democracies of Eastern Europe where unapologetically illiberal regimes gained ascendancy, championed most loudly by Viktor Orbán's Fidesz Party, in power in Hungary since 2010.

Democratic Recessions and Resistance

Clearly, the ascendancy and spread of political tribalism was accompanied by global recessions of democracy. In the euphoria of the end of the Cold War in the early 1990s, the Third Wave of Democracy that swept the former socialist countries of Central and Eastern Europe and an assortment of dictatorships in Asia, Africa and Latin America, seemed unstoppable. Francis Fukuyama, an American scholar, giddily proclaimed the end of history. By the 2010s, democratic retreat was evident in its historic heartlands and among the newer democracies, which were being pulverised by the resurgence of reactionary and right-wing populist forces and weakened by growing disillusionment – especially among the younger generations – at the minimalist efforts, ineffectiveness and corruption they saw.

There is currently a vast scholarly and popular literature bemoaning and analysing the democratic recessions of the 2010s. Democracy indexes showed sharp declines in average global scores in dozens of countries. According to a report by The Economist Intelligence Unit,[2] the scores fell for much of the 2010s. Between 2016 and 2017, they fell in eighty-nine countries, stagnated in fifty-one and did not improve in any region. According to Freedom House's *Freedom in the World Report* 2019,[3] 2018 'recorded the 13th consecutive year of decline in global freedom. The reversal has spanned a variety of countries in every region, from long-standing democracies like the United States to consolidated authoritarian regimes like China and Russia. The overall losses are still shallow compared with the gains of the late 20th century, but the pattern is consistent and ominous. Democracy is in retreat.'

Several factors accounted for the reversal of the post-Cold War democratic wave. They included the failure of democratic regimes to meet the needs of their populations and rising anger and anxieties about growing inequality. Moreover, there were the corrosive effects of massive technological disruptions and the rise of digital authoritarianism, the revival of global hegemonic rivalries, the hollowing out of democratic institutions and practices (especially protections for migrants and minorities) and the sheer exhaustion from the euphoria of the 1990s. A critical backdrop to the recession of democracy was the Great Recession of 2008–2009 that had devastated many economies and highlighted the inability of governments to deliver and safeguard economic prosperity.

But there were some bright spots. In Africa, these included the adoption of a new vibrant Constitution in Kenya in 2010, which brought closure to the deadly post-election violence of 2007–2008. In the hotly contested elections of 2017, Kenya distinguished itself by becoming the first African country and the fourth in the world where a presidential election was revoked by the judiciary. This underscored the independence of the judiciary, the growing strength of public institutions and deepening national commitment to transparency, accountability and the rule of law, thereby demonstrating that Kenyan democracy was maturing.

Several vicious dictators and notorious kleptocrats came to the end of their political rope, including President Robert Mugabe, the once-celebrated hero of the Zimbabwean liberation struggle who had descended into being an irascible octogenarian autocrat, overthrown in November 2017. Next door in South Africa was President Jacob Zuma, whose disastrous reign over the rainbow nation had culminated in state capture by corrupt forces. The African National Congress, the venerable liberation movement experiencing the proverbial challenges of transitioning into an effective governing party, ousted him in February 2018.

The decade ended with the opening up of authoritarian Ethiopia under Prime Minister Abiy Ahmed, who assumed office in April 2018 and proceeded to win the 2019 Nobel Peace Prize.

Similar stories of reform, sometimes fragile to be sure, could be told for other world regions. In the United States, the Republican Party's stranglehold over the three branches of government achieved in the 2016 elections eased when the Democratic Party won the majority of seats in the House of Representatives in 2018 and proceeded to impeach President Trump in December 2019, thereby restoring some faith in the resilience of the American constitutional system. In Latin America, reforms, sometimes frail, were registered from Ecuador to Mexico to Cuba, where the Castros finally exited the scene. The decade closed with the ousting of Bolivia's Evo Morales in December 2019, following protests against voting irregularities in his bid for a fourth term as president. In the European parliamentary election of May 2019, the much-anticipated and dreaded surge of far-right parties failed to materialise. Despite threats from China, massive and protracted protests erupted in Hong Kong from September to December in 2014, and resumed from June 2019. The first set of protests was triggered by proposed reforms to Hong Kong's electoral system and the second by the introduction of a bill that would have allowed the extradition of criminal fugitives to China.

In India, fresh from electoral victory in the general elections earlier in the year, the emboldened government of Prime Minister Modi passed a controversial citizenship law on 11 December 2019, allowing citizenship for ostensibly persecuted immigrants from Afghanistan, Bangladesh and Pakistan but excluding Muslims. It met massive resistance across the country from protesters who saw it as a dangerous homage to Hindu nationalism and an assault against the country's 200 million Muslims and the country's cherished secular Constitution.

Clearly, history comprises messy and multifaceted flows of complex and contradictory forces that abjure singular narratives. In short, the much-bemoaned phenomenon of democratic recession was accompanied by reinvigorated struggles for democratic expansion, whose trajectories continue to unfold.

In fact, only a year into the 2010s, in 2011, the world was electrified by unprecedented struggles for democracy in North Africa. Often dubbed the Arab Spring, the uprisings and rebellions toppled the region's sclerotic and kleptocratic dictatorships in Tunisia, Egypt and Libya. The firestorm spread to other parts of Africa, from Mali to Côte d'Ivoire to Uganda to Malawi, as well as to several Arab countries in the Middle East, including Saudi Arabia, Jordan, Palestine, Lebanon, Oman, Kuwait, Bahrain, Yemen and Syria. The Arab Spring soon descended into the Arab Winter, save for Tunisia and tepid reforms in some countries. A revanchist and ruthless dictatorship emerged in Egypt and ferocious civil wars broke out in Libya, Yemen and Syria.

The decade ended with reignited struggles in Sudan and Algeria that succeeded in ousting the once-indomitable dictatorships of presidents Omar al-Bashir and Abdelaziz Bouteflika, respectively. Various outcomes of the Arab Spring were to be expected. As reflected in the vast literature that has since emerged, these can be attributed to different constellations of internal political, economic, social and institutional forces and geopolitical dynamics. The Arab Spring represented the second phase in Africa's struggles for the 'second independence' that had begun in the 1980s and 1990s. This is a subject I reflected on at length in my 2014 book, *The Resurgence of Africa: Domestic, Global and Diaspora Transformations.*[4]

Some scholars and commentators credit the Arab Spring with inspiring protests for democracy and change in some parts of Europe, Asia and the Americas.[5] Whatever the accuracy of such claims, in many parts of the world the decade witnessed the revitalisation of old and new social movements that challenged prevailing configurations of power. In the United States, three movements are worth mentioning: Occupy Wall Street, Black Lives Matter and Me Too. Elsewhere, movements against authoritarianism and populism gathered momentum.

The Occupy Wall Street movement began in September 2011 in New York City. It soon spread to other American cities and cities in several countries, including Australia, Belgium, Brazil, Britain, Canada, Colombia, France, Germany, Hong Kong, India, Italy, Japan, Malaysia, Mexico, New Zealand, Nigeria, Spain, South Africa, South Korea and Turkey. Occupations, demonstrations, strikes, picketing and social media activism characterised the movement. In the United States, the movement was galvanised under the slogan, 'We are the 99 per cent'. The protests were against deepening income and wealth inequality, corporate dominance and lack of accountability, and for relief for rising student debt and the mortgage foreclosure crisis then rocking the US economy, although many in the movement prided themselves on not issuing clear demands.

The movement was met by government crackdowns encompassing heightened surveillance and arrests. In the United States, this outcome, combined with the limited involvement of minorities and the absence of a clear agenda, led to the movement's quick demise. However, it left a lasting legacy in as far as it thrust issues of rising economic and social inequality and inordinate corporate influence into the public domain and political discourse, as evident in subsequent local and national elections and the rise of the populist wings of both the Democratic and Republican parties. The changed terms of political and policy debate on inequality and corporate accountability was apparent in many other countries as well, although these did little to dent economic and social inequalities during the rest of the 2010s.

The Black Lives Matter movement also emerged in the United States and spread to other countries with long histories of entrenched anti-black racism and violence, such as Australia, Canada and the United Kingdom. It began in July 2013 following the acquittal of the vigilante killer of Trayvon Martin in 2012 and was further galvanised in 2014 by police killings of Michael Brown in Ferguson, Eric Garner in New York and Tamil Rice in Cleveland. It soon became a national movement with dozens of chapters across the country that organised protests against the endless killings of African-American men and women, girls and boys by vigilantes and the police. The movement also sought to promote and affirm African-American struggles and empowerment in other occupations.

The movement drew its inspiration from, but sought to transcend, the agendas, tactics and structures of older civil rights and other social movements in the United States. In its guiding principles and ambitions, it sought to embrace enduring Pan-Africanist aspirations. Befitting the times, it actively incorporated social media activism. In fact, it drew its name from the hashtag #BlackLivesMatter. Predictably, despite overwhelming support in the black community and sizeable segments of the white community, the movement was met with dismissive racist rhetoric trumpeting 'All Lives Matter', 'Blue Lives Matter' and 'White Lives Matter'.

The movement proceeded to flex its political muscles during the 2016 presidential primaries and elections. A country that had entered the 2010s basking in the fantasies of a postracial dispensation with the 2008 election of its first black president, the suave and cosmopolitan Barack Obama, was rudely awakened to the racist backlash of Trump's election in 2016. The election of an avowed bigot, boisterous buffoon and incorrigible liar, which brought white supremacy out of the American closet, amplified the fierce urgency of the Black Lives Matter movement's anti-racist crusade.

The juxtaposition of democratic recessions, resistance and renewal is equally evident when it comes to the Me Too movement, which also first emerged as a hashtag, following sexual harassment and assault accusations against the Hollywood mogul, Harvey Weinstein, in October 2017. Legions of celebrities, including Kenya's renowned Oscar winner, Lupita Nyong'o, revealed their dreadful encounters with Weinstein, and many other women were emboldened to expose their own sexual predators. Before long, the hashtag #MeToo gained global currency and mushroomed into a movement for women's social justice and empowerment in pursuit of the persistent dreams of generations of feminists.

The Me Too movement pushed for changes in national legislation and policies on sexual harassment and assault. As it grew and became more transnational, it broadened its demands and was translated into local languages, idioms and struggles against widely prevalent gender-based violence, gender inequality and women's underrepresentation in employment, business, media, educational institutions, government agencies and public life. In other contexts, the movement championed the emancipation of marginalised communities.

Out of the movement and the already well-established women's movements around the world, poured voluminous studies and data on the appallingly high levels of sexual violence and femicide in virtually every country. This was manifested in the deliberate killing of women and girls through intimate partner violence, torture and misogynist murders, honour and dowry-related killings, and deaths resulting from genital mutilation. There were also killings of women following accusations of sorcery and witchcraft, as a 'weapon of war' in armed conflicts and by criminal gangs, drug dealers and human traffickers, not to mention killings of women and girls because of their aboriginal and indigenous status and their sexual orientation and gender identity.

There was also femicide associated with female infanticide and gender-based sex-selection foeticide. According to a report by the United Nations,[6] in some of the most affected countries, which included Azerbaijan, Armenia, Georgia, Montenegro, Albania, Vietnam and Pakistan, gender ratios at birth ranged from 109.9 to 117.6 boys per every 100 girls. Another UN report, *Gender Equality: Striving for Justice in an Unequal World*[7] (for which I served as one of the editors), showed that by the early 2000s there were already tens of millions of missing women in Asia, led by India and China, thanks to misguided reproductive health policies and deeply entrenched patriarchal cultures. The demographic chickens of these misguided policies and cultures came home to roost in the 2010s.

The Me Too movement helped raise global awareness of and reinforced age-old struggles against sexual harassment, assault and killings and for women's empowerment. Examples included widespread protests in 2015 and 2016 against gender-based violence in Mexico, Bolivia, Colombia, Argentina and Brazil and the massive Women's March in Washington in January 2017 to protest the election of a renowned misogynist to the White House. Furthermore, there were the women's strike against femicide in Israel in December 2018, recurrent protests against the rape epidemic in India and South Africa, protests against a contentious anti-rape law in nine Japanese cities in June 2019 and demonstrations in November 2019 in France, which has one of the highest domestic abuse murder rates in Europe.

In short, the women's movement continued to make progress in the treacherous and turbulent terrain of the 2010s. One indicator was women's representation in parliament. Even in the United States, often an international laggard, women won a record number of seats in the 2018 Congressional elections (102 seats out of 435, i.e. 23.4 per cent), the highest ever in the US but below the world average. Similarly, in the 2019 British elections a record 220 female Members of Parliament were elected (out of 650 seats, i.e. 33.8 per cent).

According to the Inter-Parliamentary Union,[8] by February 2019, women comprised 24.5 per cent of parliamentarians (both houses combined – 24.6 per cent for single or lower house and 24.3 per cent for upper house). In terms of regional averages, the Americas led with 30.6 per cent, followed by Europe (29.4 per cent), sub-Saharan Africa (24.0 per cent), Asia (19.7 per cent) and Pacific (19.4 per cent), and the Middle East and North Africa were at the bottom (16.8 per cent). In terms of individual countries, the top dozen were Rwanda, Cuba,

Bolivia, Mexico, Sweden, Grenada, Namibia, Costa Rica, Nicaragua, South Africa, Senegal and Finland, in that order.

Rising Economic Disequilibrium

The aftermath of the Great Recession of 2008–2009 was one of the defining economic developments of the 2010s. The recession itself was precipitated by a financial crisis in the United States, which was triggered by the collapse of the subprime housing market bubble. It became the deepest and longest recession in the country's history since World War II. The financial crisis was attributed to lax public monetary policy, slack regulation of financial institutions, high levels of household and corporate debt, international trade imbalances and poor corporate governance and accountability. For example, in the United States, household debt rose from 77 per cent of disposable income in 1990 to 127 per cent in 2007. In some European countries, such as Denmark, Iceland, Ireland, the Netherlands and Norway, such debt even surpassed 200 per cent.

The Great Recession left a trail of wanton economic devastation, mostly in the United States and Europe. In the US, between 2007 and 2009, real GDP declined by 4.3 per cent, the S&P 500 index dropped by 57 per cent, unemployment rose to 10 per cent, home prices fell by 30 per cent, the poverty rate jumped to more than 15 per cent of the population and the net worth of American households and non-profit organisations fell by 20 per cent, from US$69 trillion to US$55 trillion. In some European countries, such as Cyprus, Greece, Ireland, Italy and Portugal, the crisis became so severe that they were forced to default on national debt and seek bailouts from the European Union, European Central Bank and the International Monetary Fund.

To contain the contagion and revive growth, many governments enacted fiscal stimulus packages and austerity measures comprising tax increases and reductions in social benefits programmes. For their part, central banks cut rates and adopted quantitative easing, an expansionary monetary policy of injecting liquidity into the economy by buying assets. Rates of recovery in the 2010s were predictably slow and uneven and varied by country and community, down to the eternal structured inscriptions of class, ethnicity/race and age.

It is generally agreed that the Great Recession accelerated the growth of economic and social inequality in the United States and around the world. This was one of its major consequences. Tens of millions of people lost their jobs, assets and livelihoods, as well as control over their lives, dignity and hope for the future. The policy responses favoured capital over labour, the wealthy at the expense of the middle and working classes, financial services rather than productive sectors. Fear, uncertainty, rage and distrust of governments captured by business and often self-serving elites flared into a political and social inferno in many countries.

The 2010s were greeted by this combustible brew. Widespread political instability and social struggles gave rise to toxic tribalism and populism. Right-wing forces most effectively mobilised and manipulated these reactionary ideologies. At the same time, there were heightened recessions of and resistances to democracy, examined in the previous sections.

Employment was particularly battered. According to the ILO's 2019 *World Employment Social Outlook*,[9] from 2011 to 2018 the world economy grew at an average rate of 3.6 per cent, a slight dip from the 3.9 per cent between 2001 and 2010. The percentage of the working-age population in employment fell during the Great Recession and its immediate aftermath and rose slowly thereafter, although by 2018 it was down to 58.4 per cent compared to 62.2 per cent in 1993. The majority of jobs were in informal employment, which in 2016 accounted for two billion jobs, or 61 per cent of all jobs. In terms of sectors, employment in manufacturing generally fell, while that in services rose; by 2018, the latter accounted for almost half of all employment.

Working conditions in both informal employment and services, including the emerging gig economy, largely remained poor. Nearly 700 million workers in low- and medium-income countries in 2018 lived in extreme or moderate poverty. The deficits in decent work remained alarmingly high, afflicting the majority of the 3.3 billion people employed globally, who suffered from persistent economic insecurity and lack of equal opportunities for their well-being. Average real wage growth remained low and fluctuated, rising in some years and falling in others.

The unemployment rate in 2018, at 5 per cent, was the same as in 2008 and lower than the 5.6 per cent in 2009. Also evident was the prevalence and in some cases growth of underemployment or labour underutilisation. Employment rates and conditions varied quite considerably according to levels of development, gender and for the youth. Overall, employment indicators tended to be worse for low-income than high-income economies and those in between, in terms of gender for women compared to men, and were particularly challenging for the youth.

For many countries, employment was a key feature of the difficult aftermath of the Great Recession and played an important role in engendering and sustaining income and wealth inequalities. Reports on growing global inequalities within and across countries abound in the academic literature, media and publications of development agencies, think tanks and NGOs.

For example, according to Credit Suisse's *Global Wealth Databook 2018,*[10] 64 per cent of the world's adult population held less than 2 per cent of global wealth, while less than 10 per cent of the wealthiest individuals owned 84 per cent of global wealth and the richest 1 per cent owned 45 per cent. The growth of high net worth individuals – those with net worth assets of more than US$1 million – was staggering.

While the largest numbers of the world's high net worth individuals (HNWIs) were in the United States (41 per cent in 2018), Europe and China (7 per cent), they rose even faster in Africa, the world's least-developed continent. According to the *World Wealth Report 2018,*[11] the size of HNWIs in Africa in 2017 reached 169,970 with a combined wealth of US$1.7 trillion (0.9 per cent out of the 18.1 million HNWIs globally and 2.4 per cent of global HNWI wealth, totalling US$70.2 trillion).

Oxfam did much to publicise the scourge of growing inequality in a series of alarming reports published to coincide with the annual World Economic Forum, the Davos jamboree of masters of the universe. Its report in 2015[12] showed that the richest 1 per cent increased their share of the world's wealth from 44 per cent in 2009 to 48 per cent in 2014, while the least well-off 80 per cent owned just 5.5 per cent. In its 2017 report, entitled *An Economy for the 99%,*[13] Oxfam bemoaned the fact that eight multibillionaires owned as much wealth as the poorest half of the world's population. Its 2019 report[14] claimed that the wealth of 2,200 billionaires worldwide had grown by 12 per cent, whereas for the poorest half it had fallen by 11 per cent.

Oxfam blamed the obscene disparities on capital, squeezing workers and producers while executives were grossly overpaid, crony capitalism and state capture, super-charged shareholder capitalism and tax avoidance by the rich. As might be expected, the debate on global inequalities was extremely heated. Inequality received its intellectual imprimatur in Thomas Piketty's academic blockbuster first published in 2013, *Capital in the Twenty-First Century,*[15] which offered a voluminous and compelling account of wealth and income inequality in the United States and Western Europe over the last three centuries.

Piketty's bestselling book received as much acclaim as criticism for its thesis, methodology and conclusions, underscoring how high the stakes were. In a lead story in its issue of 30 November 2019, *The Economist*[16] returned to the topic with a predictable verdict, 'Inequality Illusions'. It argued that the idea of soaring inequality rests on shaky analytical ground and problematic data. Nevertheless, the magazine conceded, 'And even if inequality has not risen by as much as many people think, the gap between rich and poor could still be dispiritingly high.'

In the 2010s, several global income inequality databases were created, such as the World Bank's PovcalNet, the World Inequality Database, the OECD's Income Distribution Database, the University of Texas Inequality Project Database and The United Nations University's World Income Inequality Database. Each focused on a particular set of issues. The UNDP's *Human Development Report 2019,*[17] which makes sobering reading, reflects much of this work. The report offered five key observations.

> First, while many people are stepping above minimum floors of achievement in human development, widespread disparities remain. ... Second, a new generation

> of severe inequalities in human development is emerging, even if many of the unresolved inequalities of the 20th century are declining. … Third, inequalities in human development can accumulate through life, frequently heightened by deep power imbalances. … Fourth, assessing inequalities in human development demands a revolution in metrics. … Fifth, redressing inequalities in human development in the 21st century is possible – if we act now, before imbalances in economic power translate into entrenched political dominance.

The report urged the development of a new framework for analysing inequality that goes beyond income. 'A comprehensive assessment of inequality must consider income and wealth. But it must also understand differences in other aspects of human development and the processes that lead to them'. It has to go beyond averages. 'The analysis of inequalities in human development must go beyond summary measures of inequality that focus on only a single dimension'. Moreover, it needs to go beyond today. 'Inequalities in human development will shape the prospects of people that may live to see the 22nd century'.

In the 2010s, concerns over inequalities in income, wealth, capabilities and opportunities became widespread across political divides. While gaps in basic capabilities (such as access to basic education and health) across the world narrowed, they grew in terms of enhanced capabilities (including life expectancy at older ages and access to tertiary education). In the words of the UNDP report, 'In all regions of the world the loss in human development due to inequality is diminishing, reflecting progress in basic capabilities.'

Globally, the loss fell from 23.4 per cent in 2010 to 20.2 per cent in 2018, ranging from 35.1 per cent to 30.5 per cent for sub-Saharan Africa at one end, and from 16.1 per cent to 11.7 per cent for Europe and Central Asia at the other. The percentage of access to primary and secondary education grew more rapidly than to tertiary education between 2007 and 2017, in all world regions. For sub-Saharan Africa, it grew by about 9 per cent and less than 2 per cent, respectively, so that by 2017 more than 40 per cent of the population had primary education compared to 2 per cent with tertiary education. The ratios for the developed countries were more than 95 per cent and 25 per cent, respectively.

However, not everyone benefitted equally from the rising provision of basic capacities. Millions of vulnerable populations remained trapped in the insidious horizontal inequalities of discriminatory policies and restrictive legal frameworks and by the dynamics of deeply entrenched historical, market, cultural and gender biases, which blocked them from meaningful and ameliorative social, economic and political participation. The UNDP report called for more refined and timely studies of inequality using universally recognised statistics and comprehensive inequality databases.

The Great Recession did not affect all world regions equally. As noted above, many developing countries largely escaped its worst effects, although they experienced slower growth. Many of the economies in South America went into recession, reflecting reduced demand in their main North American and European markets for their predominantly primary commodity exports.

Economic growth continued in much of Africa, save for countries like South Africa, which went into recession, but at lower rates than before. This reflected the resilience of the continent's recovery since the 1990s and its reorientation of major trading partners, from the western countries to the rising economic giants of Asia, especially China and India, where growth remained robust, as it was in Indonesia and Bangladesh. For its part, South Korea barely escaped recession.

The uneven effects and limited impact of the Great Recession on China and India pointed to an emerging phenomenon in the world economy that accelerated in the 2010s, namely, the decoupling of growth trajectories between the historically dominant economies of western Europe, the United States and Japan and the emerging economic powerhouses of the twenty-first century. This is another major consequence of the Great Recession, which became more apparent in the 2010s and led to the reshuffling of global hegemonies and hierarchies. This is discussed under the next heading.

While the heady projections of the future made in the late 2000s and early 2010s for some of the emerging economies in the BRICS (Brazil, Russia, India, China and South Africa) faded, the fact remained that these economies assumed a much greater share of global economic output, a trend that continued in the 2010s. Other configurations of leading emerging economies included MINT (Mexico, Indonesia, Nigeria, Turkey) and the Next 11 (Bangladesh, Egypt, Indonesia, Iran, Mexico, Nigeria, Pakistan, the Philippines, Turkey, South Korea and Vietnam). For example, as I noted in my book on *Africa's Resurgence*[18] referred to earlier, between 1990 and 2012 the relative share of the BRICS of world GDP increased by some 3.6 times so that they accounted for 56 per cent of world GDP growth. By 2012, the BRICS had claimed about 20 per cent of world GDP compared to 24 per cent for the European Union and 21 per cent for the United States. The BRICS accounted for 43 per cent of world reserves of foreign exchange and increased their share of total world trade to 21.3 per cent as compared to 25 per cent for the EU and 27 per cent for the US.

Shifting Global Hierarchies and Hegemonies

Clearly, global hegemonies and hierarchies shifted in the 2010s at global and regional levels. In terms of intraregional shifts, World Bank data[19] showed that, in Africa, Nigeria overtook South Africa to become the continent's largest economy in 2012 (worth US$459.4 billion compared with South Africa's US$396.3 billion). In East Africa, Ethiopia overtook Kenya as the largest economy in eastern Africa in 2015 (US$64.6 billion compared with US$64.0 billion). In terms of purchasing power parity (PPP), by 2018 the size of the Nigerian economy was

US$1,117.4 billion compared to South Africa's US$768.3 billion, while it was US$219.0 billion for Ethiopia and US$176.4 billion for Kenya. In PPP terms, in 2018 Egypt's economy was actually the continent's largest, at US$1,189.0 billion.

An even more remarkable development during the 2010s was the rising share of the global economy among middle-income countries. According to a World Bank report,[20] from the 2000s to the mid-2010s this share rose from 17 per cent to 35 per cent (4 per cent to 8 per cent for lower middle-income countries and 13 per cent to 27 per cent for upper middle-income countries). In the meantime, the share of global GDP among higher-income countries declined from 83 per cent to 64 per cent during the same period. In terms of purchasing power parity, in 2018 the middle-income countries claimed 53.6 per cent of global GDP (US$72.7 trillion out of US$135.5 trillion). The respective shares for the lower middle-income and upper middle-income countries was US$22.9 trillion and US$49.7 trillion, which translated into 16.9 per cent and 36.7 per cent of the global economy, respectively.

The biggest economic story of the decade, indeed of the previous thirty years, was the exponential rise of China. In terms of purchasing power parity, China overtook the United States as the world's largest economy in 2014. By 2018, the size of the Chinese economy towered at US$25.3 trillion compared with that of the US at US$20.7 trillion, although in terms of per capita incomes the latter was still ahead – US$63,390 compared to US$18,140. China's re-emergence as the world's largest economy returned the country to a position it had enjoyed a few centuries before. This phenomenal growth enabled China to lift hundreds of millions of people from poverty in a generation, an achievement almost unparallelled in human history.

The story of China is an integral part of Asia's resurgence as the world's economic centre and of the historic decline of Europe and North America since the first Industrial Revolution. In 2018, the five leading Asian economies – China, India, Japan, Indonesia and South Korea – accounted for 34.5 per cent of the world economy. Four of them were among the top ten economies in the world: China (US$25.3 trillion in 2018), the United States (US$20.7 trillion), India (US$10.4 trillion), Japan (US$5.6 trillion), Germany (US$4.6 trillion), Russia (US$3.9 trillion), Indonesia (US$3.4 trillion), Brazil (US$3.3 trillion), France (US$3.1 trillion) and the United Kingdom (US$3.0 trillion).

Africa seemed nowhere near achieving Asia's extraordinary feat, although it became popular in the 2010s to celebrate Africa Rising/Rising Africa. The new rhetoric of Afro-optimism clearly sought to countervail the Afro-pessimism that was rampant during the continent's 'lost decades' of the 1980s and 1990s. The media often trumpeted that six or seven of the world's ten fastest-growing economies were in Africa. In 2018 there were five (Guinea, Côte d'Ivoire, Libya, Ethiopia and Senegal).

However, the reality was that no African country had yet achieved decades of high and sustained economic growth as experienced in Asia. This was clear from the fact that the list of Africa's fastest-growing economies shifted ever so often. Many of the Asian tigers consistently achieved growth rates that were far above population growth for three decades or more. According to data from the International Monetary Fund,[21] Africa's growth rate, which reached 6 per cent in 2005, fell to 5.8 per cent in 2010 and 3.5 per cent in 2015 and rose slightly to 3.8 per cent in 2018, remained too low to achieve profound transformation in human development. It is instructive that Africa's growth rates during these years were below the averages for the developing economies as a whole (7.2 per cent in 2005, 7.4 per cent in 2010, 4.3 per cent in 2015 and 4.9 per cent in 2018).

The rise of Asia, led by China, which was consolidated in the 2010s, generated an extensive literature. Its historic transformation was attributed to all sorts of complex historical, political, socioeconomic and geopolitical factors and forces. It is possible to argue that after World War II and, for some, after independence, Asian countries constructed far more cohesive and strategic developmental states, undergirded by inclusive economic, political and social institutions and massive investments in human capital development, than other regions in the global South. Also, they aggressively pursued state capitalism, which was reinforced following the Asian crisis of 1997, despite fierce opposition and often misguided advice from the gendarmes of the Washington Consensus of neoliberal free market fundamentalism.

It was quite clear that the 2010s witnessed historic shifts in global power from Euro-America to Asia in general, from the United States as the sole post-Cold War superpower to China, the ascendant superpower of the twenty-first century, which precipitated a fierce hegemonic rivalry. One British academic and journalist, Martin Jacques, went so far as to argue in a commentary in the British newspaper, the *Guardian* that 'This decade belonged to China. So will the next one.'[22] He noted that 'Prior to the western financial crisis, it had been seen as the new but very junior kid on the block. The financial crash changed all that,' which had huge consequences for the western world's 'stability and self-confidence'.

The west, Jacques continued, had displayed:

> ... a kaleidoscope of emotions from denial, dismissal and condemnation to respect, appreciation and admiration; though there is presently much more of the former than the latter. The rise of China has provoked an existential crisis in the US and Europe that will last for the rest of this century. The west is in the process of being displaced and, beyond a point, it can do nothing about it.

Particularly galling was the rise of China from a technological copycat into an innovation juggernaut for the defining technologies of the twenty-first century, through its US$300 billion 'Made in China 2025' plan. The country also moved from being a cautious global player to asserting its power through its ambitious Belt and Road Initiative, targeted at the developing world and designed as the harbinger of a new world order.

Such shifts are very rare in world history. As noted in the previous chapter, this is the third potential shift in the last three centuries. The first was in the late nineteenth and early twentieth centuries, which saw Britain, the world's first industrial nation fade to Germany, the rising continental European industrial power. It culminated in World War I. The second arose out of the ashes of World War II, which saw the devastated imperial powers of Europe replaced by two new superpowers, the United States and the Soviet Union.

Deluged by the cacophony of daily news, it was easy to get distracted by the endless punditry in the media and the pronouncements of American and Chinese leaders, especially with America's unconventional and unhinged president with his tweetstorms. At stake was the demise of the post-World War II order that the US created and disproportionately benefitted from. It predated presidents Donald Trump and Xi Jinping and would outlive them. The US and Chinese economies were so intertwined that decoupling would be extremely costly for both countries and the rest of the world. Some believe decoupling from China 'isn't just perilous – it's impossible'; others fear 'severing U.S. – Chinese links would make it impossible to save the environment'. But hegemonic transitions have their own logic that often defy the cold calculus of costs. The 2020s would tell where the bitter rivalry between the declining and rising superpowers was headed. The rest of the world would be forced to adjust accordingly.

The 4 January 2020 edition of *The Economist*[23] offered a fascinating portrait of China's breathtaking technological advances. It showed the progress Chinese companies had made in older and imported industries, including nuclear reactors, high-speed railways, electric cars and laser technologies. The country had also gradually moved up in the microprocessing value chain and was investing heavily in robotics, the Internet of Things and artificial intelligence. In some areas, China was working hard to become a global leader, such as in 5G technology, or was already ahead, for example in the application and use of face-recognition technologies. The latter are a double-edged sword, as they facilitate the enforcement of state digital espionage or what some call algorithmic surveillance, whose implications for human rights and individual freedoms is portentous.

Emergence of Surveillance Capitalism

It was in the 2010s that the buzz about the Fourth Industrial Revolution reached a crescendo. As I noted on the website *The Elephant,*[24] the term often referred to the emergence of quantum computing, artificial intelligence, the Internet of Things, machine learning, data analytics, big data, robotics, biotechnology, nanotechnology and the convergence of the digital, biological and physical domains of life and the digitalisation of communication, connectivity and surveillance.

The 2010s saw the maturation of technological innovations from previous decades and the emergence of several new ones. Perhaps most ubiquitous was the explosion of social media networks, some of which were established in the decade before. The leading dozen social media sites were Facebook (established in 2004, with 2.45 billion users in 2019); YouTube (2005, 2 billion users); WhatsApp (2009, 1.6 billion users); WeChat (2011, 1.1 billion users); Instagram (2010, 1 billion users); QQ (1999, 823 million users); Qzone (2005, 572 million users); TikTok (2016, 500 million users); Sina Weibo (2009, 465 million); Twitter (2006, 330 million users); Reddit (2005, 330 million users); and Baidu (320 million). The United States and China each had six on this list, underscoring the global dominance of the two countries in the emerging technologies of the twenty-first century.

While more and more people and businesses embraced social media, the technophilia of the early 2010s gave way to growing technophobia about its negative impact, both real and imagined. The sins of commission and omission by social media advanced by the critics were long and varied. It was accused of fostering political polarisation, fuelling the epidemic of fake news, facilitating online stalking, harassment and bullying, reinforcing digital divides and disparities including class distinctions, gender and racial/ethnic stereotypes, compromising privacy, and endangering mental health through online addiction, depression and social disengagement, especially among the youth.

Politicians generally found social media useful when it suited their needs and promoted their interests, but deplored it when it did not. The closure of social media platforms during political protests joined the long arsenal of state authoritarianism. Social media also became a powerful weapon of electoral manipulation, as was evident in the Russian interference in the 2016 American presidential election, in which they sought to damage the candidacy of Hillary Clinton and boost that of Donald Trump, as well as in the 2016 Brexit Referendum in the United Kingdom. The scandal surrounding the data firm Cambridge Analytica, which misappropriated 87 million Facebook profiles, underlined the scale of the crisis.

Concerned by these dangers and threats to democracy and privacy, some activists called for the regulation of social media companies. In 2016, the European Union became one of the first intergovernmental agencies to do so by enacting the General Data Protection Regulation (GDPR). The European Commission declared:

> The regulation is an essential step to strengthen individuals' fundamental rights in the digital age and facilitate business by clarifying rules for companies and public bodies in the digital single market. A single law will also do away with the current fragmentation in different national systems and unnecessary administrative burdens.[25]

Given the weight of the EU, the GDPR was copied in some regulatory frameworks elsewhere. Even in the United States, where such regulations were vigorously fought, demands grew for greater self-regulation by the industry and the once-fêted technological wizards of Silicon Valley joined the hall of infamy occupied by politicians, journalists and left-wing academics. However, by the end of the decade, regulatory controls had done little to curb the apparently relentless march of cybersurveillance, and surveillance capitalism as data became a new and potentially endless gold mine.

Data-harnessing capacities would increasingly determine economic opportunities and divides among nations and industries. A key asset in this critical indicator and differentiator was evident in the global distribution of high-performance computing (HPC). In 2017, the USA had 33.8 per cent of global HPC capacity, followed by China with 32 per cent, Japan 6.6 per cent, Germany 5.6 per cent and France and the United Kingdom each with 3.4 per cent. Altogether, in terms of continents Asia had 42.4 per cent, the Americas 35.4 per cent, Europe 21 per cent and Africa and Oceania the remainder. The leading African country in this space, South Africa, had 0.2 per cent.

Big data from African countries and companies is largely stored in vast computer farms, otherwise known as the cloud, located and controlled by large global firms. This is the face of twenty-first-century digital imperialism, the transnationalisation of digital platforms owned by the major technological powers, capturing one service industry after another across the world, from transport (Uber) to accommodation (Airbnb) and combinations thereof (Expedia, Booking.com, etc). During the era of the Atlantic slave trade, Africa sold its people for trinkets, under colonialism it exported raw materials for a pittance and in the 2010s it was mortgaging its data, a dubious privilege it even paid for.

There were of course other technological developments in the 2010s. Smartphones and tablets became extremely popular consumer items. The release of the iPad by Apple founder and CEO, Steve Jobs, in April 2010 was almost as electrifying as that of the iPhone in June 2007. During the decade various other inventions were adopted, from 3D printing to cryptocurrency, to e-cigarettes that especially enticed the youth, to virtual assistants, such as Amazon's Echo, Google Home, Apple's HomePod and Samsung's Bixby. Self-driving cars were also developed.

The Rebellion of Nature

The 2010s marked a decade when nature harshly rebelled against its despoliation and gradual destruction by humans. The onslaught of extreme weather events, from hurricanes, tornadoes, cyclones, tsunamis to droughts and wildfires, to melting icecaps and rising sea levels reached apocalyptic dimensions that awakened much of the world to the existential dangers, economic damages and social devastations of environmental degradation and climate change.

Global consciousness about the perilous climatic crisis facing the planet was galvanised by scientific consensus, the indefatigable work of environmental movements increasingly animated by the youth, and renewed commitments to sustainable development goals by the international community. The synthesis reports by the Intergovernmental Panel on Climate Change (IPCC)[26] issued ever more alarming information on global warming, the culpability of human activities through the production of greenhouse gases, and the urgency of taking drastic action for mitigation and adaptation.

The decade opened on the heels of the acrimonious 2009 Copenhagen Summit, the failure of which was largely blamed on the intransigence of the developed countries led by the United States, then under the Obama administration. In the next few years a series of United Nations Climate Change conferences were held, in Mexico, South Africa, Qatar, Poland, Peru and France. The last conference led to the adoption of the Paris Agreement. It proposed keeping climate change below 2°C, although no binding emission targets were set. Subsequent conferences were held in Morocco, Germany and Poland.

In the meantime, young people galvanised the environmental movement. The fearless Greta Thunberg, who became an influential international environmental activist, forcefully represented the youth. At the 2019 UN Climate Action Summit in New York, she bluntly told world leaders: 'You are failing us ... But the young people are starting to understand your betrayal. The eyes of all future generations are upon you. And if you choose to fail us, I say: "We will never forgive you".'[27] The school strike for climate movement she initiated in late 2018 quickly spread to many parts of the world.

Unfortunately, stubborn pockets of climate change denial persisted, most alarmingly among some right-wing politicians, a group that found its loudest proselytisers in the new presidents of the United States and Brazil, Donald Trump and Jair Bolsonaro, respectively. President Trump announced that the United States would pull out of the Paris Agreement, while President Bolsonaro lashed out at European leaders who complained about deforestation in the Amazon. But even for the less recalcitrant governments, their rhetoric was often not matched by action.

To be sure, there was progress as a growing number of countries adopted renewable or sustainable energy. Investments in hydropower, solar power, wind power, bioenergy and geothermal energy increased. In the early 2010s, according to a 2018 report by the International Renewable Energy Agency,[28] 'Global annual investment in renewable energy rose steadily in 2013–2015, peaking at USD 330 billion in 2015 before falling to USD 263 billion in 2016.' Consequently, the report stated, 'Since 2012, renewable power capacity installations have exceeded non-renewables by a rising margin, representing about 60 per cent of all new power-generating capacity added worldwide in 2016.' East Asia, led by China, was at the forefront, followed by Europe. The bulk of the investment, more than 90 per cent in 2016, came from private sources.

However, the world's major polluters continued to resist cutting their emissions significantly or adequately financing global climate mitigation efforts by the developing countries. This became abundantly clear at the World Climate Change Conference held in Valencia, Spain, in December 2019, which failed to agree on concrete actions to enhance targets to reduce greenhouse gas emissions. As if in reproach and final display of nature's wrath at the end of the decade, 2019 closed with ferocious infernos torching large swathes of California and Australia.

In Memoriam

This essay was written in memory of my father, who passed away in June 2015 aged 85, and in tribute and hope for his grandchildren, including my son and daughter, who came into their own in the 2010s. Such are the sublime continuities of human life on our splendid, fragile and increasingly endangered planet. It is because I fervently believe each generation has an existential and ethical responsibility to serve as custodians of past generations, its own and future generations that I see environmentalism as one of the supreme imperatives of our time.

Notes

1. Paul Tiyambe Zeleza, 'Africa's persistent struggles for development and democracy in a multipolar world', *Canadian Journal of African Studies* (2019) 53, 1: 163.
2. The Economist Intelligence Unit, 'Free speech under attack', Democracy Index 2017. http:// www.eiu.com/Handlers/WhitepaperHandler.ashx?fi=Democracy_Index_2017.pdf&mode= wp&campaignid=DemocracyIndex2017.
3. M. J. Abramowitz, 'Democracy in Crisis: Freedom in the World 2018', Freedom House, 2018. https:// freedomhouse.org/sites/default/files/FH_FITW_Report_2018_Final_SinglePage.pdf.
4. Paul Tiyambe Zeleza, *Africa's Resurgence: Domestic, Global, and Diaspora Transformations*, Los Angeles: TSEHAI Publishers, 2014.
5. Anthony Alessandrini, 'Their Fight Is Our Fight: Occupy Wall Street, the Arab Spring, and New Modes of Solidarity Today', *Is This What Democracy Looks Like?* https://what-democracy-looks-like.org/their-fight-is-our-fight/; Nora Lafi, The 'Arab Spring' in Global Perspective: Social Movements, Changing Contexts and Political Transitions in the Arab World (2010–2014), in Berger S., Nehring H. (eds), *The History of Social Movements in Global Perspective*, London: Palgrave Macmillan, 2017; Charles W. Anderson, 'Youth, the "Arab Spring", and Social Movements', *Review of Middle East Studies,* (2013) 47(2), 150–156; Stefan Berger and Holger Nehring, *The History of Social Movements in Global Perspective,* New York: Palgrave Macmillan, 2017.
6. Claire Laurent, FEMICIDE: *The Killing of Women and Girls Around the World,* Academic Council on the United Nations System (ACUNS) Vienna Liaison Office, 2013. https://acuns.org/wp-content/uploads/2013/05/Claire-Laurent.pdf

7. UNRISD, *Gender Equality: Striving for Justice in an Unequal World,* Geneva: United Nations Research Institute for Social Development, 2005. http://www.unrisd.org/80256B3C005BCCF9/search/1FF4AC64C1894EAAC1256FA3005E7201
8. Inter-Parliamentary Union, Women in National Parliaments. http://archive.ipu.org/wmn-e/classif.htm
9. International Labour Organization, *World Employment Social Outlook Trends* 2019, Geneva: International Labour Organization, 2019. https://www.ilo.org/wcmsp5/groups/public/–dgreports/–dcomm/–publ/documents/publication/wcms_670542.pdf
10. Credit Suisse, *Global Wealth Report* 2018, 2018. https://www.credit-suisse.com/media/assets/corporate/docs/publications/research-institute/global-wealth-report-2018-en.pdf
11. Capgemini, *World Wealth Report 2019.* https://worldwealthreport.com/wp-content/uploads/sites/7/2019/07/World-Wealth-Report-2019-1.pdf.
12. Oxfam, *Wealth: Having It All and Wanting More,* Oxford: Oxfam GB, 2015. https://oxfamilibrary.openrepository.com/bitstream/handle/10546/338125/ib-wealth-having-all-wanting-more-190115-en.pdf;jsessionid=3632B6E6986C434FADD0C61E506D145F?sequence=8
13. Oxfam, *An Economy for the 99%*, Oxford: Oxfam GB, 2017. https://oi-files-d8-prod.s3.eu-west-2.amazonaws.com/s3fs-public/file_attachments/bp-economy-for-99-percent-160117-summ-en.pdf
14. Oxfam, *Time to Care,* Oxford: Oxfam GB, 2019. https://oxfamilibrary.openrepository.com/bitstream/handle/10546/620928/bp-time-to-care-inequality-200120-en.pdf
15. Thomas Piketty, *Capital in the Twenty-first Century,* Cambridge, MA: Harvard University Press, 2014.
16. *The Economist*, 'Inequality Illusions', 30 November 2019.
17. United Nations Development Program, *Human Development Report 2019,* New York: UNDP, 2019. http://hdr.undp.org/sites/default/files/hdr2019.pdf
18. Paul Tiyambe Zeleza, *Africa's Resurgence: Domestic, Global and Diaspora Transformations*, Los Angeles: TSEHAI Publishers, 2014.
19. See World Bank, World Development Indicators database. https://data.worldbank.org/indicator/NY.GDP.MKTP.PP.CD
20. World Bank, *The Changing Wealth of Nations 2018: Building a Sustainable Future,* Washington, DC: The World Bank, 2018.
21. International Monetary Fund, IMF DataMapper, 2018. https://www.imf.org/external/datamapper/ NGDP_RPCH@WEO/OEMDC/ADVEC/WEOWORLD.
22. Martin Jacques, 'This decade belonged to China. So will the next one', *Guardian,* 31 December 2019. https://www.theguardian.com/commentisfree/2019/dec/31/decade-china-west-china-ascent?CMP=Share_iOSApp_Other
23. *The Economist*, 'Chinese Technology: From the people who brought you fireworks …', 4 January 2020.
24. Paul Tiyambe Zeleza, 'The Fourth Industrial Revolution and African Universities', *The Elephant,* 17 October 2019. https://www.theelephant.info/ideas/2019/10/17/gen-z-the-fourth-industrial-revolution-and-african-universities/
25. European Union Commission, General Data Protection Regulation, 2016. https://eur-lex.europa.eu/legal-content/EN/TXT/PDF/?uri=CELEX:02016R0679-20160504&from=EN

26. The six reports of the Intergovernmental Panel on Climate Change can be found here https://www.ipcc.ch/assessment-report/ar6/
27. United Nations Department of Economic and Social Affairs, 'Greta Thunberg tells world leaders "You are failing us", as nations announce fresh climate action', September 2019. https://www.un.org/development/desa/youth/news/2019/09/greta-thunberg/
28. International Renewable Energy Agency, *Global Landscape of Renewable Energy* Finance 2018. https://irena.org/-/media/Files/IRENA/Agency/Publication/2018/Jan/IRENA_Global_landscape_RE_finance_2018.pdf

References

Coltan, Jeff D., 'The Climate Case Against Decoupling,' Foreign Affairs, September 14, 2020. https://www.foreignaffairs.com/articles/united-states/2020-09-14/climate-case-against-decoupling?utm_medium=newsletters&utm_source=on_the_ballot&utm_campaign=on_the_ballot_2020_prospects&utm_content=20200916&utm_term=prospects-OTB-021020

Reference for first quote: Farrell, Henry and Abraham L. Newman, 'Chained to Globalization,' Foreign Affairs, January/February 2020. https://www.foreignaffairs.com/articles/united-states/2019-12-10/chained-globalization?utm_medium=newsletters&utm_source=on_the_ballot&utm_campaign=on_the_ballot_2020_prospects&utm_content=20200916&utm_term=prospects-OTB-021020

First written 4–5 January 2019

9

The Coronavirus: The Political Economy of a Pathogen

The global coronavirus pandemic of 2020 triggered worldwide panic as the numbers of victims exploded and economies imploded, as physical movements and social interactions withered in lockdown, as apocalyptic projections of its destructive reach soared and as unprepared or underprepared national governments and international agencies desperately scrambled for solutions.

The pandemic exposed the daunting deficiencies of public health systems in many countries. It threatened cataclysmic economic wreckage as entire industries, global supply chains and stock markets collapsed under its frightfully unpredictable trajectory. Its social, emotional and mental toll was as punishing as it was paralysing for multitudes of people increasingly isolated in their homes as the public life of workspaces, travel, entertainment, sports, religious congregations and other gatherings ground to a halt.

Also being torn asunder were cynical ideological certainties and the political fortunes of national leaders as demands grew for strong and competent governments. The populist revolt against science and experts met its comeuppance as the deadly costs of pandering to mass ignorance mounted. At the same time, the pandemic shuttered the strutting assurance of masters of the universe as they either caught the virus or as it constrained their jet-setting lives and eroded their cushy equity portfolios.

Furthermore, the coronavirus threw into sharp relief the interlocked embrace of globalisation and nationalism, as the pandemic leapt across the world showing no respect for national boundaries and countries sought to contain it by fortifying national borders. It underscored the limits of both neoliberal globalisation, which had reigned supreme since the 1980s, and populist nationalisms, which had bestrode the world since the 2000s and had emerged partly out of the deepening social and economic inequalities spawned by the former.

These are some of the issues I reflect on in this chapter – the political economy of the coronavirus pandemic. As historians and social scientists know all too well, any major crisis is always multifaceted in its causes, courses and consequences. Epidemics are no different. In short, understanding the epidemiological dimensions and dynamics of the coronavirus pandemic is as important as analysing its economic, social and political impact. Moments of crisis always have their fear-mongers and sceptics. The role of progressive public intellectuals is to provide sober analysis.

In the Shadows of 1918–1920

The coronavirus pandemic was the latest and potentially one of the most lethal global pandemics in a long time. One of the world's deadliest pandemics was the Great Plague of 1346–1351, which ravaged large parts of Eurasia and Africa. It killed 75 to 200 million people and wiped out 30 to 60 per cent of the European population. The plague was caused by fleas carried by rats, underscoring humanity's vulnerability to the lethal power of small and micro-organisms, notwithstanding the conceits of its mastery over nature. The current pandemic shows this remains true despite all the technological advances humanity has made since then.

Over a century ago, as World War I ended, an influenza epidemic, triggered by a virus transmitted from animals to humans, devastated the globe. One third of the world's population was infected and it left 50 million people dead. It was the worst pandemic of the twentieth century. It was bigger and more lethal than the HIV/AIDS epidemic of the late twentieth century. But for a world then traumatised by the horrors of war it seemed to have left little impact on global consciousness.

Some health experts feared that COVID-19, as the novel coronavirus was officially called, might rival the influenza epidemic of 2018. However, there were those who cautioned that history is sometimes not kind to moral panics, that similar hysteria was expressed following the outbreaks in the 2000s and 2010s of bouts of bird flu and swine flu, of SARS, MERS and Ebola, each of which was initially projected to kill millions of people. Of course, nobody really knew whether the coronavirus pandemic of 2020 would rival that of the influenza pandemic of 1918–1920, but the echoes were unsettling: its mortality rate seemed comparable and so did its explosive spread.

The devastating power COVID-19 was wracking and humbling every country, economy, society and social class, although the pervasive structural and social inscriptions of differentiation still cast their formidable and discriminatory capacities for prevention and survival. In its socioeconomic and political impact alone, COVID-19 had already made history. One lesson from the 1918 influenza pandemic that applied to the current coronavirus pandemic was that countries, cities and communities that took early preventive measures fared much better than those that did not.

Doctors' Orders

After COVID-19 broke out in Wuhan, China, in late December 2019, international and national health organisations and ministries issued prevention guidelines for individuals and institutions. Most of the recommended measures reflected guidelines issued by the World Health Organization.[1] They included the need to wash hands regularly, maintain social distance, practice respiratory hygiene, staying informed and following given by healthcare providers, and national and local public health authorities. The WHO also instructed persons who were in or had recently visited (past 14 days) areas where COVID-19 was spreading to undertake protection measures, and for one to stay at home if one began to feel unwell, even with mild symptoms, until recovery. Later, the WHO and other national health agencies including the Centers for Disease Control (CDC) in the US encouraged the wearing of protective masks as a preventive measure against the spread of COVID-19.

Unfortunately, in some countries and communities, especially in the US, wearing masks became highly politicised, signalling whether one was a Democrat (for) or a Republican (against) wearing masks. 'Mask rage' joined the arsenal of partisan acrimony and polarization. Wrote *The Washington Post*:

> Mask-wearing for some people is an identifier of broader beliefs and political leanings. Like so many issues rooted in science and medicine, the pandemic is now fully entangled with ideological tribalism. This has played out before: helmets for motorcyclists, seat belts in cars, smoking bans in restaurants. All of those measures provoked battles over personal liberty.[2]

But as the fires of the pandemic raged across the so-called red states controlled by Republicans, some governors and many mayors made the wearing of masks mandatory. Even President Trump, who had derided masks and refused to be seen in public wearing one, swallowed his inflated ego.

The pandemic was not just about physical health. It was also about mental health. In *The Atlantic* magazine, one psychotherapist wrote on how to stay sane during the pandemic. She stated, 'You can let anxiety consume you, or you can feel the fear and also find joy in ordinary life, even now.' She concluded, 'I recommend that all of us pay as much attention to protecting our emotional health as we do to guarding our physical health. A virus can invade our bodies, but we get to decide whether we let it invade our minds.'[3]

A report by the United Nations noted that, 'Before COVID-19 emerged, statistics on mental health conditions (including neurological and substance use disorders, suicide risk and associated psychosocial and intellectual disabilities) were already stark.'[4] The pandemic made the situation far worse as stress, anxiety and destructive behaviours escalated, which were manifested in domestic abuse, gender-based violence, online addiction, drug and alcohol abuse, and certain other crimes including cybercrime. Various national surveys revealed high prevalence of distress ranging from 35 per cent in China to 45 per cent in the US and 60 per cent in Iran.

Specific populations were at risk in different ways. The most vulnerable were health-care workers, older adults and people with pre-existing conditions, and people in humanitarian and conflict settings. Children and adolescents were also affected as schools closed and they became susceptible to domestic abuse. In Italy and Spain 31 per cent reported feelings of loneliness, 38 per cent nervousness, 39 per cent restlessness, another 39 per cent irritability and 77 per cent difficulty concentrating. There was a gender dimension as well. In India 66 per cent of women reported being stressed compared to 34 per cent of men.

The UN report recommended three sets of interventions. First, the inclusion of mental health and psychosocial considerations in a COVID-19 national response. Second, ensuring widespread availability of emergency mental health and psychosocial support, including supporting action that strengthened social cohesion, solidarity and healthy coping, reduced loneliness and promoted psychosocial well-being and access to remote support. Third, supporting recovery from COVID-19 by building mental health services for the future, shifting resources from institutionalisation to affordable, quality mental-health care in the community and undertaking research.

Scramble for Containment

The coronavirus pandemic caught many governments unprepared or underprepared. Some even initially dismissed the scourge. This was particularly the case among populist right-wing governments, such as the administrations of President Trump of the United States, Prime Minister Johnson of the United Kingdom and President Bolsonaro of Brazil. As populists, they had risen to power on a dangerous brew of nationalist and nativist fantasies of reviving national greatness and purity, xenophobia against foreigners and manufactured hatred for elites and experts.

To right-wing ideologues, the coronavirus was a foreign pathogen, a 'Chinese virus' according to President Trump and his Republican followers in the United States, which posed no threat to the nation quarantined in its splendid isolation of renewed greatness. Its purported threat was fake news propagated by partisan Democrats or, in the case of the United Kingdom and Brazil, by disgruntled left-wing labour and liberal parties who had recently been vanquished at the polls.

Such was the obduracy of President Trump that he and his team ignored not only frantic media reports about the pandemic leaping across the world, but also ominous, classified warnings issued by the US intelligence agencies throughout January and February of 2020. Instead, he kept assuring Americans in his deranged tweetstorms that there was little to worry about, that 'I think it's going to work out fine', that 'The Coronavirus is very much under control in the USA.'[5]

Trump's denialism was echoed by many leaders around the world, including in Africa. This delayed taking much-needed preemptive action that would have limited the spread and potential impact of the coronavirus firestorm. As early as 2012 a report by the Rand Corporation had warned that only pandemics were 'capable of destroying America's way of life'.[6] The Obama administration proceeded to establish the National Security Council directorate for Global Health Security and Biodefense, which the Trump administration closed in 2018. Security establishments in many countries have generally not taken global pandemics seriously, preoccupied as they are with conventional wars, terrorism and the machismo of military hardware.

In the meantime, China, the original epicentre of the pandemic, took draconian measures to lock down Wuhan and neighbouring regions. Many politicians and pundits in 'western democracies' initially dismissed these measures as a frightful and an unacceptable example of Chinese authoritarianism. Regional and national lockdowns were embraced as a strategy of containment as the pandemic ravaged Italy, which became the coronavirus epicentre in Europe and a major exporter of the disease to several African countries.

Asian democracies, such as South Korea, Japan, Taiwan and Singapore, adopted less coercive and more transparent measures. Already endowed with good public health systems capable of handling major epidemics, which had been enhanced by lessons from the virus epidemics of the 2000s and 2010s, they developed effective and vigilant monitoring systems encompassing early intervention, meticulous contact tracing, mandatory quarantines, social distancing and border controls.

Various forms of lockdown – some severe, others more mild – were soon adopted in many countries and cities around the world. They comprised the closure of offices, schools and universities and entertainment and sports venues, as well as the banning of international flights and even domestic travel. Large-scale disinfection drives were also increasingly undertaken. *The Economist* of 21 March noted in its lead story that China and South Korea effectively used 'technology to administer quarantines and social distancing. China is using apps to certify who is clear of the disease and who is not. Both it and South Korea are using big data and social media to trace infections, alert people of hotspots and round contacts.'[7]

Belatedly, as the pandemic flared in their countries, the sceptics began singing a different tune, although a dwindling minority complained of overreaction. Befitting the grandiosity of populist politicians, they suddenly fancied themselves as great generals in the most ferocious war in a generation. Some commentators found the metaphor of war obscene, used for self-aggrandisement by clueless leaders anxious to burnish their tattered reputations and accrue more gravitas and power. For the bombastic, narcissistic and pathological liar that he is, President Trump sought to change the narrative, that he had foreseen the pandemic, notwithstanding his earlier dismissals of its seriousness.

His British counterpart, Prime Minister Johnson, vainly tried Churchillian impersonation, which provoked widespread derision in the media. Each time either of them spoke trying to reassure the public, the more it became clear they were out of their depth, that they did not have the intellectual and political capacity to calm the situation. It was a verdict delivered with painful cruelty by the stock markets they adored, which fell sharply each time they gave a press conference and announced half-baked containment measures.

Initially, many of Africa's inept governments remained blasé about the pandemic, even allowing flights to and from China, Italy and other countries with heavy infection rates. Cynical citizens with little trust in their corrupt governments to manage a serious crisis sought comfort in myths peddled on social media about Africa's immunity because of its sunny weather, youthful population, the curative potential of some concoctions – from disinfectants to pepper soup, the preventive potential of shaving beards, or the protective power of faith and prayer.

Some claimed African governments and societies were better prepared because of their experience dealing with other deadly disease epidemics, from malaria to tuberculosis, HIV/AIDS to Ebola. Others attributed the expected relatively low rate of cases to limited international travel in many of Africa's underdeveloped economies. Even more outlandish were claims of the purported immunities of African genetics. The rates of transmission and morbidity from COVID-19 among African diaspora populations, which in Britain, the US and Brazil were disproportionately higher than for the white populations, underscored the hazardous inanity of genetic arguments. According to the *Guardian*, in the United Kingdom, 'Black people are more than four times more likely to die from Covid-19 than white people.'[8] In the US, *The New York Times* lamented, 'The coronavirus pandemic has stripped bare the racial divide in the health of our nation.'[9] This was because, to quote an African-American physician, this battle found black people 'outmatched, underresourced, undersupported and undertested'.[10]

More than seven months after the pandemic had started there were indeed fewer cases of COVID-19 reported in Africa than originally anticipated and in comparison to other world regions, which fed into the dangerous delusions noted above. The fact of the matter is that the numbers were relatively low because little testing had been done in most African countries. It was not accidental that the highest numbers of people infected by the coronavirus were reported to be in Africa's most developed economies in South Africa and northern Africa, which had undertaken more testing.

The World Health Organization was not as sanguine about Africa's prospects. The WHO Regional Office for Africa warned, 'Eighty-three thousand to 190 000 people in Africa could die of COVID-19 and 29 million to 44 million could get infected in the first year of the pandemic if containment measures fail.'[11] In another report, the WHO 'expressed concern at the potential impact of COVID-19 on food security, which is likely to exacerbate the already considerable burden of malnutrition in Africa. The impact of the disease is expected to be greater among those grappling with food scarcity and malnutrition, while widespread food insecurity will likely increase due to movement restrictions.'[12]

As the concerns and outrage from civil society mounted and opportunities for foreign aid rose, some governments went into a rhetorical overdrive that engendered more panic than reassurance. It increasingly became evident that Africa needed unflinching commitment to public health and massive resources to stem the rising tide of coronavirus infections. According to one commentator in the *Sunday Nation* of 22 March, 'It is estimated that the continent would need up to $10.6 billion in unanticipated increases in health spending to curtail the virus from spreading.' He advised the continent to urgently implement the African Continental Free Trade Area and work with global partners.

In Kenya, some defiant politicians refused to self-quarantine after travelling from coronavirus-stricken countries, churches resisted closing their doors and traders defied orders to close markets. This forced the government to issue draconian containment measures on 22 March 2020, stipulating that all those who violated quarantine measures would be quarantined forcefully at their own expense, all gatherings at churches and mosques were suspended, weddings were no longer allowed and funerals would be restricted to fifteen family members.

The infodemic of false and misleading information, as the WHO called it, was of course not confined to Africa. It spread like wildfire around the world. So did the peddling of fake information and products by coronavirus fraudsters to desperate and unwary recipients. In Britain, the National Fraud Intelligence Bureau was forced to issue urgent scam warnings against emails and text messages purporting to be from reputable research and health organisations.

The coronavirus pandemic showed the fecklessness of some political leaders and incompetence of many governments. The neoliberal crusade against 'Big Government' that had triumphed since the turn of the 1980s suddenly looked threadbare. And so did the populist zealotry against experts and expertise. The valourisation of the politics of gut feelings masquerading as gifted insight and knowledge suddenly vanished as ignoble ignorance was revealed to endanger the lives of millions of people. People found more solace in the calm pronouncements of professional experts, including doctors, epidemiologists, researchers and health officials, than loquacious politicians.

Populist leaders like President Trump and Prime Minister Johnson, and many others of their ilk, had taken vicarious pleasure in denigrating experts and expert knowledge and decimating national research infrastructures and institutions. Suddenly, at their press conferences they were flanked by trusted medical and scientific professionals and civil servants as they sought to bask in their authoritative glow. But that could not restore public health infrastructures overnight, severely damaged as they were by indefensible austerity measures and pro-rich transfers of wealth adopted by their governments.

In fact, even as the pandemic ravaged their countries, populist leaders continued to undermine mitigation measures recommended by healthcare experts through misleading pronouncements and misguided actions. It is instructive to note that some of the worst effects of COVID-19 in terms of infections and deaths were in the US, Brazil, India and Russia, which were the four top countries, and Britain was one of the worst-performing countries in Europe. By 18 July 2020, the US had 3.544 million confirmed cases, Brazil 2.014 million, India 1.039 million and Russia 765,437. Altogether, the four countries represented 53 per cent of the global confirmed cases on that day, which stood at 13.876 million.[13] The bombastic denialism by the leaders of the four countries and their misguided sense of national exceptionalism had failed to inoculate their nations from the pandemic.

Economic Meltdown

When the coronavirus pandemic broke out, many countries were unprepared for it. There were severe shortages of testing kits and health care facilities. Many also lacked universal entitlement to health care and social safety nets, including basic employment rights and unemployment insurance that could have mitigated some of the worst effects of the pandemic's economic impact. All this ensured that the pandemic would unleash mutually reinforcing health and economic crises. Every economic sector was affected, from the hospitality industry to banking, manufacturing and education.

The signs of economic meltdown escalated around the world. Stock markets experienced volatility that ran out of superlatives. In the United States, from early February to 20 March 2020, the Dow Jones Industrial Average fell by about 10,000 points, or 35 per cent, while the S&P fell by 32 per cent. In Britain, the FTSE fell by 49 per cent from its peak earlier in the year, the German DAX by 36 per cent, the Hong Kong HSI by 22 per cent and the Japanese Nikkei by 32 per cent. Trillions of dollars were wiped out. In the United States, the gains made under President Trump vanished and fell to the levels left by his nemesis President Obama, depriving the market-obsessed president of one of his favorite talking points and justifications for re-election.

There are hardly any parallels to a pandemic leading to markets crumbling the way they did with the coronavirus. They did not during the 1918–1920 influenza pandemic, although they fluctuated afterwards. More recently, during the flu pandemic of 1957–1958, the Dow fell about 25 per cent, and the SARS and MERS scares of the early twenty-first century had relatively limited economic impact. However, some economic historians warned that the stock market was not always a good indicator or predictor of the severity of a pandemic.

In fact, as the pandemic spread the stock market rebounded, a clear indication of its divorce from the real economy. As Michael Steinberger put it in a long article in *The New York Times*, 'Perhaps one lesson this crisis can reinforce is that we should stop thinking of the stock market as a barometer of national prosperity. Maybe it served that function in the past, but it doesn't now. Instead, the market has become an emblem and engine of American inequality. In that sense, its performance in recent months reflects our reality all too well.'[14]

The severe economic downturn was evident as one industry after another went into a tailspin. The travel, hospitality and leisure industries, including airlines, hotels, restaurants, bars, sports, conventions, exhibitions, tourism and retail, were the first to feel the economic slump as people escaped or were coerced into the isolation of their homes. For example, hotel revenues in the United States plummeted by 75 per cent on average, worse than during the Great Recession and the aftermath of the 9/11 terrorist attacks combined. Aviation faced the biggest crisis in its history as air travel and tourism ground to a virtual halt. When the pandemic was declared in March 2020 passenger numbers fell by 58 per cent or 198 million and cargo by 19 per cent.

In 2020 tourism was expected to decline by 60 to 80 per cent compared to 2019.[15] By April 2020 industrial production had already fallen by 24 per cent in upper-middle-income countries, 22 per cent in lower-middle-income countries and 18 per cent in high-income countries. According to the United Nations Industrial Development Organization (UNIDO), firms in the textile, apparel and leather, furniture, recycling and printing, basic materials and machinery and transport industries suffered above average decreases, while firms in food processing, non-manufacturing and the chemical, plastic and rubber industries had below average decreases. Small and medium enterprises also suffered deeper declines than larger firms.[16]

Other industries soon followed suit as supply chains were scuppered, profits and share prices fell, offices were closed and staff told to work from home. Manufacturing, construction and banking were not spared. Big Technology was also affected by factory shutdowns and postponed launches of new products. Nor was the oil industry safe. With global demand falling and the price war between Saudi Arabia and Russia escalating, oil prices fell dramatically to US$20.3 a barrel, a fall of 67 per cent since the beginning of 2020. Some predicted the prospect of US$5 per barrel of oil.

The oil price war threatened to decimate smaller or poorer oil producers, from the Gulf States to Nigeria. It also threatened the shale oil industry in the United

States, with its high production costs, thereby depriving the county of its newly acquired status as the largest oil producer in the world, which had so chagrined Russia and OPEC. Many of the US shale oil companies faced bankruptcy as their production costs were fourteen times higher than Saudi Arabia's production costs and they needed prices of more than US$40 per barrel to cover their direct costs.

Falling oil prices, combined with growing concerns about climate change, dented the prospects of several oil exploration and production companies, such as the British company Tullow, which until then had ambitious projects in Kenya, Uganda and Ghana. The freeze on such projects threatened those countries' aspirations to join the club of major oil-producing nations. In early March 2020, one of Tullow's major investors, Blackrock, the world's biggest hedge fund with US$7 trillion in assets, made it clear that it was losing interest in fossil fuel investment.

Such were the disruptions caused by the coronavirus pandemic that a survey by the London School of Economics revealed '66 per cent of the panel [of experts] strongly agreed, 31 per cent agreed, 3 per cent were uncertain, and none disagreed' that the world faced a deep recession.[17] According to a survey reported by the World Economic Forum:

> The public sees coronavirus as a greater threat to the economy than to their health, new research suggests. Economic rescue measures announced by governments do not appear to be calming concern. ... The majority of people in most countries polled expect to feel a personal financial impact from the coronavirus pandemic, according to the results. Respondents in Vietnam, China, India and Italy show the greatest concern.[18]

Many economies spiralled into recession. The major international financial institutions and development agencies revised world, regional and national economic growth prospects for 2020 downwards, sometimes sharply so. Such was the gravity and uncertainty about the COVID-19 recession that growth forecasts were frequently revised. In June 2020 the IMF and World Bank produced reports that gave steep downgrades from previous projections just a few months or even weeks earlier.

The IMF's *June 2020 World Economic Outlook Update* projected global growth:

> at -4.9 percent in 2020, 1.9 percentage points below the April 2020 World Economic Outlook (WEO) forecast. The COVID-19 pandemic has had a more negative impact on activity in the first half of 2020 than anticipated, and the recovery is projected to be more gradual than previously forecast. In 2021 global growth is projected at 5.4 percent. Overall, this would leave 2021 GDP some 6 ½ percentage points lower than in the pre-COVID-19 projections of January 2020. The adverse impact on low-income households is particularly acute, imperiling the significant progress made in reducing extreme poverty in the world since the 1990s. As with the April 2020 WEO projections, there is a higher-than-usual degree of uncertainty around this forecast.[19]

The report stressed, 'Data releases since then suggest even deeper downturns than previously projected for several economies' and made seven observations. First, the pandemic had worsened in many countries, and levelled off in others. Second, there had been a synchronised, deep downturn around the world. Third, consumption and services output had dropped markedly. Fourth, mobility remained depressed. Fifth, there had been a severe hit to the labour market in which 130 million full-time jobs were lost around the world in the first quarter of 2020 and another 300 million were expected to be lost in the second quarter. Sixth, global trade had contracted by 3.5 per cent in the first quarter 'reflecting weak demand, the collapse in cross-border tourism, and supply dislocations related to shutdowns (exacerbated in some cases by trade restrictions).' Finally, inflation was weaker as it dropped for the advanced economies by 1.3 percentage points to 0.4 per cent and in the emerging and developing economies by 1.2 percentage points to 4.2 per cent.

For the advanced economies, the IMF projected growth at:

> … -8.0 percent in 2020, 1.9 percentage points lower than in the April 2020 WEO. There appears to have been a deeper hit to activity in the first half of the year than anticipated, with signs of voluntary distancing even before lockdowns were imposed. This also suggests a more gradual recovery in the second half as fear of contagion is likely to continue. Synchronized deep downturns are foreseen in the United States (-8.0 percent); Japan (-5.8 percent); the United Kingdom (-10.2 percent); Germany (-7.8 percent); France (-12.5 percent); Italy and Spain (-12.8 percent). In 2021 the advanced economy growth rate is projected to strengthen to 4.8 percent, leaving 2021 GDP for the group about 4 percent below its 2019 level.

For the emerging market and developing economies, the reported stated that:

> … downward revision to growth prospects over 2020–21 (2.8 percentage points) exceeds the revision for advanced economies (1.8 percentage points). Excluding China, the downward revision for emerging market and developing economies over 2020–21 is 3.6 percentage points. Overall, growth … is forecast at -3.0 percent in 2020, 2 percentage points below the April 2020 WEO forecast. Growth among low-income developing countries is projected at -1.0 percent in 2020, some 1.4 percentage points below the April 2020 WEO forecast, although with differences across individual countries. Excluding a few large frontier economies, the remaining group of low-income developing countries is projected to contract by -2.2 percent in 2020.

The reported concluded sombrely:

> For the first time, all regions are projected to experience negative growth in 2020. There are, however, substantial differences across individual economies, reflecting the evolution of the pandemic and the effectiveness of containment strategies; variation in economic structure (for example, dependence on severely affected sectors, such as tourism and oil); reliance on external financial flows, including

> remittances; and precrisis growth trends … These projections imply a particularly acute negative impact of the pandemic on low-income households worldwide that could significantly raise inequality. The fraction of the world's population living in extreme poverty – that is, on less than $1.90 a day – had fallen below 10 percent in recent years (from more than 35 percent in 1990). This progress is imperiled by the COVID-19 crisis, with more than 90 percent of emerging market and developing economies projected to register negative per capita income growth in 2020.

The World Bank painted a similarly grim picture in its much longer report, *June 2020 Global Economic Prospects.*

> The COVID-19 pandemic has, with alarming speed, delivered a global economic shock of enormous magnitude, leading to steep recessions in many countries. The baseline forecast envisions a 5.2 percent contraction in global GDP in 2020 – the deepest global recession in eight decades, despite unprecedented policy support. Per capita incomes in the vast majority of emerging market and developing economies (EMDEs) are expected to shrink this year, tipping many millions back into poverty.[20]

The report noted that this was the fourteenth global recession since 1870, the fourth deepest, and the most severe since the end of World War II.

> The spread of the pandemic has essentially halted international travel and disrupted global value chains, resulting in a sharp contraction in global trade. A flight to safety has triggered sharp falls in global equity markets, unprecedented capital outflows from EMDEs, rising credit-risk spreads, and depreciations for many EMDE [emerging market and developing economies] currencies. Falling demand has led to a sharp decline in most commodity prices, with a particularly substantial plunge in oil prices.

The global recession triggered by COVID-19 hit the emerging and developing economies particularly hard, especially those 'with large domestic outbreaks and those that rely heavily on global trade, tourism, commodity exports, and external financing. Per capita incomes are projected to contract deeply as a result, causing the first net rise in global poverty in more than 20 years.' The vulnerability of these economies was exacerbated by their

> … large informal sectors. Participants in the informal sector – workers and small enterprises – are often not registered with the government and hence have no access to government benefits … The impact is likely to be particularly severe on women, due to their outsized participation in sectors that are more affected by the pandemic. While the effects of the crisis continue, it is critical to implement effective delivery channels to quickly provide the support that informal workers and firms need to survive. Unconditional support programs would be advisable in many EMDEs.

Overall, the report projected that in 2020 the advanced economies would decline at a steeper rate than the EMDEs, by 7.2 per cent compared to 2.5 per cent, respectively. The euro area would suffer the biggest decline by 9.1 per cent, followed by Japan and the United States, both by 6.1 per cent. There would be huge divergences among the EMDEs. East Asia and the Pacific would grow by a paltry 0.5 per cent, Europe and Central Asia would contract by 4.7 per cent, Latin America by 7.2 per cent, the Middle East and North Africa by 4.2 per cent, South Asia by 2.7 per cent, and sub-Saharan Africa by 2.8 per cent.

Within each region prospects varied. In East Asia, China was projected to grow by 1.0 per cent, the only major economy expected to grow in 2020, followed by Indonesia at 0.0 per cent and Thailand, which was expected to shrink by 5.0 per cent. The largest economies in the other world regions all seemed destined to decline. In Europe and Central Asia, Russia was projected to contract by 6.0 per cent, Turkey 3.8 per cent and Poland 4.2 per cent; in Latin America and the Caribbean, Brazil by 8 per cent, Mexico 7.5 per cent and Argentina 7.3 per cent; in the Middle East and North Africa, Saudi Arabia by 3.8 per cent, Iran by 5.3 per cent and Egypt by 3 per cent; in South Asia, India by 3.2 per cent and Pakistan by 2.6 per cent; and in sub-Saharan Africa, Nigeria by 3.2 per cent, South Africa by 7.1 per cent and Angola by 4.0 per cent.

The World Bank expected the global economy to rebound in 2021. Growth prospects would 'depend primarily on the severity and duration of the necessary pandemic-control measures and related financial turmoil, as well as the ability of policymakers to buffer economic disruptions'. According to various scenarios, the Bank projected that recovery would be fastest in East Asia and the Pacific at 6.6 per cent (Indonesia 6.9 per cent, China 6.6 per cent and Thailand 4.8 per cent), followed by the advanced economies at 3.9 per cent (Japan 4.5 per cent, euro area 4.0 per cent and US 3.9 per cent).

In third place would be Europe and Central Asia, which would grow by 3.6 per cent (Turkey 5.0 per cent, Poland 2.8 per cent and Russia 2.7 per cent), then sub-Saharan Africa (Angola 3.1 per cent, South Africa (2.9 per cent and Nigeria 1.7 per cent). Next would be Latin America and the Caribbean, and South Asia, both of which would experience growth of 2.8 per cent (Mexico 3.0 per cent, Brazil 2.2 per cent and Argentina 2.1 per cent; India 3.1 per cent, Bangladesh 1.0 per cent and Pakistan -0.2 per cent). At the bottom would be the Middle East and North Africa, which would grow by 2.3 per cent (Saudi Arabia 2.5 per cent, and Iran and Egypt both by 2.1 per cent).

The OECD also produced a voluminous report in June 2020, which revised the projections of its March 2020 report.[21] The report began by underscoring what had become a truism: 'The spread of COVID-19 has shaken people's lives around the globe in an extraordinary way, threatening health, disrupting economic activity, and hurting wellbeing and jobs.' It went on to state, 'As long as no vaccine or treatment is widely available, policymakers around the world will continue to walk a tightrope. Physical distancing and testing, tracking, tracing and isolation (TTTI) will be the main instruments to fight the virus.'

The report noted business activity remained exceptionally weak as manufacturing and services output declined sharply, collapsing world trade fell by 3.75 per cent in the first quarter of 2020, while volatility and risk aversion and tensions in financial markets spiked. Sharp drops in revenues due to shutdowns led to widespread corporate insolvencies and bankruptcies. Emerging and developing economies faced particular hazards from the collapse of export commodity markets, capital flight and high levels of external debt. The epidemiological outlook also remained volatile as 'incomplete data and insufficient knowledge about the nature of the coronavirus made it uncertain how the pandemic will evolve'.

The OECD's projections of global economic activity did not vary markedly from those of the IMF and World Bank. It noted the global recession was extraordinarily deep and that recovery would be slow. The report noted that from 2012 to 2019 the global, G20 and OECD economies had grown by 3.3 percent, 3.5 per cent and 2.1 per cent, respectively. In comparison, the non-OECD economies had grown by 4.3 per cent. Much of the benefits of this growth were lost. To quote the report, 'Five years or more of income growth could be lost in many countries by the end of 2021. The disruption resulting from the pandemic is likely to leave long-lasting scars in many economies. Living standards have been reduced significantly ... the direct impact on people's livelihoods is particularly severe among the most vulnerable groups in society.'

In what it called a 'double hit' scenario (where there is another coronavirus outbreak), in 2020 the world, G20, OECD and non-OECD economies would contract by 7.6 per cent, 7.3 per cent, 9.3 per cent and 6.1 per cent, respectively. In a 'single hit' scenario they would contract by 6.0 per cent, 5.7 per cent, 7.5 per cent and 4.6 per cent, respectively. Under the double-hit scenario, the economies of the United States, euro area and Japan would shrink by 8.5 per cent, 11.5 per cent and 7.3 per cent, respectively; under the single-hit scenario they would shrink by 7.3 per cent, 9.1 per cent and 6.0 per cent, respectively. In the meantime, the non-OECD economies would fare slightly better. They would contract by 6.1 per cent under the double-hit scenario and 4.6 per cent under the single-hit scenario.

As for recovery, in 2021 the OECD report projected a global growth rate of 2.8 per cent, 3.1 per cent for the G20, 2.2 per cent for the OECD and 3.2 per cent for non-OECD. Under the single-hit scenario, the growth rates would be 5.2 per cent, 5.5 per cent, 4.8 per cent and 5.6 per cent, respectively. The OECD data clearly showed that the non-OECD countries led by China and India performed best pre-COVID-19, during the pandemic and would do so after the pandemic. From 2012 to 2019, China grew at the rate of 7.8 per cent, followed by India at 6.8 per cent, the US 2.4 per cent, euro area 1.6 per cent, Japan 1.0 per cent and Brazil 0.0 per cent.

In 2020, under the double-hit scenario, China was also expected to perform best (-3.7 per cent), followed by India and Japan (both -7.3 per cent), then the US (-8.5 per cent) and the euro area (-11.5 per cent). Under the single-hit scenario, performance would be led by China (-2.1 per cent), India (-3.7 per cent), Japan (-6.9 per cent), US (-7.3 per cent), Brazil (-7.4 per cent) and the euro area (-9.1 per cent). In 2021 the order in growth rates would be India (7.9 per cent), China (6.8 per cent), euro area (6.5 per cent), Brazil (4.2 per cent), US (4.1 per cent) and Japan (2.1 per cent).

The impact of COVID-19 and prospects for African economies were particularly bleak. The African Development Bank put it bluntly. 'Africa's economic prospects are weak', the Bank stated in its *African Economic Outlook – Supplement* published in early July 2020.[22]

> Real GDP in Africa is projected to contract by 1.7 percent in 2020, dropping by 5.6 percentage points from the January 2020 pre-COVID–19 projection, if the virus has a substantial impact but of short duration. If it continues beyond the first half of 2020, there would be a deeper GDP contraction in 2020 of 3.4 percent, down by 7.3 percentage points from the growth projected before the outbreak of COVID–19. Cumulatively, GDP losses could range between $173.1 billion and $236.7 billion in 2020–2021. With the projected contraction of growth, Africa could suffer GDP losses in 2020 between $145.5 billion (baseline) and $189.7 billion (worst case), from the pre-COVID–19 estimated GDP of $2.59 trillion for 2020. Some losses are carried over to 2021, as the projected recovery would be partial. For 2021, the projected GDP losses could be from $27.6 billion (baseline) up to $47 billion (worst case) from the potential GDP of $2.76 trillion without the pandemic.

According to the report, the most vulnerable countries would be those with poor health systems, dependent on international trade, volatile financial flows and commodity exports, and that were heavily indebted. As for its macroeconomic impact, the crisis had triggered a sudden uptick in inflation, increased already high fiscal deficits, raised debt burdens and would reduce remittances. Its socioeconomic impacts were also likely to be dire. The continent was inadequately prepared to handle the crisis, between 28.2 and 49.2 million more Africans could be pushed into poverty, and an estimated 30–50 million jobs could be lost.

The severe socioeconomic impacts of COVID-19 were of course not confined to Africa. All over the world the pandemic had particularly devastating effects on the labour market. Unemployment rose to staggering levels not seen in decades. Data from the International Labour Organization (ILO) was sobering. In a report published on 30 June 2020, the ILO noted that 93 per cent 'of the world's workers continue to reside in countries with some sort of workplace closure measure in place' and that 'working-hour losses have worsened during the first half of 2020, reflecting the deteriorating situation in recent weeks, especially in developing countries'.[23] Altogether, global working hours during the first quarter of 2020 had declined by 5.4 per cent over the last quarter of 2019, which was equivalent to 155 million full-time jobs. During the second quarter of 2020 the fall in global working hours reached 14.0 per cent representing 400 million jobs.

The job losses varied by income group and geographical region. During the first quarter the losses were highest in the upper-middle-income countries (9.3 per cent), followed by lower-middle-income countries (3.0 per cent), high-income countries (2.5 per cent) and low-income countries (2.4 per cent). In terms of regions, the most affected were Asia and the Pacific (9.1 per cent), followed by Europe and Central Asia (3.4 per cent), Arab States (3.1 per cent), the Americas (3.0 per cent age) and Africa (2.4 per cent). During the second quarter, lower-middle-income countries bore the brunt (16.1 per cent), then came the high-income (13.9 per cent), upper-middle-income (12.6 per cent), and low-income (11.1 per cent). The Americas shot to first place (18.3 per cent), trailed by Europe and Central Asia (13.9 per cent), Asia and the Pacific (13.5 per cent), Arab States (13.2 per cent), and Africa (12.1 per cent).

Within each region there were subregional differences. In Africa the most affected region, in both quarters, was Northern Africa (at 2.5 per cent and 15.5 per cent, respectively), while the lowest in the first quarter was Southern Africa (1.6 per cent) and in the second quarter Eastern Africa (10.9 per cent). In the Americas, South America led in both quarters (4.8 per cent and 20.6 per cent, respectively). The lowest in the first quarter was Central America (1.1 per cent) and in the second quarter Northern America (15.3 per cent). In Asia and the Pacific, Eastern Asia had the highest rate of job losses (11.6 per cent) and Southeastern Asia the lowest (2.1 per cent), while during the second quarter the highest went to Southern Asia (17.9 per cent) and lowest to Eastern Asia (10.4 per cent). In Europe and Central Asia, Southern Europe claimed the highest share (5.3 per cent) and Eastern Europe the lowest (2.6 per cent) during the first quarter, positions they retained during the second quarter (Southern Europe 18.0 per cent and Eastern Europe 11.6 per cent).

The steep declines in employment had a disproportionate impact on women both in terms of unemployment, vulnerability and stress. This is because larger proportions of women workers were in sectors hardest hit by the pandemic (40 per cent compared to 36.6 per cent for men). Women also accounted for 51.2 per cent of domestic work, which was severely affected by containment measures. Moreover, women represented 70 per cent of workers in the frontline health and social work sector. Finally, women were affected by the unequal distribution of childcare and household chores, the pressures of which increased with lockdowns and the closure of schools. The ILO report concluded, 'These disproportionate impacts on women could undo some of the gains in gender equality in the labour market and exacerbate disparities.'

The ILO made several projections for the fourth quarter of 2020. In a baseline scenario, the loss of global working hours would decline from the peak in the second quarter to 4.9 per cent, equivalent to 140 million full-time jobs. In a pessimistic scenario, the global working hour loss would be 11.9 per cent or 340 million full-time jobs. In an optimistic scenario, job losses would decline to 34 million or 1.2 per cent of global working hours.

The ILO proposed interventions anchored on four pillars. First, stimulating the economy and employment through active fiscal policy, accommodative monetary policy, lending and financial support to specific sectors, including the health sector. Second, supporting enterprises, jobs and incomes, extending social protection to all, implementing employment retention measures, and providing financial/tax and other relief for enterprises. Third, protecting workers in the workplace, strengthening occupational safety and health measures, and adapting work arrangements (e.g. teleworking). Fourth, relying on social dialogue for solution, strengthening the capacity and resilience of employers' and workers' organisations, enhancing the capacity of governments, promoting social dialogue, collective bargaining and labour relations institutions and processes, preventing discrimination and exclusion, providing health access for all, and expanding access to paid leave.

The impact of COVID-19 was equally far reaching on food and agriculture. The Food and Agriculture Organization (FAO) noted that food and nutrition security were under threat. The pandemic affected food production, agricultural and fishery supply chains and markets. Fear of contagion had implications for food demand and prices. In short,

> Border closures, quarantines, and market, supply chain and trade disruptions are restricting people's access to sufficient/diverse and nutritious sources of food, especially in countries hit hard by the virus or already affected by high levels of food insecurity … In any scenario, the most affected will be the poorest and most vulnerable segments of the population, (including migrants, the displaced, and those hit by conflict). Countries in protracted crises also suffer from underinvestment in public health, which will amplify the pandemic's impacts.[24]

The FAO noted that 820 million people around the world experienced hunger and that 'in the absence of timely and effective policies, millions more are likely to join the ranks of the hungry as a result of the COVID-19-triggered recession. That number will vary according to the severity of economic contractions, ranging from 14.4 million to 38.2 million, or even 80.3 million.' More than half (73 million) of the 135 million people facing crisis levels of acute food insecurity were in Africa. FAO expressed serious concern about the impact of COVID-19 on vulnerable communities that were already grappling with hunger. Other vulnerable groups included small-scale farmers, pastoralists, fishers and migrant and informal sector workers unable to work because of lockdowns, quarantines and panic. Also, because of school closures tens of millions of children could not access school meals. Before the pandemic the FAO itself had supported school meals programmes benefitting 85 million children in Latin America and the Caribbean alone.

The FAO recommended several proactive and mitigation measures. It urged countries, first, to meet the immediate food needs of their vulnerable populations by ensuring emergency food needs were met, adjusting and expanding social protection programmes, scaling up nutritional support, supporting management and prevention of undernourishment, and adjusting school meal programmes so as to continue delivering school meals even when schools were shut. Second, to boost their social protection programmes by 'increasing transfer amounts to people already benefitting from social assistance' and 'providing complimentary entitlements to offset loss of income by small-scale producers'. Third, to gain efficiencies and try to reduce trade-related costs by not restricting trade and mobility of commodities; reducing food waste and losses; resolving logistics bottlenecks; reviewing trade and policy options and their likely impacts; avoiding generalised subsidies for food consumers; reducing restrictions on use of stocks; reducing import tariffs; reviewing 'taxation policy to imported goods to compensate from potential cost increases (because of exchange devaluation) and assess exchange devaluation's potential impacts'.

Return of the State

As the economic impact of the coronavirus pandemic escalated, demands from the public, employers, employees and trade unions for government support intensified. The pandemic wreaked particular havoc among poor workers who could hardly manage in 'normal' times. For example, across Kenya jobs had already been lost before the coronavirus epidemic. Those in the informal economy were exceptionally vulnerable after the extensive lockdown that the government announced on 22 March. By early June, it was reported 'Over one million rendered jobless in Kenya as COVID-19 takes toll on businesses'.[25]

Many others saw pay cuts and struggled to keep afloat. Kenyan employers, workers, unions and analysts implored the government to take drastic measures to boost the economy, by providing bailouts, tax incentives and rebates and social safety nets, as well as increasing government spending. Demands were made on banks to extend credit to the private sector and for the Central Bank to lower or even freeze interest rates for six months. The government scrambled a war chest of KES140 billion to shore up the economy and avert a recession.

Elsewhere, including the rich countries, the battered middle classes had barely recovered from the Great Recession. In the United States, tens of millions of Americans were already 'only $400 away from financial hardship ... If faced with an unexpected expense of $400, 61 per cent of adults could cover it with cash, savings, or a credit card paid off at the next statement. But 27 per cent would have to borrow or sell something to pay for the expense; 12 per cent would not be able to cover the expense.'[26]

Those earning a precarious living in the gig economy faced special hurdles in making themselves heard and receiving support. With the lockdown of cities, couriers became even more essential to deliver food and other supplies, but they lacked employment rights, so that many could not afford self-isolation if they became sick. Customer service workers at airports and in supermarkets were sometimes at the receiving end of pandemonium and the anxieties of irate customers.

The COVID-19 pandemic forced dramatic shifts in government policy. The state that neoliberalism had sought to rein in came galloping back with a vengeance. The pandemic may have marked the moment when the gospel of free-market fundamentalism, mortally wounded by the Great Recession, was finally buried. A range of policy mixes were developed to contain the health-care, macroeconomic and socioeconomic impacts of the pandemic. In terms of health care, the focus was on ensuring adequate hospital capacity, provision of personal protective equipment, and building capacities for effective testing, tracking, tracing and isolation.

Fiscal interventions encompassed tax relief, subsidies to the hardest hit sectors and enterprises, expansion and extension of social insurance support and emergency relief assistance. Monetary responses consisted of asset purchase by central banks (quantitative easing), lending support and liquidity support measures, such as loans, loan guarantees and recapitalisations, and regulatory changes. Labour market responses comprised variations of the ILO recommendations noted above, from short-time work schemes and wage subsidies to cash transfers and deferment or reduction of taxes for business, especially for small and medium enterprises. The crisis forced governments to begin rethinking economic sustainability and resilience for the future in terms of structural reforms, regulations, social safety nets and inclusive growth.

Central banks began to cut interest rates aggressively as the pandemic gathered momentum. On 15 March, the US Federal Reserve cut the rate to near zero in a co-ordinated move with the central banks of Japan, Australia and New Zealand. On 12 March the Fed also announced measures to shore up financial markets, including a package of US$1.5 trillion for asset purchase and a credit facility for financial institutions; an additional US$500 billion was added four days later. At the same time, Congress began working on an unprecedented economic relief programme. The negotiations between the two political parties, the Democrats and Republicans, over the proposed stimulus bill proved bitterly contentious.

For President Trump and the Republicans it was a hard pill to swallow, given their antipathy to Big Government. It marked the fall of another ideological pillar of Trumpism and Republicanism. For some, the collapse of these pillars (the first being economic growth) marked the end of the Trump presidency, which had been exposed for its deadly incompetence, autocratic political culture and aversion to truth and transparency. Congress passed a US$2 trillion Coronavirus, Aid and Relief (CARES) Act on 27 March 2020, the largest aid package in US history, which provided US$367 billion in loans and grants for small businesses, expansion of unemployment benefits, direct payments of US$1,200 to families earning less than US$75,000, US$500 billion fund for loans to corporate America, over US$130 billion to healthcare providers, US$150 billion for state and local governments, and US$32 billion cash grants to the airline industry.

On 20 March, the UK announced that the government would pay up to 80 per cent of the wages of employees across the country who had been sent home after businesses shut their doors as part of the drastic coronavirus containment strategy. This followed the example of the Danish government, which had earlier pledged to cover 75 per cent of employees' salaries for firms that agreed not to cut staff.

Initially, these measures failed to assure the markets, which continued to plummet. But as the scale of the stimulus packages skyrocketed market jitters eased, and by mid-July many markets had recovered much of their losses in March and April.

The ILO noted,

> By the end of May 2020, over 90 countries had introduced or announced fiscal measures totalling over US$10 trillion, while a similar number have cut interest rates following the outbreak. Fiscal measures in advanced economies, averaging 5 per cent of GDP in each case, account for 88 per cent of the global fiscal stimulus... In emerging and developing economies, policy responses were similarly rapid, but the fiscal packages were much smaller. On average, fiscal stimulus measures amounted to 2.3 per cent of GDP in these countries, which reflects their more constrained fiscal environment.[27]

The upper-middle-income countries accounted for 9.5 per cent, lower-middle-income countries for 2.5 per cent and the low-income countries for 0.03 per cent. In terms of regions, Europe and Central Asia led with 42.8 per cent, followed by the Americas with 33.0 per cent, Asia and the Pacific 23.2 per cent, Arab states 0.8 per cent and Africa 0.2 per cent.

The international financial institutions and development agencies opened their own spigots of financial support. In early March, the IMF announced that it 'could provide up to US$50 billion in emergency financing to fund emerging and developing countries' initial response' and that beyond 'the immediate emergency, members can also request a new loan – drawing on the IMF's war chest of around US$1 trillion in quota and borrowed resources – and current borrowers can top up their ongoing lending arrangements.'[28]

Soon thereafter, the World Bank approved 'an increased $14 billion package of fast-track financing to assist companies and countries in their efforts to prevent, detect and respond to the rapid spread of COVID-19. The package will strengthen national systems for public health preparedness, including for disease containment, diagnosis and treatment and support the private sector.'[29] The European Central Bank quickly followed and announced a 'new Pandemic Emergency Purchase Programme with an envelope of €750 billion until the end of the year, in addition to the €120 billion we decided on 12 March. Together this amounts to 7.3 per cent of euro area GDP.'[30]

Altogether, *The Economist* estimated, by the end of March 2020 the developed countries had injected about '$7.4trn, or 23 per cent of GDP'. But it expressed caution. 'Meanwhile, orthodox stimulus tools may not work well. Interest rates in the rich world are near zero, depriving central banks of their main lever. ... What to do? An economic plan needs to target two groups: households and companies.'[31]

Some of the regional development banks also announced major infusions of funds to contain the pandemic. On 18 March, 'The Asian Development Bank (ADB) today announced a $6.5 billion initial package to address the immediate needs of its developing member countries (DMCs) as they respond to the novel coronavirus (COVID-19) pandemic.'[32] In early April, the African Development Bank 'announced a COVID-19 Response Facility that will provide up to $10 billion to African governments and the private sector to tackle the disease and mitigate suffering that results from the economic downturn and job losses'. It estimated the pandemic would cost the continent between US$22.1 billion and US$88.3 billion.

Clearly, the coronavirus pandemic had upended traditional ideological polarities. Right-wing governments competed with left-wing governments, or opposition liberal legislatures as in the United States, to craft Big Government mitigation packages. Many borrowed monetary and fiscal measures from the Great Recession playbook, some of which they had resisted when they were in opposition or not yet in office.

Moreover, the pandemic helped bring political perspective to national and international preoccupations that suddenly looked petty in hindsight. For example, as one author put it in a story in *The Atlantic,* 'it's not hard to feel like the coronavirus has exposed the utter smallness of Brexit. ... Ultimately, Brexit is not a matter of life and death, literally or economically. The coronavirus, meanwhile, is killing people and perhaps many businesses.'[33]

The same could be said of many trivial political squabbles in other countries. In the United States, stated one observer also in *The Atlantic*:

> In the absence of meaningful national leadership, Americans across the country are making their own decisions for our collective well-being. You're seeing it in small

> stores deciding on their own to close; you're seeing it in restaurants evolving without government decree to offer curbside pickup or offer delivery for the first time; you're seeing it in the offices that closed long before official guidance arrived.[34]

The author concluded poignantly, 'The most isolating thing most of us have ever done is, ironically, almost surely the most collective experience we've ever had in our lifetimes.' I can attest I have seen this spirit of co-operation and collaboration on my own campus, among faculty, staff and students. However, the pandemic also raised questions about how effectively democracy could be upheld under the lockdowns of the coronavirus. Might desperate despots in some countries try to use the crisis to postpone elections?

Hegemonic and Nationalist Rivalries

At the beginning of the coronavirus outbreak China bore the brunt of numbers of victims and victimisation. The rest of the world feared the contagion spreading from China and, before long, from other Asian countries such as South Korea, Taiwan, Singapore and Iran to where the disease had quickly diffused. This triggered anti-Chinese and anti-Asian race bashing in Europe, North America and even Africa.

For many Africans it was a source of perverse relief that the coronavirus had not originated on the continent. Many wondered how Africa and Africans would have been portrayed and treated given the long history in the western and global imaginaries of pathologising African cultures, societies and people as diseased embodiments of sub-humanity.

Disease epidemics breed xenophobia, irrational fears of the 'other'. Commenting on the 1918 influenza pandemic, in *The Wall Street Journal*, one scholar reminded us, 'As the flu spread in 1918, many communities found scapegoats. Chileans blamed the poor, Senegalese blamed Brazilians, Brazilians blamed the Germans, Iranians blamed the British and so on.'[35] One key lesson is that to combat pandemics global co-operation is essential. Unfortunately, that lesson seemed to be ignored by some governments in the COVID-19 pandemic, although, as in other pandemics, good Samaritans did also abound.

As China, South Korea and Japan gradually contained the spread of the disease, Italy and other European countries turned into its epicentre and as the contagion began surging in the United States, the tables turned. While the Asian democracies largely managed to contain the coronavirus through less coercive and more transparent ways, China took centre stage in the global narrative. As would be expected in a world of intense hegemonic rivalries between the United States and China, the coronavirus pandemic became weaponised in the two countries' superpower rivalry.

As early as 19 March, less than three months after the outbreak of the first cases of coronavirus in Wuhan, China marked a milestone since the outbreak of the coronavirus with the announcement that there were no new domestic cases; people coming from abroad had brought all the 34 new cases identified that day. An article in *The New York Times* of 19 March reported:

> Across Asia, travelers from Europe and the United States are being barred or forced into quarantine. Gyms, private clinics and restaurants in Hong Kong warn them to stay away. Even Chinese parents who proudly sent their children to study in New York or London are now mailing them masks and sanitizer or rushing them home on flights that can cost $25,000.[36]

Even before this turning point, as coronavirus cases in China declined, the country began projecting itself as a heroic model of containment. It anxiously sought to furbish its once battered image by exporting medical equipment, experts and other forms of humanitarian assistance. Such was the newfound conceit of China that, in response to Trump's racist casting of the 'Chinese virus', some misguided Chinese nationalists falsely charged that the coronavirus had started with American troops and scornfully disparaged the United States for its apparently slow and chaotic containment efforts.

Another article in *The New York Times,* on 18 March, captured China's strategy for recasting its global image.

> From Japan to Iraq, Spain to Peru, it has provided or pledged humanitarian assistance in the form of donations or medical expertise – an aid blitz that is giving China the chance to reposition itself not as the authoritarian incubator of a pandemic but as a responsible global leader at a moment of worldwide crisis. In doing so, it has stepped into a role that the West once dominated in times of natural disaster or public health emergency and that President Trump has increasingly ceded in his 'America First' retreat from international engagement.[37]

The story continued:

> Now, the global failures in confronting the pandemic from Europe to the United States have given the Chinese leadership a platform to prove its model works – and potentially gain some lasting geopolitical currency. As it has done in the past, the Chinese state is using its extensive tools and deep pockets to build partnerships around the world, relying on trade, investments and, in this case, an advantageous position as the world's largest maker of medicines and protective masks. … On Wednesday, China said it would provide two million surgical masks, 200,000 advanced masks and 50,000 testing kits to Europe … One of China's leading entrepreneurs, Jack Ma, offered to donate 500,000 tests and one million masks to the United States, where hospitals are facing shortages.

Some analysts argued that the coronavirus pandemic was accelerating the decoupling of the United States from China that had begun with President Trump's trade war launched in 2018. American hawks saw the pandemic as an opportunity to bolster their argument that China's dominance of certain global supply chains, including medical supplies and pharmaceutical ingredients, posed a systemic risk to the American economy. Many others believed that Trump's 'America First' campaign damaged not only the country's standing and its preparedness to deal with the pandemic, but also its ability to create the international solidarity required for the containment and control of the virus.

In the words of one author in *The Atlantic*:

> Like Japan in the mid-1800s, the United States now faces a crisis that disproves everything the country believes about itself. ... The United States, long accustomed to thinking of itself as the best, most efficient and most technologically advanced society in the world, is about to be proved an unclothed emperor. When human life is in peril, we are not as good as Singapore, as South Korea, as Germany.[38]

The pandemic also exposed Europe's misguided historic conceits. To quote from a long article in *The New York Times:*

> As recently as February, when European health ministers met in Brussels to discuss the novel coronavirus emerging in China, they commended their own health systems and promised to send aid to poor and developing countries. Barely a month later, the continent was overwhelmed. Instead of serving primarily as a donor, providing aid to former colonies, Western Europe became an epicenter of the pandemic. Officials once boastful about their preparedness were frantically trying to secure protective gear and materials for tests, as death rates soared in Britain, France, Spain, Italy and Belgium.[39]

Pride and lack of humility proved Europe's undoing. In the scathing words of the article:

> This was not supposed to happen. The expertise and resources of Western Europe were expected to provide the antidote to viral outbreaks flowing out of poorer regions. Many European leaders felt so secure after the last pandemic – the 2009 swine flu – that they scaled back stockpiles of equipment and faulted medical experts for overreacting. But that confidence would prove their undoing. Their pandemic plans were built on a litany of miscalculations and false assumptions. European leaders boasted of the superiority of their world-class health systems but had weakened them with a decade of cutbacks. When COVID-19 arrived, those systems were unable to test widely enough to see the peak coming – or to guarantee the safety of health care workers after it hit. Accountability mechanisms proved toothless.

COVID-19 revealed the delusions and discontents of both globalisation and nationalism. Some commentators contended that the pandemic was facilitating the process of deglobalisation more generally as countries not only locked themselves in national enclosures for protection, but also sought to become more economically self-sufficient. It is important to note that throughout history, there have been waves and retreats of globalisation. Since the nineteenth century there have been three waves of globalisation.

The first wave lasted till 1914 and was characterised by massive growth in world trade, migrations and new transport and communication technologies. It ended with World War I and the Great Depression. The second wave began after World War II during which international trade and travel expanded, and new technologies and regional and global institutions emerged. The end of the postwar boom at the turn of the 1970s brought it to an end. The third phase began with the end of the Cold War in the early 1990s, the onset of the digital revolution and the triumph of neoliberalism. World trade and interconnectivity exploded. This phase was hit hard by the Great Recession of 2008–2009, and COVID-19 may deal it a fatal blow.

Nationalism was fortified by the massive inequalities, social disaffection and rising populist anger of neoliberal globalisation. It was bolstered under COVID-19 as international travel ground to a halt, countries closed their borders and the disruption in global value chains revived dreams of self-reliance and autarky. Moments of crisis tend to strengthen the state and nationalist sentiments and chauvinism. Citizens turn their patriotic attention and attachments to the nation-state rather than the amorphous international order or institutions that lack the former's financial resources, organisational capacities and emotional appeal.

The resurgence of the leviathan at home was accompanied by the flexing of protectionist muscles abroad. *The New York Times* reported, 'At least 69 countries have banned or restricted the export of protective equipment, medical devices or medicines, according. ... The World Health Organization is warning that protectionism could limit the global availability of vaccines. ... With every country on the planet in need of the same lifesaving tools at once, national rivalries are jeopardizing access for all.'[40]

Nationalism reared its ugly head even in the European Union, where several governments re-asserted controls over border management and internal movements. The EU struggled to forge a common response, and in surveys the EU was perceived by many Europeans as irrelevant. Under the xenophobic Trump administration in the US nativism became combustible. Canada and Mexico went their own ways almost oblivious to the existence of NAFTA that had morphed into the United States-Mexico-Canada Agreement in 2018.

In Asia, the ten-member Association of Southeast Asian Nations came under 'criticism for its slow response at the start of the pandemic gripping the globe'.[41] Although regional policy convergence grew, it was hampered by different national capacities to handle the pandemic and bureaucratic inertia. Consequently, containment measures developed by individual states remained supreme.[42] Co-operation among the countries of the South Asian Association for Regional Cooperation initially amounted to several meetings, creation of an emergency fund of a paltry US$18 million in March and the removal of tariffs on medical equipment and hygiene products.

In Latin America and the Caribbean, the response of the MERCUSOR group, whose members include Argentina, Uruguay, Paraguay and Brazil, was relatively low key. It was not helped by the COVID-19 denialism of Brazil's President Bolsonaro. CARICOM responded more robustly with several emergency meetings. Yet, wrote one commentator, behind the regional consensus on the necessity of coordinated action, 'Divisive questions such as travel bans has [sic] marred efforts at coordination and, as of 13 April, CARICOM still did not have a common public health protocol and common border policy.'[43]

In Africa, regional co-ordination efforts fared no better. All too often, neighbouring countries did not co-ordinate their pandemic mitigation efforts. To be sure, intergovernmental meetings were held and plans issued, but as noted in an article on how Africa's regions had fared in tackling COVID-19, 'their efforts have had mixed results. In many cases the regional bodies haven't communicated their strategies sufficiently to the African public.'[44] In the East African Community, Tanzania, Kenya, Burundi and Rwanda adopted rapidly different approaches. The responses in ECOWAS focused on linking the scientific communities in each country, while in SADC emphasis was put on the procurement of essential medical supplies and equipment.

The African Union tried to be proactive and, through the Africa Centre for Disease Control, which sought to trace, test and track the spread of the pandemic across the continent, tried to co-ordinate its public health interventions as well as the procurement of medical supplies and donations and the standardisation and deployment of common technology platforms. But, Alden and Dunst noted, 'given the weaknesses in public health systems in many African countries and the dizzying financial shortfalls experienced by governments, the AU has had to appeal for international help to fight the pandemic'.[45] In contrast, the Arab League was lacklustre in developing a co-ordinated response to the pandemic, paralysed by longstanding internal divisions.

Thus, efforts to develop co-ordinated regional approaches to COVID-19 mitigation and adaptation largely remained tepid. Almost everywhere anxieties about the impact of the virus on national security and survival, real and imagined, were bolstered. As a result, nationalism increasingly trumped regionalism. In many countries the pandemic fuelled the racism and anti-immigration jingoism of ultra-nationalist parties and populist politicians.

Yet, by its very nature and rapid spread across boundaries, the pandemic offered a powerful rebuke against the delusions of nationalism, that it was possible to seal and safeguard the artifice of the nation-state in fortified walls of splendid isolation. The pandemic could only be managed effectively through vigorous regional and international co-operation, as well as collaboration between the public and private sectors and civil society.

Mitigation measures that were nationalistic, statist, ethnocentric and elitist were simply not enough and were doomed to fail. As noted earlier, it is instructive to note that some of the worst effects of COVID-19 in terms of infections and deaths were among some of the most nationalistic and xenophobic regimes, such as the US, Brazil, India, Russia and Britain. Thus, the coronavirus pandemic also threw into sharp relief the bankruptcy of populist nationalism. It underscored global interconnectedness, that pathogens did not respect our imaginary communities of nation-states, that the ties that bind humanity were thicker than the threads of separation.

Obituaries of globalisation that appeared everywhere seemed premature. There could be little doubt that COVID-19 presented a severe stress test for globalisation. *Harvard Business Review* observed, 'Current forecasts, while inevitably rough at this stage, call for a 13–32 per cent decline in merchandise trade, a 30–40 per cent reduction in foreign direct investment, and a 44–80 per cent drop in international airline passengers in 2020. These numbers imply a major rollback of globalization's recent gains, but they do not signal a fundamental collapse of international market integration.'[46]

An influential voice of business, *The Wall Street Journal*, was quite sanguine about the future of globalisation.

> In the midst of our current spiral, it is hard to resist such dire forecasts. But we should. … The sudden halt in commerce and travel precipitated by the outbreak will not snap back overnight, and the next few years will see a renationalization of some industries for countries that can. … But a sharp contraction caused by a pandemic is not the same as a permanent reversal of the deep and complicated global integration of supply chains, markets and daily life built up over the past two decades. Those relationships are durable and beneficial and will be difficult to sever.[47]'

Similar sentiments were expressed in *Foreign Policy* magazine:

> Many of the key drivers of globalization – shipping, data, and capital flows, our understanding of comparative advantage, and economies of scale – will not go away. But driven by a combination of changes in popular sentiment, government policy, and corporate practices, globalization will change. The coronavirus pandemic will mark not the end of an era, but its transformation.[48]

Dependence on fragile and concentrated supply chains was likely to change, economic integration might accelerate at regional and bilateral levels, and governments might pay more attention to the losers of the current globalisation.

Globalisation faced a complex future. It is important to distinguish between globalism as an ideological project of neoliberal capitalism that bestrode the globe since the 1980s, and globalisation as a historical process of increasing technological, economic, cultural, political and ideational interconnectedness and interdependence. The former was clearly in retreat, whereas the latter was not, even if some of its aspects such as trade were undermined by the pandemic.

Thus, while COVID-19 was a gift to nationalists and protectionists, it also underlined the failures of reactionary nationalism to shield the beloved followers of the populist demagogues. At the same time, the pandemic demonstrated the dangers of hyperglobalisation, which inflated the spread and impacts of COVID-19. The pandemic appeared to have hammered the last nails in the coffin of the neoliberal wave of globalisation. No one knew when the next wave would emerge or what the constellation of its regime and driving logic would be.

Education Goes Online

The coronavirus pandemic negatively affected many industries and sectors, including education, which saw the closure of schools, colleges and universities. However, fear of crowding and lockdown boosted online industries, ranging from e-commerce and food delivery to online entertainment and gaming, to cloud solutions for business continuity, to e-health and e-learning. The pandemic seemed likely to leave a lasting impact on the growth of e-work or telecommuting and other online-mediated business practices. Before it broke out, the gig economy had already been a growing part of many economies, as had e-health and e-learning.

The educational sector was one of the most affected by the coronavirus pandemic as many governments adopted the closures of schools and universities as the first line of defence. According to UNESCO data, by the end of March 2020, 193 countries had imposed closures that affected 1.6 billion learners at all levels, representing 91.3 per cent of all learners. By mid-July the number of countries with closure had reduced to 107, affecting 1.1 billion learners, which was 60.9 per cent of the total.[49]

The impact of the closure of educational institutions was wide-ranging, as evident from an avalanche of studies and reports in the academic media and from education ministries and UNESCO. Schools and tertiary institutions, including universities, had to undertake crisis planning. They were forced to analyse existing and potential pandemic crisis risks and their capacities and resources for risk mitigation, identify and try to overcome patterns of access to education exacerbated by the transition to distance learning, mobilise multiple internal and external stakeholders and plan effectively for the reopening of educational institutions.

School closures meant that teachers and students had to adapt to new modes of distance teaching and learning. Parents had to adjust juggling between work obligations and income generation, and home schooling. This raised the issue of the pitfalls and potential of family and intergenerational learning, and the partnership between the home and the school. To quote a report by UNESCO:

> In particular, in addition to supporting children's distance and online home-based learning, many families, depending on their contexts, also rediscovered the joy of learning from one another about how to stay healthy and safe, cope with stress

> and uncertainty, strengthen their bonds and acquire new knowledge and skills. In this situation, home has become the centre of learning for all family members. ... Therefore, the education response to the crisis could also be seen as an opportunity to take into account and position family and intergenerational learning more centrally in the distance and online online school education model.[50]

This would entail developing take-home packages, using media campaigns through TV, radio and social media to guide parents, and combining adult literacy programmes with family learning strategies.

A key challenge in transitioning from face-to-face to distance teaching and learning centred on levels of institutional readiness in terms of technology, content, pedagogical and home support, remote supervision and monitoring and assessment methodologies. There were wide discrepancies among institutions within and between countries that reflected prior investments and capacities, learning platforms, teacher training and proficiency and curriculum development. Also apparent were social inequalities in terms of access to electronic devices and bandwidth, based on class, gender, age and location, as well as reliable electricity supply. Online instruction also raised issues of data privacy and security for learners and teachers, and supporting 'teachers to plan and facilitate teachers, and engage parents and caregivers'.[51]

Moreover, the closure of educational institutions affected the health and nutrition of learners. It was estimated that 365 million primary-school children were missing out on school meals, which affected their health, growth and development, and wellbeing. There were also the threats of increased household work, physical inactivity, stress, anxiety and mental health, as well as the heightened opportunity for domestic violence, online abuse and harassment.[52] Compounding the social and emotional well-being of learners and young people was sensationalist media reporting, which 'fueled the spread intolerance, racism, xenophobia, and hate crimes'.[53]

These pressures made it more imperative to provide reliable and accurate information about COVID-19 as well as support and care for teachers and learners. Moreover, educational institutions, communities and families needed to build social and emotional learning (SEL) skills and impart them to children, youths and adults all the time. The mainstreaming of these skills in the curriculum was also recommended.

Equally critical was supporting teachers and educational personnel, many of whom showed great creativity and resilience. According to UNESCO, the pandemic affected at least 63 million primary- and secondary-school teachers, and millions more in tertiary institutions. They needed support and recognition in terms of access to relevant, quality professional development, job security and timely compensation, provision of psychosocial support, their inclusion in developing COVID-19 responses, supporting teachers' initiatives and communities of practice, and ensuring that relationship between teachers and learners was maintained.[54]

The challenges outlined above were faced by the university sector. Universities were expected to manage the pandemic for their own institutions and contribute to the mitigation capabilities of their societies. Some transitioned to emergency online teaching and learning, and webinars and academic conferences proliferated. The pandemic exposed striking digital and financial divides among institutions and students in educational quality and access in general and for online and blended teaching and learning in particular.

Also, many universities saw their enrolments drop sharply, and faced severe financial difficulties that led to drastic cost-containment measures, including cuts in benefits and job losses even for permanent or tenure-track faculty. The situation for international students was particularly dire as campus and border closures left many of them stranded. The mental health of students and employees, which was already a serious concern, was exacerbated by the anxieties and uncertainties engendered by the pandemic.

Universities responded to these challenges and pressures in various ways. Many sought to strengthen the structures, systems and resources to support online learning, and began planning for the recovery phase and repurposing of education for the future, which would most likely combine face-to-face, online and blended learning. They responded to mental health challenges by strengthening counselling services, providing teletherapy, wellness coaching, establishing resilience courses, programmes and training, raising awareness through outreach, providing information and conducting webinars, and preventing stigma against mental-health care.

In many cases the pandemic also reinforced partnerships with other universities, the public and private sectors, civil society organisations, and philanthropic, international and intergovernmental agencies. Out of the collaborations came interventions that sought to strengthen institutional capacities and provide resources for relief, recovery and resilience. This included supporting faculty development and training, research capacity, technological infrastructure and online instruction, and student aid.

Universities also used their assets to help society manage the crisis. Some used their campuses and medical schools to provide health services and quarantine centres. Several made innovations and produced hygiene products and personal protective equipment. Many undertook research on the epidemiology of the coronavirus, biomedical treatments and the socioeconomic impacts of the pandemic, and provided advisory services to governments. They produced data, modelling and software to map the spread and impact of the pandemic for more effective tracing and tracking and public policy responses. On mental health they sought to raise awareness and provide psychosocial support to the wider society, in conjunction with other providers in society, undertook research on mental health and provided policy interventions.

For their part, African universities demonstrated remarkable commitment and capabilities to respond to COVID-19. First, many transitioned to online teaching and learning. Second, they embarked on much-needed research and produced innovations. Third, they strengthened partnerships among each other and with other national, regional and global actors. Fourth, they contributed to the development of transformative economic and social policies and interventions. Fifth, they began to rethink the future of higher education.

Huge challenges of course remained for universities in Africa and elsewhere in terms of limited financial, infrastructural, human and research resources. There were also glaring inequalities of access along the differentiations of class, gender, ethnicity, religion, age, location and other social markers. Some were left staring at the abyss of collapse. But many showed great resilience in managing the worst global health and economic crisis in a century. At the same time they demonstrated a capacity for creativity and innovation and to reinvent the future of higher education.

Home Alone

Home isolation was recommended by epidemiologists as a critical means of what they called 'flattening the curve' of the coronavirus pandemic. Its economic impact was well understood, less so its psychological and emotional impact. While imperative, social isolation exacerbated the growing 'loneliness epidemic', as some called it, especially in the developed countries. This epidemic was already becoming a serious health-care crisis before the pandemic. In the words of one author,

> Research has shown that loneliness and social isolation can be as damaging to physical health as smoking 15 cigarettes a day. A lack of social relationships is an enormous risk factor for death, increasing the likelihood of mortality by 26 percent. A major study found that, when compared with people with weak social ties, people who enjoyed meaningful relationships were 50 percent more likely to survive over time.[55]

The problem of loneliness is often thought to be prevalent among older people, but in countries such as the United States, Japan, Australia, New Zealand and the United Kingdom it is young adults who suffer most from loneliness. In the US the proportion of those reporting loneliness in 2019 was highest among Gen Z (79 per cent), followed by millennials (71 per cent), Gen X (65 per cent), Boomers (50 per cent) and the Silent/Greatest generation (38 per cent). Loneliness also seemed to be correlated with income (77 per cent of those earning US$25,000 or less compared to 53 per cent earning US$100,000 or more), living status (69 per cent of those living alone compared to 51 per cent living with another) and gender (58 per cent for females and 63 per cent for males).[56]

Research shows that the feeling of loneliness is not a reflection of physical isolation. Rather, it is about the meaning and depth of one's social engagements. Social media exacerbates loneliness among the Millennial and Gen Z generations. Many studies have pointed out that social media, increasingly ubiquitous before the pandemic, was reinforcing social disconnection, which is at the root of loneliness. This is because, while social media facilitates instant communication and makes people more densely connected than ever, it offers a poor substitute for the intimate communication and dense and meaningful interactions humans crave and get from real friends and family. It fosters shallow and superficial connections, surrogate and even fake friendships and narcissistic and exhibitionist sociability.

But during the pandemic, technology also helped to foster social interactions. It helped to mitigate social and physical distancing and became indispensable for many people, not just for work but in maintaining relationships with friends and family. To quote one author writing in *The Atlantic*, 'As more employers and schools encourage people to stay home, people across the country find themselves videochatting more than they usually might: going to meetings on Zoom, catching up with clients on Skype, FaceTime with therapists, even hosting virtual bar mitzvahs.'[57] Jointly playing video games, watching streaming entertainment or holding virtual family meetings, video chats, dinner parties and even weddings and funeral services opened up bonding opportunities during the pandemic. On my birthday in May 2020, a surprise virtual party was held for me attended by family, friends and colleagues scattered around the world. Several times a week I played online games with my daughter in Atlanta (she always beat me!). I had more interactions with many other family members in different countries than ever before.

Loneliness is difficult to define. It should not of course be confused with solitude. Moreover, loneliness cannot be attributed solely to external conditions as it is often rooted in one's psychological state. But the density and quality of social interactions matters. The current loneliness epidemic reflects the irony of a vicious cycle, a nexus of triple impulses. In cultures and sensibilities of self-absorption and self-invention, some people invite or choose loneliness as a marker of self-sufficiency or social success, while the Internet makes it possible for people to be lonely and lonely people tend to be more attracted to the Internet.

Besides the growth and consumption of modern media and its disruptive and isolating technologies, structural forces reinforce loneliness. They include the spread of the nuclear family, an invention that even in the United States has a short history as a social formation. This is evident in sociological studies and demonstrated in the lead story in the March 2020 edition of *The Atlantic*, 'The Nuclear Family was a Mistake', by David Brooks, a columnist at *The New York Times*. The article showed that for much of American history people lived in extended clans and families, whose great strengths were their resilience and role as a socialising force. The decline of multigenerational families dates to the development of an industrial economy and reached its apogee after World War II between 1950 and 1975, when the extended family began falling apart, again due to broader structural forces.

One does not have to agree with the author's analysis of what led to the profound changes in family structure. Certainly, women did not benefit from the older extended family structures, which were resolutely patriarchal. However, it is a fact that currently more people live alone in the United States and many other countries, including those in the developing world, than ever before. The author stressed, 'The period when the nuclear family flourished was not normal. It was a freakish historical moment when all of society conspired to obscure its essential fragility.'

He continued, 'For many people, the era of the nuclear family has been a catastrophe. All forms of inequality are cruel, but family inequality may be the cruelest. It damages the heart.' He urged society 'to figure out better ways to live together'. The question that arose was what would the impact of social distancing be, as demanded by the coronavirus pandemic, on the loneliness epidemic and prospects of developing new and more fulfilling ways of living together.

Another question worth pondering is: What would be the likely long-term impact of COVID-19 on social relations and interactions including family formations? There was some evidence that the loneliness epidemic in the US worsened. An article in *Time* magazine reported that surveys in April 2020 showed between a third and almost half of American adults felt lonelier than usual. A similar trend was reported elsewhere.

> SocialPro's survey of 1,228 people ages 18 to 75 predominantly living in English-speaking countries found that at least 20 per cent of respondents from each age group polled were lonelier than usual as a result of coronavirus. Millennials were among the most likely age groups to feel lonely before COVID-19, research shows, and that's no different now; 34 per cent of millennials in the survey said they were 'always or often' lonelier due to the pandemic.[58]

People with pre-existing mental health conditions, such as anxiety, mood and substance abuse disorders were 'likely to have their symptoms worsen on account of the pandemic', observed a Nigerian physician and public health expert.[59] The national lockdowns and physical distancing preventive measures 'have spurred an observed increase in addictive coping strategies, such as the abuse of alcohol, drugs, tobacco and online gaming.' This resulted in increased domestic violence mostly against women and children, marriage breakdowns and suicides. To curb these behaviours some countries, including several in Africa, placed restrictions on the sale of alcohol.

There was an explosion of advice guides on how to stave off loneliness and isolation during COVID-19. They stressed the importance of keeping to a schedule; staying informed; staying active; doing something meaningful such as writing, art and home projects; distracting yourself through reading, watching television and movies, creating or listening to music, taking virtual tours and playing online games; planning for the future; practising self-compassion and showing compassion to others; calling and contacting relatives and friends; checking community offers for assistance; and seeking mental health when needed.[60]

Whither the Future

Moments of profound crisis, such as the one engendered by the coronavirus pandemic, attract soothsayers and futurists. The American magazine, *POLITICO*, invited about three dozen thinkers to envision the long-term impact of the pandemic.[61] They all offered intriguing reflections. For community life, some suggested the personal would become dangerous, a new kind of patriotism would emerge, polarisation would decline, faith in serious experts would return, there would be less individualism, and there would be changes in religious worship and the rise of new forms of reform.

As for technology, they suggested that regulatory barriers to online tools would fall, healthier digital lifestyles would emerge, there would be a boom in virtual reality, the rise of telemedicine, the provision of stronger medical care, government would become Big Pharma and science would reign again. With reference to government, they predicted that Congress would finally go digital, Big Government would make a comeback, government service would regain its cachet, there would be a new civic federalism and revived trust in institutions, the rules we lived by wouldn't all apply, and that we should expect a political uprising.

In terms of elections, they foresaw electronic voting going mainstream, Election Day would become Election Month and voting by mail would become the norm. For the global economy, they forecast that more restraints would be placed on mass consumption, stronger domestic supply chains would grow and the inequality gap would widen. As for lifestyle, they anticipated there would be a hunger for diversion, less communal dining, a revival of parks, a change in our understanding of 'change', and the tyranny of habit no more.

Of course, only the future will tell. History teaches us that after watershed events, including pandemics, the new futures that emerge carry a heavy imprint of the past with them.

Notes

1. World Health Organization, 'Coronavirus disease (COVID-19) advice for the public.' https://www.who.int/emergencies/diseases/novel-coronavirus-2019/advice-for-public
2. Lori Rozsa, Chelsea Janes, Rachel Weiner and Joel Achenbach, 'The battle over masks in a pandemic: An all-American story', *The Washington Post*, 19 June 2020. https://www.washingtonpost.com/health/the-battle-over-masks-in-a-pandemic-an-all-american-story/2020/06/19/3ad25564-b245-11ea-8f56-63f38c990077_story.html
3. Lori Gotlieb, 'Dear Therapist's Guide to Staying Sane During a Pandemic', *The Atlantic*, 17 March 2020.
4. United Nations, *Policy Brief: COVID-19 and the Need for Action on Mental Health*, 20 May 2020. https://www.un.org/sites/un2.un.org/files/un_policy_brief-COVID_and_mental_health_final.pdf

5. Tamara Keith and Malaka Gharib, 'A Timeline of Coronavirus Comments From President Trump And WHO', National Public Radio, 15 April 2020. https://www.npr.org/sections/goatsandsoda/2020/04/15/835011346/a-timeline-of-coronavirus-comments-from-president-trump-and-who
6. Uri Friedman, 'We Were Warned', *The Atlantic,* 18 March 2020. https://www.theatlantic.com/politics/archive/2020/03/pandemic-coronavirus-united-states-trump-cdc/608215/
7. *The Economist,* 'Closed', 21 March 2020.
8. 'Black people are more than four times likely to die from Covid-10 than white people', *Guardian,* 7 May 2020. https://www.theguardian.com/world/2020/may/07/black-people-four-times-more-likely-to-die-from-COVID-19-ons-finds?CMP=Share_iOSApp_Other
9. Linda Villarosa, '"A Terrible Price": The Deadly Racial Disparities of COVID-19 in America', *The New York Times,* 29 April 2020. https://www.nytimes.com/2020/04/29/magazine/racial-disparities-COVID-19.html?referringSource=articleShare
10. 'How COVID-19 is a perfect storm for black Americans', *The Washington Post,* 26 April 2020. https://www.washingtonpost.com/opinions/2020/04/26/we-must-address-social-determinants-affecting-black-community-defeat-COVID-19/
11. World Health Organization, 'New WHO estimates: Up to 190 000 people could die of COVID-19 in Africa if not controlled', 7 May 2020. https://www.afro.who.int/news/new-who-estimates-190-000-people-could-die-COVID-19-africa-if-not-controlled
12. World Health Organization, 'COVID-19 could deepen food insecurity, malnutrition in Africa', 14 May 2020. https://who-africa.africa-newsroom.com/press/coronavirus-africa-COVID19-could-deepen-food-insecurity-malnutrition-in-africa
13. WHO Coronavirus Disease (COVID-19) Dashboard 18 July 2020. https://COVID19.who.int
14. Michael Steinberger, 'What is the stockmarket even for any more?' *The New York Times,* 29 April 2020. https://www.nytimes.com/interactive/2020/05/26/magazine/stock-market-coronavirus-pandemic.html
15. UNCTAD, *How COVID-19 is changing the world: A statistical perspective,* Committee for the Coordination of Statistical Activities, 2020. https://unstats.un.org/unsd/ccsa/documents/COVID19-report-ccsa.pdf
16. UNIDO, 'Coronavirus: the economic impact', 10 July 2020. https://www.unido.org/stories/coronavirus-economic-impact-10-july-2020
17. Romesh Vaitilingam, 'How economists view the policy response to the COVID-19 so far', London School of Economics, 31 March 2020. https://blogs.lse.ac.uk/businessreview/2020/03/31/how-economists-view-the-policy-response-to-the-COVID-19-crisis-so-far/
18. World Economic Forum, 'Most people see COVID-19 as an economic crisis first, health risk second, survey finds', 18 March 2020. https://www.weforum.org/agenda/2020/03/COVID-19-public-perception-economic-health-crisis-coronavirus-pandemic-ipsos/
19. International Monetary Fund, *June 2020 World Economic Outlook Update.* https://www.imf.org/-/media/Files/Publications/WEO/2020/Update/June/English/WEOENG202006.ashx?la=en

20. World Bank, *June 2020 Global Economic Prospects*, Washington, DC: World Bank, 2020. https://openknowledge.worldbank.org/bitstream/handle/10986/ 33748/ 9781464815539.pdf
21. *OECD Economic Outlook*, Volume 2020, Issue 1. https://read.oecd-ilibrary.org/economics/oecd-economic-outlook/volume-2020/issue-1_0d1d1e2e-en#page41
22. African Development Bank, *African Economic Outlook – Supplement,* 7 July 2020. https://www.afdb.org/en/documents/african-economic-outlook-2020-supplement
23. ILO Monitor, *COVID-19 and the world of work*, 5th ed, 27 May 2020. https://www.ilo.org/wcmsp5/groups/public/@dgreports/@dcomm/documents/briefingnote/wcms_749399.pdf
24. FAO, 'Q&A: COVID-19 pandemic – Impact on Food and Agriculture'. http://www.fao.org/2019-ncov/q-and-a/impact-on-food-and-agriculture/en/
25. Paul Wafula, 'Over one million rendered jobless in Kenya as COVID-19 takes toll on businesses', *The East African*, 5 June 2020. https://www.theeastafrican.co.ke/business/COVID19-Over-a-million-rendered-jobless-in-Kenya/2560-5571598-format-xhtml-13v1usc/index.html
26. Eric Rosenbaum, 'Millions of Americans only $400 away from financial hardship. Here's why', CNBC, 23 May 2019. https://www.cnbc.com/2019/05/23/millions-of-americans-are-only-400-away-from-financial-hardship.html
27. ILO Monitor, *COVID-19 and the world of work*, 5th ed, 27 May 2020. https://www.ilo.org/wcmsp5/groups/public/@dgreports/@dcomm/documents/briefingnote/wcms_749399.pdf
28. IMF, 'Coronavirus economic planning: Hoping for the best, prepared for the worst', 12 March 2020. https://blogs.imf.org/2020/03/12/coronavirus-economic-planning-hoping-for-the-best-prepared-for-the-worst/
29. World Bank, 'World Bank Group Increases COVID-19 Response to $14 Billion To Help Sustain Economies, Protect Jobs,' 17 March 2020. https://www.worldbank.org/en/news/press-release/2020/03/17/world-bank-group-increases-COVID-19-response-to-14-billion-to-help-sustain-economies-protect-jobs
30. Christine Lagarde, 'Our response to the coronavirus emergency', ECB blog, 19 March 2020. https://www.ecb.europa.eu/press/blog/date/2020/html/ecb.blog200319~11f421e25e.en.html
31. *The Economist*, 'Fighting the Slump', 21 March 2020.
32. Asian Development Bank, 'ADB Announces $6.5 billion Initial Response to COVID-19 Pandemic', 18 March 2020. https://www.adb.org/news/adb-announces-6-5-billion-initial-response-COVID-19-pandemic
33. Tom McTague, 'The Coronavirus Brings Political Perspective', *The Atlantic,* 11 March 2020. https://www.theatlantic.com/international/archive/2020/03/coronavirus-COVID19-brexit-united-kingdom-politics/607687/
34. Garret M. Graff, 'What Americans Are Now Doing is Beautiful', *The Atlantic,* 19 March 2020. https://www.theatlantic.com/ideas/archive/2020/03/inspiring-galvanizing-beautiful - spirit-2020/608308/
35. Jonathan D. Quick, 'What we can learn from the 20th century's deadliest pandemic', *The Wall Street Journal,* 6 March 2020. https://www.wsj.com/amp/articles/what-we-can-learn-from-the-20th-centurys-deadliest-pandemic-11583510468

36. Damien Cave and Tiffany May, 'World Feared China Over Coronavirus. Now the Tables Are Turned', *The New York Times,* 19 March, 2020. https://www.nytimes.com/2020/03/19/world/asia/coronavirus-china-united-states.html?referringSource=articleShare
37. Stephen Lee Myers and Allysa J. Rubin, 'Its Coronavirus Cases Dwindling, China Turns Focus Outward', *The New York Times,* 18 March 2020. https://www.nytimes.com/2020/03/18/world/asia/coronavirus-china-aid.html?referringSource=articleShare
38. Anne Applebaum, 'The Coronavirus Called America's bluff', *The Atlantic,* 15 March 2020. https://www.theatlantic.com/ideas/archive/2020/03/coronavirus-showed-america-wasnt-task/608023/
39. David D. Kirkpatrick, Matt Apuzzo and Selam Gebrekidan, 'Europe Said Was Pandemic Ready. Pride was its Downfall', *The New York Times,* 20 July 2020. https://www.nytimes.com/2020/07/20/world/europe/coronavirus-mistakes-france-uk-italy.html?referringSource=articleShare
40. Peter S. Goodman, Katie Thomas, Sui-Lee and Jeffrey Gentleman, 'A New Front for Nationalism: The Global Battle Against a Virus', *The New York Times,* 10 April 2020. https://www.nytimes.com/2020/04/10/business/coronavirus-vaccine-nationalism.html?referringSource=articleShare
41. Jim Gomez, 'ASEA Ministers Endorse New COVID-19 Fund', *The Diplomat,* 10 April 2020. https://thediplomat.com/2020/04/asean-ministers-endorse-new-COVID-19-response-fund/
42. Riyanti Gelante, et al., 'The ASEAN's Response to COVID-19: A policy science analysis', https://www.researchgate.net/profile/Jonatan_Lassa1/publication/341309394_The_ASEAN per cent27s_Responses_to_COVID-19_A_Policy_Sciences_Analysis/links/5ed084c9299bf1c67d26f4ef/The-ASEANs-Responses-to-COVID-19-A-Policy-Sciences-Analysis.pdf?origin=publication_detail
43. Chris Allen and Charles Dunst, 'COVID-19: Latin America and the Caribbean and MERCOSUR and CARICOM', London School of Economics. http://www.lse.ac.uk/international-relations/centres-and-units/global-south-unit/COVID-19-regional-responses/Latin-America-and-COVID-19
44. Liesl Louw-Vaudran and Mohamed Diatta, 'How Have Africa's Regions Fared in Tackling COVID-19?' Institute for Security Studies, 8 July 2020. https://allafrica.com/stories/202007110122.html
45. Chris Allen and Charles Dunst, 'COVID-19: Africa and the African Union', London School of Economics, http://www.lse.ac.uk/international-relations/centres-and-units/global-south-unit/COVID-19-regional-responses/Africa-and-COVID-19
46. Steven A. Altman, 'Will COVID-19 have a Lasting Impact on Globalization?' *Harvard Business Review,* 20 May 2020. https://hbr.org/2020/05/will-COVID-19-have-a-lasting-impact-on-globalization
47. Zachary Carabell, 'Will the Coronavirus Bring the End of Globalization? Don't Count on It', *The Wall Street Journal,* 20 March 2020. https://www.wsj.com/articles/will-the-coronavirus-bring-the-end-of-globalization-dont-count-on-it-11584716305
48. Richard Fontaine, 'Globalization Will Look Very Different After the Coronavirus Pandemic', *Foreign Policy,* 17 April 2020. https://foreignpolicy.com/2020/04/17/globalization-trade-war-after-coronavirus-pandemic/

49. UNESCO, 'Global monitoring of school closures caused by COVID-19'. https://en.unesco.org/COVID19/educationresponse
50. UNESCO, 'Unlocking the potential of family and intergenerational learning'. https://unesdoc.unesco.org/ark:/48223/pf0000373512
51. UNESCO, 'Distance learning strategies in response to COVID-19 school closures'. https://unesdoc.unesco.org/ark:/48223/pf0000373305
52. UNESCO, 'Health & nutrition during home learning'. https://unesdoc.unesco.org/ark:/48223/pf0000373277
53. UNESCO, 'Nurturing the social and emotional wellbeing of children and young people during crises'. https://unesdoc.unesco.org/ark:/48223/pf0000373271
54. UNESCO, 'Supporting teachers and educational personnel during times of crisis'. https://unesdoc.unesco.org/ark:/48223/pf0000373338
55. 'The Voices of the Loneliness Epidemic', *In Time We Trust,* 10 March 2020. http://www.rachidakiki.com/the-voices-of-the-loneliness-epidemic/
56. Jamie Ducharme, 'COVID-19 is Making America's Loneliness Epidemic Even Worse', *Time,* 8 May 2020. https://time.com/5833681/loneliness-COVID-19/
57. Marina Koren, 'Social Distancing Could Change Our Relationship With FaceTime', *The Atlantic,* 14 March 2020. https://www.theatlantic.com/science/archive/2020/03/social-distancing-coronavirus-videochat-facetime/608038/
58. Jamie Ducharme, 'COVID-19 is Making America's Loneliness Epidemic Even Worse', *Time,* 8 May 2020. https://time.com/5833681/loneliness-COVID-19/
59. Adaeze a Oreh, 'Impact of COVID-19 loneliness on mental health', *Punch,* 26 May 2020. https://www.msn.com/en-xl/news/other/impact-of-COVID-19-loneliness-on-mental-health/ar-BB14AmnM
60. Arlin Cuncic, 'How to Cope with Loneliness during the Coronavirus Pandemic', *verywellmind,* 27 March 2020. https://www.verywellmind.com/how-to-cope-with-loneliness-during-coronavirus-4799661
61. *POLITICO Magazine,* 'Coronavirus Will Change the World Permanently. Here's How', 19 March 2020. https://www.politico.com/news/magazine/2020/03/19/coronavirus-effect-economy-life-society-analysis-COVID-135579

First written 21–22 March and revised 18–20 July 2020

10

Mobilising the Diaspora for Sustainable Development

Over the last half millennium, Africa has been central to the construction of the modern world in all its dimensions – economic, political, ideological, cultural and demographic – although it has not benefitted much from this progress partially because of the manner of its integration into the world system: first, through the Atlantic slave trade; then through imperialism and colonialism; and, since independence, through the exploitative marginalisations of Cold War superpower rivalries in the 1960s and 1970s, the economic and political assaults of neoliberalism in the 1990s and 2000s, and the rekindled hegemonic contestations of a rising China and declining United States in the 2000s and 2010s.

However, such are the contradictory trajectories of history that these same processes have resulted in Africa's global presence. Today, African-descended peoples are on every continent in various concentrations. They are products of centuries of coerced and free migrations that resulted in the formations of disparate African diaspora populations around the world. Africa's old and new diasporas, or historic and contemporary diasporas, constitute one of the continent's most valuable assets. The continent needs to mobilise its diasporas to navigate the depredations of the world system and pursue its historic dreams of economic, political, social and cultural development as an equal global player, rather than as a perpetual pawn.

The subject of Africa's engagements with its diasporas is very dear to me as a scholar and member of Africa's 'new diasporas', the millions of people who have migrated out of their countries of origin to other countries around the world, especially those in the global North. In my case, I left my native country in 1977 after my undergraduate studies and I spent the following four decades in Britain, Canada, Jamaica, Kenya and the United States of America. For the past fifteen years, I have published extensively on the subject, including more than a dozen academic articles and a major book, *In Search of African Diasporas: Testimonies and Encounters,*[1] based on research conducted over a five-year period in sixteen countries in the Americas, Europe and Asia.

African diasporas and African governments are increasingly aware and committed to promoting the contributions of the vast new diasporas in the pursuit of sustainable development across the continent. By the new diasporas, I refer to those who left the continent from the twentieth century, as distinct from the historic diasporas, who dispersed in earlier centuries. For both groups, of course, there have been different waves, destinations and engagements with the continent. There are also intra-African diasporas.

In this chapter, I seek to do four things. First, I provide a brief overview of Pan-Africanism, in which contemporary diaspora engagements ought to be located. Second, I identify some of the analytical issues in examining Africa's engagements with its diasporas. Third, I focus on diaspora contributions to sustainable development by looking at the forms of diaspora contributions in general and economic contributions in particular. Finally, I share a diaspora project, in which I have been intimately involved, in mobilising the intellectual resources of the diaspora. This is the Carnegie African Diaspora Fellowship Program. It grew out of a research project I conducted on the African-born academic diaspora in Canada and the United States and how it could be marshalled as an intellectual remittance pipeline in the revitalisation of African higher education.

The Pan-African Movement and Project

Pan-Africanism was born and bred in the diaspora in which the collective racialised subjugation and the consciousness of Africanness first developed. This burgeoning transnational identity, as an object of terror and derision on the one hand and the basis of struggle and agency on the other, spread along the major routes of the old triangular slave trade in the Atlantic world.

Pan-Africanism was originally an elitist movement confined to scholar-activists, but it gradually became an aspect of the mass anti-colonial and civil rights movements of the post-World War II era. It was eventually institutionalised in post-independence regional integration schemes in Africa and the Caribbean, and in state actors' interventions in the post-Civil Rights societies of the Americas where the African diaspora populations are often minorities or marginalised. For example, in the US they are a minority; in Brazil they are a majority but marginalised.

As Pan-Africanism became more regionalised and nationalised, and acquired state power or influence in the 1960s, it lost much of its transatlantic and global reach and revolutionary ambition. Its primary thrust also shifted, from struggles for cultural and political citizenship to struggles for social and economic empowerment; from humanistic to developmentalist discourses; and from a preoccupation with the civilisational presence of Africa and its diasporas in the world concert of cultures to their standing in the polarised geopolitical order of the Cold War and later the asymmetrical hierarchies of globalisation.

From its inception, Pan-Africanism has always been a transnational movement, encompassing Africa and its global diasporas. This transnationalism and globalism have been a source of both strength and weakness, as the peoples they embrace have lived and continue to live in diverse historical geographies and political economies. Over its long history, various versions of Pan-Africanism emerged. I identify six versions.

First, there is transatlantic Pan-Africanism. Its proponents imagined a Pan-African world that linked continental Africa and its diaspora in the Americas. Second, there is what can be called Black Atlantic Pan-Africanism. This version confines itself to the African diasporic communities in the Americas and Europe, excluding continental Africa, as articulated in Paul Gilroy's influential book *The Black Atlantic*,[2] in which the cultural creativity and connections of the African diaspora in the US and Britain are celebrated, while continental Africa is largely ignored (and so is Afro-Latin America).

Third, there is continental Pan-Africanism. This version is primarily focused on the unification of continental Africa. Then there are the Pan-Africanisms that restrict themselves to the peoples of the continent north and south of the Sahara, respectively. The construct of sub-Saharan Africa is Eurocentric in its origins, rooted in the Hegelian civilisational dismissal and denigration of 'sub-Saharan' Africa and its peoples, but it finds resonance among many Africans and global institutions. For its part, Pan-Arabism incorporates northern Africa and the peoples of western Asia or the so-called Middle East. President Gamal Nasser saw Egypt belonging to the three circles of Pan-Africanism, Pan-Arabism and Pan-Islamism.

Finally, there is global Pan-Africanism. This version embraces Africa and its diasporas around the world, what I call in my work Afro-America, Afro-Europe and Afro-Asia. It was evident at the UN World Conference against Racism held in Durban in 2001. At the turn of the twenty-first century, global Pan-Africanism spread on the rising waves of global migrations, transnational social movements, intensified economic flows and new information and communication technologies that compressed time and space between continents, countries and communities.

Each version of Pan-Africanism, as a discourse or a movement, developed at a different time, in a different way and in different locations. For example, while transatlantic Pan-Africanism grew as a movement of ideas with little formal organisation apart from periodic conferences, and predated, indeed, spawned continental Pan-Africanism, the latter first found institutional fulfillment with the formation of the Organisation of African Unity (OAU) in 1963.

The formation of the OAU represented the triumph of continental integration over transatlantic solidarity. In 2002, the OAU gave way to the African Union, a much more robust organisation and more committed to the pursuit of development, democracy and human rights than its predecessor, which had been preoccupied with the politics of decolonisation, national sovereignty and presidential camaraderie.

In 2005, in a gesture to global Pan-Africanism, the AU designated the diaspora as Africa's sixth region and allocated it representation in the Economic and Social Council. This paved the way for the global Pan-Africanism of the twenty-first century.

The connections and reverberations between these Pan-Africanisms were and continue to be intricate, complex and contradictory, spawning narrow territorial nationalisms and broad transnational movements, including dozens of regional integration schemes. Often complementing and constraining the Pan-African movements were other transnational movements, those organised around religion, for example, or colonial linguistic affiliations.

During its long and turbulent history over the course of the twentieth century, Pan-Africanism encompassed various political, cultural and intellectual movements based on a series of shared presumptions and objectives. On the one hand, it sought to liberate Africans and the African diaspora from racial degradation, political oppression and economic exploitation, and on the other to promote unity and solidarity among African peoples in political, cultural and economic matters.

Pan-Africanism incorporated ideas derived from the experiences of and struggles against slavery, colonialism and racism, as well those of democracy, Marxism and socialism and nationalism, from various parts of the imperial, colonial and postcolonial worlds. Thus, almost from the very beginning there were different articulations of Pan-Africanism as an imaginary of the perils and possibilities of the African condition on the continent and in the diaspora.

The solidarities and schisms encompassed the different spatial and social geographies of Africa and the diaspora: between the imperial divisions of Anglophone, Francophone and the Lusophone worlds; between elite and mass expressions; national and transnational commitments; ethical and epistemic imperatives; radical and reformist projects. These dynamics were manifest at every moment, in every region and even country – for example, in the contestations between the Du Boisean congresses and Garveyite conventions in the US, in which elitist and populist invocations and socialist and capitalist ideologies vied for supremacy; and in Africa, between Nkrumah, who advocated immediate continental unity, and Nyerere, who preferred regional integration as a stepping-stone to continental unity.

In short, it can be said that in its long and chequered history Pan-Africanism has been as much an intellectual movement (about the conception of Africa and Africanness in the modern world) as it has been an ideological movement (about unity and the construction of vibrant African and diaspora states and societies in an unequal and exploitative world). Deeply intertwined are the intellectual and ideological dimensions and dynamics of Pan-Africanism. In that regard, knowledge production and higher education in Africa constitute powerful arenas for the articulation and advancement of Pan-Africanist projects, paradigms and possibilities.

Africa's Contemporary Engagements with its Diasporas

While the old preoccupations of Pan-African activists persist, for African states and societies there is greater interest in the question of diaspora contributions to the continent's perennial quest for self-determination, development and democracy. This has directed increased attention to the new diasporas formed out of postcolonial global migrations rather than the historic diasporas formed out precolonial migrations to the Americas, Europe and Asia.

In examining diaspora contributions to the development of their countries of origins, it is evident that this involves a variety of economic, political, social and cultural activities channelled through formal and informal networks in the homeland, hostland and the international system. Diaspora contributions to development can be both direct and indirect and undertaken by individuals and groups located in the hostland, homeland or organised through transnational networks.

Voluntary as well as profit considerations motivate the diaspora. While individual activities are important, especially for remittances, diaspora engagements are most efficacious through collective organisation. Diaspora organisations include hometown associations, ethnic associations, alumni associations, religious associations, professional associations, development NGOs, investment/business groups, national development groups, welfare/refugee groups, supplementary schools and virtual organisations (digital diasporisation).

Clearly, the question of diaspora and development involves three interconnected dynamics: development in the diaspora; development through the diaspora; and development by the diaspora. Not only have diasporas become more conscious of their power and potential, interest in the role of diasporas has increased among governments in both the sending and receiving countries and among international organisations, from the UN and its various agencies, including the International Organization for Migration, to the World Bank and the African Development Bank.

The reasons for this growing interest in diaspora contributions to development relate to remittances, return, resources, recognition and reputation. The volume of remittances often exceeds Official Development Assistance (ODA). Return migration, whether temporary, permanent or circulatory, turns 'brain drain' into 'brain gain' and 'brain circulation'. Diasporas possess multifaceted resources that need to be better mobilised and deployed. Diasporas tend to display dual loyalties to their countries of origin and settlement. Engaging them effectively has reputational benefits for all involved.

Mainstreaming diasporas in development effectively involves several strategies: through knowledge-building activities that include research and mapping exercises and pilot projects; by strengthening diaspora technical and organisational capacities through training and knowledge exchange programmes and networking initiatives; supporting the organic formation of, rather than imposing, umbrella diaspora organisations; maximising diaspora participation in terms of partnership selection procedures; funding schemes; forging equal not paternalistic or token collaborations in project development and implementation; actively including diasporas by recruiting diaspora individuals in development agencies; and developing a formal consultation process with diaspora associations. The diversity diasporas bring fosters innovation in often-homogeneous development agencies and practices.

Previously negative views of diasporas and development, of the developmental impact of migration, have been tempered by an appreciation of its benefits, although a lot remains to be done to improve understanding of these processes, and to promote policy coherence and co-ordination as well as international dialogue and co-operation. Because of the evident economic and political influence of many diasporas, governments are increasingly courting them by creating agencies and even ministries for diasporic affairs.

The growing recognition of the diaspora as part of the domestic political community is concretely manifested by conferring dual citizenship to its members. According to one survey,[3] by 2007 there were 115 states and independent territories that allowed citizens abroad to vote in domestic elections; by 2018, there were 127 countries; by 2010, fifteen African countries had set up diaspora-related institutions and ministries in order to deal more professionally with diaspora-led development-related issues; by the end of the 2010s, thirty-two African countries allowed dual citizenship. The formal recognition and incorporation of the diaspora in homeland affairs allows the diaspora to increase its claims and influence.

Diaspora engagements with their homelands are often complex, contradictory and always changing so that it is hard to generalise about the behaviour and activities of any particular diaspora. Diaspora communities, like all communities, are highly differentiated according to the social inscriptions of gender, class, ethnicity, religion and ideology.

Diaspora Political, Social and Economic Contributions

Diasporas can exert significant political influence, both positive and negative, on their countries of origin and residence as well as international institutions like the UN, through protest, public relations campaigns and diplomatic pressure. Politically savvy diaspora groups use a variety of activities and instruments to mobilise public opinion in the hostland for their causes by working with hostland civil society groups, from community-based organisations to non-governmental organisations, from traditional social movements including labour, religious and women's associations, to new social movements ranging from environmental to human rights activists.

Their tactics cover conventional rallies, marches, concerts and boycotts, and public relations campaigns in the traditional and digital media. The mobilisational capacities of the diaspora partly depend on the nature of the hostland's political regime. The more democratic the hostland, the greater the opportunities, all things being equal, for diaspora activists and struggles to exercise diplomatic pressure on it to adopt foreign policies that favour the diaspora's homeland.

The capacity of diasporas to become influential political constituents and important interest groups in their countries of residence is often proportional to their political weight in the electoral process, their ability to affect the outcome of local and national elections because of their numbers, resources or influence. Through diplomatic pressure, diasporas can help legitimise or delegitimise their homeland government and political processes.

The role of diasporas in African politics is complex and contradictory. In a study I did several years ago on the role and impact of diasporas on African conflicts,[4] I found that different diasporas at different moments were as much perpetrators of conflicts as they were purveyors of peacemaking and participants in post-conflict reconstruction.

Diasporas acquire and possess social and cultural capital – attributes and attitudes, skills and sensibilities – that can be mobilised for the development of their countries of origin. The social, cultural and professional experiences, values, skills and assets acquired by diasporas inform their perception and participation in the affairs of their countries of origin.

Diasporas located in developed and democratic societies can develop routine economic, social, cultural and political activities and practices that can be leveraged for development and democratisation in their countries of origin. Moreover, diasporas have access to extensive transnational political, social and cultural networks that can be mobilised for the development and democratisation of their homelands. These include knowledge and media networks, cultural institutions, and ideologies and imaginations through which the cultural and social landscape of the homeland can be re-imagined, revitalised, modernised and globalised.

The worth of diaspora social and cultural capital in the homeland tends to be realised through civic-oriented activities, which can help enhance the capacities and structures of local civil society organisations. A fascinating area concerns digital diasporisation, the use of the Internet and social media to maintain connections, build networks and for advocacy.

The range of economic contributions from the diaspora includes remittances, philanthropy, human capital and investment. According to a World Bank study,[5] from 1990 to 2018 remittance flows to the developing countries were larger than Official Development Assistance and more stable than private capital flows. The data in the study shows that, in 2000, global remittance inflows stood at US$126,750 billion, out of which US$74,767 billion went to low- and middle-income countries. By 2010, remittances had reached US$459,722 billion, with US$343,044 billion going to low- and middle-income countries. According to the projections for 2019, remittances rose to US$706,625 billion, out of which US$550,523 billion went to low- and middle-income countries. Africa received US$84,280 billion. The leading ten recipients were, in order: Egypt with US$26,352 billion (8.8 per cent of GDP); Nigeria US$25,368 billion (5.7 per cent of GDP); Morocco US$7,070 billion (5.8 per cent of GDP); Ghana US$3,723 billion (5.5 per cent of GDP); Kenya US$2,855 billion (2.9 per cent of GDP); Senegal US$2,495 billion (9.9 per cent of GDP); Tunisia US$1,936 billion (5.3 per cent of GDP); Zimbabwe US$1,773 billion (8 per cent of GDP); Uganda US$1,507 billion (5 per cent of GDP); and Mali US$964 million (6.8 per cent of GDP).

Thus, in many African countries remittances are the most important and stable source of capital inflows, in some case exceeding both ODA and FDI. For example, in 2014 in Morocco, remittances made up 673 per cent of FDI and 425 per cent of ODA; in Egypt, 467 per cent of FDI and 225 per cent of ODA; and in Cape Verde, 929 per cent of FDI and 103 per cent of ODA.

Migrants and diasporas send remittances for a variety of motives using different mechanisms. Occasionally, remittances are generated by coercive means, when a home government imposes demands for remittances. As far as migration decisions are often part of an explicit or implicit contract between the migrant and the remaining household, migrant remittances are part of enlightened self-interest. Diasporas send remittances to improve the consumption levels of family members, in anticipation of reciprocal assistance, as part of co-insurance arrangements, or to repay loans and investments in their human capital.

Whatever the source, diaspora remittances increasingly play a crucial role in sustaining livelihoods, basic services and economic growth in many developing countries. Financial transfers occur through formal channels – Western Union, Money Gram and banks. Remittances also occur through the informal sector and informal means.

The cost of sending money to developing countries is much higher than the Sustainable Development Goal target of 3 per cent. In 2017, the average cost of sending a remittance of US$200 was 7.2 per cent, varying between a low of 5.4 per cent for South Asia and a high of 9.1 per cent for sub-Saharan Africa. Hence, the growing pressure to lower these costs for Africa. The African Foundation for Development in the UK has gone further by campaigning for tax relief for remittances similar to domestic charity donations.

The diasporas can also serve as a major philanthropic player in their own right or in helping to mobilise philanthropy in the hostland for their homeland. Diaspora philanthropy organisations are particularly important for subsequent diaspora generations who may not have the direct family and social connections in the homeland that first-generation diasporans do. Thus, while the latter dominate in remittance flows, the historic diasporas and later diaspora generations may gravitate to diaspora philanthropy to channel their capital, skills and services to the homeland.

For many African countries, their overseas diasporas constitute one of the largest sources of human capital for development. Africa suffers from the world's highest rates of skilled labour emigration. Homeland governments and international development agencies have increasingly come to value the potential of the diaspora communities and expertise for development.

The deployment of diaspora human capital often involves repatriation, which can be permanent, temporary or circulatory in nature. Diaspora circulation often includes what some call 'homeland tourism' and return visits. One can also think of the mobilisation of this capital in both physical and virtual modes. I conclude this chapter with a brief discussion of a programme that I have been involved in, the Carnegie African Diaspora Fellowship Program (CADFP).

Diaspora economic outlays to the homeland can involve various levels and forms of business investments as well. Diasporans often possess deep affective capital for their homelands, their commitment tends to be long-term, they are more likely than other investors to think out of the box and they can harness long-term contacts in the homeland. Diaspora investment decisions are based on expectations of financial, emotional and social-status returns. Thus, diasporans exhibit strong country-of-origin bias and a sense of origin-country duty, derive 'psychic income' from investing in the homeland and raise their status in the diaspora by doing so.

Diaspora investments can range from purchasing equity or lending to local businesses to direct investments in industry and services. In June 2017, Nigeria pioneered the issuing of a diaspora bond for US$300 million to finance development projects. The bond was oversubscribed by 130 per cent. Diasporas can also serve as reputational intermediaries and provide transnational connections for businesses in the hostland and homeland.

The impact of diaspora contributions is neither uniformly positive nor negative, but often variable depending on the specific context. The inflows of remittances, philanthropy and human capital from the diaspora are inherently contradictory. Remittances are insufficient to compensate for the losses of human capital from Africa in the first place. Their benefits are selective and they carry with them social and cultural baggage. They can increase dependency, engender economic distortions and deepen social and regional inequalities, which may hinder development because they are unpredictable, undependable and encourage the consumption of goods with high import content. Diasporas do not control how their resources might be used in the homeland, which may be channelled towards conflict.

Diaspora philanthropy and repatriation of human capital may have some of the same potentially negative effects. Diaspora attitudes and attitudes towards them in the homeland may introduce new or reinforce old class and ethnic stratifications, resentments and divisions. Returning diasporans sometimes exhibit insufferable superiority complexes and project a 'development aid' mindset, or the proverbial 'been to' mentality lamented in the African literature of the 1960s and 1970s, which is deeply resented. Also, elites and even ordinary people in the homeland harbour their own complexes and resentments against the diasporans for abandoning the homeland when it was in crisis, which can erupt once the diasporans return. Such friction and hostility can exact a toll on development efforts by delaying or thwarting them altogether.

Mobilising Intellectual Remittances: CADFP

I had long been convinced through my research on African diasporas that the diaspora constitutes a huge asset for the continent. As noted earlier, the diaspora played a pivotal role in the development of Pan-Africanism, which incubated the territorial nationalist movements across the continent that led to decolonisation. In 2011, the Carnegie Corporation of New York (CCNY) approached me to do research on the African-born academic diaspora in the United States and Canada. In 2012, this was followed by research on how the academic diasporas are perceived by African higher education institutions, from vice chancellors to academic staff or faculty in southern, West and East Africa.

The project sought to determine the size and scope of the African-born academic diaspora in the two countries, understand the dynamics for diaspora engagement with institutions of higher education in Africa and identify ways to promote productive and sustainable engagements between the two. I submitted the final report to CCNY at a convening of various stakeholders in February 2013.

The programme was launched in September 2013, with a novel structure in international higher education exchanges, which consists of four organs. CCNY provides funding (US$13 million had been paid by 2018, in four cycles of funding) and the Institute for International Education offers management and logistical support. The Advisory Council, which comprises leading African academics and administrators on both sides of the Atlantic and which I chair, sets strategic direction and leadership, and my university – first in the United States and now USIU-Africa in Kenya – hosts the Secretariat that provides overall co-ordination.

The programme operates in six 'Carnegie' countries – Ghana, Nigeria, Kenya, Uganda, Tanzania and South Africa. In 2019, three other countries – Ethiopia,

Rwanda and Senegal – with universities belonging to the African Research Universities Alliance, were added. The programme seeks to reverse the continent's much lamented 'brain drain'. We believe the academics at these universities represent a huge asset for the continent in meeting the challenges of African higher education and exploiting its opportunities in a rapidly changing global landscape. As is well known, Africa suffers from an acute shortage of qualified academics.

By February 2020, the programme had received 1,100 project requests from 206 accredited African universities. Altogether, 465 fellowships were funded and hosted by more than 150 universities in the nine African countries. Data shows that the programme has helped to build the capacities of African higher education institutions by increasing curriculum offerings, graduate programming and research production. Surveys completed shortly after programme completion demonstrated that the average fellowship contributed two to three courses to host institutions. After participating in the CADFP, alumni continued to co-develop curricula with African institutions.

According to a comprehensive review of the programme's alumni released in mid-2019, up to five years after fellowships 55 per cent of fellows continued to collaborate on capacity-building with 115 institutions beyond their host institutions, located in a total of sixteen countries. Post-fellowship, many also sought funding with African institutions and for other Africa-related research. Seventy percent of respondents reported that they had travelled to Africa in the past year to visit an African institution using resources from their own institutions and other sources.

Two-thirds of the fellows continued research collaboration in terms of joint applications for research grants and publications. Twenty-three fellows reported a combined total of over US$1,250,000 in non-CADFP funding for Africa-related research. Over 60 fellows received US$450,000 from home institutions to support Africa-related research.

Many fellows also continued mentoring graduate students. Fellows supported their network of graduate students, extending the reach of African students. By offering resources and feedback, they enabled students to tap into new ideas and expand their academic capacities. Some fellows were instrumental in securing funding for African graduate students by leveraging home institution support. In addition, fellows supported African faculty in their network through sustained mentorship.

Furthermore, in their academic communities, hosts reported changes since participating in the CADFP. For example, hosts found that students in their academic institutions were more motivated to pursue advanced degrees and adopted research best practices from the fellows. Additionally, hosts indicated that disseminating and applying knowledge from the CADFP in their communities was an important outcome. Community workshops and public lectures based on CADFP collaborations, both during and post-fellowship, developed the knowledge base of community members.

Further, through the CADFP, close to two-thirds (64 per cent) of respondents reported improvements in their hosts' ability to set up collaborations with other institutions. Forty-three percent of respondents reported instituting formal links between their home and African institution that led to improvements in African higher education. About one-third of fellows also established institutional links between their hosts and other institutions. Fellows described leveraging networks they had prior to the CADFP to set up connections between hosts and other African institutions. In expanding fellowship projects to partner institutions and having better practice in collaborating with other organisations, hosts described universities as better prepared to develop new linkages.

Overall, 87 per cent of the fellows reported to have developed more interest in supporting African higher education systems; 76 per cent as being more capable of supporting African higher education systems; and 72 per cent as having more knowledge of African higher education systems. Clearly, there is a huge demand by African institutions for diaspora academics and there is a need to expand beyond fellowships to other modalities of engagement to appeal to different stakeholders.

Based on CADFP's experience, success and lessons learned the time was ripe to implement one of the key priorities from the first Higher Education summit held in Dakar in March 2015. This was the establishment of the 10/10 Programme to sponsor 1,000 academics in the diaspora, both from the historic and new diasporas from anywhere in the world across all disciplines, every year, to anywhere across the continent.

Conclusion

The diaspora in all its dimensions is indispensable for building capacities in African countries to realise their lofty ambitions articulated in national, regional and global instruments, such as Kenya's Vision 2030, the African Union's Agenda 2063 and the United Nation's Sustainable Development Goals.

More than any other external community, the diaspora represents a priceless asset comprised of people with the necessary affective commitments and social and economic capital as partners of the peoples and governments across our beloved continent in the pursuit of integrated, inclusive, innovative and sustainable development. The last is imperative for Africa to reclaim the twenty-first century as truly ours, unlike the previous few centuries that pulverised us with the barbarisms of slavery and colonialism and the depredations of neocolonialism. Sustainable development is essential to meet the needs and potential of Africa's exploding population to ensure that the youth bulge turns into a positive demographic dividend rather than a Malthusian nightmare. The diaspora will further augment Africa's global demographic weight and development potential.

In addition to the nearly 1.2 billion people currently on the continent, Africa's global diaspora, both the historic and new diasporas, comprises more than 150 million people. This resource is too important for the continent to ignore or waste. In short, Africa and its global diasporas are each other's keepers, their fates bound by the inextricable ties of the past, present and future.

Notes

1. Paul Tiyambe Zeleza, *In Search of African Diasporas: Testimonies and Encounters*, Durham, NC: Carolina Academic Press, 2012.
2. Paul Gilroy, *The Black Atlantic: Modernity and Double Consciousness*, Cambridge, MA: Harvard University Press, 1993.
3. World Population Review, 'Countries That Allow Dual Citizenship 2020'. https://worldpopulationreview.com/country-rankings/countries-that-allow-dual-citizenship
4. Paul Tiyambe Zeleza, 'The Role of African Diasporas in Reconstruction', in Cassandra R. Veney and Dick Simpson (eds), *African Democracy and Development: Challenges for Post-Conflict African Nations*, Lanham, MD: Lexington Books, 2012: 185–218.
5. World Bank Group, *Leveraging Economic Migration for Development, World Bank Board Briefing Paper*, Washington, D.C: World Bank Group, 2019. https://www.knomad.org/sites/default/files/2019-08/World%20Bank%20Board%20Briefing%20Paper-LEVERAGING%20ECONOMIC%20MIGRATION%20FOR%20DEVELOPMENT_0.pdf

An original version of this essay was delivered as the keynote address, Kenya Diaspora Home Coming Convention 2017, Strathmore University, Nairobi, on 13 December 2017.

III

Africa's Political Dramas

11

Mandela's Long Walk with African History

The death of Nelson Mandela on 5 December 2013 provoked an outpouring of mourning, celebration and commentary around the world that was unprecedented for an African leader. Glowing tributes gushed from world leaders, and major magazines and newspapers carried special features on his extraordinary life and legacy. He was showered with lavish praise as a great man, titan, colossus and conscience of his nation and the world, for his magnanimity, moral courage and dignity. For his resilience, patience and passion; for his charisma, charm, regal countenance and common touch; for his humility, visionary and political brilliance; and above all, for his spirit of forgiveness and reconciliation, believed to have been the driving force behind the South African 'miracle' that steered the beloved country from the abyss of a racial bloodbath. Several African countries, including Nigeria, Kenya and Tanzania, declared three days of mourning and in several European countries and the United States flags were flown at half-mast in national mourning for Mandela.

Everyone, it seems, sought to bask in Mandela's reflected glory, including many African leaders who compared quite unfavourably with him for their mendacity, self-aggrandisement and dictatorial tendencies. However, there were critics, including some in South Africa and among the African left, who accused Mandela of having failed to dismantle the South African apartheid economy, which had left millions of black people – especially the unemployed youth – in grinding poverty. Reconciliation, they argued, rescued whites from seriously reckoning with apartheid's past and its legacies and deprived blacks of restitution. Mandela's death forced South Africans to reflect on the post-apartheid state he helped create. Deprived of Mandela's aura, some believed, the ANC's monopoly on power would erode. Such critical assessments of Mandela's legacy could only be expected to grow, but in the immediate aftermath of his death, they were drowned by outflows of endearment.

The Myth and the Man

It was hard to remember that Mandela had once been widely reviled in much of Euro-America as a terrorist as much as he was revered in Africa and the progressive world as a revolutionary figure. He was now everyone's venerated hero, a man sanctified, a transcendent myth, his place in African history stripped of its messy contexts and multiple meanings, his life and legacy of protracted struggle reshaped into a universal redemptive tale of reconciliation. His iconic image of lofty leadership lifted a world mired in pettiness; it was a resounding reproach to the small-minded leaders most countries were cursed with. The various Mandelas commemorated offered different opportunities to people, politicians and pundits in the global North and in the global South – absolution from the barbarous crimes of imperialism for the former and affirmation of their humanity for the latter and a reminder of the heady dreams of independence.

As with the day he was released from prison in 1990, many will remember where they were when they heard the news of Mandela's death. I remember 11 February 1990 as if it were yesterday. I sat glued to the television anxiously for the live broadcast of Mandela's release. I told my then six-year-old daughter this was one of the most memorable days for my generation and she would live to remember it, too. I choked with tears of joy, anger, sadness, pride, anticipation and other bewildering emotions as we watched the tall, smiling, dashing and unbowed Mandela walking out of Victor Verster Prison beside his wife, Winnie, a militant in her own right who had suffered so much and done a lot to keep his memory alive. They walked with defiant dignity, holding hands, and with clenched fists raised. The announcement of his death, although long anticipated because of his age and grave illness, came more unceremoniously. It arrived as a news alert on my iPad as I was working on some memo in my office. However, it was no less momentous for it marked the end of an era, of Africa's long twentieth century.

Predictably, the traditional and social media were awash with tributes, reminiscences and verdicts on Mandela the person, the politician and the symbol. In the United States and Britain, politicians, pundits and celebrities fell over themselves to find the words laudatory enough to describe Mandela as the epitome of global moral authority, of humanity at its best, the last in the hallowed canon of twentieth-century saintly liberators, from Mahatma Gandhi to Martin Luther King. Such encomiums were to be expected for a world hungry for the goodness, forgiveness, trust and optimism that Mandela exuded so masterfully. Conveniently forgotten was the fact that the British and American governments had upheld the apartheid regime for decades and condemned Mandela's African National Congress as a terrorist organisation. Many of us remember that Ronald Reagan and Margaret Thatcher had resolutely defended the apartheid regime and fiercely condemned the ANC and its leaders, including Mandela. In the United States, ANC leaders were officially regarded as terrorists until 2008!

The sanctified portrait of Mandela belied the exceedingly complex and contradictory man and historical figure that Mandela was and the true measure of his life and legacy. Anyone who has read Mandela's autobiography, *Long Walk to Freedom*,[1] and the equally voluminous biographies, including Anthony Sampson's *Mandela: The Authorised Biography*[2] and Martin Meredith's *Mandela: A Biography*,[3] knows he was not the caricatured figure of the popular media who rose from clan royalty to the South African presidency and global political celebrity, appropriately purified by twenty-seven years of imprisonment. Rather, his greatness arose from the very complexities and contradictions of his life and times, how he embodied them, experienced them, articulated them, learned from them, manipulated them, deployed them and tried to transcend them. He was not much of a father to his children, but he became a beloved father of the nation. He had several failed marriages but his warm embrace seduced the public. He was a ruthless political operator as much as he was a self-effacing leader. The very texture of daily life and struggle under apartheid cultivated in him, rather than bitterness, an empathy that allowed him to effectively deal with his jailors and negotiate with his Afrikaner opponents in the transition from apartheid to democracy.

Moreover, Mandela's unflinching loyalty to his comrades in the liberation movement sometimes blinded him to their limitations, with adverse consequences – as exemplified by his two immediate successors. And there was the loyalty he had exhibited to the unsavoury leaders of states who had supported the anti-apartheid struggle, such as Libya's Muammar Gaddafi and Nigeria's Sani Abacha. The early Mandela was known for being impetuous and boisterous; the later Mandela could be fiercely stern, coldly calculating and compellingly charming in order to seize opportunities and advance his aspirations. At age thirty-three, he declared that he would be South Africa's first black president, but when he finally did achieve this goal at seventy-six he forswore the grandiosity of office so beloved by many leaders in Africa and elsewhere. However, there were constants in his life. He remained supremely proud and confident of himself and his African heritage, and his commitment to South Africa's liberation struggle was steadfast.

Many have remarked on Mandela's remarkable understanding of the nature of politics and the performance of power that enabled him to embody the nation better than many of his fellow founding fathers of African nations and his two successors. Above all, he was praised for his lack of bitterness after spending twenty-seven years in jail and his embrace of forgiveness and reconciliation. The manner in which this issue is discussed often serves to advance the redemptive narrative of Mandela's road to political sainthood. Only he and his closest confidants of course know how he truly felt. Post-apartheid reconciliation may or may not have been a romantic attribute of Mandela the man; it was certainly a pragmatic imperative for Mandela the nationalist leader. Mandela's life and legacy cannot be fully understood through the psychologising and symbolic discourses preferred in the popular media and hagiographies. It could be argued that he and his comrades were able to sublimate their personal anger and bitterness because the liberation struggle was too complex, too costly, too demanding, too protracted and too important to do otherwise. Reconciliation was both a tactic and a necessity because of the dynamics of the liberation struggle in South Africa.

This is to suggest that, like all great historical figures, Mandela can best be understood through the prism of his times and the political, economic, social and cultural dynamics and conditions that structured it. Mandela changed much in his long life but it was a life defined by the vicissitudes of African nationalism. For those who do not know much about African history, or are wedded to exceptionalist notions of South African history, they would be surprised to learn the parallels Mandela shares with the founding fathers of many other independent African nations, in whose rarefied company he belongs. In fact, his historic significance and the eruption of grief over his death and gratitude for his life in the Pan-African world and elsewhere can partly be explained by the fact that he was Africa's last founding father.

Decolonisation – the first step of African nationalism

The decolonisation drama started in Egypt in 1922, with the restoration of the monarchy there and limited internal self-government, and finally ended in 1994 with the demise of apartheid in South Africa. In the long interregnum, decolonisation unfolded across the continent, reaching a crescendo in the 1950s and 1960s. In 1960 alone, often dubbed the year of African independence, seventeen countries achieved their independence. The colonial dominoes began falling, from North Africa (Libya 1951) to West Africa (Ghana 1957) to East Africa (Tanzania 1961) before reaching southern Africa (Zambia and Malawi 1964). The settler colonies of southern Africa were the last to fall, starting with the Portuguese colonies of Angola and Mozambique in 1974, followed by Rhodesia in 1980 and Namibia in 1990. South Africa, the largest and mightiest of Africa's settler colonies, finally joined this place in African history in 1994. Nelson Mandela is cherished because of his and his country's long walk with African history.

Mandela embodied all the key phases, dynamics and ideologies of African nationalism, from the period of elite nationalism before World War II when the nationalists made reformist demands on the colonial regimes, to the era of militant mass nationalism after the war when they demanded independence, to the phase of armed liberation struggle. Many countries achieved independence during the second phase through peaceful means. Others were forced to wage a protracted armed struggle. The variations in the development and trajectories of nationalism were marked by the way each individual colony had been acquired and administered; the traditions of resistance in each colony; the presence or absence of European settlers; the social composition of the nationalist movement; and the nature and ideologies of the leadership. Similarly, there were different ideological orientations and emphases. Some nationalists espoused secular or religious ideologies. Among the former there were competing liberal, socialist and Marxist ideologies that would later frame postcolonial development agendas.

All along, African nationalism unfolded in a rapidly changing world. It was most critically affected by the Great Depression and World War II; the emergence of the superpowers and the Third World; and the growth of Pan-Africanism and civil rights struggles in the diaspora. Independence marked the triumph of the first out of the five humanistic and historic objectives of African nationalism, namely, decolonisation. The other four objectives included nation-building, development, democracy and regional integration. In as much as contemporary Africa is largely a product of struggles for independence and their complex, changing and contradictory intersections with colonialism, imperialism and globalisation, Mandela's life and legacy as a historic figure were conditioned by the contexts and imperatives of nationalism. Like many of Africa's founding fathers, Mandela's life spanned much of South Africa's existence as a nation, traversed the various phases of the country's nationalist movement and embodied the trajectories of postcolonial Africa.

The birth of a freedom fighter

Mandela was born in 1918, a mere eight years after the founding of South Africa as a nation out of four separate settler colonies and an assortment of conquered African states and societies, and six years after the formation of the African National Congress. He was thirty when the country's racist settler regime gave way to the uncompromising racial barbarity of apartheid, in 1948. In the early 1940s, he was one of the founders of the ANC Youth League that sought to radicalise and rescue the ANC from its reformist politics. When the ANC adopted its Programme of Action in response to the establishment of apartheid, he became the leader of the Defiance Campaign in the early 1950s. In 1955, he was among 156 activists to be tried in one of the longest political trials in South African history, which lasted from 1956 to 1961. Following the Sharpeville Massacre in March 1960, the liberation movement decided to shift to armed struggle and Mandela was charged with the formation of the ANC's Umkhonto we Sizwe (Spear of the Nation).

In 1963, Mandela and nine other leaders, including Walter Sisulu, his mentor, and Govan Mbeki, the father of future President Thabo Mbeki, were charged with sabotage at the infamous Rivonia Trial. During the trial, on 20 April 1964, Mandela uttered his immortal words from the dock: 'I have fought against white domination and I have fought against black domination. I have cherished the ideal of a democratic and free society in which all persons live together in harmony and with equal opportunities. It is an ideal I hope to live for and to achieve. But if needs be, it is an ideal for which I am prepared to die.'[4] Thus Mandela was not an advocate of Gandhi's or King's non-violent resistance, not because he was not a man of peace, but because he correctly understood that in the South African context, fighting against an obdurate racist settler regime required all available tactics, from mass protest to armed resistance. For him multiple tactics had to serve the overall strategy of achieving national liberation. In short, as a freedom fighter he was simultaneously a political leader and a guerrilla leader. Under the ANC's broad and tolerant political umbrella, he worked with traditionalists, liberals, socialists, communists and Black Consciousness activists, both before and after his long incarceration.

Mandela outlived apartheid by nearly twenty years. His story is broadly similar to that of other African nationalists. Some progressed from peaceful protest to armed liberation struggle. They included the nationalists of Algeria, Kenya, Mozambique, Angola, Guinea Bissau and Zimbabwe. Many of those who led their countries to independence were also born either just before or after their countries had been colonised. Examples include Jomo Kenyatta, Kenya's first president, born at least six years before Kenya became a British colony in 1895, and who outlived colonialism by fifteen years by the time he died in 1978. Kwame Nkrumah of Ghana was born in 1909, and also outlived colonialism by fifteen years. Félix Houphouët-Boigny, the first president of Côte d'Ivoire, was born in 1905 and died in 1993, thirty-three years after the end of French colonial rule. Léopold Sédar Senghor, Senegal's first president who ruled for twenty years, was born in 1906 and died in 2001, outliving colonialism by forty-one years. In my own homeland, Hastings Kamuzu Banda, who was reportedly born in 1898, a few years after the country was colonised, lived to rule Malawi for thirty-years from 1964 to 1994 and died in 1997.

The long and large lives of many of Africa's founding fathers, including Nelson Mandela, represent a historic rebuke to the destructive conceits of European colonialism. Notoriously, Ian Smith, the prime minister of the settler colony of Southern Rhodesia, which became Zimbabwe, and other European colonists, did not 'believe in black majority rule in Rhodesia – not in a thousand years'. Set against many of his fellow founding fathers, Mandela stands out for his singular contribution to democratic politics. He relinquished power after only one five-year term in office. Many others were overthrown in coups, as was Nkrumah, or died in office, like Kenyatta and Houphouët-Boigny. Before Mandela, the only other African leaders to voluntarily leave office were Senghor of Senegal and Nyerere, the founding president of Tanzania.

Mandela's example shines all the brighter when compared to his nemesis in Zimbabwe, Robert Mugabe, once a widely admired liberation hero, who had been president for thirty-three years after independence when Mandela died.

Mugabe and the likes of President Yoweri Museveni of Uganda, then in power for twenty-seven years – the same number of years Mandela spent in apartheid jails – and still going, represented the dinosaurs of African politics on a continent that had been undergoing various forms of democratic renewal since the turn of the 1990s. The democratic struggles were in part influenced by the effect of South Africa's transition to democracy and Mandela's enlightened exit from office after only five years.

Reconciliation and Nation-building

The lateness of South Africa's decolonisation, it can be argued, helped to compress the sequentiality, as it turned out for the early independent states, of the five objectives of African nationalism. While those states had achieved decolonisation, they had struggled hard to build a unified nation out of the territorial contraptions of colonialism, which had enjoyed statehood without nationhood. They had come to independence in an era when development, democracy and regional integration were compromised by weak national bourgeoisies, relatively small middle classes and the Cold War machinations of the two superpowers, the United States and the Soviet Union.

Mandela's South Africa benefitted from both the positive and negative experiences of postcolonial Africa, the existence of a highly organised and vociferous civil society and the end of the Cold War, which gave ample space for the growth of democratic governance and the rule of law. But the new post-apartheid state was held hostage to the dictates of the negotiated settlement between the ANC and the apartheid regime, which had arisen out of the strategic stalemate between the two sides. By 1990 South Africa had become ungovernable, but the apartheid state was not vanquished as had happened in Angola and Mozambique. This, combined with the global triumph of neoliberalism in the post-Cold War era, guaranteed the powerful interests of capital in general and the white bourgeoisie in particular against any serious economic restructuring, despite the great expectations of the masses and the ambitions of successive development plans by the new government. Those plans ranged from the Reconstruction and Development Programme to Growth Employment and Redistribution to the Accelerated and Shared Growth Initiative.

Nevertheless, the post-apartheid state achieved much faster growth than the apartheid regime ever did. The country witnessed massive expansion of the black middle class and the ANC government fostered the growth of a black bourgeoisie through its Black Economic Empowerment programme, much as the apartheid regime before it had cultivated the Afrikaner bourgeoisie through apartheid affirmative action. There was also some reduction in poverty, although huge challenges remain in terms of high levels of unemployment and deepening inequality. Interestingly, at the time of writing, South Africa lagged behind much of the continent in terms of rates of economic growth. This was in part because of the lingering structural deformities of the apartheid economy in which the peasantry had been virtually destroyed, and because the labour-absorptive capacity of the economy was limited by its high cost structures. Moreover, South Africa suffered from relatively low levels of skill formation for an economy of its size because of the apartheid legacy of poor black education.

It was expected that South Africa would be overtaken by Nigeria as Africa's largest economy, which happened in 2014. The continent's rapid growth, reminiscent of the immediate post-independence years, which was dubbed by the world's financial press 'Africa Rising', gave rekindled hopes for the establishment of democratic developmental states that might realise the remaining goals of African nationalism.

Thus, Mandela's political life and legacy resemble in significant ways that of other African founding fathers, and South Africa's trajectory mirrors that of other African countries, notwithstanding the differences of national historical and geopolitical contexts. It is worth remembering that Mandela's rhetoric of reconciliation was a staple among many African founding presidents in the immediate post-independence years. Jomo Kenyatta used to preach reconciliation, urging Kenyans to forgive but not forget the ills of the past as a way of keeping the European settlers and building his nation, which had been fractured by the racial and ethnic divisions of colonialism. Even Mugabe in the euphoric days after independence urged reconciliation between white and black Zimbabweans, before domestic political challenges forced him to refurbish his revolutionary credentials by adopting radical land reform and rhetoric.

Reconciliation was such a powerful motif in the political discourses of transition to independence among some African leaders because of the imperatives of nation-building, the second goal of African nationalism. It was also a rhetorical response to the irrational and self-serving fears of imperial racism that, since Africans were supposedly eternal wards of whites and incapable of ruling themselves, independence would unleash the atavistic violence of 'intertribal warfare' from which colonialism had saved the benighted continent, and there would be a retributive cataclysm of white massacres in the post-settler colonies. Instead of comprehensive accountability for apartheid and its normative institutional violence, which constituted crimes against humanity, post-apartheid South Africa pursued 'truth and reconciliation', which individualised both the victims and perpetrators and transformed the logic of crime and punishment of the Nuremberg Trials into the logic of crime and confession, justified tendentiously in the name of *ubuntu*.

Mandela bookends Nkrumah in Africa's independence struggles. Nkrumah fired the Pan-African imagination; Mandela gave it its most memorable consummation. The former was a key architect of Pan-Africanism, a cosmopolitan intellectual activist whose diaspora associates included W.E.B. Dubois, George Padmore and C.L.R. James, whereas the latter was largely a homegrown pragmatic revolutionary whose long incarceration and struggles revitalised the intricate Pan-African connections between the continent and its diaspora.

In the United States, the anti-apartheid struggle offered the Civil Rights movement its most powerful and successful intervention in American foreign policy. The Congressional Black Caucus (CBC) that emerged in the mid-1970s out of growing black political representation, together with TransAfrica, spearheaded the anti-apartheid sanctions campaign that galvanised the country, from churches to college campuses. Over the past two centuries, African-American mobilisation over Africa has been greatest where the intersection of imperialism and whiteness as concrete and symbolic constructs, national and international projects and policies, have been most pronounced and where Africa advocacy is likely to yield significant domestic dividends.

For the CBC, passing anti-apartheid legislation was imperative not only because this was a popular cause in the black community and increasingly throughout the country, it also offered them an opportunity to demonstrate and raise their power and profile in the halls of Congress, which would enable them to advance their domestic agenda. So widespread and powerful did the movement become that Democratic and even Republican politicians scurried to prove their anti-apartheid credentials. In 1986, after nearly two decades of black Congressional representatives sponsoring sanctions bills, the CBC registered a historic victory, when it succeeded in getting the Comprehensive Anti-Apartheid Act passed, over President Ronald Reagan's veto. This marked the apotheosis of African-American influence on US policy towards Africa, which was not to be repeated any time soon. Mandela's release in 1990 and subsequent visits to the United States were widely celebrated as the return of a native son. This was true in other parts of the diaspora, from the Caribbean to Latin America, Europe to Asia.

It is therefore easy to understand the iconic status of Mandela and the overflow of emotion his death provoked in the Pan-African world. The fact that President Obama started his politics as a student at an anti-apartheid rally, and acknowledged his indebtedness to Mandela's exemplary life and struggle, was a poignant thread in the thick ties that bind Africa and the diaspora in the struggle for emancipation from racial tyranny and dehumanisation. For the rest of the world, Mandela's life and legacy resonated deeply because his progressive nationalism was fundamentally a struggle for human freedom and dignity, for social justice and equality. It is not hard to see why that would be universally appealing to a world rocked by the horrendous devastations of the twentieth century, a century of emancipatory, ambiguous and destructive mass movements, of mass culture, mass consumption, mass education and mass media, as well as mass war and mass murder. The genocidal regimes of Hitler and Stalin and the overlords of imperial Europe dominated the first part of that long century. In the second half, the long arc of history swung towards the liberators from the South, such as Gandhi and Mandela, and from the imperial heartlands themselves, such as Martin Luther King. That, I would submit, is Mandela's global historical significance – he was a major player in the most important political movement of the twentieth century, decolonisation. And for that, his place in history is assured.

Notes

1. Nelson Mandela, *Long Walk to Freedom,* New York: Little Brown & Co., 1994.
2. Anthony Sampson, *Mandela: The Authorised Biography,* New York: HarperCollins, 1999.
3. Martin Meredith, *Mandela: A Biography*, London: Simon & Schuster, 2010.
4. Nelson Mandela, Statement from the dock at the opening of the defence case in the Rivonia Trial, 20 April 1964. http://db.nelsonmandela.org/speeches/pub_view.asp?pg=item&ItemID=NMS010&txtstr=prepared%20to%20die

First written 8 December 2013

12

The Zuma Saga and the Postcolonial Reckoning of South Africa

A political earthquake that was unthinkable in 2017 finally consumed President Jacob Zuma in February 2018. He had survived years of outrageous scandals and increasingly deafening calls for his resignation that would have sunk a less wily politician. The last days of the Zuma presidency were characterised by nerve-racking intrigue, impatience, anxiety and great anticipation. Hours before his resignation, the embattled president gave a rambling and defiant speech claiming victimhood and bewilderment at his fate.

But faced by the extraordinary resolve of the ANC, a party he had led for a decade and which had long shielded him from accountability, President Zuma resigned on 14 February rather than face a no-confidence vote the next day. His proverbial nine lives finally ran out as he faced his ninth vote of no confidence, and he was destined to lose. It was a wildly welcomed Valentine's gift to the troubled rainbow nation. His humiliating rendezvous with history marked a befitting end to a treacherous leader who had robbed South Africa of the storied heroism of its protracted anti-apartheid struggle.

Zuma's legendary corruption made him the anti-Mandela, the absolute opposite of the canonised founding president of democratic South Africa who had bestrode the world stage as a moral colossus. He was also the anti-Mbeki, the antithesis of the cerebral architect of the post-apartheid government. President Mandela benevolently left power after one term; President Mbeki was ousted ignominiously before the end of his second term. Mbeki lost to the forces loyal to his former deputy, Jacob Zuma, whom he had fired in 2005 over corruption allegations.

Yet, it should not be forgotten that it was President Mbeki who had brought Zuma from the backwaters of provincial leadership in KwaZulu-Natal to national prominence as his deputy. Like many insecure or calculating African leaders, Mbeki picked an incompetent sidekick who would bring with him his ethnic and factional base of supporters. But his choice later came to bite him and wreck the beloved country. Even so, ten years after Mbeki's ouster the chickens came home to roost for Zuma himself. Unlike Mbeki, who had readily resigned despite his misgivings, Zuma sought to cling to power. Consequently, Mbeki left with his reputation intact, whereas Zuma's was in tatters.

Under President Zuma, South Africa lost its proud halo as a much-beloved and promising post-liberation society and descended into the proverbial postcolonial African state. The myth of South African exceptionalism, deeply etched in the imaginaries of both apartheid and democratic South Africa, finally burst. Zuma exhibited all the unsavoury characteristics of Africa's notorious Big Men: patrimonialism, paranoia, profligacy, populism and pettiness. The litany of his scandals was depressingly long: there was the shady arms deal of the late 1990s; the disgrace of the rape case in 2006; the larceny of Nkandla; and the destructive state capture of Guptagate.

Zuma cultivated criminal patronage networks, oversaw the debasement of state institutions and eroded the integrity of public life and trust in politics. His deeply embarrassing personal and political behaviour robbed the country and its citizens of their hard-won dignity. And he left behind a dismal economic record: 27.7 per cent unemployment; the country's credit rating at junk status; the budget deficit at 4.3 per cent of GDP, the highest since 2009; an anaemic rate of economic growth, which had fallen from 3.1 per cent in 2008 to a projected 0.7 per cent in 2017. Some twenty-six years after the end of apartheid, ten per cent of the population, predominantly white, still controlled 90 per cent of the economy.[1]

In the meantime, inequality deepened, although its racial edges were slightly blunted by the rise of the black middle class. According to a World Bank survey of 154 countries in 2019,[2] South Africa enjoyed the dubious distinction of having the worst Gini coefficient (0.63).

It could be argued that the Zuma saga was part of a much larger story. It reflected the challenges of redressing massive historic inequalities that faced a ruling coalition transitioning from a protracted liberation struggle to democracy, led by a new political class seeking to anchor its political prowess on the levers of economic power. As in other postcolonial societies, the state became a key instrument of accumulation for the political class and aspiring national bourgeoisie.

The political class that was incubated by African nationalism was not the first in South Africa to travel this road. The original robber barons of South Africa go back to Cecil John Rhodes, the mining magnate and Prime Minister of the Cape Colony, who had helped to engineer the South African War of 1899–1902 to seize the goldfields of the Transvaal. In turn, the Afrikaner nationalists, who had lost the war that led to the formation of South Africa in 1910, inherited the political kingdom of settler colonialism. They spent the next several decades turning political power into economic power, through the affirmative action of a racial segregation that placed whites at the top, the expansion of state capital by means of the creation of state enterprises, and discriminatory support for Afrikaner business interests. This culminated in the formalisation of apartheid in 1948, which consolidated South Africa's brutal regime of racial capitalism and the fortunes of the Afrikaner bourgeoisie.

For the new political class that emerged out of the liberation struggle, access to state power offered immense opportunities for personal and collective accumulation. As I argued in an essay commemorating Nelson Mandela's life following his death in December 2013, 'Mandela's Long Walk with Africa' (see Chapter 11 in this volume):

> South Africa's protracted liberation struggle followed the contours of nationalist struggles across the continent. Following the demise of apartheid in 1994, the country was destined to traverse the well-trodden path of postcolonial Africa, notwithstanding the illusions of South African exceptionalism spawned by settler colonial racism, that South Africa was an outpost of European civilisation in darkest Africa.

Presidents Mandela and Mbeki came to embody the limits of South Africa's neoliberal capitalist transition, which was quite galling for the ANC, a party steeped in the promissory rhetoric and aspirations of profound socioeconomic transformation embedded in African nationalism and socialist ideology. Despite economic growth, the expansion of the black middle class and emergence of a black bourgeoisie from the largesse of Black Economic Empowerment policy, poverty and unemployment remained entrenched for the majority of black South Africans. President Mbeki bore the brunt of the growing disaffection, as President Mandela withdrew from public life into the rarefied existence of a saintly icon for a world bereft of great leaders of high moral stature and dignity.

This is the context in which President Mbeki's 'recall' by an increasingly disenchanted ANC alliance occurred in September 2008, about nine months before the end of his second term. They had lost faith in him despite the growth of the economy at an average annual rate of 4.5 per cent, expansion of the black middle class, and his continental leadership as the proponent of the African Renaissance, architect of NEPAD and a key player in transitioning the Organisation of African Unity into the African Union. His vociferous opponents found his apparent elitism and aloof intellectualism unappealing and his HIV/AIDS denialism appalling. They gravitated to his more flamboyant, populist and ill-educated deputy, whom he had dismissed several years earlier. Jacob Zuma was hailed as the 'people's president', who would bring the fruits of freedom to the impoverished and expectant masses.

Thus, for many, President Mbeki's ousting was a cause for celebration, a tribute to party democracy and a harbinger of better days for the masses who had not yet seen the fruits of decolonisation. In short, great hopes were pinned on the

Zuma presidency by radicals in the ruling tripartite alliance of the ANC, the South African Communist Party and Congress of South African Trade Unions. Many local newspapers and elite opinion were critical of Mbeki's removal. They saw it as a sign that the once mighty liberation party had lost its soul under the strains of governing, that it marked the beginning of South Africa's descent into dangerous postcolonial populism.

History was to prove the sceptics right. In fact, before long some of President Zuma's loudest supporters lost faith in his kleptocratic regime. They included the controversial Julius Malema, who served as President of the ANC Youth League from 2008 to 2012, and Zwelinzima Vavi, General-Secretary of COSATU from 1999 to 2015. Both became bitter critics of President Zuma's government. Malema went on to form the Economic Freedom Fighters (EFF) following his expulsion from the ANC.

The events surrounding President Mbeki's exit pointed to the fracturing of the ANC alliance, the sharpening of ideological dissensions within the party, which could no longer be papered over by the uniting heroism of the liberation struggle and the ANC's fabled love of unity. As elsewhere in postcolonial Africa, South Africa was undergoing the complex and challenging transition from liberation politics to postcolonial governance. It was of course not doomed to follow the familiar and tortuous postcolonial path of other African states. As I wrote on 19 September 2008, the day after President Mbeki resigned, in an essay entitled, 'The Fall of Thabo Mbeki: Whither South Africa?',[3] 'The ANC may rue the day they rolled this dangerous political dice and precedent.'

High levels of corruption compounded President Zuma's poor record of performance. The ANC began to wake up from its slumber of complicity as its electoral appeal began to plummet. In the General Election of 2014, it won 62.15 per cent of the vote compared to 65.90 per cent in 2009, which translated into a loss of fifteen seats in the 400-member National Assembly. The real shocker came with the municipal elections of August 2016, which the ANC won with 53.9 per cent of the vote, the lowest level since 1994. The two major opposition parties, the Democratic Alliance (DA) and the EFF, garnered 26.9 per cent and 8.2 per cent, respectively. The opposition parties seized control of three major metropolitan areas, namely, Nelson Mandela Bay, Tshwane and Johannesburg. This was a severe rebuke to the ANC, which seemed poised to shed its urban roots and identity and become a rural party.

The rising political cost of continued support for the reviled Zuma presidency increasingly became apparent to the ANC and its allies. Attempts by the beleaguered president to engineer dynastic succession through the candidacy of his ex-wife, Dr Nkosazana Dlamini Zuma, ruffled more ANC feathers. Despite her impressive credentials as an accomplished politician, a long-serving member of the Cabinet under all South African presidents and chairperson of the African Union, she was narrowly defeated by Cyril Ramaphosa at the ANC's 54th National Conference in December 2017. Two months later, President Zuma finally fell from power, convulsed by the emboldened forces of opposition to his rule in the party he had served for decades and which had long protected him from his litany of transgressions.

President Zuma survived for so long because of the structure of the South African electoral system. It is based on closed-party-list proportional representation, in which the electorate votes for a party rather than an individual candidate. Parliamentary seats are apportioned to each party based on its proportion of the popular vote. Each party then allocates seats to a preselected list of candidates. Under such a system, members of parliament are less beholden to voters than toeing the party line. This gives the party leadership, including the president, enormous powers of control.

But it also means that changes in party leadership quickly translate into loss of political power for the unsuccessful faction and its leaders, in often fiercely contested party elections. In such systems, the presidency of the leading party determines the presidency of the country because it is parliament that elects the president. This is why the ANC's 'recall' is such a powerful weapon because failure to heed it can lead to a parliamentary vote of no confidence. This is what happened in South Africa's dominant party system in 2008 and 2018 with the sudden ouster of presidents Mbeki and Zuma. Thus, Zuma survived for so long because of the electoral and party system. But he was ousted because of South Africa's vibrant political culture as manifested in the values, beliefs, orientations and aspirations of the demos.

As is often the case with moments of major political change, the investment in the new leader as the saviour of the nation tends to be excessive. President Ramaphosa inherited daunting challenges and great expectations. Some placed stock in the fact that he had been President Mandela's preferred successor, that he was a multi-millionaire business tycoon less likely to be corrupt (he was reportedly worth about half a billion dollars) and would therefore be better at managing the economy than his predecessors. Also, as a former trade union leader, he supposedly understood the working class, and as a skilful negotiator he was expected to navigate through the treacherous quicksands of competing interests. Some even talked of a 'Cyril Spring'.

However, others pointed to the skeletons in the new president's closet. There was his unsavoury role in the Marikana massacre in 2012, for which he later apologised and was absolved by an official inquiry. President Ramaphosa was at that time a director of Lonmin, the platinum mining company where a violent police response to a miners' strike had left thirty-four workers dead and scores injured in one of the worst massacres in recent South African history.

President Ramaphosa would be no miracle worker in rescuing South Africa from its structural deformities of uncompetitive corporate monopolies, high unemployment and low skills, deep inequalities and widespread poverty and pervasive corruption. However, he could not do worse than President Zuma, but that was a low bar. Salvaging the country and its economy from the enormous challenges left by the Zuma presidency was likely to take time. Ramaphosa's rise underscored the resilience of the South African democracy, the stubborn independence of its judiciary, and the indefatigability of its expansive and noisy civil society that had brought President Zuma to heel and forced the ANC to reckon with its slide into ignominy, from the proud party of Mandela into the despised cabal of Zuma. Thus, Ramaphosa was part of the desperate rebranding of the ANC ahead of the 2019 General Election. The ANC's political renewal was of course possible, but not guaranteed. What was more certain was the fact that South African society had been reinvigorated, its democratic and developmental hopes given a fresh start.

After the wreckage of the 'Zunami' South Africa recovered some of its lost shine as a political beacon in an increasingly illiberal world of dangerous populisms. The ANC's resolve to oust President Zuma, notwithstanding its belatedness, was unimaginable in the Republican Party in the United States, which had sold its soul to an unprincipled, pompous and perfidious huckster called Donald Trump. It was also unlikely in many African countries, which continued to be held hostage by sleazy dictators who routinely abolished term limits, rigged elections and looted their nations' meagre resources.

The transition in South Africa, following the demise of the Mugabe dictatorship in Zimbabwe and the apparent dismantling of President José Eduardo dos Santos's kleptocratic dynasty in Angola, seemed to suggest the possible resurgence of the winds of democratic change in southern Africa. One hoped such winds did not represent passing clouds destined to dissipate swiftly but that they would spread to the rest of the region and the continent. As we say in southern Africa, indeed, the struggle continues.

Notes

1. Anna Orthofer, 'Wealth Inequality in South Africa: Evidence from survey and tax data', REDI3x3 Working Paper 15, June 2020. http://www.redi3x3.org/sites/default/files/Orthofer%202016%20REDI3x3%20Working%20Paper%2015%20-%20Wealth%20inequality.pdf
2. World Bank, 'The World Bank in South Africa', 10 October, 2019. https://www.worldbank.org/en/country/southafrica/overview
3. Paul Tiyambe Zeleza, 'The Fall of Thabo Mbeki: Whither South Africa?' 20 September 2008. http://www.zeleza.com/blogging/u-s-affairs/fall-thabo-mbeki-whither-south-africa

First written 16 February 2018

13

Zimbabwe's Political Crisis: A Tale of Failed Transitions

President Robert Mugabe, once the celebrated hero of Zimbabwe's protracted liberation struggle who descended into an irascible octogenarian dictator, finally lost power when the army overthrew him on 15 November 2017. He was placed under house arrest together with his much-reviled wife, notoriously known as 'Gucci Grace' or 'DisGrace'. It was an unusually slow-motion and sanitised coup, reflective of the unpopularity of coups in an increasingly democratic Africa. However, it also underscored the fact that President Mugabe's demise arose out of an internecine struggle for power among the ruling elite. This suggested the limits of fundamental change in the immediate post-Mugabe era for the long-suffering masses of Zimbabwe.

In announcing the coup non-coup, the army claimed to be targeting 'criminals' around the doddering president. A day afterwards, the beleaguered leader was even shown meeting the army commander, General Constantino Chiwenga, and two days later he attended a college graduation ceremony. However, no one was fooled that a coup had not taken place. Support for the dreaded autocrat quickly evaporated in the ruling party itself, which called for his resignation and threatened impeachment if he refused. Another three days later, the once fearful nation recovered its repressed collective voice and erupted in euphoric celebration of the end of President Mugabe's authoritarian rule, which had destroyed a proud nation and robbed it of its potential, prosperity and prospects.

The Mugabe era had begun with so much promise in 1980 after a bloody liberation struggle that had lasted almost two decades. It ended thirty-seven years later in almost unimaginable ignominy, leaving behind a trail of economic mismanagement, widespread impoverishment and millions of emigrants, not to mention the intangible but no less palpable wounds of national trauma, humiliation and disillusionment. Much of the commentary in the African and international media largely focused on the epic failures of the president and the outrageous foibles of his avaricious and ambitious wife. Specifically, they concentrated on the spectacular mistake President Mugabe made in firing his once close and loyal confidant, Vice President Emmerson Mnangagwa, in an apparent bid to prepare his wife as his successor.

There can be little doubt that the president and his wife had finally overreached and sealed their fate by unleashing forces that they could no longer control. But the dramatic moment being witnessed in Zimbabwe was rooted in a longer and far more complex history, which transcended the fatal flaws of the president, his wife and the country's other leaders, however critical their respective roles may have been. It could be argued that this particular conjuncture in Zimbabwe represented the confluence of three failed transitions.

Zimbabwe's Problematic Transition

The first was the problematic transition from the liberation struggle to a developmental postcolonial state arising out of the country's decolonisation in the era of neoliberalism. The second was the challenge of shifting from an authoritarian to a pluralistic order when the winds of democratisation, for the 'second independence', began blowing across the continent. The third concerned the management of intergenerational contestations for power in anticipation of the post-Mugabe era.

For many Africans of my generation and our parents' generation, Zimbabwe occupies a special place in our collective political imaginary, as do other countries that also achieved their freedom through prolonged wars of independence, such as Algeria, Angola, Mozambique and South Africa. We remember and cherish the heroism of the liberation struggle against settler colonialism, the immense hopes of reconstruction and social transformation for the masses promised by the liberation movements and their 'socialist' ideologies. The high costs of the liberation struggles spawned great expectations of the future, which were invested in the larger-than-life figures of liberation movement leaders such as Robert Mugabe. But the transition from liberation struggle to national governance proved much more difficult than anticipated.

In the case of Zimbabwe, a plethora of explanations were advanced as the challenges of the transition became increasingly evident. Zimbabwe descended into a dictatorship and violently suppressed the opposition. This included a vicious clampdown in 1983 called Operation Gukurahundi, in Matabeleland, the stronghold of the Ndebele minority ethnic group and the main opposition party, the Zimbabwe African People's Union (ZAPU), led by Joshua Nkomo. An estimated 20,000 people were killed. My family then lived in the region's largest and the country's second-largest city, Bulawayo, where they witnessed the persecution. In 1987, ZAPU agreed to join the ruling party, the Zimbabwe African National Union–Patriotic Front (ZANU–PF).

To the ideologues of the regime and its ardent external supporters, Zimbabwe was a victim of an orchestrated plot by western countries, led by the former colonial master, Britain, bent on frustrating the country's progress. Evidence indeed abounds of western and British complicity and duplicity in Zimbabwe's difficult transition from a racist settler society to a postcolonial state and society. Any attempt to reform the society, especially to undertake radical land reform and redistribute resources and opportunities, was greeted with vitriol in the western media.

President Mugabe and the new regime's socialist inclinations bore the brunt of venomous and thinly veiled racist attacks. Lest we forget, the 1980s witnessed the renewal of the Cold War by the post-Keynesian and unrepentantly right-wing regimes of Prime Minister Margaret Thatcher in the United Kingdom and President Ronald Reagan in the United States. At the same time, the Zimbabwe government and its army of supporters in the Pan-African world and left-wing circles used the rhetoric of nationalism and socialism to deflect criticism against the Mugabe regime. They still do, pointing to any morsel of success to excuse the excesses of the regime.

In the 1980s, during which Zimbabwe achieved considerable progress in economic growth and social development, it was possible to mask the regime's creeping political intolerance and rising economic incompetence. Indeed, transformation and tyranny reinforced each other as the country entered its second decade of independence in the 1990s. The regime became more autocratic and adopted a more radical land reform programme as it faced a growing and credible political opposition coalesced around the Movement for Democratic Change (MDC), and as its capacity to manage let alone rescue the economy from its inherited structural deformities declined.

A more comprehensive accounting of Zimbabwe's economic and political crises from the turn of the 1990s would have to consider the contexts and conjunctures, processes and patterns of Zimbabwe's trajectory and transition from settler colonialism to a developmental postcolonial state. The country's current crisis was rooted in the failures of that transition. As with any postcolonial state, the new Zimbabwe government in 1980 was confronted by the complex challenges of turning the triple dreams of *independence* – nation-building, development and democracy – into reality. And having waged a protracted war of liberation, which entailed the mobilisation and politicisation of the peasantry, these dreams went beyond the aspirations of the urban elites and working class for the neocolonial transformation that had bedevilled decolonisation elsewhere on the continent.

But unlike many countries that had achieved their independence in the 1950s and 1960s, Zimbabwe attained its independence during a period characterised by global economic crisis and the ascendancy of neoliberalism. The first severely limited the primary commodity- and export-driven economic growth enjoyed by many of the newly independent countries in the 1960s, while the second entailed the 'rolling back' of the state in severely curtailing the developmentalist ambitions of the new government.

To be sure, in the early post-independence years Zimbabwe's record of achievement in the provision of social services, especially education and health care, was very impressive. But it was unsustainable following the imposition of Structural Adjustment Programmes (SAPs), which – as in much of Africa – took a heavy toll on the economy, particularly in social services and formal and public sector employment.

In fact, the austerities of SAPs galvanised the increasingly pauperised urban middle classes and the rural masses still awaiting the benefits of decolonisation into protests and agitation, which crystallised into struggles for democratisation, for the 'second independence'. If structural adjustment dented the revolutionary credentials and developmentalist capacities of the Zimbabwean state, the struggles that the SAPs engendered diluted the state's democratic claims and exposed its authoritarianism.

The monopoly of power enjoyed by the liberation movement, notwithstanding its fierce internal conflicts, began to crack in the 1990s as the working and professional classes in the cities, the weakest link in the liberation movement, turned into a vocal civil society demanding the full rights of political citizenship to promote civil liberties and protect their declining economic fortunes. However, structural adjustment was not the source of all the problems for the political class and the deformed state they had inherited from the white Rhodesians.

The liberation movement had inherent spatial and social contradictions, which became increasingly evident. The spatial divisions were between the rural and urban areas as well as regions (as between Matabeleland and Mashonaland) and within each region. The merger of ZAPU and ZANU–PF in 1987, after the violent campaign in Matabeleland, sought to defuse the regional tensions, although they did not disappear. In fact, they mutated into new forms.

No less critical were the urban-rural divisions, in so far as it was the rural peasants who had largely fought in the liberation war but the leadership and immediate beneficiaries of independence were the urban professional elites. The latter had a class interest in consolidating their power by promoting their accumulation of wealth, to fashion an economic base for the political power they had acquired.

The biggest opportunities for wealth accumulation were in land – real estate in the cities and farms in the countryside. Land was of course central to the peasantry, the backbone of the liberation struggle, and to the nationalist memories of violent dispossession by the forces of settler colonialism, as well as to the imaginary of independence. But land resettlement for the peasantry, especially for the poor peasantry, was not pursued aggressively until the late 1990s. This has often been attributed to the constraints imposed by constitutional safeguards of the Lancaster House Agreement that favoured market-based land transactions and resettlement. Further, a shortage of resources and the failure of the British government to provide sufficient funds to honour its pledges have been faulted.

It would seem that at stake were also the accumulative interests of powerful segments of the political class. They wanted the land for themselves. This balancing act – land for the masses and for the aspiring national bourgeoisie – found succour in the increasingly empty ideological language of socialism. This rhetoric was out of touch with not only the realities in Zimbabwe and the interests of the political class itself but also with the intolerant demands of neoliberalism and structural adjustment and the unfolding demise of global socialism.

Struggles for Democratisation

By the late 1990s, the comrades in power could no longer fool their beloved masses in the rural areas and the restive armies of unemployed educated youths in the cities. The workers flexing their industrial muscles discovered a new political voice through mushrooming civil society organisations and the MDC. Thus, in the course of the 1990s, Zimbabwe faced another complex and challenging transition arising out of the emergence of a powerful pro-democracy movement coalesced around the MDC: how to manage the transition to democratisation.

The struggles for the 'second independence' were of course raging across the continent and different modalities of transition to democracy were taking place. In short, the 1980s and 1990s represented an exceptionally complicated moment in Africa's protracted struggles for freedom. It was a moment driven by complex, sometimes contradictory and rapidly changing factors spawned by unpredictable events and new social movements and visions, anchored in the specific histories, social structures and conditions of each country. National, regional and international forces converged unevenly and inconsistently and economic and political crises reinforced each other, altering the terrain of state–civil society relationships, the structures of governance and the claims of citizenship.

In several one-party states, from Kenya to Malawi, the incumbent regimes legalised opposition parties and authorised multiparty elections through amendments to the existing Constitutions. The opposition forces were not strong enough to force regime capitulation, but had raised the costs of authoritarian governance, making it unsustainable. In other countries, especially in parts of Francophone Africa and South Africa, the transition to democracy was effected through national conferences in which members of the political class and the elites of civil society came together to forge a new political and constitutional order. There was also the path of managed transition pursued by military regimes, which tried to oversee and tightly control the process and pace of political reform, in which military dictators replaced their uniforms with ill-fitting civilian attire.

None of these modalities fit Zimbabwe. The country was certainly not a military dictatorship and it adhered to the trappings of constitutional pluralism. The winds of democracy had begun blowing hardly a decade after the country had achieved its independence. Compared to the countries that had gained independence in the 1950s, 1960s and 1970s, the reservoir of post-independence euphoria was still considerable and had not dissipated. Also, given the freshness of the memories of the liberation struggle, the ruling party still enjoyed an overwhelming legitimacy for power.

Clearly, liberation war credentials elevated claims to power and served as a powerful sanction against opposition claimants who could be dismissed or discredited as accomplices of the white settlers and western interests. The government and its ideologues increasingly attacked the MDC on these grounds. In fact, in 2002 and 2008 some army leaders openly declared that they could not salute a leader who had not participated in the liberation struggle. This made Zimbabwe's transition to democracy in the late 1990s and early 2000s, when other countries were making the transition, exceptionally difficult.

The problematic dynamics of the two transitions – from settler colonialism to postcolonial governance and from the commandist politics of the liberation movement to the democratic politics of a post-liberation society – reinforced each other as the new century unfolded. A central feature of the unfolding crisis of governance and development in Zimbabwe was the implementation of a radical land reform programme from 1998 and especially after the government lost the constitutional referendum in early 2000 by 55 per cent to 45 per cent.

Zimbabwe's growing conundrum, as a former settler colony in search of a viable future and looking into the mirror it held to South Africa, attracted intense political emotions. Both countries captured most poignantly, indeed painfully, the highly racialised, exploitative and abusive encounter in modern times between Europe and Africa that had been spawned by European imperialism and colonialism. It is not surprising that both the foes and friends of the Mugabe regime looked to South Africa to provide international leadership on the 'Zimbabwe question'. To some in South Africa, the Zimbabwe crisis served as a warning of the dangers of African nationalist demagoguery; to others, an impetus for the country to undertake extensive land reforms and socioeconomic transformation if it wanted to avoid Zimbabwe's fate.

The aims of the land reform programme were multiple and varied: to resettle more peasants, and rekindle ZANU–PF's revolutionary credentials both locally and regionally – locally, with a new generation, including the unemployed youths who were too young to be war veterans, in whose name the land seizures were undertaken; and regionally, where the ANC coalition governing a reformist post-apartheid South Africa had abandoned any pretensions to a project of revolutionary socioeconomic transformation. The radical land reform programme sought to bolster ZANU–PF and weaken the MDC ideologically and operationally, by undermining the latter's nationalist claims and character – still a compelling card in the post-settler society – and its appeal in the rural areas, where the bulk of the population lived.

A little-remarked aspect of the white settler farm invasions during this period is that they led to the displacement of tens of thousands of workers from neighbouring countries, especially Malawi and Mozambique, some of whom had been in Zimbabwe for more than a generation. In effect, the rural areas were being emptied of both European and African settlers. The urban areas also boasted large populations who could trace their origins to neighbouring countries, which may partly have driven the attempts to disenfranchise urban residents, who constituted the backbone of the MDC.

Thus, a new form of Zimbabwean citizenship was being constructed based on nativist or autochthonous rather than residential claims. This underscores what was at the heart of the Zimbabwean conundrum. How to restructure, develop and democratise a former settler colony that relied on migrant labour from within and without, which necessitated massive land alienation and left behind legacies of high structural unemployment, racial disenfranchisement and dispossession, and militarism and the use of political violence as weapons of both control and liberation. In short: how to construct an inclusive citizenship and subject state power and the political class to democratic accountability.

By the end of the 1990s, both rural and urban discontent were growing. Indeed, the rural areas bore the brunt of economic decline engendered by the draconian regime of structural adjustment imposed with missionary zeal by the gendarmes of global capitalism – the World Bank and the International Monetary Fund. This was compounded by political terror as the increasingly besieged regime sought to shore up its dwindling legitimacy and tattered revolutionary credentials by tightening its grip on the peasantry, its symbolic and substantive basis of power. The costs of the economic crisis, as manifested in food shortages and the politicisation of food relief efforts, finally broke the patience of the peasantry.

Connecting the two, the peasantry and the working classes, the rural and the urban areas and the country's other spatial and social divides, including the ethnicised divisions between the old political geographies of Mashonaland and Matabeleland, which the Mugabe regime had manipulated to weaken the opposition and maintain its iron grip on power, was the draconian Operation Murambatsvina. Officially translated as Operation Clean Up, but literally translated as 'getting rid of the filth', through it the government sought to drain the cities, including Harare, the capital, of political opposition. The operation was launched in 2005 and affected more than two million people. The bulk of the MDC's parliamentary seats from previous elections were located in the cities.

This criminal evacuation programme, which was widely condemned within Zimbabwe and internationally, including by the United Nations, led to the destruction of the informal sector in the cities and the displacement of hundreds of thousands of people, many of whom flocked to the increasingly destitute rural areas. This not only exacerbated rural poverty, but also helped dissolve some of the social and political boundaries, both real and imagined, between the rural and urban areas and dwellers, which raised *national* consciousness and reinforced opposition to the former liberation heroes turned into predators in power.

But escalating violence, intimidation and voting irregularities enabled ZANU–PF to win the parliamentary elections of 2000 and 2005. Predictably, monitors from the Southern African Development Community (SADC) pronounced the elections 'free and fair', whereas western monitors cried foul. The elections of 2005 were more violent than those of 2000, an indication to some of the continued popularity of ZANU–PF. In reality, they reflected the effectiveness of ZANU–PF political terror and the ineffectiveness of the MDC, its inability to articulate a credible message of national transformation.

The violence and polarisation became even more evident in the election of March 2008. Preliminary indications were that the MDC was poised for victory both in the parliamentary and presidential elections. The government unleashed massive intimidation against the opposition and their supporters and perpetrated voter fraud, which provoked widespread condemnation at home and abroad. Both SADC and the United Nations tried to intervene.

It took more than a month before the final results were declared after being doctored to prevent a run-off – the winner needed more than 50 per cent for outright victory. Finally, on 2 May, the Zimbabwe Electoral Commission announced that the MDC leader, Morgan Tsvangirai, had received 47.9 per cent of the vote, trailed by President Mugabe who had received 43.2 per cent; the rest had gone to minor candidates. For the parliamentary elections, the MDC secured 100 seats and the breakaway MDC-Mutambara ten seats, while the ruling ZANU–PF garnered ninety-nine seats. In the Senate, ZANU–PF claimed fifty-seven seats, MDC twenty-four and MDC-Mutambara twelve.

Despite international condemnation and interventions, violence and intimidation against the opposition continued, which saw dozens of people killed. The MDC decided to withdraw from the second round of presidential elections scheduled for 27 June 2008. President Mugabe won 85.51 per cent of the vote in a much-reduced turnout placed at 42.37 per cent. He was sworn in immediately after the results were announced. The regional bloc and the African Union called for a Government of National Unity (GNU) between ZANU–PF and the MDC, which was eventually formed in early 2009 and under which Morgan Tsvangirai became prime minister.

It was a bloated government with two deputy vice presidents, two deputy prime ministers, thirty-one ministers, eight ministers of state, twenty deputy ministers and nine provincial governors. Its large size was not matched by its efficacy, nor were the political divisions overcome. Indeed, as with most marriages of convenience, it was a fragile, acrimonious and temporary union that crumbled several years later.

To be sure, under the GNU, the economy recovered from the economic crisis of the 2000s that had been characterised by endemic shortages of goods, hyperinflation measured in the trillions, the collapse of educational institutions and health facilities, massive unemployment and migrations of an estimated three to five million to South Africa and other neighbouring countries, as well as Europe and North America.

The GNU benefitted ZANU–PF and fatally weakened the MDC. Governments of national unity tend to enervate opposition parties as governments in waiting, remove checks and balances and turn parliament into a rubber stamp for the executive. They also tend to marginalise civil society organisations as critical players in so far as GNU agreements are usually confined to the contending political parties. Further, elections as vehicles for popular participation, political choice and accountable governance are undermined.

In short, critics complained that the GNU in Zimbabwe had undermined democracy by rewarding power-hungry politicians from the ruling and opposition parties, sabotaged political accountability and the pursuit and promotion of human rights, and had given the country a false sense of stability and progress. In the daily grind of political compromises and the country's pervasive culture of corruption that soon infected the MDC itself, during its five years of power-sharing the party became diminished as it lost its political innocence in the popular imagination. The GNU whitewashed President Mugabe's wily dictatorship, which pocketed its achievements and left the untested and outmanoeuvred MDC tarnished with the debris of the two unfinished transitions.

In the election of 31 July 2013 under the new Constitution approved in a referendum in March 2013, the MDC suffered an inglorious defeat. ZANU–PF won 159 seats in the National Assembly to the MDC's twenty-one (and the two parties won thirty-seven and twenty-one seats for women, respectively) and thirty-seven to twenty-one seats in the Senate. In the presidential elections, President Mugabe was returned to office with 61.09 per cent of the vote to Mr Tsvangirai's 34.94 per cent. Despite protestations from the latter and his supporters, as well as from some international observers, the African Union declared the elections 'free, honest and credible'. African leaders and other autocratic fellow travellers around the world congratulated the reinvigorated hoary autocrat of Zimbabwe. The AU even honoured him by appointing him its Chairperson in 2015–2016.

Divisions in the Ruling Party

The political respite that came with the containment of the MDC proved short-lived. Assured of its political dominance, ZANU–PF turned inwards and intraparty contestations over the post-Mugabe era heated up. As in many other dictatorships in postcolonial Africa, openly discussing the president's frailty and demise were taboo. However, everyone knew the old man was on his last legs as evidence mounted of his growing physical and mental infirmity. Predictably, the struggle centred on the position of the vice presidency in which intra-Shona, ethnic, generational and gender cleavages reared their ugly heads. Ideology had long ceased to be a factor, notwithstanding the invocations of tired socialist rhetoric and empty obeisance to protecting and promoting the 'revolution'.

The intra-ZANU conflict increasingly centred on the war veterans, and the post-liberation generations coalesced around two key protagonists. On the one hand was the then seventy-five-year-old vice president, Emmerson Mnangagwa, the cunning and ruthless 'Crocodile', infamous for orchestrating the Matabeleland massacres of 1983. On the other was the Generation 40 faction of post-liberation apparatchiks and looters beholden to the president's wife, the combative fifty-two-year-old Grace Mugabe, who had since acquired an insatiable hunger for power in addition to her earlier shopping addiction.

Both sought to oust Joice Mujuru, a renowned war veteran in her own right, as vice president, which happened in December 2014. Soon after, Mujuru was expelled from ZANU–PF. Mnangagwa and Grace Mugabe fell into openly bitter jostling for power within ZANU–PF and for the president's ear. The latter enjoyed the upper hand of marital intimacy and the support of the G40, while the former had the support of the war veterans and, most crucially, the military.

The reckoning came following the ousting of Mnangagwa as vice president on 8 November 2017. For the military and political elite that had accumulated vast wealth in an increasingly impoverished country and enjoyed political power for decades, the prospects of Grace Mugabe and the G40 supplanting them was anathema. They struck back on 15 November. The hapless president quickly discovered that the weary population was not on his side as it marched in the streets of Harare with an ecstasy not seen since independence. Even his party seemed more interested in protecting its hold on power and economic interests than in protecting him. Party branches passed no-confidence votes in him and an emergency meeting was called to formally remove him as party leader. As with many dictators, power whooshed out of the once-beloved and long-dreaded president's hands like air out of a deflating balloon.

The immediate trigger of President Mugabe's fall came from the regime's failure to manage the transition from the nation's octogenarian founder to a successor and new political dispensation. The fratricidal conflict in ZANU–PF between the two generations meant that the future of the country of my birth, whose struggles for liberation I cherish and whose bright future I yearn for, would be a troubled one.

The vicious struggle between the two factions was less about charting a more productive future for the country and more about safeguarding their ill-gotten wealth built on the deepening poverty of millions of workers and peasants, not to mention the immiseration of significant sections of the middle classes. In short, both factions had profiteered from President Mugabe's political repression and economic plunder.

In 1980, the people of Zimbabwe believed passionately in the promises of the liberation struggle. Over the next decades, they were progressively betrayed by the failures of the transitions to build an integrated, inclusive, innovative and sustainable democratic and developmental state and society. However, this is a resilient nation richly endowed with human talent and natural resources. It will rise from the downward spiral of Mugabe's dysfunctional regime. But it will not be easy or happen any time soon.

Written 18 November 2017

14

Kenya's Election Watershed and the Promise of African Democracy

On 1 September 2017, the Supreme Court of Kenya issued its much-anticipated decision on the presidential election held on 8 August. By a majority 4–2 decision, the court annulled the re-election of incumbent President Uhuru Kenyatta. The court declared that the presidential election 'was not conducted in accordance with the Constitution and the applicable laws'. Specifically, the Supreme Court cited irregularities and illegalities committed by the Independent Electoral and Boundaries Commission (IEBC) in the transmission of the results and stated that this had affected the integrity of the election. It ordered a fresh presidential poll within sixty days.

As was to be expected, the court judgment was greeted by celebration and condemnation in the opposition and ruling party strongholds, respectively. Early indications were that there was some disquiet in business circles as the stock market and Kenyan shilling tumbled immediately following the announcement of the court decision. Crucially, the political leaders and media pundits respected and accepted the court ruling, notwithstanding their predictable disagreements and differences.

This was a watershed development in Kenyan and African political history. It was the first time that a presidential election in an African country had been revoked by the judiciary (and the fourth time in the world).[1]

This development compared in its significance, since the dawn of Kenya's 'second independence', to the elections of 2002 that had marked a milestone in Kenya's protracted and bumpy road to democracy. It effectively represented a landmark consummation of the new democratic Constitution of 2010, which had emerged out of the unprecedented 2007–2008 post-election violence that had rocked this lovely and proud nation.

Thus, the decision by the Supreme Court demonstrated the maturing of Kenyan democracy, the consolidation of a functioning democracy. It underscored the independence of the judiciary, the growing strength of public institutions and deepening national commitment to transparency, accountability and the rule of law. It gave Kenya a priceless opportunity to restore public faith and trust in the judiciary, one of the three critical organs of government and good governance. Trust in public institutions is indispensable for national cohesion and imperative for sustainable development.

The next sixty days promised to provide a supreme test for the Kenyan political class and civil society, of whether the country and its demos would move forward or stall in its complex and exacting journey of constructing an integrated, inclusive, innovative and sustainable democratic developmental state and society. There was little doubt that passions would run high in the next two months of new presidential campaigns. The danger lay in allowing heated party competition to degenerate into violent political polarisation. The two main contestants, President Uhuru Kenyatta and Raila Odinga, understood the high stakes for the future of their beloved country. In their initial remarks after the court issued its judgment, they rightly stressed the need for peace.

On the day the judgment was made many issues remained unclear. Would the election be conducted by the same IEBC as currently constituted? The court had twenty-one days to give its detailed judgment, while the new elections had to be held in sixty days. Did that give enough time for the current or reconstituted IEBC to make the necessary corrective actions, should they be required? Would the contestation be confined to the presidential election, or would it open a Pandora's Box of endless and costly litigation over the other offices contested in the general elections – for county governors, members of county assemblies, senators, special women representatives and members of parliament?

The court's decision also shone a spotlight on the dubious role of international election monitors, including those from the European Union, the Commonwealth, the African Union and the USA's Carter Center, which were quick to endorse the results of the presidential elections. Altogether, there were at least ten international observer missions that largely hailed the elections as free and fair. A similarly blinkered view was echoed in the so-called international media, as evident in an editorial in *The New York Times*, which stated:

> Kenya's national elections last Tuesday were closely watched around the world, less for the results than for the threat of violence that has marred past elections. Barack Obama, whose father was a Kenyan, had been among those urging the county's leaders to 'reject violence and incitement.' That has not happened … Mr. Odinga has once again fanned the embers of ethnic strife. That is disgraceful and unnecessary. International monitors from the African Union, the United States and Europe said they witnessed no foul play … All observers have urged Mr. Odinga and other losing candidates to refer any allegations of fraud to the commission and the courts.[2]

There were of course honourable exceptions, such as the long critical article on the Kenyan elections in the 8 August issue of *The New York Review of Books,* in which Helen Epstein bemoaned the widespread cover-up.

> Kenya is notorious for corruption, and virtually all prior elections had been marred by rigging ... When Kenya's electoral commission announced on August 11 that President Uhuru Kenyatta had won another five-year term with over 54 percent of the vote, observer teams ... commended the electoral process and said they'd seen no evidence of significant fraud. Congratulations poured in from around the world and Donald Trump praised the elections as fair and transparent. But not everyone was happy. Raila Odinga, leader of the opposition National Super Alliance party, or NASA, declared the election a sham as soon as the results began coming in ... Signs that something weird was going on emerged well before the election ... Election day brought more problems.[3]

Interestingly, soon after the Supreme Court announced its decision, diplomats in Kenya representing two dozen western countries praised 'the Court's independent review', for demonstrating 'Kenya's resilient democracy and commitment to the rule of law'.[4] They were trying to salvage the discredited western democracy monitoring enterprise.

Kenya's civil society organisations were more divided in their evaluation of the integrity of the elections. They, too, had lessons to learn. Clearly, the custodians of democracy in Africa could not and would not be outsiders, especially not those from Euro-America whose ideological and geopolitical interests often trumped commitments to democracy in the global South. Africa carries the additional burden of racist stereotyping and denigration in the western imaginary. International organisations, including the United Nations, cannot guarantee African democratisation any more than the Trusteeship Council of the League of Nations promoted African decolonisation.

Democracy in Africa can be promoted only by the five estates within each country – the executive, legislative and judicial branches of government properly and effectively discharging their respective roles, as well as the media and civil society who maintain eternal vigilance of hard-won democratic freedoms, rights and responsibilities. The sixth estate, comprised of subregional and regional agencies, is potentially another critical underwriter of democratisation, as long as its agencies desist from the age-old dishonourable habit of electoral rubber-stamping for the president rather than the people's Pan-African solidarity.

The lessons for the rest of the continent were clear. I suspect that many in Gabon, Zambia, Uganda, Burundi, Rwanda and Angola, to mention just a few countries that held elections in 2017, wished they were Kenyans. I believed large numbers of Africans at home and in the diaspora would hail Kenya for this historic decision. Unfortunately, many lived in countries without robust judiciaries to protect the citizenry from electoral irregularities and illegalities. The Supreme Court in Kenya reassured the country's citizens of the integrity of their votes.

The lessons of the Kenyan elections went beyond Africa. Numerous comments in *The Washington Post*[5] on the annulment of the Kenyan presidential election compared the USA elections unfavourably to Kenya's. Since 2000, American elections have given its people and the world two presidents who lost the popular vote. The first was President Bush, who was crowned in 2000 from the Hanging Chads of Florida by a highly politicised and partisan Supreme Court. The second was the incomparably incompetent and unpopular President Trump who ascended to office in 2017 thanks to the outmoded and undemocratic system of the electoral college. He lost the popular vote by nearly three million to his opponent, Senator Hillary Clinton. Neither outcome would be possible in Kenya's electoral system, which requires the winner to garner 50+1 and 25 per cent of votes in at least twenty-four of the country's forty-seven counties, as demonstrated by an independent and non-partisan Supreme Court.

The first day of September 2017 would be remembered as the day Kenya's democratic Constitution became fully alive. The rest of the continent could only hope for their own moments of progressive constitutional, electoral and political reckoning. Thus, whatever the future held for the new presidential election, Kenya had already made history for itself and for our democratically challenged continent. Perhaps the country that invented the electronic banking system of Mpesa would export the model of accountable, transparent, credible, free and fair elections undergirded by a strong and independent judiciary and vibrant civil society to struggling democracies and stubborn dictatorships on the continent.

Notes

1. Joe Ombuor, 'Kenya third country in the world and first in Africa to annul a presidential election', *The Standard,* 2 September 2017. https://www.standardmedia.co.ke/article/2001253337/kenya-third-country-in-the-world-and-first-in-africa-to-annul-a-presidential-election#
2. The *New York Times,* 'The Real Suspense in Kenya', The Editorial Board, 13 August 2017. https://www.nytimes.com/2017/08/13/opinion/the-real-suspense-in-kenya.html
3. Helen Epstein, 'Kenya: The Election & the Cover-Up', *The New York Review of Books,* 30 August 2017. https://www.nybooks.com/daily/2017/08/30/kenya-the-election-and-the-cover-up/
4. Jacob Ngetich, '20 Western Envoys Welcome Supreme Court Ruling', *The Standard,* 2 September 2017. https://www.standardmedia.co.ke/kenya/article/2001253340/20-western-envoys-welcome-supreme-court-ruling-call-for-fair-election
5. Rael Ombuor and Paul Schemm, 'Kenya's Supreme Court annuls presidential election result for irregularities, orders new vote', *The Washington Post,* 1 September 2020. https://www.washingtonpost.com/world/kenya-supreme-court-cancels-presidential-election-result-for-irregularities-orders-new-election/2017/09/01/ceee81d6-8ef4-11e7-84c0-02cc069f2c37_story.h

First written 1 September 2017

15

Malawi's Political Earthquakes

Nullification of the Presidential Election

The much-anticipated ruling of Malawi's Constitutional Court was sombrely delivered to an anxious, tense and polarised nation on 3 February 2020. In a unanimous decision, the court nullified the hotly contested and rigged presidential election of 21 May 2019. It was a brilliant legal victory for the opposition parties and a profound political watershed for the country.

The level of public anticipation and apprehension was so high that in many parts of the country businesses, schools, offices and public transport were closed or suspended. It felt like a national holiday. Like millions of spellbound Malawians at home and in the diaspora, I was glued to the radio. It made watching the impeachment trial of President Trump in the US Senate, where the Republicans save two had refused to allow additional witnesses and documents, seem farcical in comparison. So much for mature and emerging democracies!

In a lengthy judgment comprising more than 500 pages, but summarised in a proceeding that was broadcast live to an anxious nation, the court noted that it was alive to the enormous importance of the case. This was the first time in the country's history that a presidential election had been subjected to a court dispute and such a historic ruling. The court stressed that the Constitution called for an open, transparent and accountable government through the democratic choice exercised by its citizens. The Constitution under the Bill of Rights guaranteed and entrenched the right to vote.

It affirmed that elections must be managed with all due diligence and integrity and conducted in a fair and transparent manner. Clearly, this had not been the case with the 21 May 2019 presidential election. In more than ten hours of reading the summary judgment, the court systematically demolished the arguments of the respondents. It had identified substantial compromise of citizens' voting rights and of the principles and processes of free and fair elections.

The magnitude of the irregularities and anomalies was so widespread, systematic and grave that the results had been compromised and could not be trusted as a true reflection of the will of the voters.

In a meticulous and masterly exhibition of jurisprudence and judgement, the judges painstakingly outlined and analysed all the issues in contention and the applicable laws, and interrogated relevant legal precedents from other countries. The defence of the respondents against the charges of the petitioners was left in tatters. They lost on the important issues of proof in an election case and the processes of election management. The court found that the Malawi Electoral Commission (MEC) had committed multiple breaches against several pertinent sections of the Constitution and had even created illegal processes, thereby raising serious doubts about the validity of the election results. In its ruling, it called for the appointment of new officers for the Commission.

On 27 May 2019 the deeply compromised Electoral Commission had declared the incumbent – Professor Peter Arthur Mutharika of the ruling Democratic People's Party (DPP) – the winner, with 38.57 per cent of the popular vote. Dr Lazarus Chakwera of the Malawi Congress Party (MCP), the age-old Independence Party, had garnered 35.41 per cent, and Dr Saulos Chilima had garnered 20.24 per cent for the insurgent United Transformation Movement (UTM), formed in 2018 by the country's former vice president. Four other minor candidates shared the rest.

The results had provoked angry nationwide protests led by the followers of the two main opposition parties and civil society organisations, most notably the Human Rights Defenders Coalition (HRDC), which paralysed the major cities in the months that followed. The protesters had accused the DPP and MEC, led by Dr Jane Ansah, of gross electoral fraud. They called for President Mutharika and Dr Ansah to be ousted, the latter under the #AnsahMustFall campaign, and demanded fresh elections. DPP supporters responded with counter-demonstrations, state-sanctioned intimidation and support rallies for the beleaguered Chair of the MEC, led by women functionaries of the regime. Sporadic violence broke out in several areas.

The country was on fire, staring into the abyss of ungovernability. Public order virtually collapsed in some parts of the country as the discredited police lost their authority. Even the president could no longer travel freely to many parts of the country outside his ethnic laager, including the capital, Lilongwe, without a convoy of heavily armed military vehicles. The popularity of the Malawi Defence Force had risen and a few misguided elements even seemed to yearn for the dangerous respite of a military coup. Predictably, businesses and the economy were shuttered.

The other institution in which the disaffected and inflamed masses had placed their political desires and demands for electoral justice was the judiciary. Within a week after the general elections were held, the two opposition parties had filed separate petitions with the High Court for the nullification of the presidential elections over alleged irregularities and mismanagement of the electoral system.

The odour of electoral malfeasance was detected days after the election, as stories of rigging started circulating, buttressed by delays in announcing the results. Soon, a new word entered Malawi's political vocabulary: Tipp-Ex, a brand of correction fluid which had been used to alter vote results sheets. The elections had been Tipp-exed, Mutharika was the Tipp-Ex president and the overwrought social media went into overdrive. On 25 May the UTM called for the nullification of the election, while the DPP requested the immediate release of the election results and the MCP applied for a judicial review of the presidential election results from several districts and constituencies.

The MEC proceeded first to release the results of the parliamentary election and briefly withheld results of the presidential vote for a few more days, which raised much suspicion. The influential and quasi-religious body, the Public Affairs Committee (PAC), issued a press statement on 30 May 2019 stating categorically that the elections lacked credibility. The next day, on 31 May, the two main opposition parties filed separate election cases, which were consolidated by the High Court four days later because they were similar.

Efforts by lawyers for the Electoral Commission and the ruling party first to dismiss the case and later to extend the time for disclosures of documents and information by the second respondent (the Malawi Electoral Commission) to the second petitioner (Lazarus Chakwera of the MCP) were curtailed. The case was referred to select High Court judges sitting as a Constitutional Court (such a court does not exist as a separate entity). The court also dismissed several applications by the Attorney General in August and September for sanctions and an injunction against political demonstrations.

Thus began the months-long election case that was broadcast live and transfixed the troubled nation. The hearings commenced on 8 August and ended on 20 December 2019, a duration of sixty-one days, and according to the Constitution judgment had to be rendered within forty-five days. The third of February 2020 marked the forty-fifth day. The court hearings, with all their gravity and levity, enraptured the population as no other event since the transition from the one-party dictatorship to multiparty democracy in the early 1990s. They raised national awareness about election laws and processes and democratic rights and responsibilities. The country's crass and corrupt ruling cabal was exposed for all its impunity, iniquity and ineptitude.

Some lawyers and pundits were applauded, others damaged their reputations with their mediocrity and mendacity. Similarly, some witnesses were celebrated and others were ridiculed ignominiously. The latter included an insufferably arrogant cabinet minister who flaunted a fake doctorate (unearned accolades are so beloved by African elites), but couldn't mention his alma mater, a term he even did not seem to know. In the meantime, large demonstrations and counter-demonstrations continued.

The country seemed to be spiralling out of control and the acrimony between the ruling and opposition parties intensified. The PAC called for dialogue on the electoral stalemate, to no avail. Appeals for an open and inclusive dialogue by the foreign diplomatic missions of Germany, Ireland, Japan, Norway, the United Kingdom and the United States also proved ineffectual.

The court hearings systematically revealed blatant manipulation and mismanagement of the electoral process and system. The submissions by the lawyers of the opposition parties vigorously argued that the Electoral Commission had breached its duty and infringed on the petitioners' and citizens' political rights under various sections of the Constitution. They concluded, 'The irregularity and fraud in the elections were substantial and significant that they affected the integrity of the elections.'[1]

The petitioners sought the nullification of the presidential election of 21 May 2019 and the declaration of Peter Mutharika as president-elect as invalid, null and void. In their lengthy submissions, the respondents accused the petitioners of relying on hearsay evidence and claimed, 'There were no irregularities or other factors that beset the election and that even if any were there and they did not affect the result of the election.'[2] They requested dismissal of the petitions with costs.

In January 2020, the drama continued as the nation eagerly awaited the ruling of the Constitutional Court. Two particular events caught public attention and provoked wrath. One was a visit by the European Union's Election Observation Mission during which they announced plans to release their report on the 21 May election. This was met with outrage by the opposition parties, civil society and the public; the EU team was forced into a hasty retreat. The second was a shocking leak in mid-January 2020. It was reported that on 28 November 2019 the Chief Justice had lodged a formal complaint with the Anti-Corruption Bureau (ACB) about a bribery attempt targeting the judges hearing the case for the nullification of the presidential election. It was reported that there were two culprits, one in the private sector and the other in the 'arms of Government'.[3] The latter had yet to be named by the time of the court judgment. But on 22 January, the ACB ordered the arrest of Thom Mpinganjira, a leading business tycoon. However, later that same night, his lawyers managed to get an order from a magistrate in another city quashing the arrest warrant. Several days later, on 28 January, a High Court judge ordered the re-arrest of Mpinganjira and for disciplinary action to be taken against the errant magistrate and lawyer. The case underscored both the rot and rectitude of the country's besieged judicial system.

As 3 February 2020 approached, everyone wondered which face of the courts would show up. Few dates in any nation's history mark pivotal moments. In Malawi's history, they include 3 February 1915, when the leader of the first major uprising against colonial rule, John Chilembwe, an American-educated Baptist pastor, was killed. Chilembwe Day is commemorated every 15 January. Another key date is 3 March 1957, the day the British colonial government declared a state of emergency to quell nationalist agitation by arresting leading nationalists, which provoked more protests. The day is marked as a national holiday, called Martyrs' Day in honour of the nationalist heroes who sacrificed their lives in the protracted struggle for decolonisation.

Then there is, of course, 6 July, Malawi's Independence Day. In the postcolonial era, 14 June 1993 marked a significant day when a referendum was held to abolish President Banda's ruthless MCP dictatorship and introduce multiparty democracy. The referendum was approved by nearly 65 per cent of the voters. My parents' generation had fought for the 'first independence', mine was in the forefront of the 'second independence'. In recognition of my own role in the democratic struggle, the opposition party, the United Democratic Front appointed me Shadow Minister, but I turned down a Cabinet appointment when the party won the elections in May 1994. Unfortunately, my initial misgivings about the leadership and integrity of President Bakili Muluzi's ten-year corrupt and lacklustre administration were borne out.

A day of infamy in Malawi's political trajectory under the 'Second Republic' is 20 July 2011, when nationwide protests broke out against economic mismanagement and creeping political authoritarianism by the DPP government led by the late President Bingu wa Mutharika, the elder brother of the incumbent president. The draconian crackdown against the demonstrations over the next several days resulted in nearly twenty people killed, another fifty-eight injured and up to 275 arrested. The country was shaken to its knees. The hapless president never regained his political footing and, less than a year later, on 5 April 2012, he died of a heart attack at the age of seventy-eight. The landmark verdict nullifying the presidential election would mark 3 February 2020 as another milestone in the history of this incredibly beautiful, but badly governed and desperately poor country. One of Malawi's most renowned intellectuals, Thandika Mkandawire, noted for his caustic wit, told a Malawian friend that visiting Nairobi in December 2019 served as a grim reminder of Malawi's lost fifty years of independence, much as one might find visiting the Asian economic tigers a sobering testimony to Africa's lost years of independence.

Malawi followed Kenya, where on 1 September 2017 the Supreme Court had annulled the country's presidential election held on 8 August 2017. In fact, in its judgment the Malawi Constitutional Court frequently referred to the Kenyan case. Cancelling presidential elections is extremely rare given the high levels of substantiality of evidence required in such cases. Thus, Malawi had joined an exclusive club of world democracies. Annulment of an election represents a grave indictment of the electoral body. The Constitutional Court was unsparing in castigating the Malawi Electoral Commission for its incompetent and improper management of the entire presidential election process.

Towards the Presidential Election Rerun

The court called for fresh elections within 150 days. The offices of the president and vice president were returned to the status quo before the 21 May election, thereby reinstating Vice President Chilima and retaining President Mutharika until new elections. Parliament was urged to meet within twenty-one days to pass legislation on new presidential, parliamentary and local elections and maintain the principle of concurrent tripartite elections every five years.

As happened in Kenya after the presidential election was annulled on 1 September 2017, the annulment in Malawi was greeted by jubilation from the leaders and followers of the opposition parties and trepidation from those affiliated to the ruling party, including some professionals and former activists who had sold their souls for tarnished pieces of silver. In the days leading to the Constitutional Court ruling, political and religious leaders, the security services, foreign diplomatic missions as well as the United Nations and the African Union appealed for calm and urged citizens to accept the court's decision.

Many hoped President Mutharika would try to salvage his tattered reputation by gracefully accepting the court decision, as his predecessors had: President Banda when he lost the 1993 referendum, and President Muluzi, who lost an ill-guided attempt at a third term.

As became evident in Kenya, annulling a presidential election did not guarantee a smooth re-election process. In fact, in Kenya the opposition had proceeded to boycott the election, so that the incumbent, President Uhuru Kenyatta, cruised to victory unopposed. This was unlikely to happen in Malawi. In fact, what might be in question was not whether the main contending parties would contest the fresh presidential election, but how. Would the opposition parties proceed separately as before or form an electoral alliance to fight the fresh election?

In its ruling, the Constitutional Court found that no candidate in the 21 May 2019 presidential election had secured a majority and proclaimed that from the next election only a candidate who secured 50+1 would be deemed elected as president. Parliament was asked to make the necessary amendments to the electoral law. In 2017, the DPP supported by a minority party had blocked the Presidential, Parliamentary and Local Government Amendments Bill that would have allowed a 50+1 electoral system.

The ruling might facilitate much-needed political realignment. Many urged the two leading parties, UTM and MCP, to seriously pursue forming a possible coalition to beat the DPP and any coalition it might cobble together. They argued that Malawi could not afford to mortgage its future to the DPP, a party that had degenerated into an incompetent, sleazy, tribalistic, nepotistic and kleptocratic cabal. Creating meaningful and durable political coalitions require leadership and compromise that is quite rare among politicians.

There are of course many other electoral systems, including single-member or multi-member constituencies under which there are several variants. Majoritarian, proportional or mixed majoritarian and proportional features can also complement them. Malawi needed to introduce an electoral system that best promoted proportionality of seats to votes, accountability to constituents, interethnic and interreligious conciliation and minority office-holding. The decentralisation and devolution of power from a highly centralised presidency also needed to be on the table.

Incidentally, it was the first-past-the-post system that had allowed the election of President Trump, who lost the popular vote to Senator Hillary Clinton by 2,868,686. Similarly, commenting on Brexit a day after Britain left the European Union, a British journalist wrote in the *Guardian*:

> How did a matter of such momentous constitutional, economic and cultural consequence come to be settled by a first-past-the-post vote and not by a super-majority? .... There is much that is historically unjust about the British state, but very little of that injustice derives from the EU. ... It was the task of the Brexit campaign to persuade the electorate otherwise. In the referendum, they succeeded with 37 per cent, enough to transform our collective fate for a generation at least.[4]

Malawi was being offered a historic opportunity to reclaim its future, to change direction and fulfill the dreams of millions of its people who had fought for the 'second independence'. The opposition parties and politicians who succeeded in nullifying the presidential election were under pressure not to seek to become a reincarnation of the discredited DPP regime, greedily awaiting their chance to 'eat' from the paltry state coffers. They owed it to history, to the past, current and future generations of citizens of this aggrieved country, to pursue and realise persistent yearnings for the creation of a truly sustainable democratic developmental state and society.

Creating a sustainable democratic developmental state

As we have learned from development studies, and the histories and economies of some Asian countries, creating such a state and society is not a mystery. It is not a matter of ethnicity or race or nationality, neither is it dictated by the peculiarities of culture or the imagined genius of a particular civilisation, let alone the endowments of natural resources. Rather, it is determined by the quality of institutions and leadership, the development of human capital and the prevalence of the social capital of trust. The future of Malawi, like other African countries, centres on confronting many challenges and seizing new opportunities. Two stand out.

First, is the need to undertake profound political reforms including that of the electoral system. The newly empowered masses must maintain pressure on politicians to embrace the politics of policy differences rather than ethnic chauvinism, let alone personal self-aggrandisement. They must resist the self-serving machinations and shenanigans of the political class. As we have learned in African studies and from the rise of contemporary political populisms around the world, ethnicity (or race), overlaid by all manner of regionalisms, is often a more powerful predictor of political loyalties and voting behaviour than class and social interests.

However, ethnicity itself is a complex phenomenon. 'Moral ethnicity' differs from 'political ethnicity'. The former represents a complex web of social obligations and belonging, whereas the latter reflects the competitive confrontation of 'ethnic contenders and constituencies' for state power and national resources. As I wrote elsewhere,[5] both are socially constructed, but one as an identity, the other as an ideology. Ethnicity may serve as a cultural public for the masses estranged from the civic public of the elites, a sanctuary that extends its comforts and protective tentacles to the victims of political disenfranchisement, economic impoverishment, state terror and group rivalry. In other words, it is not the existence of ethnic groups (or racial groups) that is a problem in itself, a predictor of social conviviality or conflict, but their political mobilisation. This is the struggle Malawians committed to a more inclusive future have to fight.

Malawi's current first-past-the-post or winner-take-all system is one of the root causes of political instability. It facilitates minority presidencies. Since the dawn of multiparty democracy in 1994, there had been six elections. Only in two of these did the elected president garner more than half the votes of the electorate (1994, Bakili Muluzi 46.15 per cent; 1999, Bakili Muluzi 52.34 per cent; 2004, Bingu wa Mutharika 35.97 per cent; 2009, Bingu wa Mutharika 66.17 per cent; 2014, Peter Arthur Mutharika 36.4 per cent; 2019, Peter Arthur Mutharika 38.57 per cent).

The second major challenge is that the awakened citizenry must force the political class to attend to the country's tenacious crises of mass poverty, low economic growth and rising inequality. There is a pressing need for strategic and sustainable interventions in the traditional primary, secondary and tertiary sectors and what some call the quaternary sector, or the knowledge sector, comprising high-quality education and training, research and development and the advancement of science, technology and innovation.

In short, a future democratic government needs to focus steadfastly on economic growth and transformation by overcoming the country's enduring legacies of underdevelopment as it simultaneously embraces, even if belatedly, the unrealised potentialities of the old industrial revolutions and the possibilities of the Fourth Industrial Revolution. At stake is the need to raise the country's human development index by ensuring the provision of what the United Nations Development Program calls 'basic capabilities' while moving towards enhanced capabilities. Especially critical is reducing power imbalances and gender inequality, as well as promoting youth employability and decent work.

Malawi's development deficits are glaring indeed, ranging from persistent poverty for the rural and urban masses, to poor physical and social infrastructures, to abysmally low levels of education at all levels, to extensive unemployment and underemployment. Each time I visit the country, I am struck by how little the cities where I grew up in the 1960s and 1970s have changed. I joke to my relatives and friends that I cannot get lost in Lilongwe, Blantyre or Zomba, although I left the country forty-three years ago! When I visited in December 2019, together with my family, including my son and his fiancée, it was disconcerting to see that the primary and secondary schools I had attended looked so dilapidated; they were depressing and pale replicas of the fine institutions I had graduated from.

Thus, getting the politics right is only a prelude to getting the economics right for the well-being and dignity of Malawian citizens. The good news from the ruling of the Constitutional Court annulling the presidential election was that an indispensable first step had been taken. That day would be remembered as a turning point in the country's tortured political history. Perhaps it would come to be known as Constitutional Democracy Day.

One of my relatives, a young, bright and highly educated professional, said the whole saga had left her proud to be a Malawian. This was a moment of reckoning for the country, she said, when Malawians became active citizens, abandoning the docility of bystanders in the political game created, controlled and manipulated by self-serving, cynical, corrupt and crafty politicians. Her fervent hope was that the citizenry, now informed and inspired by their active involvement in a signal political event, would not retreat to the political sidelines as passive observers.

Opposition Wins Election Re-run

On 27 June 2020, Malawi became the first country in Africa where a presidential election re-run was won by the opposition that defeated the ruling party 59 to 40 per cent. Kenya had claimed the distinction of being the first African country to nullify a presidential election. However, in Kenya the ruling party had proceeded to win the election re-run, which had been boycotted by the opposition. Malawi's unprecedented political feat sprang from eight powerful forces.

First, it was a tribute to the protracted and unrelenting struggles of its people for democratic governance. For a year they had persevered with mass demonstrations against the wanton theft of their votes, despite threats and repression by the beleaguered and discredited government. They were sick and tired of the crass, corrupt, inept and ethnocentric leadership of the Democratic Progressive Party (DPP) in power since 2004, save for a brief interlude. The two-year interval was the presidency of Joyce Banda following the death of Bingu wa Mutharika in April 2012 and the election of Peter Mutharika, the late Bingu's brother, in May 2014.

Second, it reflected Malawi's political culture of collective nationalist pride that goes back to decolonisation. No region or ethnic group in Malawi claims ownership of the independence struggle, as is the case, for example, in Kenya where the Kikuyu claim the Mau Mau struggle that led to independence. The Malawian nationalist movement fought on two fronts, against British colonialism and against settler colonialism of the Central African Federation of Rhodesia and Nyasaland. Malawi was the poorest of the three colonies in the federation that included Zambia (Northern Rhodesia) and Zimbabwe (Southern Rhodesia). It was a labour reserve for southern Africa, a political economy that gave rise simultaneously to a regionalist and nationalist outlook, a propensity to embrace regional developments and forge a distinctive national path.

In the struggles for democratisation, for the 'second independence' in the 1980s and early 1990s, Malawi's political culture was buoyed by the emergence of strong social movements. These movements coalesced most prominently around the Public Affairs Committee and the Human Rights Defenders Coalition. Formed in 1992 as a pressure group of religious communities and other forces, the PAC became a highly respected and influential political actor. While the PAC functioned as a civil interlocutor for democracy, the HRDC flexed its political muscles in organising mass protests.

Complementing Malawi's political culture was the third force, political socialisation. As in much of Africa, regional and ethnic political mobilisation and polarisation had deepened after independence as the capacities of the political class to deliver the developmental and democratic promises of *ufulu* (Uhuru) declined and their appetites for primitive accumulation escalated. However, the nationalist memories and aspirations for nation-building lingered. The DPP's openly ethnocentric and exclusionary regime had come to be deeply resented. The country's robust media, both the traditional and new social media, provided ample space to vent against the intensifying regional, ethnic and religious divides.

Reinforcing the complex and contradictory dynamics and demands of the country's political culture and political socialisation was, fourth, the emergence of a fiercely independent judiciary that refused to be intimidated by the executive branch of the country's tripartite system of government. As noted above, not only was the judgment of the Constitutional Court annulling the presidential election unanimous, it was upheld by the Supreme Court on 8 May 2020 against a misguided and embarrassing appeal by the DPP and Malawi Electoral Commission. In their deliberations, the courts demonstrated admirable, methodical and brilliant jurisprudence. Most critical was the ruling that the winner in presidential elections should amass over 50 per cent of the valid votes cast.

At a stroke, a fatal dagger was struck at the heart of regional and ethnic politics and of the DPP's electoral shenanigans, for no party could any longer win by only mobilising its base. The opposition parties, led by the independence party, the Malawi Congress Party and the recently formed United Transformation Movement, quickly entered into a powerful alliance. The DPP also forged an alliance with the party that had won the first democratic election of 1994, the United Democratic Party, out of which the DPP had split.

Desperate and ill-guided efforts by the DPP government to fire the Chief Justice and his deputy a little over a week before the elections provoked national, regional and global outrage from the Chief Justice and lawyers associations as well legal scholars and activists, in a valuable expression of African and international solidarity. The legal community in the country organised unprecedented nationwide demonstrations. It had been an act of political sabotage which would bring utter humiliation to the DPP leader, Peter Mutharika, himself a lawyer and former university professor of law for more than four decades in Tanzania, Ethiopia and the US.

The strength of the opposition movement against the DPP's kleptocratic and dynastic rule was facilitated, fifth, by a generational shift in the country's politics. Like most African countries, Malawi's population is predominantly young. The median age for the country's 20.1 million people in 2020 was 16.5 and 66.7 per cent were below the age of 24. This meant that the vast majority of the country's population had no memories of Dr Banda, the founding president, or of his dictatorial regime from 1964 to 1994. What they knew was the ineptitude and putrescence of the governments of the Mutharika brothers.

Ravaged by poverty, unemployment and underemployment, the youth were hungry for more accountable and development-oriented government. They had been the backbone of the widespread protests that rocked the country following the rigged election of May 2019. They were particularly galvanised by the charismatic vice president, Dr Saulos Chilima, who was born nine years after Malawi's independence. They could not relate to the octogenarian and antediluvian DPP leader, President Mutharika, born in 1940.

The new government also represented a generational shift. The new president, Dr Lazarus Chakwera, was born in the twilight years of colonialism and came of age after independence. All his predecessors had been products of colonialism from which they inherited some of their perverted political and psychological dispositions. He was also the first graduate of the country's first university, the University of Malawi, to ascend to the presidency. The first president, born in the

1890s, had received his university education in the US and Britain; the second and fourth did not attend university; the third and fifth also went to overseas institutions as they had grown up when Malawi had no university.

President Chakwera's election seemed to signal the end of the diaspora allure and grip over the Malawi presidency started by Dr Banda. President Banda had returned to Malawi to join the nationalist movement after spending forty-three years abroad. The Mutharika brothers had returned to rule also after decades in the diaspora. Presidents Bakili Muluzi (1994–2004) and Joyce Banda (2012–2014) were homegrown. So was President Chakwera, although he did graduate studies in the US.

The role of the diaspora noted above underscored the sixth context of Malawian politics and transitions, namely, the impact of external developments. The Constitutional Court had been inspired by the nullification of the presidential election in Kenya in 2017. Earlier, in the 1990s, during the struggle for democratisation, Malawi's opposition movement had been invigorated by the ouster of President Kaunda in 1991 in neighbouring Zambia through a democratic election. It had been galvanised, too, by the momentous demise of apartheid in South Africa, the subregional metropole of southern Africa that, from the late nineteenth century, had drawn millions of workers from the labour reserves of the region, including Malawi.

More recently, two developments had cast their shadows on the Malawian political and developmental imagination. First, was the meltdown of Zimbabwe under the incompetent and venal Mugabe dictatorship, a spiral that has continued under his successor, President Mnangagwa. Zimbabwe was once a major destination for Malawian migrant workers and a country that in the first decade of independence was seen as a model of democratic developmentalism, notwithstanding the heavy structural legacies of settler colonial capitalism.

Second, was the stronger economic growth of Malawi's neighbours – Tanzania in the north, Zambia in the west and formerly war-torn Mozambique enveloping the southern part of the country. Further afield was Botswana, one of Africa's most impressive stories of postcolonial success. In my own personal family, we had roots and relatives in all these countries. Our family story was quite common among many Malawians. This partly explains the intolerance for petty ethnic identities.

Thus, given Malawi's regional tentacles generated by the history of migrant labour, reinforced by the transport and communication networks of a landlocked country and the thick circuits of contemporary media, many Malawians were acutely aware of regional developments. They were frustrated and angered by the fact that their country seemed to lag behind their southern African neighbours in terms of development. They blamed it, rightly, on poor leadership and bad governance, exacerbated by a culture of mediocrity and low national expectations.

The professionalism of the military was the seventh critical factor in Malawi's remarkable electoral transition. Since independence, and at crucial moments, it had consistently maintained loyalty to the Constitution of the Republic rather than to the President as Commander-in-Chief. They had done so in 1992 during the referendum on multiparty democracy and in the subsequent two years. Similarly, in 2012 they facilitated the ascendancy of the estranged vice president, Joyce Banda, when a DPP-led cabal was planning an unconstitutional takeover to install the president's brother, Peter Mutharika. From the annulment of the election in 2019 till the re-run they had provided security for peaceful protests.

The coronavirus pandemic provided the eighth context against DPP rule. As elsewhere, COVID-19 exposed the glaring incapacities of the state and the depth of socioeconomic inequality in the country. When the government sought to impose a lockdown in April 2020 to contain the spread of the pandemic, the HRDC went to court and won an injunction against the lockdown. The HRDC argued that the government had not undertaken consultations or provided measures to cushion the poor and most vulnerable against the impact of the lockdown.

Protests by small-scale traders, most of them young people, demanded government support in terms of cash handouts and food to help them manage the harsh effects of a lockdown. Underlying these protests was a general lack of faith in the government's capacity to manage the crisis, which fed into the narrative of government corruption and incompetence. In short, even during, or despite, the most devastating health and economic crisis to hit the country and the world in decades, there was little trust in a state that was likely to oversee the devastation of the economy and society as the pandemic continued to spread after the election.

Lessons for Africa

Thus, the opposition rode to election victory on the back of sweeping dissatisfaction and disaffection with Malawi's democratic dispensation since 1994. The 23 June 2020 election re-run itself revealed five remarkable developments, lessons and possibilities, some of which had implications for Africa as a whole.

First, the new Malawi Electoral Commission delivered on its mandate with impeccable integrity in record time. The Commission was sworn in on 9 June under the leadership of a relatively young, dynamic and incorruptible chairperson, Justice Chifundo Kachale. He replaced the partisan Dr Jane Ansah. Within three weeks the new MEC was able to deliver the country's most credible presidential election since the first post-independence multiparty elections of 1994.

This result underscored the importance of appointing competent, credible, committed and ethical professionals to national bodies and functions, and the power of transparency. Unlike before, the election results were announced at each polling station and broadcast live to an anxious nation. People, including schoolchildren, could do the maths. While the official announcement came on the night of 27 June, within a day of the election the winner and the magnitude of his victory was known. Personally, I started celebrating on the afternoon of 24 June.

Second, the election was held without international observers, whether the European Union, Commonwealth, African Union, Southern African Development Community, United Nations or other self-appointed guardians of democracy from individual nations such as the United States. These bodies had betrayed Malawians before.

Third, the election was conducted without foreign funding. Malawi relied on its own admittedly depleted budget, spurning the ubiquitous 'donor support' that the arrogant purveyors of the mercy industrial complex wave at so many supplicant African governments to conduct one of the most basic functions of sovereignty – elections. It is humiliating when African governments seek financial support and political validation for their elections from the cynical and self-serving election observer industry that grew following the democratic wave at the turn of the late 1980s and early 1990s.

Fourth, the election result showed that despite the power of incumbency that had been ruthlessly exploited by the DPP government, an organised, disciplined and smart opposition could win. Talking to some of the leaders of the opposition alliance and their supporters, I was impressed by their steely determination and calm confidence that they would prevail. The opposition alliance leaders had crisscrossed the country, never taking the voters for granted or trying to buy them with cheap gimmicks, handouts and empty promises.

Fifth, the election succeeded in breaking the vicious grip on Malawian politics held since 1994 by two families: the Bakili Muluzi political dynasty, in which the former president had transacted his son, Atupele Muluzi, who succeeded him as leader of the UDF, to every possible political alliance, including as the running mate of DPP's Peter Mutharika, to gain power and save the father from a long-running corruption case; and the Mutharika brothers, who had succeeded each other as party leaders and, after a brief interlude for Peter Mutharika as noted earlier, as presidents.

In the days after the election results were announced, the atmosphere in Malawi was filled with giddy excitement and great expectations. But the excitement would inevitably dissipate and the high expectations would encounter disappointments. I remember the intoxicating euphoria of 1994 only too well. In May that year I had returned from seventeen years of self-imposed exile to partake in the exhilarating dance of democracy.

The Struggle for a Democratic Developmental State

The Chakwera government represented, potentially, the dawn of what could be called Malawi's Third Republic. The first was the era of Dr Banda; the second comprised the twenty-six years of the Muluzi-Mutharika dynasties. These conjunctures in Malawian history coincided, with some discrepancies, with the three eras of development and democracy in postcolonial Africa. In my work, I call the first the era of authoritarian developmentalism (1960–1980); the second the era of neoliberal authoritarianism (1980–2000); and the third the dawn of the era of possible democratic developmentalism (since 2000).

The era of authoritarian developmentalism

As I have written more elaborately elsewhere,[6] the era of authoritarian developmentalism was characterised by the intensification of statism (the growth of state power) and developmentalism (the pursuit of development at all costs). The escalation of statism after independence was accentuated by the underdeveloped nature of the indigenous capitalist class and the weak material base of the new rulers. The state became their primary instrument of primitive accumulation. Also important to remember is that the legitimacy of the postcolonial state lay in unlocking the huge colonialist backlog of development for the expectant masses.[7]

State intervention in the organisation of economic, social, cultural and political processes intensified as the contradictions deepened and became more open. As the crisis of growth and accumulation began escalating globally in the 1970s, the postcolonial state assumed a progressively more precarious and openly repressive character with frequent coups and rearrangements of ruling cliques, endless constitutional revisions and human rights violations, and suppression of democratic freedoms. To be sure, until the mid-1970s, African countries had experienced relatively rapid rates of economic growth and development, notwithstanding significant differences between countries, sectors and social classes, gender and generation, as well as ideological divergences and disputes among and within countries.

The era of neoliberal authoritarianism

The structural and ideological underpinnings of authoritarian developmentalism were reinforced by the onset of neoliberalism at the turn of the 1980s, which ushered in Africa's 'lost decades' of the 1980s and 1990s. The era of Structural Adjustment Programmes (SAPs) threatened to undo the developmental promises and achievements of independence, to dismantle the postcolonial social contract and to abort the nationalist project of Africa's renewal after centuries of slave trade followed by colonialism. The rise of SAPs reflected the global ascendancy of neoliberalism, which emerged as an ideological response to the world economic crisis of the late 1960s and early 1970s that had ended the postwar boom.

Neoliberalism marked the collapse of the 'Keynesian consensus' and the political coalitions that had sustained it, and the rise to power of conservative, free-market-oriented governments in the leading industrial economies. SAPs were pursued with missionary zeal by the international financial institutions and western governments, and were imposed on African countries often with the connivance of the African political class or significant factions thereof. SAPs called for currency devaluation, interest and exchange rate deregulation, liberalisation of trade, privatisation of state enterprises, withdrawal of public subsidies and retrenchment of the public service – in short, for a minimalist state and an extension of the market logic to all spheres of economic activity.

The results were disastrous for African economies. The euphoria of independence gave rise to unrelenting 'Afro-pessimism'. The collapse of the independence social contract provoked massive and sustained struggles for the 'second independence', for democratisation, which gathered momentum in the 1990s and scored significant victories at the turn of the 2000s. This ushered in the possibilities of the third era of democratic developmentalism.

The era of democratic developmentalism

The resumption of economic growth in the 2000s and 2010s, reprising the growth rates of the 1960s and first half of the 1970s, brought hope back as encapsulated in the narrative of Africa Rising/Rising Africa. However, the match between economic growth and development remained elusive as socioeconomic inequalities deepened, industrialisation proved elusive and the value chain of African economies remained low. Similarly, the marriage between democracy and development was hardly consummated in many of the emerging illiberal democracies. Africa's wily ruling classes sang the performative and symbolic tunes of minimalist democracy as they subverted the substantive and expansive score of social democracy.

The historiography of Malawi's postcolonial political economy broadly fits into this trajectory. The Banda presidency straddled the first two eras, while the quarter of a century after multiparty democracy was introduced coincided with the second and third eras. In other words, Malawi – like most African countries – has been struggling to establish a democratic developmental state that could produce economic growth and foster integrated, inclusive, innovative and sustainable development. The challenge for the Chakwera government would be to build and sustain such a state.

The developmental state of Thandika Mkandawire

The great Malawian intellectual, Thandika Mkandawire, who passed away on 27 March 2020 at the age of seventy-nine, produced some of the most iconic work on the African developmental state with which the policy-makers and think tanks of the Chakwera government could fruitfully engage. Thandika, as we all lovingly called him, firmly believed in the existence of an ideological–structural nexus for building developmental states in Africa. He argued that developmentalism had an ideological imperative in that it required making development aspirations hegemonic and creating structural components that would encompass state capacities – institutional, technical, administrative and political – to implement effective and transformational development policies.

Clearly, it is imperative to strengthen the administrative apparatus of the state while at the same time building strong state–society synergies. Thandika's work brilliantly debunked many of the conventional diagnoses and prescriptions for development. The latter tend to be based on ahistorical determinisms of geography, culture and history. At one time race and ethnicity were posited as explanations for why some nations develop and others don't, why some are rich and others poor, but they are no longer entertained in the academy. More compelling are explanations that focus on institutional arrangements and the construction of inclusive economic, political and social institutions.

As I wrote in a recent essay, 'Countries with extractive institutions have not fared as well in achieving sustained growth and development. To the quality of institutions, I would add two other critical factors: the quality of human capital and the quality of the social capital of trust'.[8] By the turn of the 2000s, authoritarian developmentalism belonged to the dustbin of history because Malawians and other Africans had and continued to wage protracted struggles for democracy.

A democratic developmental state is one that embodies the principles of electoral democracy, ensures citizens' participation in the development and governance processes, and fosters growth and development. The democratic developmental state is defined by its objectives and its institutional characteristics, including the 'autonomy' of state institutions, which enable it to define and promote its strategic developmental goals and its 'embeddedness', that is, its ability to form alliances with key social groups in society that can help it to achieve its developmental goals.

In short, a democratic developmental state is characterised by institutional autonomy and coherence and inclusive embeddedness operating in a democratic order. This order is marked by competitive and accountable electoral systems and has the capacity to promote development and growth. The construction of democratic developmental states requires Africa to confront and control several sets of challenges and opportunities. At the domestic level there is the need to revitalise the nationalist project by reconstructing the state, rebuilding citizenship, renewing the social contract, reconstructing society and rejuvenating integrated and inclusive economies – in other words, to manage the nexus of state, market and civil society as effectively as possible.

This is the challenge and opportunity that would face the victorious Chakwera–Chilima alliance voted into government by Malawi's expectant masses exhausted by underdevelopment, poverty, inequality, tribalism and regionalism, marginalisation and social despair, compounded by COVID-19. Thandika, who remained resolutely committed to the five humanistic and historic agendas of progressive African nationalism – decolonisation, nation-building, development, democracy and regional integration – would have expected no less from the Chakwera–Chilima electoral victory.

Thandika always believed in the agency of Malawians and Africans everywhere, at home and in the diaspora. His compatriots vindicated him in the June 2020 presidential election re-run, while the diaspora did so through the Floyd protests examined in Chapter 5. Malawi had a rare chance to construct a developmental democratic state and society. But progress was not guaranteed.

Notes

1. *Nyasa Times,* 'Chilima & Chakwera Vs Mutharika & EC – Final Judgment', 3 February 2020. https://www.nyasatimes.com/chilima-chakwera-vs-mutharika-ec-final-judgment/
2. Chem'bwana Nkolokosa, 'Mutharika files court response to discredit evidence of Chilima, Chakwera in polls case: 'Petitioners fail to prove alleged irregularities', *Nyasa Times,* 22 July 2019. https://www.nyasatimes.com/mutharika-files-court-response-to-discredit-evidence-of-chilima-chakwera-in-polls-case-petitioners-fail-to-prove-alleged-irregularities/
3. Wongani Chiuta, 'Chief Justice reports to ACB attempt to bribe judges in Malawi election case', *Nyasa Times,* 12 January 2020. https://www.nyasatimes.com/chief-justice-reports-to-acb-attempt-to-bribe-judges-in-malawi-election-case/
4. Ian McEwan, 'Brexit, the most pointless, masochistic ambition in our country's history, is done', *Guardian,* 2 January 2020. https://www.theguardian.com/politics/2020/feb/01/brexit-pointless-masochistic-ambition-history-done?CMP=Share_iOSApp_O
5. Paul Tiyambe Zeleza, 'Holding a Nation Hostage to a Bankrupt Political Class', *Pambazuka,* 4 January 2008. https://www.pambazuka.org/global-south/holding-nation-hostage-bankrupt-political-class
6. Ibid.
7. Paul Tiyambe Zeleza, 'What Happened to the African Renaissance? The Challenges of Development in the Twenty-First Century', *Comparative Studies of South Asia, Africa and the Middle East* (2009) 29 (2): 155–170.
8. Paul Tiyambe Zeleza, 'Africa's persistent struggles for development and democracy in a multipolar world', *Canadian Journal of African Studies* 53 (1) (2019): 1–16.

First written 3 February and revised 28 June 2020

IV

Africa's Persistent Mythologisation

16

Why I was Afraid of the African Disease of Ebola

Wherever I turned, there was Ebola. In the newspapers and magazines, on television and radio and across the ubiquitous social media. Ebola. I sweated, shook and cringed in mortal fear. Such an ugly word, fearsome in its primal sound, so African, so dark and so black. Since Africa is one country, beware of going to Africa, the media screamed. Never mind that occasional mentions of the disease indicated that it was confined only to Liberia, Sierra Leone and Guinea, three out of Africa's fifty-four countries. But what did they know about world geography? Africa was Africa. That was the problem with political correctness, denial of inconvenient truths. This was an African disease. It afflicted Africa, that benighted land of biblical agonies, of inexplicable scourges, of unimaginable suffering, of epidemics and pandemics, of AIDS.

I was afraid of Ebola because I am an African. I was not one of the nearly 1.1 billion Africans actually living on the continent. What difference did it make that all of western and eastern Europe, China, India and the United States would fit into Africa? It was regarded as one sorry place, home to all those hapless people living in trepidation of Ebola. I was part of Africa's large global diaspora numbering in the tens of millions. But I remain an African, so I was scared of my susceptibility to the disease that is so African. I lived in the United States and I was terrified because, as I wrote this, months after the panic started, Ebola had already killed one person, an African who had travelled to Africa and infected one health-care worker.

I wondered how many people had since died of other diseases – heart disease, malignant cancers, lung disease, brain disease, accidents or unintentional injuries, Alzheimer's disease, diabetes, influenza and pneumonia, kidney disease and suicide, the ten leading causes of death in the United States, responsible for nearly 1.86 million deaths in 2011, three-quarters of all deaths in the country. Where was the panic for all those deaths, some of which were surely preventable and premature? But that was beside the point. Those were normal deaths. Ebola was terrifying in its monstrosity. It was a disease out of Africa.

I was afraid of Ebola because I, too, come from Africa. I watched the gory images of deaths from Ebola in Africa. I listened to the pundits pontificating about the millions it would kill in Africa, the need to close US borders from Africa. I shuddered at seeing President Obama, whose father came from Africa (or was it Kenya?) being called President Ebola. I was stunned when a student refused to go on a study abroad trip to Spain because it is close to Africa. Hadn't one Ebola case already been diagnosed there? I was speechless when well-meaning colleagues wondered why I was going to Africa; they had never heard the names of the actual countries to which I was going.

I was afraid of Ebola because it was robbing me of my African authenticity when I failed to give special insights into the nature of the disease to inquiring colleagues or the media, about the culinary delights of eating monkey meat that had apparently sparked Ebola and the strange primeval customs that helped spread it like wildfire. The fact that I was not a medical doctor, or from the three affected countries, did not matter. I was an African. Or, had I become too Americanised to understand my African disease heritage? Maybe I was not Americanised enough to speak authoritatively about things I knew little about, not even when it came to that simple place with a single story, called Africa.

I was afraid of Ebola for bringing back to centre stage the Afro-pessimists with their perennial death wishes for the continent. In recent years, they had lost some traction to the narratives of a 'rising' Africa. I was afraid of Ebola because it had quarantined me in the denigrated Africa of the western imagination, in the diseased blackness of my body. Ebola had robbed the American public of Africa's multiple stories, of the continent's splendid diversities, complexities, contradictions and contemporary transformations. Ebola was indeed a deadly panic. It threatened civilisation, as we knew it.

Or, were my fears about Ebola misplaced? Was it about something else deep in the western psyche I couldn't understand, perhaps going back to the Black Death of the fourteenth century that had wiped out nearly one-third of Europe, the influenza pandemic of 1918 that had killed tens of millions of people, or the genocide of native peoples in the Americas brought about by European diseases? But questions offered little solace in the avalanche of grim stories about the African plague of the year, Ebola. As someone who earns a living as an educator, I was afraid of Ebola because it was an enemy of critical and balanced thinking about Africa, about disease, about our common humanity.

First written 11 October 2014

17

Trump's Shithole Africa: The Homogenisation and Dehumanisation of a Continent

In January 2018, Haiti and Africa became the butt of President Trump's pathologically racist and profusely obscene verbal assaults. During a White House meeting with Congressional leaders on immigration, he dismissed Haiti and the entire African continent as undesirable 'shithole' countries. The comments provoked a firestorm of global condemnation, from the United Nations to the African Union. Several African countries, such as Botswana and Senegal, summoned US ambassadors to issue official diplomatic protests. Social media exploded with incredulity, outrage and bitterly satirical hashtags celebrating the beauty and humanity of the disparaged peoples and their lands.

Within the United States itself, reaction to President Trump's racist, xenophobic and undiplomatic diatribe was filtered through the poisonous partisan divide that had eroded civil discourse and made American politics so dysfunctional. Democrats, including members of the Congressional Black Caucus, denounced the President's vulgar and vile remarks unequivocally and pushed for a censure resolution, while defensive Republicans kept silent or prevaricated, except for a handful of Black Republicans, such as Mia Love, the first Haitian American elected to Congress, and Tim Scott, the lone African-American Republican in the Senate. Representative Love rebuked the president and demanded an apology and Senator Scott expressed deep disappointment.

The predictable political script of outrage and support for the president's divisive comments was replicated in the media. Outraged liberal pundits excoriated him for his racism, but his right-wing cheerleaders heartily defended him for his realism. Elsewhere, among African and Haitian immigrants and across Africa itself, many were shocked but not surprised. So was I.

The reasons for my lack of surprise were outlined at length in two essays, one written in March 2016, seven months before the US election, entitled 'Republicans, Racists and the Obama Derangement Syndrome' (Chapter 2 in this book), and the other, 'The Tragedy and Farce That Is Trump's America', written a day after the November elections (Chapter 3 in this volume). Trump's obnoxious, moronic and dangerous racist buffoonery appealed to and embodied the Republican Party's underbelly of white supremacy and neofascist obsession to 'Make America White Again'.

Trump's derogatory dismissal of shithole Haiti and Africa reflected enduring tendencies in the American social imaginary about Africa and its diasporas. This is to suggest that, as outraged as we might have been about Trump's provocative and pusillanimous pronouncements, the Trump phenomenon transcended Trump. The spectre of racism, whose pernicious and persistent potency Trump had brazenly exposed to the world, had haunted America from its inception with the original sin of slavery, through a century of Jim Crow segregation and the past half-century of post-civil rights redress and backlash.

The disdain expressed for Haiti and Africa in the president's vicious verbal assault was a projection of an angry racist project to roll back the limited gains of the Civil Rights struggle and settlement of the 1960s that had animated the Republican Party's Southern Strategy and politics ever since. In short, international relations and perceptions of foreign nations are often driven as much by geopolitical interests and developments as they are by prevailing domestic politics. For multicultural societies the shifting dynamics of interethnic and interracial relations should not be underestimated. The intersection of domestic and foreign affairs tends to reflect, reproduce and reinforce national and global racial hierarchies.

Ever since millions of enslaved Africans had landed on the shores of the Americas, a historic tragedy that lasted for four centuries and involved the largest forced migration in world history, negative images of Africa had become crucial to the construction of justificatory racist ideologies and racial discrimination against the African diaspora. The alleged primitivity and undesirability of Africa were used as a hammer to bludgeon the enslaved Africans and their descendants into suffering complexes of racial inferiority, to make them ashamed of their ancestral continent, to make them appreciate being in America and acquiesce to their subjugation.

The racist opprobrium attached to Haiti goes back to the turn of the nineteenth century. Once one of the richest slave plantation societies in the Americas, Haiti has never been forgotten or forgiven as the first country in the Americas, indeed in history, where a revolution by an enslaved population succeeded. The Haitian Revolution, which lasted from 1791 to 1803, spawned independence struggles across Latin America and threatened the lucrative slave systems that had built the economies of the Americas, including that of the United States, and fuelled the industrialisation of the Atlantic powers, including Britain, the world's first industrial nation.

The United States and most European states refused to recognise and quarantined Haiti for decades. In 1825, France, the former colonial power, in exchange for recognition of the damage caused by the revolution, demanded an indemnity of 90 million francs, equivalent to more than US$40 billion today. These draconian external pressures, combined with the newly liberated country's own internal dysfunctions, crippled Haiti's development prospects and made it a poster child for the costs of black independence in the Americas. The United States itself occupied Haiti for nineteen years from 1915 to 1934, to enforce its economic and political interests on the island.

Thus, in the Euro-American imaginary and discourse, both Africa and Haiti serve as potent signs of otherness, of eternal inferiority, of being less than. At every measure in the positivist master references of progress, from levels of historicity to humanity, civilisation to culture, economics to ethics, sociality to sexuality, they are always found lacking and lagging behind Euro-America. This was the import of Trump's description of Haiti and African countries as shithole, an image that evoked utter depravity, deprivation and destitution, of countries, societies and peoples living in unimaginable squalour, bereft of skills, of a people who were beyond the pale in making white America Great Again.

Never mind that, in 2012, 41 per cent of African-born immigrants in the United States[1] had bachelor degrees and above (64 per cent for Egyptians and 61 per cent for Nigerians in the US), compared to 28 per cent for the overall foreign-born and 33 per cent for native-born Americans. At the other end, while nearly a third of the overall foreign-born population in the US (32 per cent) had less than a high-school education, this applied to only 12 per cent of the African-born population in the US (compared with South Africa's 3 per cent, Nigeria's 4 per cent and Egypt and Kenya's 5 per cent each). Thus, Africans were among the most educated immigrants in the United States.

It could be pointed out that Trump's tirade ignored the actual history of the United States, the fact that it had been built by centuries of unpaid labour by millions of enslaved Africans and immigrants from Europe and Asia. Despite these contributions, at the beginning of the new Republic, citizenship was racialised and gendered. According to the Naturalization Act of 1790, one of the first bills passed by Congress, citizenship was a privilege of free white males. Clearly, the United States has a long history of restrictive and racist immigration policies, which tend to flare up during moments of nativist angst and insecurity.

In Trump's bigoted and juvenile vocabulary, many of the immigrants in the nineteenth and twentieth centuries had come from the 'shithole' countries of the day and were regarded as undesirables in Anglo-Saxon America. For example, the Italians and Irish who had flocked in their millions were not deemed 'white', Asians were barred from entering the United States by a series of laws including the Chinese Exclusion Act of 1882 (which wasn't repealed till 1943), and the

Immigration Act of 1917 barred immigration from the Asia-Pacific region. The 1924 Immigration Act imposed a 2 per cent nationality quota based on the 1890 census. This was intended to limit immigration from non-Anglo-Saxon countries.

Trump's presidency was and continued to be propelled by an upsurge of virulent nativism and xenophobic nationalism, which erupts periodically in American history during moments of profound socioeconomic changes and crises. Demographically, the United States is becoming less white. Populations of African, Asian and Latino descent have grown rapidly and, according to some estimates,[2] they are poised to become a majority by 2044.

For more than three decades, neoliberal globalisation had ravaged the livelihoods of tens of millions of American workers. The neoliberal restructuring of the economy and society spawned the populism led by super-rich billionaires, like Trump, who do not care about the poor and middle classes. Populists of Trump's ilk sought to racialise the deepening class inequalities. But racialised populist politics offered cold comfort to pauperised whites.

The Trump phenomenon, political rhetoric and policy agenda was a product of a more specific conjuncture. Backlash against the Obama presidency and what it represented fuelled it. Lest we forget, Trump was the godfather of birtherism, the racist lie that Obama was not American-born, a real American, that he was born in Kenya. In the dog-whistle politics of the United States, the racial meaning was obvious: Obama, the *African*, was an illegitimate president, unfit to rule and represent white America.

The African-American public intellectual, Ta-Nehisi Coates, captured this impulse marvellously in several brilliant essays, including 'My President Was Black'[3] and 'The First White President'.[4] Coates argued, powerfully and persuasively in my view, that the Trump phenomenon was fuelled by the pervasive and racist backlash against the first black president from those committed to reclaiming a vanishing America of white privilege and white supremacy. The Trump presidency, in turn, was propelled by an obsessive drive to dismantle former President Obama's legacy. The ghost of Obama haunted Trump, throwing him into frequent spasms of delirious derangement. Journalists ran out of adjectives to describe his personal mendacity and apparent madness.

The Trump presidency provoked widespread resistance from the majority of Americans, who had never voted for him in the first place, and who hoped to retake their country, to continue making it a more perfect union as dreamt by generations in their struggles for inclusive citizenship. Trump may have dominated the news headlines with his tweetstorms, but he enjoyed the lowest approval ratings of any president in the history of polling. Just as he had empowered racists to hate again with impunity, he had inspired even more Americans to fight for decency. But even though Trump had reinforced a sense of moral superiority among liberals, it was too self-serving.

When it came to the homogenisation of Africa and dehumanisation of Africans, the lines between the angels and the devil were blurred. This is reflected in a large literature on the invention of Africa and the construction of distorted images about Africa. It is clear that Africa suffers from what the renowned Nigerian novelist, Chimamanda Ngozi Adichie, called 'the danger of a single story'.[5] The single-story syndrome rests on several tropes: excessive selectivity, sensationalism, stereotyping and use of special vocabulary. Typically, the stories on Africa in the western media and oftentimes in the African media itself, are highly selective, focused on the sensational, have little nuance and use vocabulary reserved for African events, even if the phenomenon is not particularly African. For example, there is the ubiquitous use of the words 'tribe' and 'tribal' to describe African phenomena, problems or practices, which no one uses to describe their European equivalents, as I wrote in a satirical essay twelve years earlier, entitled 'Angelina Jolie Discovers Africa'.[6]

The propensity to reduce Africa to a single story is based on the homogenisation of the continent, the pervasive tendency to strip it of its bewildering complexities. This, too, is deeply rooted in the social imaginaries of Africa of both the foes and friends of the continent. But these shortcomings are also evident within the continent itself and in the Pan-African discourses of affirmation. As many critics in African studies have observed, a lot of journalistic and scholarly writing on the countries, societies and peoples of this vast continent is lazy. This is to urge the liberal media and academics to engage in critical self-reflection on how they represent Africa.

The continent is often reported as a country, eliding the vast differences among its fifty-four countries and the sheer size of its landmass and scale and diversity of its histories, societies, economies, cultures, polities and ecologies. 'Africa', or that favorite cartographic label of Africanist scholarship and the overseers of global geopolitics, 'sub-Saharan Africa', often prefaces titles of academic books even when the study is about a very specific place or community.

In 2013, the British newspaper, the *Guardian,* poignantly captured the careless homogenisation of the continent in an article entitled, 'Africa is not a Country'.[7] The piece looked at articles published on the continents of Asia and Africa, in 2012 and 2013 respectively, and on the three major countries in each of them. For Asia, 2,948 articles mentioned only 'Asia', 16,090 mentioned China, 8,829 mentioned India and 8,481 mentioned Japan. In contrast, for Africa, 5,443 mentioned only 'Africa', 6,824 mentioned South Africa, 2,615 mentioned Egypt and 2,169 mentioned Nigeria. Thus, nearly a third (31.9 per cent) of the articles mentioned only 'Africa' compared to less than one-tenth (8.1 per cent) that mentioned only 'Asia'.

It goes without saying that, in the literature, levels of specificity and differentiation for Europe, not to mention the United States itself, are a lot more pronounced. In other words, Europe and North America and increasingly Asia do not suffer from the simplifications and inanities of the single-story syndrome that afflicts Africa. It can be argued that the homogenisation of Africans facilitates their dehumanisation because it strips them of the intricate and individual tapestries of their lives.

The homogenisation of Africa is evident in its cartographic contraction, too. The global maps that most people see tend to follow the Mercator projection invented in the sixteenth century, which inflates the size of Europe and the northern continents. In this mapping, Africa is shown as the same size as Greenland, when the continent is in fact fourteen times larger. When I taught in the United States and Canada, I used to show students maps based on more accurate projections.[8] These indicate that the United States, Europe (excluding Russia), China, India and Japan would fit into the vast landmass called Africa, the second-largest continent in the world.

The kind of cartographic, cultural, political and paradigmatic homogenisation and oversimplification of our vast continent in the popular media and scholarly literature is what sustains the diminution and dehumanisation of Africa and Africans. We and our international friends might want to begin removing the ideological and intellectual oxygen that sustains and inflates the racist bigotry upon which an ignorant Trump can hang his 'shithole Africa', by thinking and writing about, and celebrating, the splendid diversities of our beloved continent and its peoples.

Thus, in the discursive realm – the world of producing ideas and images – we must continue the historic project of deconstructing Eurocentrism. This project was started by African intellectuals on the continent and in the diaspora half a millennium ago, following the tragic encounter between Europe and Africa that led to the establishment of the modern world system with its economic inequalities and racial hierarchies. In the diplomatic realm, the African Union and African governments must raise the costs of denigrating the continent and its diasporas through the symbolic acts of summoning American ambassadors and recalling their ambassadors to the United States until the American government apologises.

Symbols and words matter, otherwise the world would not have been so riled up by Trump's invective. In the economic realm, we need to reprise the Sullivan principles against apartheid for the twenty-first century – American businesses must respect African sovereignty and speak out against the would-be leader of Global Apartheid.

Notes

1. Christine P. Gambino, et al., *The Foreign-Born Population from Africa*, U.S. Census, 1 October 2012. https://www.census.gov/content/census/en/library/publications/2014/acs/acsbr12-16.html
2. William H. Frey, 'New Projections Point to a Minority Majority Nation in 2044', Brookings, 12 December 2014. https://www.brookings.edu/blog/the-avenue/2014/12/12/new-projections-point-to-a-majority-minority-nation-in-2044/
3. Ta-Nehisi Coates, 'My President was Black', *The Atlantic,* January/February Issue, 2017. https://www.theatlantic.com/magazine/archive/2017/01/my-president-was-black/508793/
4. Ta-Nehisi Coates, 'The First White President', *The Atlantic,* October 2017 Issue. https://www.theatlantic.com/magazine/archive/2017/10/the-first-white-president-ta-nehisi-coates/537909/
5. Chimamanda Ngozi Adichie, 'The Danger of a Single Story', TEDGlobal 2009. https://www.ted.com/talks/chimamanda_adichie_the_danger_of_a_single_story
6. Paul Tiyambe Zeleza, 'Angelina Jolie Discovers Africa', *Africa Resource*, 7 July 2006. https://www.africaresource.com/essays-a-reviews/essays-a-discussions/144-angelina-jolie-discovers-africa
7. Nicolas Kayser-Bril, 'Africa is not a country', *Guardian*, 24 January 2014. https://www.theguardian.com/world/2014/jan/24/africa-clinton
8. 'Africa: bigger than you think! Greenland: much smaller', *EarthPowernews.* http://www.earthpowernews.com/africa-bigger-than-you-think/

Essay first written 13 January 2018

18

Black Panther and the Persistence of the Colonial Gaze

On 30 March 2018, I finally watched the much-hyped film, *Black Panther*. I had read numerous reviews and commentaries in the American media and some in the African press that had enthused about the exceptional entertainment value and historical significance of the film. *Black Panther* earned the distinction of being the second-highest grossing film of 2018 and one with a predominantly black cast (it eventually grossed US$1,347 million globally). It became an international blockbuster, putting the lie to the Hollywood myth that 'black' films have no crossover transnational appeal.

In the African-American community, the film became an iconic cultural moment, even movement, marked by viewing parties, reaffirmations of African fashion and hairstyles and reclamations of black pride. Wakanda was elevated to the emblematic modernity and technological superiority of an imagined African nation. For the literati among the frothy pundits, the technoculture and science fiction of *Black Panther* marked the coming of age of Afro-futurism, the bold re-envisioning of Afro-diasporic pasts and futures.

Thus the film bore the great weight of racial representation, of the brilliant possibilities of the past, present and future for African peoples on the continent and in the diaspora. It carried this burden because of the paucity of black films in Hollywood; it was a burden it ultimately failed to uphold because it was too much for one film to bear.

While I found the film interesting even engrossing in parts, I was underwhelmed. In fact, I left the theatre quite troubled by the pervasive tropes of colonial discourse that frame the film despite its eagerness to invoke a progressive Pan-African aesthetic. The tropes of the colonial gaze are signalled at the outset. We are told that Wakanda is a 'tribal' nation-state. None of Africa's major precolonial states – from the ancient Nile valley civilisations to the great empires of western Africa, not to mention others elsewhere on the continent – were 'tribal' states; they were multi-ethnic or, to use contemporary terms, multicultural and multinational states and societies. And contemporary African states, formed out of the historical geography of European colonialism, are almost invariably multi-ethnic, multicultural and multireligious. The term 'tribe' is the 'N' word of colonial denigration for African societies. There is nothing authentic or liberating about referring to African communities as 'tribal', a term which evokes atavistic identities and primordial politics.

The representations of Wakanda reek with other Eurocentric stereotypes. The accession to and defence of the throne are marked by ferocious and bloody fights. The contestation between the king of Wakanda, T'Challa, the Black Panther and his estranged African-American cousin and interloper, Erik Kilmonger, degenerates into the 'intertribal' warfare of colonial folklore, together with the Tarzanian animalistic chants by the neighbouring kingdom that comes to intervene. There are also the shields, spears and gyrations of old Hollywood films about 'tribal' African warfare.

The bodies of several of the characters are duly adorned with the 'tribal markings' of *National Geographic* among 'native peoples' in remote corners of the globe; one even spots an elongated mouth disk! Equally disconcerting are the fake accents, the poor attention paid to African languages, all of which produces a dangerously simplistic and homogenised representation of the continent.

Wakanda reproduces the colonial discourse of Africa as the black continent. As I have written extensively elsewhere, the conflation of Africa with sub-Saharan Africa is an invention of Eurocentric colonial discourse, of the Hegelian homogenisation, diminution and dehumanisation that 'Africa proper' is sub-Saharan Africa, the habitus of the Negro, which is 'the land of childhood, which lying beyond the day of self-conscious history, is enveloped in the dark mantle of Night'.[1]

In other words, despite all its best counter-hegemonic efforts, Wakanda's Africa is quintessentially sub-Saharan Africa, the truncated Africa of Eurocentric cartography, of Europe's ultimate other. *Black Panther* offers us an Afrocentric projection of an Africa invented by the racialised and racist realities and rhetoric of American history and society. It is not a reflection of the bewildering complexities, contradictions and diversities of Africa itself.

A fascinating contrast can be seen in the scenes that represent South Korea, in which that country's urban modernism is evident and unencumbered by the scenes of rural dwellings and pastoral landscapes depicted in Wakanda. While portraits of an urban skyline are latched onto aerial overviews of Wakanda, much of the action in the film, save for the technological centre where Sheri works, takes place in the countryside under the cascading waterfalls and on the savanna grasslands of traditional portraits of Africa. The urban scene in Afro-futuristic Wakanda towards the end of the film is in a crowded and rundown street. The downtowns of many contemporary African cities are far glitzier than that.

Even the attempts at capturing gender equality in Wakanda seem to fall flat. To be sure, some of the women in the film are remarkably brave, but they primarily serve as support cast in male battles for power in a deeply patriarchal society. In fact, they largely seem devoid of personal lives, their ferocity reminiscent of the female Amazon warriors of nationalist and colonial historiographies.

The stereotypes do not stop with the African society and scenes. They are evident in the representation of the African-American community and characters. Kilmonger, the usurper to the throne from the diaspora, is the proverbial Angry Black Man moulded by the ubiquitous violent desolation of the inner city and America's imperial wars. Even the last scene, when the UFO-looking plane lands on a basketball field, invokes the dystopia of the 'hood as the thuggish youngsters talk about dismembering and selling its parts.

The two whites who are featured are no better than cartoon characters. One is the crooked and unscrupulous buffoon, Klaw; the other is a mild-mannered CIA operative, Everett, who is initially incredulous about the technological achievements of Wakanda. It is as if Wakanda's technological prowess is incomplete without the white colonial gaze, not through engagement or confrontation with a powerful Euro-American state but two hapless individuals. Kilmonger kills Klaw, whereas Everett becomes part of the salvation of the ousted king, T'Challa. If only the CIA had such an honourable history in Africa!

Thus, *Black Panther* is at best a tribute to the Afrocentric imaginary of Africa and, at worst, it assiduously reproduces colonial stereotypes about Africa. Pan-African solidarity needs more nuanced imaginative creations and recreations of African societies and their diasporas that transcend the familiar and discredited tropes of colonial discourse.

In an era when the burgeoning African film industry is thriving (Nigeria's Nollywood is now the world's second-largest film industry after India's Bollywood), the Pan-African world deserves far better than the simple and singular stories of Hollywood's *Black Panther*, however entertaining and commercially successful they may be.

Notes

1. G.W.F. Hegel, *The Philosophy of History*, trans. J. Sibree, introduction C.J. Friedrich, New York: Dover Publications, 1956: 91.

First written 31 March 2018

19

The Decolonisation of African Knowledges

Introduction

It is truly a pleasure to be back at this lovely campus ten years after I gave the keynote address at the same institution. A lot has happened in the intervening ten years. I was then a department head at the University of Illinois, Chicago. I have since been to three other universities, as a college dean in California, then vice president for Academic Affairs in Connecticut, and am now vice chancellor of a wonderful international and innovative university in Kenya.

The University of the Free State has changed and grown. So has the world at large witnessed remarkable transformations. President Mbeki then led South Africa. Barack Obama was a little-known US senator. Facebook was only three years old, Twitter a year old and Instagram was three years away from being launched. Forest Whitaker won Best Actor at the Oscars for *The Last King of Scotland* and the Dixie Chicks won Album of the Year at the Grammys. The interminable wars in Afghanistan and Iraq were in their fourth year. The World Cup in South Africa was three years away. But a lot has not changed. Poverty, disease, inequality, environmental degradation and global warming remain pressing global challenges. The spectres of racism, bigotry and xenophobic nationalisms have arisen from the ravages of neoliberal globalisation and stalk many parts of the world with impunity, from Brexit UK to Trump's America, not to mention the carnage in Syria and South Sudan and the migration and refugee crises across the Mediterranean.

My presentation ten years earlier focused on the development of African studies in the Euro-American academy, surveying its institutional, ideological and intellectual tendencies. I was then deeply immersed in the field, having served recently as Director of the Center for African Studies for eight years at the University of Illinois at Urbana-Champaign and published two volumes on *The Study of Africa.*[1] I was tempted to update my presentation, but realised that since my reincarnation into higher levels of university administration I have not kept pace with developments in African studies. So I thought I should share broad reflections on the issue of knowledge production more generally, a subject that has preoccupied me for more than three decades. It has acquired a new urgency since my relocation to the continent after spending twenty-five years in North America and as a university leader involved in academic and policy discussions about the role of higher education for our beloved continent's integrated, inclusive and innovative sustainable development.

In this presentation, I focus on two interconnected issues. First, the unfinished project of decolonising African knowledges. This is partly in homage to the social and academic struggles currently raging across South African universities. These struggles are familiar to many of us raised in the academies of postcolonial Africa in the 1960s, 1970s and 1980s. This is to underscore how much you can learn from the rest of the continent; it is a gentle reminder against the dangers of South African exceptionalism. Second, I examine the continent's positioning in global knowledge production, which is relatively weak. Thus, as we concentrate on the project of decolonising African knowledges, we should pay equal attention to raising the volume and value, quantity and quality of African knowledge production. The two are interconnected in so far as the decolonised African Academy is best placed to serve as a robust centre for producing knowledges that are both locally relevant and add to the global stock of knowledge.

The Project for Knowledge Decolonisation

Ever since Africa's modern encounters with Europe in the fifteenth century, African thinkers have confronted the epistemic challenges of Eurocentrism, not to mention the existential and economic threats of European imperialism more generally. Eurocentrism frames African humanity and history as less than, mimetic and perpetually infantile and becoming Europe. The epistemological, ontological and historiographical tropes of Eurocentrism permeate intellectual and popular discourses on Africa, which distort, disparage and demean African realities, lives and experiences. Predictably, Eurocentrism has elicited countervailing affirmations of Africa and Africanness, of African purity, parity and personhood; defiant assertions of African difference from Europe, sameness with Europe and authenticity without Europe.

The impulses and imperatives for refashioning the Eurocentric narratives on, about and for Africa have mutated during the long historical geographies of slavery, colonialism and neocolonialism. These three moments constitute the conjunctures through which the unequal exchanges and engagements, confrontations and contestations between the African and European worlds were produced and reproduced. Clearly, the way these eras were experienced in different parts of Africa varied. Consequently, the trends, tempos and textures of responses and resistances to Eurocentric knowledges and reclamations and reconstructions of Africa-centred knowledges differed.

The struggles over the who, what, when, where and whys of African knowledges, about the producers, content, periodicity, spatiality and meaning of studying, researching and knowing this most ancient and infinitely complex and diverse constellation of peoples called Africa, are dateless. They go back millennia to the emergence of African social thought long before the tragic encounters of Africa and Europe in modern times. The historical geographies of these epistemological and ontological battles vary across Africa in their manifestation and intensity. They tend to be captured by the term 'decolonisation'.

Both as a temporal condition and analytical or discursive term, decolonisation dominated African countries in the heady days of nationalist struggles and the immediate aftermath of independence. The imperatives and contestations over the reorganisation of national political, economic, cultural and social life, including education, were particularly heightened in the early decades of the post-colony. For the majority of African countries this happened from the 1950s to the 1980s. It is not surprising that the debates about the decolonisation of knowledge, of the curriculum and academic texts, of scholarly and popular discourses, of modes of being and speech, are currently so hotly contested in South Africa, the last country to join the ranks of postcolonial African states following the end of the grotesque system of apartheid in 1994.

The term 'decolonisation' is both illuminating and limiting, combining as it does epistemic desires for decentring Eurocentric knowledges, but it often inadvertently centres the latter in the archives of African knowledges in all its consuming deconstructive drive. This is to argue that just as colonialism is not the sum total of African history, Eurocentrism should not be allowed to overwhelm African knowledges of their capaciousness. In this presentation, I would like to argue that Africa has different libraries, of which the Eurocentric is only part of one. A project that seeks to liberate African knowledges must begin by understanding the variety, development and intersections of Africa's multiple libraries. It must go beyond Afrocentric injunctions of proclaiming eternal difference, and recognise the enduring and complex conversations of cultures and ideas within Africa itself and between the continent's societies and civilisations and those of other continents beyond modern Europe.

This is to make a simple proposition: let us truly immerse ourselves in African and global histories of knowledge. This injunction is of course predictable coming from a historian. I urge us to take seriously the study of African and world histories, not to apologise for Africa's centrality certainly to itself and also to the world, in our efforts to recentre Africa and its knowledges and decentre Eurocentrism and provincialise Europe. In this regard, let me outline, in broad strokes, Africa's key libraries that go back at least two thousand years. What I propose is to provide a broad overview of African intellectual historiography.

In discussing the history of ideas it is important to note that the economies and cultures of knowledge production are an integral part of complex and sometimes contradictory, but always changing, institutional, intellectual, ideological and individual dynamics and predilections that unfold at interlocking national and transnational, or local and global levels. Knowledge production unfolds in the shifting intersections of political economy, historical geography and epistemological and ontological constructs.

Africa's Four Libraries

I identify four libraries that emerged during the four broad phases in African historiography, each of which embodied various tendencies. The first phase is the ancient era that spawned the Afro-Christian, Afro-Islamic and griot libraries. The second phase is the slave trade era that gave rise to the colonial library. The third era is the colonial period during which the colonial library was consolidated. We are in the fourth phase, the post-independence era, during which the four libraries are locked in fierce contestation. The question is, what are the prospects for a new library to emerge out of the synthesis of these four?

Libraries of the Ancient Era

The ancient era was dominated by three successive and co-existing traditions: that of the Afro-Christian library, the Afro-Islamic library and the griot library. The first is brilliantly represented by the great theologian and philosopher, St Augustine, from present-day Algeria. His writings profoundly influenced the development of Christianity. He saw history as inevitably universal and meta-historical in that it entails movement towards divine providence. There were other thinkers and theologians, from Tertullian to Origen located in Alexandrian Egypt, whose works were part of the corpus of early Christian theology and historiography. The ecclesiastical writings and histories of Christian Africa extend to Ethiopia, where chronicles such as *Kebra Negaste* (Glory of Kings) were produced, proclaiming dynastic glory in a religious idiom.

The Afro-Islamic library is also represented by an illustrious list of African thinkers and writers from northern to western to eastern Africa. As with their Christian counterparts, African Muslim scholars played a major role in the development of Islamic theology and philosophy, as well as in the transmission of knowledges from classical Greece and Rome and from Asia (such as Arabic numerals, which were actually Indian) to western Europe, following the establishment of what have variously been called Muslim, Moorish or African empires in the Iberian peninsula in the early eighth century. One of the most renowned figures in this tradition is Ibn Khaldun, from present-day Tunisia, who is regarded by many as one of the greatest historians of all time. His history of the world provided the first serious challenge to providential history. His work postulated a cyclical theory of history, anticipated modern historical methodology and influenced interpretations of Maghreb history well into the twentieth century. It is to Khaldun that we owe one of the earliest surviving fragments of the history of the Mali Empire.

Muslim scholars from North Africa and West Africa itself produced numerous works on West African societies, among them the famous *Ta'rīkh al-Sūdān* and *Ta'rīkh al-Fattāsh,* both produced in Timbuktu in the seventeenth century, and the *Kano Chronicle* and the *Gonja Chronicle* produced in modern-day Ghana in the eighteenth century. In East Africa, you have similar chronicles, such as the *Kilwa Chronicle. I*t is not an exaggeration to say that comprehension of Arabic and *Ajami* writings (writing using Arabic script) are fundamental to understanding African history and historiography. Numerous archives continue to be discovered and preserved.

It is out of the Islamic tradition that Africa's, and some of the world's, oldest universities emerged. They include Ez-Zitouna in Tunis, founded in 732. Next came al-Qarawiyyin, established in Fez in 859 by a young migrant female princess from Qairawan (Tunisia), Fatima Al-Fihri. The university attracted students and scholars from Andalusian Spain to West Africa. Then, in 969, Al-Azhar mosque university was established in Cairo, the same year that the city was founded by the Fatimid dynasty from the Maghreb. It came to be regarded as the most prestigious centre of Islamic education and scholarship and attracted the greatest intellectuals of the Muslim world, including Ibn Khaldun who taught there. Another major early Islamic university was Sankore in Timbuktu, founded in the twelfth century. Save for the last, the other three universities have survived to this day.

The third tradition is what I call the griot library. Griots, known by different names in various societies, were highly trained custodians of oral traditions and narratives. Their recollections sought to link the past and the present, construct collective worldviews and identity, educate the youth, express political views and provide entertainment and aesthetic pleasure. Studies show griots had many other functions besides being genealogists and historians; they were also advisers to rulers, patrons, spokespersons, diplomats, mediators, interpreters and translators, musicians, composers, teachers, exhorters, warriors, witnesses, praise-singers and ceremony participants during namings, initiation, courtship, marriages, installations and funerals. In West Africa, griots first emerged at least a thousand years ago and since then their role has changed.

The griot library is often mistaken as being quintessentially African, as much as writing is seen as the preserve of Europe. The existence and development of Africa's Afro-Christian and Afro-Islamic libraries should put to rest the misguided notion that African knowledge production, or what some people call indigenous knowledges, can be confined to orality. Christianity and Islam are as indigenous to their long-term African followers in northern, western and eastern Africa as they are to the long-term followers of these religions in Europe and Asia. Lest we forget, clerics in Christian Ethiopia were writing centuries before the inhabitants of the British Isles had been converted to Christianity and learned the Roman alphabet. Similarly, Islam reached Ethiopia before it arrived in most parts of Asia, including the so-called Middle East.

The Slave Trade Era Library

The emergence of the colonial library can be dated to the second era in African historiography, the period from the fifteenth to the nineteenth centuries, characterised by the Atlantic slave trade and incipient colonialism. The three libraries identified above continued to exist and develop and engaged the new historiographical traditions in complicated ways. From the rising colonial library emerged the Eurocentric and the vindicationist traditions.

Much of the early European writings on Africa consisted of colourful and often inaccurate travel writing. Later, more self-consciously historical writings developed but they often used the travel literature as their sources. Much of this work was unapologetically Eurocentric, especially as the Atlantic slave trade expanded and the need to justify it grew. Africa was increasingly portrayed as 'primitive', and as the drums of imperialism began beating, its salvation was seen to lie in European overlordship or outright conquest.

Eurocentrism was given its philosophical imprimatur in Hegel's *Philosophy of History*[2] in which he declared, categorically, that Africa 'is not a historical continent; it shows neither change nor development', and that the portion that showed historical light, according to his judgement, namely, North Africa, was not really a part of this benighted continent. Thus was born the racist truncation of Africa into the sub-Saharan cartographic contraption. In the meantime, North Africa was encapsulated into Orientalism, so brilliantly dissected by Edward Said.[3]

In reaction, western-educated scholars in West Africa and the African diaspora began producing histories that emphasised African civilisations and achievements. The vindicationist tradition found a powerful voice in Olaudah Equiano's *The Interesting Narrative of the Life of Olaudah Equiano.*[4] Even more scholarly and combative were the works of the great Liberian scholar, Edward Blyden, whose trilogy – *A Vindication of the African Race, The Negro in Ancient History and Christianity, Islam and the Negro Race*[5] – published in the mid-nineteenth century set the tone for much twentieth-century nationalist and Pan-Africanist thought and historiography.

Besides these large civilisational histories, West African intellectuals also published national histories, such as Samuel Johnson's influential and classic *History of the Yorubas.*[6] From the diaspora came the writings of Alexander Crummell and in the early twentieth century those of W. E. B. Dubois, most memorably his *The*

World and Africa,[7] and W. L. Hansberry,[8] who conducted lifelong research on the image of Africa and Africans by classical Greco-Roman writers. These histories defended the humanity and historicity of Africans. I recall the electrifying impact some of these works had on me when I first read them as an undergraduate student.

The Colonial Era Library

The third period emerged in the twentieth century. The colonial library flourished. But this library embodied contrasting historiographical traditions. The Eurocentric, or what I call imperialist, tradition dominated. Challenging it were the nationalist and radical traditions. Each of these traditions differed both in their interpretations and in methodology, in the type and way they used sources. Imperialist and nationalist historiographies represented almost diametrically opposed views of African history. To the former, African history began with the arrival of Europeans, a narrative that turned colonialism into a decisive moment, whereas to the latter African history stretches for millennia and colonialism is a parenthesis, an episode, a footnote in Africa's long history, as Ade Ajayi so memorably put it in his famous essay of 1968.[9]

Consequently, imperialist historians mostly discussed, in positive light, the policies of colonial governments and the activities of colonial auxiliaries, from European merchants to missionaries to the settlers. When Africans appeared in their narratives, it was to condemn their societies and cultures, or to chronicle their westernisation or modernisation. Those who resisted colonial conquest or colonial rule were depicted as atavistic whereas those who collaborated or accepted the colonial regime were praised for their foresight and wisdom. In fact, in-depth study of African societies was largely left to anthropology. With its functionalist-positivist paradigms and ethnographic present, it exonerated, if not extolled, colonialism.

However, the production of historical knowledge was not an imperial monopoly even in the darkest days of colonialism. This is because the colonial project was always contested. The perennial struggles over the organisations of the colonial economy, politics and culture created spaces for the production of anti-imperialist knowledges by the proponents of Africa's ancient libraries. There were also anti-colonial critics in the imperial metropoles themselves.

The vindicationist tradition of the slave trade era mutated into a fully fledged nationalist historiography, which focused on African agency, adaptations, choices, experiences, initiatives and resistance against colonialism. The methodological forte of nationalist historiography lay in its discovery of new sources of data. Oral tradition, historical linguistics, evidence from the natural sciences and historical anthropology joined the written and archaeological sources prized by Eurocentric historiography as valid sources for historical research and reconstruction.

Decolonisation created favourable conditions for the production of nationalist historiography as new universities were established, research funds became available, historical associations were formed, journals launched and publishers scrambled for the latest research findings. Famous schools emerged, most prominently the Ibadan school, which denounced the shortcomings of missionaries and colonial governments and launched the influential Ibadan History Series, and the Dar es Salaam school, which popularised dependency approaches that stressed, to use the title of Walter Rodney's famous book, *How Europe Underdeveloped Africa*.[10]

Nationalist historians chronicled the rise and fall of Africa's ancient states and empires, long-distance trade, migrations and the spread of religions, and critiqued colonial policies, celebrated the growth of nationalism and reincorporated Egypt and North Africa into the mainstream of African history. The nationalist perspective spread to universities in the global North where African studies programmes mushroomed.

The Post-Independence Era Library

From the 1970s, the fourth phase – the post-independence era – began to unfold from the momentary euphoria of decolonisation. Not surprisingly, the nationalist tradition began to face challenges from radical perspectives. Critics charged that nationalist historiography focused on the 'voices' of the ruling classes, rather than the 'masses'. It was also pointed out that nationalist historiography was too preoccupied with showing that Africa had produced organised polities, monarchies and cities just like Europe, so that it wrote African history by analogy and subsumed it into the logic or teleology of European history. It failed to probe deeper into the historical realities of African material and social life before colonial rule. As for the colonial period, nationalism was made so 'overdetermining' that only feeble efforts were made to provide systematic analyses of imperialism, its changing forms and their impact, not to mention the processes of local class formation and class struggle.

The radical traditions that railed against the nationalist tradition and its now largely discredited nemesis, the imperialist tradition, included the Marxist, dependency, feminist, ecological and postcolonial traditions. Marxist influence grew with the triumph of radical liberation movements in the early 1970s in southern Africa and the adoption of Marxism as a developmentalist ideology by several African political parties and states. In addition, were western intellectuals who were dissatisfied with bourgeois liberalism and western imperialism in what was then called the Third World before it was rechristened the global South.

Marxist scholars examined the processes of production, social formation and class struggle, as well as the complex mediations and contradictory effects of imperialism in modern Africa. Marxist historiography, broadly defined, came in different theoretical and national configurations. Some of the Marxist-inspired work was schematic, doctrinaire and pretentious. However, some of the work was rich and enlightening. Particularly impressive were the studies on labour and workers, agriculture and peasants and the changing structures of Africa's incorporation into the world economy.

Marxists often did not regard dependency scholars and writers as fellow travellers. Indeed, there was much theoretical and ideological bloodletting between the two, but they shared more affinities than differences in their emphasis on exploitative economic structures and processes. The Marxists preferred to concentrate on the internal dynamics of African societies, whereas the dependistas were more interested in the external dynamics of Africa's contemporary underdevelopment. They blamed it on Africa's incorporation into the periphery of the world capitalist system, initially during the era of the slave trade, followed by direct colonialism, then neocolonial or multilateral imperialism. Throughout, the structures of internal underdevelopment were reproduced through unequal exchange and outflow of surpluses, which engendered external dependency for capital, markets and technology.

Despite some of the insightful work the various approaches inspired there was one glaring omission: their coverage of gender and women's history was poor. From the turn of the 1970s, feminist historians began to challenge women's marginalisation in African historiography, a challenge buoyed by the growth of the women's movement. Some African feminists relentlessly attacked the epistemological hegemony of western feminism, criticising the very foundational categories of 'gender', 'woman' and the 'body', arguing that these categories must be subjected to critical analysis and privilege the categories and interpretations of African societies.

Perhaps the most famous interventions were those made by Ifi Amadiume and Oyeronke Oyewumi, in their books *Male Daughters, Female Husbands*[11] and *The Invention of Women: Making African Sense of Western Gender Discourses,*[12] respectively. From the 1980s, there was an explosion of feminist-inspired histories, many of which simply sought to restore women to history, to record women's activities and experiences in the conventional themes of African historiography and some to engender African historiography as a whole. Feminist scholarship inspired new research work, including highly sophisticated studies on development, sexualities and gendered identities.

For its part, the ecological tradition began to reshape understanding of the various periods and phenomena in African history as dynamic processes. These processes involve complex interactions between humans and habitat, nature and society, history and geography, reflect how the physical environment and human agency are mutually constitutive, in that people's creativity and thought produce places as much as places produce people's cultures and identities, and illustrate the deep effects of ideologies of power on the landscape and vice versa.

Influenced by postcolonial ideas, many environmental historians increasingly stressed the complexity and contradictions of environmental change and the variability of outcomes. Inter-related work has dwelt on African environmental ideas, ideologies, movements and conflicts. Included are environmental feminists, who seek to decipher the gendered perceptions and constructions of environmental changes and adaptations.

The 1980s and 1990s also saw the postcolonial tradition and its affiliated 'posts' – postmodernism and poststructuralism. Analyses inspired by the 'posts' shared a distrust of the 'meta-narratives' of nation, class and sometimes gender and the positivism and dichotomies of modernist history. They insisted on the hybridity, contingency, decentredness, ambivalence and the centrality of discourse in historical experience. Let me point out in passing that African scholars have had a complex and problematic relationship with the 'posts', one characterised by advocacy, ambivalence and antagonism.

The claims of the 'posts' often sound both familiar and strange. Familiar because they have spent their entire careers deconstructing western and modernist claims to truth, to the universal and to chronicling the clashes and convergences of cultures and the loss of certainties. Also, strange because many of them believe passionately, bred as they were with the enduring dreams of African nationalism – self-determination, development and democratisation – in the possibilities of historical agency, the necessity of Africa's regeneration.

Clearly, taking the long view, African knowledges are constituted from different libraries, each with a variety of paradigmatic traditions. I asked earlier, what are the prospects for an integrated library to emerge out of the synthesis of the four libraries examined in this presentation? This begs another set of questions: Is such a project necessary? Who will undertake it? A starting point, surely, would be for our academic leaders, our scholars and students to immerse themselves in the rich traditions of African society and thought going back centuries and millennia. If nothing else, that would help put Eurocentrism in its place as just one of the strands in our intellectual history, which we must continue to combat whenever it rears its ugly head, and assert that it is not the sum total or foundational matrix of our knowledge systems.

Placing Africa in World History

For those of us who are historians, and I believe that every student across the continent should be taught African history regardless of their major, we have to continue recovering and reconstructing Africa's long history, the oldest in the world, but also inserting it into global history, into the history of humanity. The immense achievements of African historiography over the past half-century are quite evident. The apotheosis of the African historiographical revolution was the publication of two rival compendiums, each in eight volumes, namely, the *UNESCO General History of Africa* (1981–1993)[13] and the *Cambridge History of Africa* (1975–1986).[14] The *General History* brought together the largest group of historians ever assembled to work on a research project. Today, thousands of studies are published every year on every aspect of African histories, societies, politics, cultures, economies and ecologies by the tens of thousands of academics who spend their professional lives researching, thinking and writing their pieces about this gigantic continent Africa.

Nevertheless, studies of African phenomena, processes and problems have yet to rid themselves entirely of the epistemic erasures, omissions, fabrications, stereotypes and silences of Eurocentrism. The struggles to liberate African knowledges will have to continue resting on a triple intellectual manoeuvre: provincialising Europe, which has monopolised universality; universalising Africa beyond its Eurocentric provincialisation; and reading histories of other continents on their own terms. No amount of historiographical conceit can hide the fact that Europe has not always been the dominant part of the world, or Europeans the most numerous members of the human species.

The rise of Europe to global dominance is recent: until the mid-eighteenth century, the Muslim world was dominant in much of the Afro-Eurasian world. In recent times, global power shifted gradually from Euro-America to Asia, as China returns to the global economic power it enjoyed several centuries ago. Moreover, the notion of the West must be deconstructed: there is no industrial Britain without the Atlantic slave trade, and the Americas including the United States are inconceivable without the massive contributions of Africans.

This is to suggest that African historians must take seriously the challenge of placing African history in world history, in the history of our species, *Homo sapiens.* Conventional history covers only the last 5,000 years, a flash in the span of human evolution and existence on this beautiful and fragile planet of ours. It is from this continent that the world's *Homo sapiens* evolved and scattered across the globe. Thus, Africa is at the heart of human history: it is the continent where humans have lived the longest, and where they underwent and made many of the fundamental transformations and innovations that characterise modern humans and social life.

Long conceptions of human history offer the world and us an immense opportunity to recentre Africa in global and human history and deepen our understanding of African history itself. Conceiving and writing the remarkable history of humanity requires us to focus on key moments and transformations. Different authors focus on, and will select, different thematic anchors. For me, a history of *Homo sapiens* would have to include at least four critical elements. First, changes in production that affected our material lives, including agriculture and manufacturing and their ecological interactions and implications. Second, changes in modes of communication, including the development of languages and exchange systems. Third, changes in the human imagination, including the development of religions and the arts. Finally, changes in modes of power, including the constructions and hierarchies of imperialism, race, nationality, ethnicity, class, gender, sexuality and other social inscriptions of difference and control.

Raising Africa's Knowledge Production

I conclude with reflections on a critical challenge facing Africa when it comes to knowledge production, which we ought to give weight to as we continue fighting against Eurocentrism. As I noted earlier, I see connections between the two, between the development of fully decolonised African universities and the establishment of robust and globally competitive knowledge-producing institutions. Here I address, briefly, the issue of Africa's position in global knowledge production.

My remarks are drawn from my most recent book, *The Transformation of Global Higher Education, 1945–2015.*[15] The book examines the development of higher education on every continent over the past seventy years. I identify five major sets of changes, namely, massification, privatisation, internationalisation, shifts in knowledge production, and rising pressures for accountability. Below I deal with the shifts in knowledge production and how they manifest themselves in Africa.

Before sharing with you data on Africa's global research profile, let me identify some of the key changes in global knowledge production. First, there is the massive reorganisation of knowledge production, dissemination and consumption. This transformation is partly evident in the expansion and emergence of new disciplines, sub-disciplines and inter-, trans- and multidisciplinary fields of study. New interdisciplinary formations, ranging from environmental studies to Big Science, have grown. This has led to shifts in the positioning and status of different academic fields both inside and outside the academy. Generally, in many countries, STEM and professional fields such as Business Studies have eclipsed the Humanities; the fate of the Social Sciences has tended to wax and wane between the 'two cultures'.

Second, there have been remarkable shifts in global knowledge hegemonies and hierarchies. The dominance of the developed countries of Europe, North America and Japan has progressively declined while that of the emerging economies, especially in Asia, has grown. North America's share of global research and development (R&D) declined from 37.9 per cent in 1994 to 28.9 per cent in 2013, while Europe's fell from 31.4 per cent to 22.7 per cent. In the meantime, it rose for Asia from 26.6 per cent to 42.2 per cent and to a much smaller extent for Latin America and the Caribbean, from 1.9 per cent to 3.5 per cent.

The proportions of the developed countries in the growth and distribution of researchers and publications also fell relative to the emerging economies, especially China. The latter more than doubled its share of world publications, from 9.9 per cent in 2008 to 20.2 per cent in 2014. Asia as a whole raised its share, from 24.2 per cent in 2002 to 39.5 per cent in 2014. For North America, the decline was from 34.2 per cent to 28.6 per cent and for Europe 45.5 per cent to 39.3 per cent between 2002 and 2014. Thus, Asia is now the global leader both in the volume of knowledge production and number of researchers.

Third, in the midst of these transformations the modes of scholarly knowledge production, dissemination and consumption have also been undergoing changes, facilitated by the rise of new information and communication technologies. ICTs have become increasingly pervasive in higher education because of growing student demand, rising evidence of their benefits and institutional strategies for revenue growth and branding. Technology-enhanced learning has brought new pedagogical opportunities and challenges. Some have welcomed the innovative capacities of ICT in the processes of learning and teaching, research and scholarship, professional service and public engagement. However, others dread its disruptive potential for the business model of on-campus education.

ICT has also transformed the role of libraries and dynamics of academic publishing. The explosion of information is reconfiguring the role of libraries as repositories of information into nerve centres of digitised information communication and raising the need for information literacy. Similarly, academic publishing is being transformed by the acceleration, commercialisation and digitalisation of scholarly communication. Technology simultaneously opens new opportunities for researchers to collaborate and disseminate their output more widely, while at the same time it strengthens the role of powerful gatekeepers outside the academy, as evident in the growth of global firms that dominate the academic publishing and database industry.

Fourth, the academic profession is itself undergoing disruptions. Overall, there has been a progressive shift towards more top-down institutional governance, and the ranks of professional managers and even presidents, rectors, or vice chancellors without academic backgrounds are swelling in several parts of the world. The edicts of managerialism are increasingly undermining academic autonomy and freedom. It is clear that the decreasing influence of academics on institutional decision-making, combined with deteriorating conditions of work, have led to declining institutional loyalty. The growing disempowerment of academics as well as their casualisation constitute key factors in the apparent declining educational quality of higher education institutions around the world.

Both academics and academic work are also becoming more fragmented. This is a product of the institutional, professional and instructional unbundling of faculty roles. Significant changes have taken place in the social composition of academics, including the rising proportion of female academics, although gender disparities in terms of disciplines, conditions of work, remuneration and status persist. The academic workforce has also become more casualised and stratified as institutions seek to cut costs by reducing the number of permanent faculty and expand the ranks of part-time or adjunct faculty. In the United States, for example, adjunct faculty now make up nearly 80 per cent of the professoriate – a reversal from a generation ago.

Unfortunately, Africa scores the lowest on all global research indicators, including its share of R&D, gross domestic expenditure as a share of GDP, and its proportion of world researchers, researchers per million inhabitants and world scholarly publications. But Africa enjoys one dubious distinction – African scholars boast the world's highest share of publications with international authors, especially from the United States, France and the United Kingdom. Clearly, African academic knowledge systems, like our economies, suffer from limited regional integration and high levels of external dependency. That is a challenge we must overcome if our higher education systems are to contribute to integrated, inclusive and innovative sustainable development.

Conclusion

The struggles for the transformation of higher education that we are witnessing across the continent encompass many dimensions. It is imperative that the various key stakeholders in African higher education, from governments to the public to parents and to students, faculty, staff and administrators in the academic institutions themselves, raise the value proposition of African higher education for twenty-first century African societies, economies and polities. This requires commitment to what I call the 4As, 4Cs, 4Is and 4Rs.

The 4As refer to availability (of institutions), access (to institutions), affordability (of institutions) and accountability (by institutions). The 4Cs refer to comprehensiveness (provision of holistic education that develops the whole person), curiosity (cultivation of lifelong learning), community (fostering civic values) and capabilities (developing soft skills and attributes beyond technical, job-specific and generic cognitive skills, especially communication and critical-thinking skills, problem-solving, empathy, creativity, self-confidence and intercultural, international, interdisciplinary and information literacies).

The 4Is refer to inclusion (valuing institutional diversity – class, gender, ethnicity, religion, disability, sexuality, etc.), innovation (cultivating creative and entrepreneurial mindsets), integration (building cohesive teaching, learning and research communities) and impact (fostering cultures of continuous assessment). The 4Rs refer to relevance (of scholarly knowledges for the economy, society and times), retention (ensuring development and success for students, faculty and staff), research (unwavering commitment to both basic and applied knowledge production and evidence-based decision-making) and rigour (in all activities to ensure academic excellence, operational excellence and service excellence).

Only then will our universities fully contribute to the 'Africa Rising' narrative, turning it from dependence on the fluctuating fortunes of primary commodity prices towards sustainable knowledge-driven economies and societies; from the fleeting bliss of abundance experienced by only the wealthy few into the reality of well-being for the many. Higher education is a powerful engine for building the kind of Africa we all wish to live in and of which we can be proud. It is indispensable to fulfilling the dreams of generations of struggles against imperial and neocolonial exploitation and marginalisation, and realising the enduring aspirations of our peoples, in all their splendid diversities, for emancipation, empowerment and advancement. With that, the continent may finally realise Kwame Nkrumah's vision, expressed prematurely at the height of decolonisation, that the late twentieth century would be Africa's, and turn the twenty-first century into one that is truly ours.

Notes

1. Paul Tiyambe Zeleza (ed.), *The Study of Africa, Volume 1: Disciplinary and Interdisciplinary Encounters; Volume 2: Global and Transnational Engagements,* Dakar: CODESRIA Book Series, 2006.
2. G.W.F. Hegel, *The Philosophy of History,* trans. J. Sibree, introduction C.J. Friedrich, New York: Dover Publications, 1956: 91.
3. Edward Said, *Orientalism*, New York: Random House, 1979.
4. Olaudah Equiano, *The Interesting Narrative of the Life of Olaudah Equiano or Gustavus Vassa, The African: Written by Himself,* Mineola, New York: Dover Publications, 1999 [1789].
5. Edward Blyden, *A Vindication of the African Race: Being a Brief Examination of the Arguments in Favor of African Inferiority, Monrovia, 1857; The Negro in Ancient History,* Mansfield Centre, Connecticut: Martino Fine Books, 2020 [1869]; and *Christianity, Islam and the Negro Race,* Mansfield Centre, Connecticut: Martino Fine Books, 2016 [1887].
6. Samuel Johnson, *The History of the Yorubas from the Earliest Times to the Beginning of the British Protectorate*, London: Forgotten Books, 2012 [1921].
7. W.E.B. Dubois, *The World and Africa: Inquiry Into the Part Which Africa Has Played in World History,* New York: International Publishers Co., Inc, 1979 [1947].
8. William Leo Hansberry, *Africa & Africans as Seen by Classical Writers,* Washington, DC: Howard University Press, 1977.
9. J. F. Ade Ajayi, 'The Continuity of African Institutions under Colonialism', in T. O. Ranger (ed), *Emerging Themes of African History: Proceedings of the International Congress of African Historians held at University College, Dar es Salaam, October* 1965. London: Heinemann, 1968: 189–200.
10. Walter Rodney, *How Europe Underdeveloped Africa,* Washington, DC: Howard University Press, 1981 [1972].
11. Ifi Amadiume, *Male Daughters, Female Husbands: Gender and Sex in an African Society,* London: Zed Press, 1987.
12. Oyèrónké Oyewùmí, *The Invention of Women: Making an African Sense of Western Gender Discourses*, Minneapolis: University of Minnesota Press, 1997.
13. UNESCO, *General History of Africa*, London: Heinemann, 1981–1993.
14. *Cambridge History of Africa,* Cambridge: Cambridge University Press, 1975–1986.
15. Paul Tiyambe Zeleza, *The Transformation of Global Higher Education,* 1945–2015, New York: Palgrave Macmillan, 2016.

Delivered as a public lecture, The Decolonization of African Knowledges, 9th Africa Day Lecture, University of the Free State, Bloemfontein, South Africa, 24 May 2017.

20

Reckoning with the Pasts and Reimagining the Futures of African Studies for the Twenty-first Century

This text was first presented as a keynote address at the Social Sciences Research Council Training Workshop, USIU-Africa, Nairobi, Kenya 7 January 2019. It appears in the African Peace Network Lecture Series, No 4.

Introduction

When I was asked to give the keynote address, I readily agreed not simply because I am the vice chancellor of this fine university but also because I am a student and scholar of the humanities and social sciences. But agreeing was easier than deciding what to say. I finally settled on framing my remarks around three anniversaries in 2019.

The first is the fiftieth anniversary of the contentious annual meeting of the US African Studies Association (ASA) in Montreal, at which African and African-American scholar-activists confronted the mostly conservative, white and male-dominated leadership of the ASA. The Montreal crisis was an outburst – in the academic arena – of the intertwined movements of African decolonisation and American civil rights, which were destined to recast the global order and US domestic politics. In short, I would like to share some reflections on the trajectory of African Studies since independence.

The second anniversary that I am mindful of is that my own university, USIU-Africa, is celebrating its fiftieth anniversary this year. This will provide a segue into some reflections on the development of African universities since independence. In so far as the Social Sciences are embedded in the institutional architecture of universities with their triple mandates – teaching and learning, research and scholarship and public service – their fate is inextricably linked to the changing contexts and conditions of higher education.

The third momentous event this year is the 400th anniversary of the arrival of the first enslaved Africans in what is today the United States of America. The story of the historic African diasporas captures most poignantly the place of Africa and Africans in the changing configurations of the world system. Since the ascendancy of Euro-American hegemony that was immeasurably facilitated by the exploitation of Africa, African social thought, as Samir Amin, the great Egyptian intellectual calls it, has been preoccupied with African positioning in the world.

I begin my presentation with a brief intellectual biography. Second, I proceed to outline some key features of the African Studies enterprise that I was engaged in for the bulk of my professional life in North America. Third, I underscore the importance of embracing the diaspora and diaspora studies in the globalisation of African Studies. Fourth, I share brief observations about the challenges and opportunities facing African universities. I conclude with a few remarks on the project of decolonising African knowledges.

Notes on a Personal Journey

The three anniversaries are threaded together in the tapestry of my personal and professional life. This is another way of saying that intellectual history, the history of ideas and knowledge-producing institutions, in short, the processes of knowledge production, is often inscribed by our social biographies as structured by intersecting institutional, ideological, intellectual dynamics. I was educated as an undergraduate student in Malawi in the early 1970s in the waning years of the euphoria of independence. I became a graduate student in Britain and Canada in the late 1970s and early 1980s when the promises of Uhuru had withered under the harsh glare of authoritarian and corrupt regimes.

As undergraduate students, we were caught up in the excitement of the struggles to decolonise the Humanities and Social Sciences, to establish vibrant African universities, to reclaim indigenous knowledges and fashion African agency out of the continent's 'triple heritage', as Ali Mazrui would later call it. Mazrui borrowed this notion from Kwame Nkrumah's treatise on the African personality. Nkrumah, in turn, was indebted to the writings of Edward Blyden in the nineteenth century, who saw African civilisation as a confluence of indigenous, Christian and Islamic streams.

Thanks to the indefatigable nationalist scholars at Africa's flagship universities, from Dar es Salaam to Nairobi, Ibadan to Dakar, Cairo to Cape Town, and the publications of eager young writers mushrooming through Heinemann's African Writers Series, we discovered the infinite intellectual joys of African histories and literatures. We were exposed to the angry denunciations of modernisation theories by dependency scholars, preeminent among them Walter Rodney, whose book *How Europe Underdeveloped Africa*[2] became our bible. Aided by Frantz

Fanon's searing indictment of the political class, *The Wretched of the Earth*, we discovered that the postcolonial emperors were naked.[3]

We transferred our hopes for the realisation of the historical and humanistic dreams of African nationalism – decolonisation, nation-building, regional integration, democracy and development – to the radical liberation movements of southern Africa and socialist movements elsewhere. By the time I was writing my doctoral dissertation, we had found solace in Marxism and various insurgent social and intellectual movements from feminism to environmentalism.

I finished my PhD in 1982 and experienced the rest of the 1980s from two institutional locations. First, as a young lecturer at the University of the West Indies, where my Pan-African intellectual sensibilities and passions were forged. I was conscious that I took a position once occupied by the great Walter Rodney. Second, I worked at Kenyatta University in Kenya. At both universities, I was nurtured and mentored by some of the most accomplished scholars of the first post-independence generation who had committed their lives to the decolonisation of the academy and were enraged by the apparent betrayal of the dreams of independence. It was during these eight years that my intellectual passions and ideological proclivities were sharpened.

I was truly fortunate to learn from the best about the need for uncompromising intellectual rigour and the transformative possibilities of acknowledging one's deep ignorance, which cultivates a spirit of intellectual striving and humility. From my mentors, I came to appreciate the power of prodigious reading and immersion in the intellectual traditions and literatures of whatever field I was working on. Mentorship is an indispensable part of building social capital, empowering the upcoming generation and keeping the older generation relevant! Good mentors, just like good teachers, learn as much from their mentees and students as the latter learn from them. This process of co-learning requires cultivating meaningful and mutually respectful engagement.

In 1990, I joined the trek to the global North where I spent the next twenty-five years in the intellectual battlefields of Canada and the United States. By then it was clear that the promises of Uhuru had descended into the lost decades of the 1980s and 1990s, ravaged by the market fundamentalist gospel of neoliberalism. The draconian regime of Structural Adjustment Programmes peddled by the international financial institutions racked African economies, societies and educational systems.

In the 1980s, many a young scholar abandoned the African academy altogether. Some found salvation in consultancies or drifted to greener pastures abroad. This difficult moment undermined the capacity of African universities to maintain primacy in the study of their own continent as they had tried to since the 1960s. The decolonisation project virtually collapsed in the maelstrom of the massive devaluation of academic labour. Globally, the end of the postwar boom and the ascendancy of the dispiriting and destructive strictures of neoliberalism proved a fertile ground for the deconstructionist paradigms of the 'posts' – postmodernism, poststructuralism and postcolonialism. The distrust of meta-narratives found supporters among some African scholars.

For my part, these developments and experiences reinforced my radical inclinations and informed three areas of research that became my preoccupations – economic history, gender studies and human rights studies. Later, I was to develop interests in other fields. This underscores the fact that our intellectual proclivities often reflect our times, prevailing ideologies and struggles, dominant intellectual traditions and institutional contexts. In short, much of our individual scholarship is enmeshed in specific historical geographies, current political economies and generational aspirations and anxieties. This observation is an invitation to self-reflexivity.

Regardless of our divergent intellectual and ideological orientations in the 1980s and 1990s, I found that we were all forced to reckon with the apparent failures of African independence and, for those of us lodged in the heartlands of the global North, the assaults of Afro-pessimism were particularly debilitating. A few joined the bandwagon of vicious Africa critics saying that Africa was a 'hopeless' continent, as *The Economist* infamously put it in one of its lead stories in 2000.[4]

The new African diaspora academics suffered from an acute form of the Duboisian 'double consciousness' spawned by the contradiction between their high academic achievements and an inferiorised identity in America's unyielding racial hierarchy, and between their alienation from Africa and the need to come to terms with their Africanity and to promote Africa. This produced three types of intellectuals, as noted by the Kenyan diaspora scholar, Njubi Nesbitt: the comprador intelligentsia (who cynically use their Africanity to authenticate the neocolonial and neoliberal agendas of the international financial institutions); the postcolonial critics (who see themselves as liberal interpreters of Africa to Euro-America and vice versa); and the progressive exiles (who seek to develop a dignified Pan-African identity and solidarity).[5]

At the turn of the new century began the tentative resurgence of Africa, the reconfiguration of global power with the rise of emerging economies, especially China's relentless march to becoming the world's largest economy, a position it had only relinquished for a couple of centuries following the triumph of European imperialism. There were also the massive disruptions of every economic and social sector, including higher education, brought by new information technologies.

I witnessed these developments from three pedestals. First, as the director of one of the largest centres of African Studies in the United States, at the University of Illinois at Urbana-Champaign, a position I assumed in 1995. That is when I became deeply immersed in African Studies and wrote extensively on the subject.

This was a crucial part of my gravitation to the field of intellectual history, my fourth preoccupation. Second, twelve years later in 2007, I became chair of the Department of African American Studies at the University of Illinois at Chicago. My interests in Diaspora Studies, which had germinated years before, were cemented by this experience. This became my fifth area of research. Finally, in 2009, I was appointed dean of the Bellarmine College of Liberal Arts at Loyola Marymount University in Los Angeles. This marked my foray into the private university sector and higher academic administration and my drift from African Studies to higher education as a whole, as I oversaw a broad range of social science and humanities disciplines and centres.

The expansion of my intellectual and institutional horizons received an immeasurable boost when I became vice president for academic affairs at Quinnipiac University in Connecticut, which involved working with the university's nine colleges. This nourished my research interests, culminating in my most recent book, *The Transformation of Global Higher Education*: 1945–2015, the first single-authored book I am aware of that examines the development of higher education on every continent over the seventy years of the postwar era.[6]

My story is not unique for members of my generation. Many of us have experienced the pain and pleasures of intellectual nomadism. We have been part of Africa's brain formation, brain drain, brain gain and brain circulation; we have followed the trails of colonialism, neocolonialism and globalisation; and we straddle Africa and the diaspora. As the younger generation of African academics takes over from us, I hope they will follow the injunction some of us have tried to follow from Ali Mazrui, one of the giants of African letters. In his celebrated television series, *The Africans: A Triple Heritage,* he implored us, echoing Alexander Pope: 'A little modernity is a dangerous thing. Drink deep or taste not the western spring.'[7] I would rephrase it: 'A little scholarship is a dangerous thing. Drink deep or taste not the academic spring.'

The Africas of African Studies

When I became Director of the Center for African Studies at the University of Illinois in August 1995, two things immediately struck me. First, out of the more than eighty Africanists in the university, only one was African American and there were only a handful of African immigrants. I realised African Studies was a white-dominated field, although it had not always been that way.

Second, in November 1995 I attended my first meeting of the African Studies Association (ASA) on US soil. There was a special session devoted to an incendiary article by Philip Curtin – one of the doyens of African Studies – published in *The Chronicle of Higher Education*, titled 'The Ghettoization of African History'.[8] He decried the growing numbers of Africans and African Americans teaching African

History and the consequent 'lowering' of standards. The session, attended by more than three hundred people, was the most contentious I had ever seen. The second lesson I learned was that the field of African Studies in the US was highly racialised and racially fraught.

I decided to delve into the history of African Studies in the US and later around the world. In 1997, I published a book, *Manufacturing African Studies and Crises,* which was followed by a series of articles.[9] It became clear to me that after World War II, two versions of African Studies emerged in the American academy: what I call 'Euro-American African Studies', and the older tradition of 'Afro-American African Studies', which it eclipsed. The former triumphed not because of its superior intellectual products but because of the greater support it received from the federal government as part of the National Defense Act of 1958 that launched funding for Area Studies programmes at American universities. Also, the major foundations, such as Rockefeller and Ford, jumped into the fray and directed much of their funding to the historically white colleges and universities (HWCUs).

My research showed that African Studies in the United States, as I wrote in one article:

> has been in a perpetual state of crisis since its institutionalisation in the 1950s. The crisis is rooted in the unyielding intellectual, institutional and ideological solitudes and bitter contestations among the producers and consumers of Africanist knowledge who are divided by the inscriptions and hierarchies of race and nationality, locational and spatial affiliations, epistemological orientations and ambitions. Particularly destructive is the continuing gulf between African American and European American Africanists and between the latter and African scholars. For African Studies to survive, let alone thrive, these solitudes must be confronted directly and transcended.[10]

The contestations ranged from divergent claims of the field's own history to conceptions of Africa itself, to epistemic preoccupations. While African Studies was pioneered at the historically black colleges and universities (HBCUs) in the nineteenth and early twentieth centuries by African-American scholar-activists such as W.E.B. Dubois, arguably the greatest black intellectual of the twentieth century, conventional histories of African Studies from the 1960s gave 'paternity' of the field to the historically white colleges and universities and white professional academics, such as Melville Herskovits. Clearly, histories of academic institutions and fields are used to stake positions, mark boundaries and to confer authority in the perennial struggle for intellectual, material and reputational resources.

African Studies entered the segregated corridors of the HWCUs after World War II out of three key imperatives. First was the security imperative. The area studies project was part of the Cold War rivalry between the United States and the former Soviet Union. Proverbial American ignorance of what was christened the 'Third World' in the 1950s, comprising the newly independent countries of Asia and Africa and the United States' turbulent backyard, Latin America, was increasingly seen as dangerous for a superpower locked in mortal combat with the USSR to win hearts and minds around the world.

Second, there was the epistemological imperative to internationalise knowledge in the American academy while simultaneously reinforcing the supremacy of the Eurocentric disciplines. The Social Science and Humanities disciplines strutting into the American academy remained resolutely ethnocentric. They concocted from sanitised American and European experiences universal models and theories that blissfully ignored the reality and diversity of global histories and geographies, cultures and societies, polities and economies. The area studies project enabled the disciplines to both retain their epistemic superiority and acquire new testing sites for the affirmation of their supposedly eternal theoretical probity.

Third, given the centrality of race and racism in American society and social imaginary, the development of area studies was invariably tied to the fate of ethnic minorities. Euro-American African Studies inherited the pervasive 'scientific racism' that coloured much of the work on Native Americans, African Americans and other marginalised populations. The exclusion of these populations from American political and cultural citizenship necessitated the separation of their ancestral cultures and continents from disciplinary narratives. Ironically, it also propelled the exclusion of racial minorities from the area studies programmes themselves in the spurious name of objectivity.

Euro-American African Studies benefitted from two other trends after World War II. As I argued in another paper, the growing commoditisation and corporatisation of academic culture:

> forced and facilitated the divorce of academics from social movements, civic engagement and public intellectualism. Intellectual life became increasingly professionalized thanks to the explosive postwar expansion of university education and the growth of middle-class comforts, consciousness and conservatism, all of which spawned a social science research culture that valorized objectivity, detachment and a mindless chase for theory. This expedited the separation of African studies from domestic African American constituencies and reinforced the use of deductive methods and models, in which Africa was reduced to a testing site for theories manufactured with faddish regularity in the American academy.[11]

The second trend was the emergence of the development industry. I had interrogated modernisation theories in my earlier work in the 1980s on economic history. I noted how the language of development in the British Empire emerged with the Colonial Development Act of 1929, which was further elaborated by the Colonial Development and Welfare Act of 1945.[12] Development discourse was part of the ideological armoury of colonialism. By the late 1920s, the narrative of colonialism as a civilising mission was already losing its Social Darwinian currency. It was finally buried in the aftermath of the ghastly barbarisms of World War II. In the context of the Cold War in which the Soviet Union and Marxist ideologues blamed Third World poverty on colonial exploitation and imperialism, liberal western scholars found succour in modernisation paradigms and prayed to the gospel of W.W. Rostow's *The Stages of Economic Growth: A Non-Communist Manifesto.*[13]

Development discourse gave area studies, including Euro-American African Studies, the prescriptive muscle of the massive development industry. The paradigmatic and political gulf between the two solitudes of the HBCUs and HWCUs in African Studies widened. In the latter, the field drifted to policy and development-oriented research and professional encounters with Africa, away from posing the large civilisational and cultural questions and popular engagement valued by Pan-African intellectuals and many in the HBCUs. Moreover, while the Africa of the Afro-American tradition was continental, that of the Euro-American African Studies was largely truncated to the sub-Saharan contraption: a conception of Africa deeply rooted in Eurocentric thought.

This was sanctified by the German philosopher Friedrich Hegel who infamously dismissed 'Africa proper' as 'the land of childhood which, lying beyond the day of history, is enveloped in the dark mantle of Night'.[14] 'Africa proper' excluded North Africa, which was within the bosom of history. Hegel's ghost roamed the corridors of African Studies centres in the HWCUs. As centre director at Illinois, where North Africa was incorporated into the Center for Middle Eastern Studies, I fought this Hegelian separation and diminution of Africa and sought to reclaim the entire continent as 'Africa proper'.

Ironically, in the 1960s African Studies departments in the HWCUs were the main beneficiaries of struggles for civil rights. As I noted in a paper on the development of African Studies, African American Studies and Africana Studies,

> there were intense reverberations between decolonisation in Africa and civil rights in the US, which had epistemological and institutional consequences. Both independence and decolonisation brought more African and African American students and faculty to predominantly white American universities. Independence brought more Africans to the US seeking education to develop their postcolonial nations, while the civil rights movements opened doors for African Americans to enter white-dominated institutions, as well as migrants from Third World regions.[15]

The racial minorities entering the white campuses encountered racism and curricular exclusion. For African-American and African students, this engendered struggles for studies of the histories and cultures of African peoples across the Atlantic. Thus:

> the African American studies movement was both an ally and a foe of African studies. Many a reluctant university administration was forced to develop African

> studies programs in direct response to the institutional, intellectual and ideological challenges posed by militant African American students ... whose demands for courses on the Black experience soon turned into calls for Black studies departments, centers, institutes, or programs that should both be independent and involved in community service.[16]

In short:

> by challenging Eurocentric paradigms and the rigid barriers between academic disciplines, the African American studies movement helped legitimize the study of non-Western cultures and multidisciplinary and interdisciplinary studies ... But by pointing to the configuration of European American power and domination in the American academy, even in African studies and emphasising the collective black experience, it challenged African studies in which the study of Africa and the African America and the African diaspora more generally were strictly separated.[17]

As more African academics arrived on American campuses in the 1980s and 1990s, fleeing authoritarian states and impoverished universities, a third Africa entered the American academy, which had complex, often contradictory relationships with the two longstanding Africas. The entry of African-born academics offered African Studies both an opportunity and a challenge. On the one hand, I wrote:

> ... many were not always sensitive to the racial dynamics and demands of American society and the academy; some even internalized the dominant's society's negative stereotypes of African Americans, which often made them accomplices with European Americans in America's eternal racial war, for which they were sometimes rewarded with preferential hiring and promotion over African Americans.[18]

However, the longer the African migrants stayed in the United States and as their children navigated the treacherous racial quagmire of low expectations for peoples of African descent, the more they increasingly gravitated towards African-American grievances. These were reinforced by their own longstanding grumblings about the marginality of African voices in African Studies and the gatekeeping functions of white scholars in publications on their countries of origin.

Out of these complex dynamics and other structural developments in the American academy, including growing fiscal constraints that generated pressures for consolidation of academic programmes in some universities, the institutional architecture and intellectual division of labour in African Studies began to creak. Joint programmes of African and African American Studies started emerging on many campuses. Although there were tensions over nationality, gender, discipline and modalities of public engagement, which manifested themselves principally over faculty searches, course scheduling and extra-curricular programming, the trend towards more comprehensive Africana studies became unmistakable.

I was part of this trajectory when I became chair of an African American Studies department as it sought to expand its African curriculum. In 2008, I became president of the African Studies Association, and in my presidential address the following year I spoke on 'African Diasporas: Towards a Global History'.[19] I urged the African Studies community to incorporate Diaspora Studies and abandon parochial Eurocentric approaches to the study of Africa and US-centric methods to the study of African global diasporas. I had previously argued at length on the need to globalise African Studies in several books, including *Rethinking Africa's Globalization. Vol. 1: The Intellectual Challenges* and *The Study of Africa Vol. 1: Disciplinary and Interdisciplinary Encounters* and *Vol 2: Global and Transnational Engagements.*[20]

Volume 1 of *The Study of Africa* examines how the continent has been studied in all the major Humanities, Social Science disciplines and interdisciplinary fields since the nineteenth century. Volume 2 interrogates African Studies in different world regions, including Asia-Pacific (China, India, Japan and Australia), Europe (Britain, France, Germany and Russia) and the Americas (Brazil, Caribbean and United States), as well as international and global frames of analysis.

Space does not allow me to elaborate on the two books, except to encourage you to buy them! Suffice to say, each region and nation has developed its own Africa in terms of intellectual preoccupations, ideological tendencies and institutional organisation. This often reflects the history of relations between the country concerned and African countries, the dominant intellectual traditions and the country's relative positioning in global scholarship and affairs.

Thus, African Studies within each discipline and across various world regions has its own distinctive features, which is an argument against facile homogenisation and the tendency to put the United States on a global pedestal. I get worried when some critics inadvertently recentre or reinscribe American hegemony by assuming that it is the global centre of African Studies. I was recently reminded of this by an article that complained about the 'gentrification of African studies', as if this was a new phenomenon.[21] Indeed the dominant version of African Studies in the United States, Euro-American African Studies, was never established to serve Africa, or even its own African diaspora, the second largest in the world after Brazil.

Embracing the Diaspora

The diaspora has always played an important role in modern African history. As I noted in an essay on diaspora knowledge production: 'the diaspora has been a critical site of knowledge production on Africa for a long time ... As both a place and a project, a cultural and cognitive community, the diaspora has provided an unusually fertile space for imagining and writing on Africa ...'.[22]

During the late nineteenth and early twentieth centuries, as colonialism reconfigured the global civilisational presence of Africans and reconnected Africa to its diaspora, the diaspora became crucial to the (re)constructions of Africa as an idea, Africa as an object of study, Africans as academics and Pan-Africanism as a project.

In short, the HBCUs where the Kwame Nkrumahs and Nnamdi Azikiwes attended college in the 1930s – the HWCUs were not yet open to them – 'were in the forefront of producing both knowledge and personnel, counter-hegemonic discourses and developmental capacities for the diaspora itself and Africa.'[23] The HBCUs continue to employ a significant proportion of African-born academics today. The political contributions of the historic diaspora are significant. As I remarked in an address on the diaspora in November 2018, 'The first thing to note when discussing the political contributions of the diaspora to Africa's transformation is the fact that the African nationalisms that brought about decolonisation were incubated by the transatlantic Pan-African movement that first emerged in the diaspora.'[24]

Contemporary African governments and communities value the diaspora for its economic contributions, especially remittances. The new diaspora is Africa's biggest donor, eclipsing official development assistance and investments from the US, EU and China, not to mention the purveyors from the entertainment industry of the mercy development complex, who feast on African commiseration. In 2017, diaspora remittances reached US$69.5 billion. If one adds diaspora philanthropy, investment and human capital flows, the scale of diaspora socioeconomic contributions becomes truly staggering.

As previously noted, the historic diaspora has been an intellectual asset. The new diaspora constitutes a source of intellectual capital – an intellectual remittance – that Africa needs to mobilise more systematically and strategically. I have been involved in this endeavour for some years, borne out of my own diaspora condition and fascination with the field of Diaspora Studies. This fascination began in the 1990s and became stronger in the 2000s as I increasingly reflected on my personal and professional circumstances, not to mention those of my family. The joint appointment I held at the Pennsylvania State University in the departments of history and African and African American studies reinforced my understanding of the complex institutional history and academic politics of African American studies.

It was while I was at Penn State that I embarked on my global project on the African diaspora, which was aided by a generous grant from the Ford Foundation, which enabled me to travel over a period of four years to sixteen countries in South America, the Caribbean, Europe and Asia to research the history of African diasporas. Out of these amazing trips, I published an academic travelogue, *In Search of African Diasporas: Testimonies and Encounters.*[25] In the mid-2000s I began publishing essays and books in which I sought to understand both our theoretical conceptualisation of the diaspora and the historical mapping of the diaspora.[26] For the latter, I became interested in three things: the patterns of dispersal of African peoples around the world; the processes of diaspora formation in different regions; and the changing dynamics of diaspora engagement with Africa.

One of the greatest joys of my intellectual life is that my diaspora work led to my being commissioned by the Carnegie Corporation of New York in 2011–2012 to undertake a study on the African academic diaspora in Canada and the United States. The purpose was to determine their size and scope, their patterns of engagement with African higher education institutions and these institutions' perspectives on how best to build effective modalities of engagement for mutual benefit.[27]

In 2013, we established the Carnegie African Diaspora Fellowship Program (CADFP) under an innovative model in international education exchanges involving four organs: the Carnegie Corporation providing funding, the International Institute for Education providing administrative and logistical support, the Advisory Council of prominent African academics and administrators in Africa and the diaspora providing strategic direction, and USIU-Africa hosting the Secretariat. To date, the programme has exceeded expectations. It has awarded fellowships to 385 diaspora academic projects. Altogether, 187 African universities have applied to host a fellow and 107 universities have been selected (discussed in more detail in Chapter 10).

Clearly, there is huge demand by African institutions for diaspora academics and there is a need to expand beyond fellowships to other modalities of engagement to appeal to different stakeholders. Based on CADFP's experience, success and lessons learned, it was decided at the First Higher Education Summit held in Dakar in March 2015 to establish the 10/10 Programme, which would sponsor 1,000 academicians in the diaspora, both from the historic and new diasporas anywhere in the world across all disciplines, every year, to anywhere on the continent.

In pursuit of this agenda, CADFP, in collaboration with various partners, including USIU-Africa, organised a conference at Harvard University in March 2017 that brought together key stakeholders from government, business, universities and philanthropic organisations to explore the establishment of the 10/10 Programme. A follow-up meeting was planned to be held in Nairobi in late 2019 (it was later postponed) to reflect on the Dakar Summit, refine the key action points of the Harvard meeting and launch the Consortium of African Diaspora Academic Programmes.

Revitalising African Universities

In my work on African universities, I have identified three broad periods: what I call the golden era, which lasted from the 1950s to the mid-1970s; the crisis era, from the late 1970s to the turn of the 2000s; and the recovery era, the first decades of the twenty-first century. The golden era was characterised by the excitement of building new universities and expanding old ones, vigorous efforts to decolonise the disciplines, stable, if not vibrant, state support, and relatively good relations between the intelligentsia and the political class.

The crisis era was marked by the financial assaults of Structural Adjustment and the political onslaught of authoritarianism. Universities were no longer seen as essential to the national project but as bastions of subversive 'foreign' ideologies and student radicalism. Many had long fulfilled their original mission to create an Africanised cadre for the civil service, which in any case was being decimated under SAPs. The old systems, structures and stabilities of African higher education disappeared and academics increasingly became casualties. Battles of various kinds and intensities were waged within and outside universities, over missions and mandates, legitimacy and their status as producers, disseminators and consumers of scientific and scholarly knowledge.

As African economies began their hesitant recovery in the 2000s and the importance of knowledge economies and societies was trumpeted, a period of reform began accompanied by the explosive growth of the university sector. We identified the broad contours of the reform agenda, centred on five issues, in the two-volume study, *African Universities in the Twenty-First Century*, which I co-edited. First, the philosophical foundations and mission of African universities. Second, the challenges of quality control, funding and governance. Third, the dynamics of teaching and learning and the volume and value of knowledge production. Fourth, the role of universities in the pursuit of the historic project of African nationalism and in helping to manage and resolve the crises of development. Fifth, their capacity to promote the Pan-African project and pursue more equitable internationalisation for African higher education systems.'[28]

As indicated at the beginning of this chapter, USIU-Africa was celebrating its golden anniversary in 2019. As noted in my book, *The Transformation of Global Higher Education*,[29] when the university was being established in 1969, there were only 170 universities across the continent, 35 of which were private. The number of universities increased to 446 in 1989, out of which 112 were private. In the 1990s, 338 new institutions were established and in the 2000s another 647. By 2015, private universities outnumbered public universities, 1,639 to 972.

In 2018, according to the World Higher Education Database,[30] there were 1,682 universities in Africa. The majority were private. Clearly, this was nothing short of phenomenal. Yet, in global terms, Africa had the smallest number of universities of any region, except Oceania. Worldwide there were 18,772 higher education institutions, putting Africa's share at 8.9 per cent. Asia boasted the largest share at 37 per cent, followed by Europe, with 21.9 per cent, North America at 20.4 per cent and Latin America and the Caribbean with 12 per cent.

Equally revealing was the data on enrolments. In a presentation at the Annual Conference of Kenya's Commission for University Education in October 2018, I noted that according to UNESCO data, enrolments in Africa remained relatively small. The total number of students in African higher education institutions in 2017 stood at 14,654,667.7 million, out of 220,704,239.5 million worldwide, or 6.6 per cent, which was less than the continent's share of institutions.[31]

Forty-five per cent of the African students were in northern Africa. To put it more graphically, Indonesia had nearly as many students in higher education institutions as the whole of sub-Saharan Africa (7.98 million to 8.03 million). Enrolment rates told the story differently. In 2017, the world's average enrolment rate was 37.88 per cent, compared to 8.98 per cent in sub-Saharan Africa and 33.75 per cent in northern Africa. Only Algeria and Mauritius boasted enrolment rates higher than the world average: 47.72 per cent and 38.84 per cent, respectively. Kenya's stood at 11.66 per cent in 2016 behind twelve other African countries that had data.

Clearly, we have a long way to go. In 2017, the enrolment rate of the high-income countries was 77.13 per cent, for upper-middle-income countries it was 52.07 per cent, for the middle-income countries 35.59 per cent and for lower-middle-income countries 24.41 per cent. The proverbial development case of South Korea is instructive. As pundits never tire of pointing out, in 1960 the country's level of development was comparable to that of some African countries: its enrolment rate in 2017 was 93.78 per cent! And China, the emerging colossus of the world economy, had a rate of 51.01 per cent. Put simply, not enough Africans are going to university.

However, the challenge is not simply to grow the number of universities, which is essential for our countries to meet the pressures of the youth bulge, the fastest-growing in the world, but to grow in a smart and sustainable way. Much of the growth in Africa's higher education sector has been haphazard. This has predictably led to declining educational quality. Equally critical is the question of research, the other key product of higher education institutions. Here, too, African countries and universities face many challenges.

According to data from UNESCO, in 2013 gross domestic expenditure on research and development (R&D) as a percentage of GDP in Africa was 0.5 per cent compared to a world average of 1.7 per cent and 2.7 per cent for North America, 1.8 per cent for Europe and 1.6 per cent for Asia. Africa accounted for a mere 1.3 per cent of global R&D. In 2018, global spending on R&D reached

US$1.7 trillion, 80 per cent of which was accounted for by only ten countries. In first place, in terms of R&D expenditure as a share of GDP, was South Korea with 4.3 per cent, and in tenth place was the United States with 2.7 per cent.

In terms of total expenditure, the United States led with US$476 billion followed by China with US$371 billion. What was remarkable was that, among the top fifteen R&D spenders, expenditure by the business sector was the most important source, ranging from 56 per cent in the Netherlands to 71.5 per cent in the United States. In contrast, for the fourteen African countries that UNESCO had data, business as a source of R&D was more than 30 per cent in three countries, led by South Africa with 38.90 per cent, and was less than 1 per cent in four countries. In most countries, the biggest contributor to R&D was either government or the outside world. The former contributed more than 85 per cent in Egypt, Lesotho and Senegal and more than 70 per cent in another two countries, while the latter contributed a third or more in four countries. Higher education and private non-profit hardly featured.

Not surprisingly, other research indicators were no less troubling. In 2013, Africa as a whole accounted for 2.4 per cent of world researchers, compared to 42.8 per cent for Asia, 31.0 per cent for Europe, 22.2 per cent for the Americas and 1.6 per cent for Oceania. Equally low was the continent's share of scientific publications, which stood at 2.6 per cent in 2014, compared to 39.5 per cent for Asia, 39.3 per cent for Europe, 32.9 per cent for the Americas and 4.2 per cent for Oceania. The only area in which Africa led was in the proportion of publications with international authors. While the world average was 24.9 per cent, for Africa it was 64.6 per cent, compared to 26.1 per cent for Asia, 42.1 per cent for Europe, 38.2 per cent for the Americas and 55.7 per cent for Oceania. Thus, African scholarship suffers from epistemic extraversion and limited regional integration, much as is the case with our economies.

Conclusion

In short, the project of building the continent's research capacities remains as pressing as ever. This has to be an essential part of the decolonisation project. It is gratifying that decolonisation of African knowledges is back on the agenda among faculty and students in many of our universities, especially in South Africa. I was privileged to give a public lecture on the subject at the University of the Free State in May 2017 (see Chapter 19).[32]

We must strive to build a new library out of Africa's four major libraries (see again Chapter 19). We must also ponder: what will this library look like in the era of Big Science and the digitalisation of knowledge, work and social life, in an era of artificial intelligence, the Internet of Things, robotics, biotechnology, nanotechnology and so on?

The project of decolonising and reconstructing African studies, of creating richer, more accurate and transformative African knowledges fit for the twenty-first century, will not go too far if the epistemic, spatial and social dynamics of knowledge production retain their historic hierarchies and structural inequalities. These are some of the issues that ought to guide the diverse communities that study Africa on the continent and around the world. The struggle indeed continues.

Notes

1. Kwame Nkrumah, *Consciencism: Philosophy and Ideology for Decolonization,* New York: Monthly Review Press, 1964.
2. Walter Rodney, *How Europe Underdevelopment Africa*, Washington, DC: Howard University Press, 1974.
3. Frantz Fanon, *The Wretched of the Earth,* Harmondsworth: Penguin, 1963.
4. *The Economist,* 'Hopeless Africa', 11 May 2000. https://www.economist.com/leaders/2000/05/11/hopeless-africa.
5. F. Njubi Nesbitt, 'African Intellectuals in the Belly of the Beast: Migration, Identity and the Politics of Exile', *African Issues*, 30, 1 (2002): 70–75.
6. Paul Tiyambe Zeleza, *The Transformation of Global Higher Education, 1945–2015*, New York: Palgrave Macmillan, 2016.
7. Ali Mazrui (writer and narrator), *The Africans: A Triple Heritage* (documentary), British Broadcasting Corporation, 1986.
8. Philip Curtin, 'The Ghettoization of African History,' *The Chronicle of Higher Education*, March 3, 1995.
9. Paul Tiyambe Zeleza, *Manufacturing African Studies and Crises* (Dakar: CODESRIA Book Series, 1997).
10. Paul Tiyambe Zeleza, 'The Perpetual Solitudes and Crises of African Studies in the United States Today', *Africa Today*, 44, 2 (1997): 193–210.
11. Paul Tiyambe Zeleza, 'The Past and Futures of African Studies and Area Studies', *Ufahamu* XXV, 2 (1999): 12.
12. Paul Tiyambe Zeleza, 'The Political Economy of British Colonial Development and Welfare in Africa', *Transafrican Journal of History* 14 (1985): 139–161.
13. Walt Whitman Rostow, *The Stages of Economic Growth: A Non-Communist Manifesto,* Cambridge UK: Cambridge University Press, 1960.
14. G.W.F. Hegel, *The Philosophy of History*, J. Sibree (trans.), introduction C.J. Friedrich, New York: Dover Publications, 1956: 91.
15. Paul Tiyambe Zeleza, 'From African Studies and African American Studies to Africana Studies in the United States', *Afrika Focus* 24, 2 (2011): 15.
16. Ibid., 15.
17. Ibid., 15.
18. Ibid., 18.
19. Paul Tiyambe Zeleza, 'African Diasporas: Towards a Global History', *African Studies Review* 53, 1 (2010): 1–19.

20. Paul Tiyambe Zeleza (ed), *The Study of Africa, Volume 1: Disciplinary and Interdisciplinary Encounters*, Dakar: CODESRIA Book Series, 2006; Paul Tiyambe Zeleza (ed), *The Study of Africa, Volume 2: Global and Transnational Engagements,* Dakar: CODESRIA Book Series, 2006.
21. Haythem Guesmi, 'The gentrification of African studies', *Africa is a Country,* 22 December 2018. https://africasacountry.com/2018/12/the-gentrification-of-african-studies.
22. Paul Tiyambe Zeleza, 'The Political Economy of British Colonial Development and Welfare in Africa, *Transafrican Journal of History* 14 (1985): 139–161.
23. Ibid., 219.
24. Paul Tiyambe Zeleza, 'Leveraging Africa's Global Diasporas for the Continent's Development', presentation at the conference on Contribution of the Diaspora to Sustainable Blue Economy for National Development and International Solidarity, University of Nairobi, Kenya, 26 November 2018.
25. Paul Tiyambe Zeleza, *In Search of African Diasporas: Testimonies and Encounters,* Durham, NC: Carolina Academic Press, 2012.
26. The journal articles include the following: Paul Tiyambe Zeleza, 'Rewriting the African Diaspora: Beyond the Black Atlantic', *African Affairs* 104, 1 (2005): 35–68; 'The Challenges of Studying the African Diasporas', *African Sociological Review* 12, 2 (2008): 4–21; 'Africa and Its Diasporas: Remembering South America', *Research in African Literatures* 40, 4 (2009): 142–164; 'Reconceptualising African Diasporas: Notes from an Historian', *Transforming Anthropology* 18, 1 (2010): 74–78; and 'African Diasporas: Towards a Global History', *African Studies Review* 53, 1 (2010): 1–19. For book collections see the following: Paul Tiyambe Zeleza, 'The African Academic Diaspora: The Struggle for a Global Epistemic Presence', in Paul Tiyambe Zeleza (ed.), *The Study of Africa Volume 2: Global and Transnational Engagements,* Dakar: CODESRIA Book Series, 2007, 86–111; Paul Tiyambe Zeleza, Diaspora Dialogues: Engagements between Africa and Its Diasporas, in Isidore Okpewho and Nkiru Nzegwu (eds.), *The New African Diaspora: Assessing the Pains and Gains of Exile,* Bloomington and Indianapolis: Indiana University Press, 2009, 31–60; Paul Tiyambe Zeleza and Cassandra R. Veney, 'African Diasporas, Immigration and the Obama Administration', in Dinesh Sharma and Uwe P. Gielen (eds), *The Global Obama: Crossroads of Leadership in the 21st Century*, New York and London: Routledge, 2013, 99–114; and Paul Tiyambe Zeleza, 'The African Diaspora's Role in Forging US-Africa Relations', in Cassandra R Veney (ed.), U.S.–*Africa Relations from Clinton to Obama,* Lanham, MD: Lexington, 2014, 169–200.
27. Paul Tiyambe Zeleza, *Engagements between African Diaspora Academics in the U.S. and Canada and African Institutions of Higher Education: Perspectives from North America and Africa,* Report for the Carnegie Corporation of New York, 3 January 2013. https://p.widencdn.net/af4g73/Engagements-between-African-Diaspora- Academics-and-Africa--Final-Report-2-for-distirbution.
28. Paul Tiyambe Zeleza and Adebayo Olukoshi (eds.), *African Universities in the 21st Century. Volume 1: Liberalisation and Internationalisation,* Dakar, Pretoria: CODESRIA Book Series and University of South Africa Press, 2004; *African Universities in the 21st Century, Volume 2: Knowledge and Society,* Dakar, Pretoria: CODESRIA Book Series and University of South Africa Press, 2004.

29. Paul Tiyambe Zeleza, *The Transformation of Global Higher Education, 1945-2015*. New York: Palgrave Macmillan, 2016.
30. World Higher Education Database. https://www.iau-aiu.net/World-Higher-Education-Database-WHED
31. Paul Tiyambe Zeleza, 'Positioning Universities as Engines of Innovation for Sustainable Development and Transformation', presentation at the 2nd Biennial Conference on the State of Higher Education in Kenya, Commission for University Education, 30 October–2 November 2018, Nairobi, Kenya.
32. Paul Tiyambe Zeleza, 'The Decolonization of African Knowledges', 9th Africa Day Lecture, University of the Free State, Bloemfontein, South Africa, 24 May 2017.

V

Disruptions in Higher Education

21

The Six Capacity Challenges of African Universities

In the first two decades of the twenty-first century, African higher education underwent profound changes. In the 1960s and 1970s, universities on the continent were few in number, small in scale and elitist, with the limited mandate of producing cadres for the Africanisation or indigenisation of the newly independent state apparatuses. In the 1980s and 1990s, during the scourge of Structural Adjustment Programmes, they were regarded as costly irrelevances at best, or bastions of political unrest at worst. After the 2000s, they were seen as essential for the creation of knowledge economies and societies, indispensable for human capital development and turning Africa's unprecedented youth bulge into a demographic dividend rather than a Malthusian nightmare.

Yet, the continent's higher education sector is plagued by huge capacity deficits and challenges that threaten its survival, sustainability and contribution to the continent's historic and humanistic project for democratic and development transformation. Since the late 1990s, I have been immersed in research on African universities and knowledge production on Africa. I have published several books and numerous articles and given dozens of conference presentations on these subjects. The books include two edited volumes on *African Universities in the Twenty-First Century* (2004)[1] and another two volumes on *The Study of Africa* (2008).[2] Among the presentations, the most significant might be the Framing Paper[3] I was commissioned to write for the First African Higher Education Summit held in Dakar, Senegal, in March 2015.

My reflections have also been immensely enriched by my work in university administration since 1994 and most recently as vice chancellor of an African university; also, as a member of several higher education governing boards, including the Administrative Board of the International Association of Universities and as Chair of the Advisory Council of the Carnegie African Diaspora Fellowship Program that provides fellowships for African-born academics in Canada and the United States to work with universities in six African countries.

From these scholarly, administrative and governance vantage points, I have distilled six key capacity challenges facing African higher education: institutional supply, resources, faculty, research, outputs and leadership. Overcoming these challenges and creating quality education is essential for the sector's contribution to the creation of globally competitive, inclusive, integrated, innovative, successful and sustainable democratic developmental states and societies envisioned in the African Union's Agenda 2063, the United Nation's Sustainable Development Goals and numerous national and regional visions.

The previous chapter discussed two of these capacity challenges, namely, institutional supply and research productivity. I showed that Africa's share of global higher educational institutions, enrolments and research indicators is the lowest in the world. Thus, Africa needs more universities and massive expansion in research production and productivity. Private universities have grown rapidly in response to escalating student demand and incapacity of public institutions to meet it. Increasingly, higher education has come to be viewed as a private rather than as a public good.

However, expanding the supply of educational institutions must be matched by investments in physical and technological infrastructures without which the slide in quality will continue. It must also be accompanied by improving access, equity and affordability, especially for marginalised communities and women. Worldwide, gender parity in tertiary education was achieved by 2000 and stood at 1.10 in 2013. Then, Africa remained the only region where gender parity had yet to be attained. Its gender parity index was 0.85 in 2013.

When it comes to research, a few African countries dominate, such as South Africa, Egypt, Nigeria and Kenya, but many countries are negligible in the production of knowledge. The vast majority of the continent's universities cannot be considered research universities and contribute very little to knowledge production, which is one of the key functions of the university.

Research productivity is essential for higher education to contribute to sustainable development and in the global competition for talented students, top faculty, scarce resources and reputational capital. Not surprisingly, most African universities do not feature in international higher education rankings, whatever one may think of the validity of such rankings.

Resource Deficits

The development of higher education institutions and research requires massive resources that many African countries simply do not have. In fact, the number of institutions has grown faster than resources and as a result quality has suffered. Without the necessary physical and electronic infrastructures for quality education and the financial capacity to recruit and retain qualified faculty, many universities are no better than glorified high schools.

As in many parts of the world, African universities have increasingly become neoliberal institutions characterised by what I call the 8Cs:

1. Corporatisation of management (application of sometimes inappropriate business practices in the leadership and management of universities).
2. Consumerisation of students (student expectations and institutional treatment of students, as consumers in a market transaction, rather than as learners in an educational environment).
3. Casualisation of faculty (growth of adjuncts due to, in Africa, shortage of qualified faculty).
4. Commercialisation of learning (imposition of high student tuition charges).
5. Commodification of knowledge (application of proprietary knowledge production and consumption norms).
6. Computerisation of education (spread of IT in teaching and learning, research and scholarship).
7. Corrosion of academic freedom (erosion of institutional autonomy and freedom of inquiry).
8. Connectivity of institutions (growing pressures and opportunities for inter-institutional collaborations in higher education and external partnerships).

Governments and governing boards pressure universities to cultivate new revenue streams, including 'cost-sharing', marketing institutional services and fundraising. Yet, few African universities have developed adequate fundraising capacity. Typically, they employ a couple of people or so, whereas similar institutions elsewhere employ scores and even hundreds. Also, we live in cultures where philanthropy is often confined to supporting relatives or religious organisations rather than institution-building.

In Search of Faculty

The rapid growth in the number of universities has outstripped the supply of faculty. In several parts of the global North, such as the United States, there are more people with terminal degrees than there are academic jobs. Across Africa, there is a severe shortage of qualified faculty. In Kenya, for example, according to data from the Commission for University Education in 2018, there were 18,005 faculty in the country's seventy-four universities and colleges, but only 34 per cent had doctoral degrees. This is equivalent to the number of faculty at any three of the large universities in the US.

The severe shortages of faculty result in universities relying on adjuncts, that is, faculty with permanent appointments in one institution who teach in multiple institutions. (In the US, about three-quarters of faculty are now adjunct because of academic labour oversupply and the efforts of financially beleaguered universities to cut costs by reducing the ranks of permanent faculty.) The predictable result is limited engagement between faculty and students, which leads to the declining quality of teaching and learning.

In many countries, the casualisation of academic labour reflects the erosion of middle-class incomes for academic professionals. Compounding the declining status of academics is the progressive shift towards more top-down institutional governance, in which the edicts of managerialism are increasingly undermining academic autonomy and freedom.

Quality of Outputs

The growing massification of higher education across Africa, while desirable, has not been accompanied by a rising quality of outputs because of the capacity deficits already noted. Besides the production of research knowledge, a critical output of universities is of course its graduates. As the costs and competitiveness among higher education institutions increase, demands have grown for accountability from all the affected constituencies, for universities to prove their value in the quality of their graduates.

An important measure is the employability of graduates. Reports on graduate employability show that there are glaring mismatches between what universities are producing and what economies need, resulting in graduates spending years 'tarmacking', unemployed and underemployed. A 2016 British Council Report, *Universities, Employability and Inclusive Development covering Ghana, Nigeria, Kenya and South Africa,*[4] makes sobering reading. The African media is full of stories of graduate underemployment and unemployment. The growing mismatch between the quality of graduates and the needs of employers and Africa's 'rising' economies has become a source of apprehension.

Concerns and pressures over the quality of outputs from universities have led to the development of national quality assurance and regulatory regimes. Gone are the days when universities were largely left alone as arbiters of their own standards. In some countries, quality assurance was initially targeted at private institutions on the faulty assumption that all was well with the public institutions. In addition to regional quality assurance agencies, such as the African Quality Assurance Network, the number of national quality assurance agencies across the continent grew from nine in 1990 to twenty-one in 2012 to thirty-two in 2015.

Nevertheless, questions remain on the extent to which the proliferation of quality assurance systems has led to improvements in the quality of higher education. In many African countries, regulatory agencies adopt authoritarian and accusatory practices instead of interactive, collaborative and iterative processes. They tend to be too interventionist, prescriptive and pursue outdated notions of education quality. For example, in some systems there is an inordinate emphasis on the nature of examinations rather than on continuous assessments and the acquisition of competency-based and lifelong learning skills. Some even decree faculty promotion standards and qualifications of members of governance bodies.

Governance and Leadership

I noted in the Dakar Summit Framing Paper that 'the challenges facing African higher education institutions require sophisticated management and effective governance systems. ... Clearly, there is need to recruit and train higher education administrators who are smart leaders, skilled managers, successful fund raisers and savvy public figures.'

The Dakar Summit Declaration and Action Plan[5] itself identified the 'Promotion of institutional autonomy and academic freedom' as a core principle. Unfortunately, the infectious and insidious authoritarian culture of the postcolonial one-party state persists in many institutions and higher education systems in which regulatory agencies, governing boards and management seek to rule by decree and directives.

Yet, shared governance is central to the success of higher education institutions. It entails institutional leadership at all levels that puts a premium on what I call the 3Cs of effective academic leadership (collaboration, communication and creativity), in pursuit of the 3Es (excellence, engagement and efficiency) and based on the 3Ts (transparency, trust and trends in higher education).

Revitalising African Higher Education

The challenges and opportunities facing African higher education institutions are evident from the analysis above. Clearly, there is a need to: expand enrolments without sacrificing academic quality; increase and improve funding and financial management; raise the volume and value of research productivity; strengthen the educational quality and employability of university graduates; develop effective and collaborative regulatory cultures of quality assessment and improvement; and enhance the quality of institutional leadership and governance.

All the key constituencies, principally, governments, the private sector, civil society and the universities themselves must forge a grand compact on African higher education. Governments have a special fiscal responsibility in the revitalisation of African higher education as an engine of growth, development and transformation. Massive investments in the sector are required. The universities cannot generate these resources all by themselves. The continent's elites, many of whom are products of Africa's universities during the golden years, have a special role to play. The ranks of high net worth individuals across the continent[6] are skyrocketing. The HNWIs increased by 19 per cent between 2006 and 2016, reaching 145,000. They are expected to rise by 36 per cent and reach 198,000 by 2026. How many of them invest in the African higher education sector as do their counterparts in the global North? The great private Ivy League and flagship public universities of the US with their massive endowments were built by philanthropic and public support. Harvard's endowment of USUS$38.3 billion in 2018 was more than the GDP of nearly forty African countries. Lest we forget, the oldest US universities were built in colonial and postcolonial times when it would have been easier for American elites to invest in sending their children to the more established and prestigious, at the time, British and other European universities. Many from our African elites take enormous pride in sending their children to overseas universities, even mediocre ones, shunning local universities for their apparent low quality, notwithstanding the fact that many of them are products of these very institutions.

It is also critical to promote, in the words of the Dakar Summit's Declaration, 'diversification, differentiation and harmonisation of higher education systems at the national, institutional and continental/regional levels and assure the quality of educational provision against locally, regionally and internationally agreed benchmarks of excellence'.

The Dakar Summit urged African governments and regional economic communities to:

> develop deliberate policies that designate some universities as research universities that drive the higher education sector to meet national development objectives. … These research universities will produce the relevant knowledge and skilled labor capacity the continent's key institutions – governance, trade, defense, agriculture, health, finance and energy – need to succeed.

The articulation and harmonisation of higher education systems goes beyond national borders. It is imperative for Africa to promote international academic mobility for students, academic staff, academic credits and qualifications within the continent. This entails strengthening and implementing existing regional conventions. Also in need of strengthening and operationalisation are protocols for the mutual recognition of academic and professional qualifications. A critical element of this process is the need to develop an African credit transfer system.

I believe the six capacity challenges identified in this essay can be overcome. The good news is that higher education around the world, not just in Africa, is in a state of crisis, transition or disruption – choose your term – which opens opportunities for African educators to reinvent higher education systems that befit their needs and contexts and the unforgiving and unpredictable demands of the twenty-first century.

Notes

1. Paul Tiyambe Zeleza and Adebayo Olukoshi (eds), *African Universities in the 21st Century. Volume 1: Liberalization and Internationalization; Volume 2: Knowledge and Society,* Dakar and Pretoria: CODESRIA Book Series and University of South Africa Press.
2. Paul Tiyambe Zeleza (ed), *The Study of Africa. Volume 1: Disciplinary and Interdisciplinary Encounters. Volume 2: Global and Transnational Engagements*, Dakar: CODESRIA Book Series, 2007.
3. http://www.trustafrica.org/en/publications-trust/books-and-ebooks?download=410:african-higher-education-summit-revitalising-for-african-s-future
4. British Council, *Universities, Employability and Inclusive Development: Repositioning Higher Education in Ghana, Nigeria, Kenya and South Africa*, 2016. https://ereadiness.kenet.or.ke/sites/default/files/ctools/Graduate%20employability%20final%20report.pdf
5. Dakar Summit Declaration and Action Plan, March 2015. http://www.trustafrica.org/images/Executive%20SummaryFINAL.pdf
6. AfrAsia Bank, *The AfrAsia Bank Africa Wealth Report 2018*. https://www.afrasiabank.com/media/3205/africa-wealth-report-2018.pdf.

First written 15 June 2018

22

Rethinking the Value Proposition of University Education: The Challenge of Employability

In the last chapter, I wrote on the six capacity challenges facing African universities: institutional supply, resources, faculty, research, outputs and leadership. In this chapter, I focus on one critical aspect of the outputs of our universities, namely, the employability of our graduates. To be sure, universities do not exist simply for economic reasons, for return on investment, or as vocational enterprises. They also serve as powerful centres for contemplation and the generation of new knowledges, for the cultivation of enlightened citizenship, as crucibles for forging inclusive, integrated and innovative societies and as purveyors, at their best, of cultures of civility, ethical values and shared well-being.

Nevertheless, the fact remains that higher education is prized for its capacity to prepare its beneficiaries for jobs and professional careers. Thus, employability is at the heart of the value proposition of university education; it is its most compelling promise and unforgiving performance indicator. The evidence across Africa, indeed in many parts of the world, is quite troubling as mismatches persist, and in some cases appear to be growing, between the quality of graduates and the needs of the economy. This often results in graduate underemployment and unemployment.

The Employability Challenge

Two powerful megatrends will determine Africa's development trajectory in the twenty-first century. The first is the continent's youth bulge, and the second, the changing nature of work. Employability is the nexus between the two, the thread that will weave or unravel the fabric of the continent's future, enabling it to achieve or abort the enduring historic and humanistic project for development, democracy and self-determination.

As we all know, Africa's youth population is exploding. This promises to propel the continent towards either a demographic dividend of hosting the world's largest and most dynamic labour force or a demographic disaster of rampant insecurity and instability fuelled by hordes of ill-educated and unemployable youths. According to United Nations data,[1] in 2017 the continent had 16.64 per cent (1.26 billion) of the world's population, which is slated to rise, on current trends, to 19.93 per cent (1.70 billion) in 2030, 25.87 per cent (2.53 billion) in 2050 and 39.95 per cent (4.47 billion) in 2100.

The African Development Bank[2] succinctly captures the challenge and opportunity facing the continent:

> Youth are Africa's greatest asset, but this asset remains untapped due to high unemployment. Africa's youth population is rapidly growing and expected to double to over 850 million by 2050. The potential benefits of Africa's youth population are unrealised as two-thirds of non-student youth are unemployed, discouraged, or only vulnerably employed despite gains in education access over the past several decades.

Thus, the youth bulge will turn out to be a blessing or curse depending on the employability skills imparted to the youth by our educational institutions, including universities. Across Africa in 2017, children under the age of fifteen accounted for 41 per cent of the population and those fifteen to twenty-four for another 19 per cent. While African economies have been growing, the rate of growth is not fast enough to absorb the masses of young people seeking gainful employment. Since 2000, the rate of employment has grown at an average rate of 3 per cent. Africa needs to double this rate or more to significantly reduce poverty and raise the general standards of living for its working people.

Not surprisingly, despite some improvements in the early twenty-first century, the employment indicators for Africa continue to be comparatively unsatisfactory. For example, International Labour Organization data[3] shows that in 2017 the unemployment rate in Africa was 7.9 per cent compared to a world average of 5.6 per cent; the vulnerable employment rate was 66.0 per cent to 42.5 per cent; the extreme working poverty rate was 31.9 per cent to 11.2 per cent; and the moderate working poverty rate was 23.6 per cent to 16.0 per cent, respectively.

This data underscores the fact that much of the growth in employment in many African countries is in the informal sector where incomes tend to be low and working conditions poor. In sectoral terms, there appears to be a structural decline in agricultural and manufacturing employment and a rise in service sector jobs. Yet, in many African countries, both the declining and rising sectors are characterised by a high incidence of vulnerable, informal and part-time jobs.

The structural shifts in employment dynamics across much of Africa differ considerably from the historical path traversed by the developed countries. But the latter, too, are experiencing challenges of their own as the so-called Fourth Industrial Revolution unleashes its massive and unpredictable transformations. In fact, the issue of graduate employability, as discussed in the next section, is not a monopoly of universities in Africa and other parts of the global South. It is also exercising the minds of educators, governments and employers in the global North.

The reason is simple: the world economy is undergoing major structural changes, which are evident everywhere even if their manifestations and intensity vary across regions and countries. As deeply integrated as Africa is in the globalised world economy, it means the continent's economies are facing double jeopardy. They are simultaneously confronting and navigating the asymmetrical legacies of the previous revolutions and the unfolding revolution of digital automation, artificial intelligence, the Internet of Things, biotechnology, nanotechnology, robotics and so on in which the old boundaries of work, production, social life and even the meaning of being human are rapidly eroding.

The analysis above should make it clear that employability cannot be reduced to employment. Employability entails the acquisition of knowledge, skills and attributes, in short, capabilities to pursue a productive and meaningful life. To quote the influential *Universities, Employability and Inclusive Development* report by the British Council,[4] 'Employability requires technical skills, job specific and generic cognitive attributes, but also a range of other qualities including communication, empathy, intercultural awareness and so forth. … Such a perspective guards against a reductive "skills gap" diagnosis of the problems of graduate unemployment.' The challenge for universities, then, is the extent to which they are providing an education that is holistic, one that provides subject and technical knowledges, experiential learning opportunities, liberal arts competencies and soft and lifelong learning skills.

In addition to the attributes, values and social networks acquired and developed by an individual in a university, employability depends on the wider socioeconomic and political context. Employability thrives in societies committed to the pursuit of inclusive development. This entails, to quote the report again:

> a fair distribution of the benefits of development (economic and otherwise) across the population and allows equitable access to valued opportunities. Second, while upholding equality of all before the law and in terms of social welfare, it also recognises and values social diversity. Third, it engages individuals and communities in the task of deciding the shape that society will take, through the democratic participation of all segments of society.

In short, employability refers to the provision and acquisition, in the words of an employability study undertaken at my university, USIU-Africa in 2017:

> of skills necessary to undertake self-employment opportunities, creation of innovative opportunities as well as acquiring and maintaining salaried employment. It is the capacity to function successfully in a role and be able to move between occupations. … employability skills can be gained in and out of the classroom and depend also on the quality of education gained by the individuals before entry into the university. As such the role of the university is to provide a conducive environment and undertake deliberate measures to ensure that students acquire these skills within their period of study.

Universities and Employability

As noted in the previous chapter, the African media is full of stories about the skills mismatch between the quality of graduates and the needs of employers and the economy. Many graduates end up unemployed or underemployed for years after graduation. In the meantime, employers complain bitterly, to quote a story in *University World News*,[5] that 'unprepared graduates are raising our costs'. The story paints a gloomy picture: 'The Federation of Kenya Employers (FKE) – a lobby group for all major corporate organisations – says in its latest survey that at least 70 per cent of entry-level recruits require a refresher course in order to start to deliver in their new jobs. As a result, they take longer than expected to become productive, nearly doubling staff costs in a majority of organisations.'

The situation is no better in the rest of the region. The story continues, noting that a study of the Inter-University Council for East Africa 'shows that Uganda has the worst record, with at least 63 per cent of graduates found to lack job market skills. It is followed closely by Tanzania, where 61per cent of graduates were ill prepared. In Burundi and Rwanda, 55 per cent and 52 per cent of graduates respectively were perceived to not be competent. In Kenya, 51per cent of graduates were believed to be unfit for jobs.' The situation in Kenya and East Africa clearly applies elsewhere across Africa.

However, the problem of employability afflicts universities and economies in the developed countries as well. Studies from the US and UK are quite instructive. One is a 2014 Gallup survey[6] of business leaders in the United States. To the statement, 'higher education institutions in this country are graduating students with the skills and competences that my business needs', only 11 per cent strongly agreed and another 22 per cent agreed, while 17 per cent strongly disagreed and another 17 per cent disagreed and the rest were in the middle. In contrast, in another Gallup survey[7] also conducted in 2014, 96 per cent of the provosts interviewed believed they were preparing their students for success in the workforce. Another survey by the Association of American Colleges and Universities[8] highlighted the discrepancy between students' and employers' views on graduates' preparedness. 'For example, while 59 per cent of students said they were well prepared to analyse and solve complex problems, just 24 per cent of employers said they had found that to be true of recent college graduates.'

In Britain, research commissioned by the Edge Foundation[9] in 2011 underscored the same discrepancies. The project encompassed twenty-six higher education institutions and nine employers. The report concluded:

> While there are numerous examples of employers and HEIs working to promote graduate employability in the literature and in our research, there are still issues and barriers between employers and many of those responsible for HEI policy, particularly in terms of differences in mindset, expectations and priorities. There are concerns from some academics about employability measures in their universities diminishing the academic integrity of higher education provision. There is also frustration from employers about courses not meeting their needs.

Specifically, the reported noted, 'Employers expect graduates to have the technical and discipline competences from their degrees but require graduates to demonstrate a range of broader skills and attributes that include team-working, communication, leadership, critical thinking, problem solving and often managerial abilities or potential.' One could argue that this is indeed a widespread expectation among employers, whether in the developed or developing countries.

Predictably, in a world that is increasingly addicted to rankings as a tool of market differentiation and competition, national and international employability rankings have emerged. One of the best known is the one by *Times Higher Education*,[10] whose 2019 edition lists 250 universities from forty-one countries. As with the general global rankings of universities, the rankings are dominated by American institutions, with six in the top ten and fifty-five overall, followed by French universities with eighteen, German and British universities with sixteen, Dutch with ten and Australian and Chinese with nine (excluding four in Hong Kong). Africa has only three universities in the league, all South African: the University of the Witwatersrand, Johannesburg, listed at 212; Stellenbosch University at 230; and the University of Cape Town at 231.

What, then, are some of the most effective interventions to enhance the employability of university graduates? There is no shortage of studies and suggestions. Clearly, it is critical to embed employability across the institution, from the strategic plan to curriculum design, to the provision of support services such as internships and career counselling. The importance of carefully crafted student placements and experiential and work-related learning cannot be overemphasised. We can all borrow from each other's best practices duly adapted to fit our specific institutional and local contexts.

Co-operative education, which combines classroom study and practical work, has long been touted for its capacity to impart employability skills and prepare young people to transition from higher education to employment.

Work-integrated learning and experiential learning encompass various features and practices, including internships, placements and service learning. In the United States and Canada, several universities adopted co-operative education and work integrated learning in the first decades of the twentieth century. The movement then spread to many parts of the world. The World Association of Cooperative and Work-Integrated Education (WACE),[11] which was founded in 1983, currently has 913 institutions in fifty-two countries.

The Developing Employability Initiative (DEI),[12] a collaboration comprising thirty higher education institutions and over 700 scholars internationally, defines employability as 'the ability to create and sustain meaningful work across the career lifespan. This is a developmental process which students need to learn before they graduate.' It urges higher education institutions to embed employability thinking in their teaching and learning by incorporating basic literacy, rhetorical literacy, personal and critical literacy, emotional literacy, occupational literacy and ethical, social and cultural literacy. The DEI has developed a suggestive framework of what it calls essential employability qualities (EEQ). These qualities:

> are not specific to any discipline, field, or industry, but are applicable to most work-based, professional environments; they represent the knowledge, skills, abilities and experiences that help ensure that graduates are not only ready for their first or next job, but also support learners' foundation for a lifetime of engaged employment and participation in the rapidly changing workplace of the 21st century.

Graduates with an EEQ profile are expected to be communicators, thinkers and problem-solvers, inquirers and researchers, collaborators, adaptable, principled and ethical, responsible and professional and continuous learners.

Equipping students with employability skills and capacities is a continuous process in the context of rapidly changing occupational landscapes. I referred earlier to the disruptions caused by the Fourth Industrial Revolution, which will only accelerate as the twenty-first century unfolds. Automation will lead to the disappearance of many occupations – think of the transport industry with the spread of driverless cars, sales jobs with cashless shops, or medical careers with the spread of machine and digital diagnoses. However, new occupations will also emerge, many of which we cannot even predict, a prospect that makes the skills of a liberal arts education and lifelong learning even more crucial.

We should not be preparing students for this brave new world in the same manner that many of us were educated for the world of the late twentieth century. To quote Joseph Aoun, President of Northeastern University in the US, a university renowned for its co-operative education, let us provide 'robot-proof higher education', one that 'is not concerned solely with topping up students' minds with high-octane facts. Rather, it calibrates them with a creative mindset and the mental elasticity to invent, discover, or create something valuable to society.'[13] The new literacies of the new education include data literacy, technological literacy and human literacy encompassing the humanities, communication and design.

Achieving the ambitious agenda of equipping university students with employability skills, attributes, experiences and mindsets for the present and future requires the development of effective and mutually beneficial, multifaceted and sustained engagements and partnerships between universities, employers, governments and civil society. Within the universities themselves, there is a need for institutional commitment at all levels and a compact of accountability between administrators, faculty and students.

This entails developing robust systems of learning assessment, including verification of employability skills, utilisation of external information and reviews, integration of career services and cultivating strong cultures of student, alumni and employer engagement, representation and partnerships in assuring programme relevance and quality. Pursuing these goals is fraught with challenges, in terms of striking a balance between the cherished traditions of institutional autonomy and academic freedom, in engaging employers without importing the insidious cultures of the 8Cs of the neoliberal academy mentioned in the previous chapter. They are: corporatisation of management, consumerisation of students, casualisation of faculty, commercialisation of learning, commodification of knowledge, computerisation of education, corrosion of academic freedom and connectivity of institutions.

The challenges of developing and fostering employability skills among students in our universities are real and daunting. However, as educators we have no choice but to continue striving, with the full support and engagement of governments, intergovernmental agencies, the private sector, non-governmental organisations and civil society organisations, to provide the best experiential and work-integrated learning we can without compromising the enduring and cherished traditions and values of higher education. The consequences of inaction or complacency, of conducting business as usual, are too ghastly to contemplate: they would condemn the hundreds of millions of contemporary African youth and the youths yet to be born to unemployable and unliveable lives. That would be an economic, ethical and existential tragedy of monumental proportions for which history would never forgive us.

Notes

1. United Nations, *World Population Prospects: Key findings and advance tables*, 2017 Revision. https://population.un.org/wpp/publications/Files/WPP2017_KeyFindings.pdf
2. African Development Bank Group, *Jobs for Youth in Africa: Catalyzing youth opportunity across Africa,* March 2016. https://www.afdb.org/fileadmin/uploads/afdb/Images/high_5s/Job_youth_Africa_Job_youth_Africa.pdf
3. International Labour Organization, *World Employment Social Outlook: Trends* 2018. http://www.ilo.org/wcmsp5/groups/public/---dgreports/---dcomm/---publ/documents/publication/wcms_615594.pdf

4. British Council, *Universities, Employability and Inclusive Development: Repositioning Higher Education in Ghana, Kenya, Nigeria, South Africa,* 2016. https://ereadiness.kenet.or.ke/sites/default/files/ctools/Graduate%20employability%20final%20report.pdf
5. Gilbert Nganga, 'Unprepared Graduates are Raising Our Costs', *University World News,* 20 June 2018. https://www.universityworldnews.com/post.php?story=20180620145937689
6. Gallup, 'Many Business Leaders Doubt Colleges Prepare Students', February 2014. https://news.gallup.com/poll/167630/business-leaders-doubt-colleges-prepare-students.aspx
7. Allie Grasgreen, 'Ready or Not', *Inside Higher Ed,* 26 February 2014. https://www.insidehighered.com/news/2014/02/26/provosts-business-leaders-disagree-graduates-career-readiness
8. Casey Fabris, 'College Students Think They're Ready for the Work Force. Employers Aren't so Sure', *The Chronicle for Higher Education,* 20 January 2015. https://www.chronicle.com/article/College-Students-Think/151289
9. *Employers' perceptions of the employability skills of new graduates,* London: Edge Foundation, 2011. https://www.educationandemployers.org/wp-content/uploads/2014/06/employability_skills_as_pdf_-_final_online_version.pdf
10. *Times Higher Education,* 'Best universities for graduate jobs: Global University Employability Ranking 2019'. https://www.timeshighereducation.com/student/best-universities/best-universities-graduate-jobs-global-university-employability-ranking.
11. https://waceinc.org/
12. Developing Employabiity Educator Site, https://developingemployability.edu.au/about/
13. Joseph Aoun, Robot-Proof: Higher Education in the Age of Artificial Intelligence, Cambridge MA: MIT Press, 2018. https://mitpress.mit.edu/books/robot-proof

This is an abridged version of a keynote address delivered at Malawi's First International Conference on Higher Education, 27 June 2018.

23

Africa, Internationalisation and the Global Context

Introduction

I argue in my book published in 2016, *The Transformation of Global Higher Education: 1945–2015*:[1]

> As might be expected, views differ widely on the forces that drive internationalisation, the activities that constitute it, the competencies it promotes, the values it creates, the processes that sustain it, the respective roles of key constituencies within and outside the universities and its effects on the core functions of the higher education enterprise, namely, teaching, scholarship and service.

Scholars are not even agreed on what internationalisation means 'because of the diversity and complexity of its rationales, activities, stakeholders and providers at the international, national, sectoral and institutional levels.'[2]

The African higher education system exhibits contradictory tendencies in which the traditions of internationalisation and indigenisation continue to vie for supremacy. Internationalisation is deeply embedded in the African higher education landscape, because during the colonial era the few African universities that were established were modelled on those in the imperial metropoles. After independence, when the bulk of the continent's universities were created, the institutional, intellectual and ideological dependency and mimicry of European, increasingly complemented by American, higher education patterns, processes and practices, by African universities, persisted. At the same time, nationalist demands and pressures grew for the decolonisation, regionalisation and localisation of African universities and knowledge production.

This is what I would like to explore in this chapter, how these contradictory tendencies are evident in multiple ways at regional, national and institutional levels. It is divided into two parts. First, I seek to frame internationalisation by briefly outlining its structural contexts, motivations and rationales and manifestations and modalities. I also examine in this section the regional dimensions and actors of internationalisation, the seductions and sanctions of rankings and the geographies and hierarchies of knowledge production and collaboration. In the second part, I share some reflections on the persistent struggle in African higher education institutions between the forces of globalisation and localisation, the complex and contradictory nexus of glocalisation in Africa's knowledge production systems.

Framing Internationalisation

Shifts in global political economies and the international division of intellectual labour fundamentally structure the growth and transformation of universities and systems of knowledge production. Among the key driving forces of change are social transformation, including demographic dynamics, business and industry demand, government policies and institutional pressures and priorities. Also notable is the globalisation and regionalisation of policy mimicry, notwithstanding the persistence of regional and national differences reflecting the complexity of local realities.

The motivations and rationales for internationalisation are multifaceted. They include national development and demographic imperatives. In the contemporary world, transnational education in the global North provides an important outlet for unmet and specialised demands from the emerging economies and countries of the global South, with its bulging youthful populations. In the meantime, in the increasingly ageing countries of the global North, importing students from the global South is critical to universities facing a youth demographic squeeze. Clearly, internationalisation in different regions reflects divergent logics of supply and demand for students, faculty and financial and reputational capitals.

There is an assortment of economic, political, social, cultural and academic imperatives and rationales. Economically, internationalisation is often justified in terms of preparing students for careers in a globalised economy, enhancing national development and competitiveness and as a means of generating extra-institutional income. Politically, it is valourised for promoting international understanding and global citizenship in an increasingly polarised and dangerous world. Its sociocultural imperative lies in the need to cultivate intercultural literacy in progressively multicultural societies.

There are also specific institutional rationales. Many universities pursue internationalisation for financial reasons, as a critical revenue stream, since foreign students tend to be charged higher fees than local students are. It is maintained that internationalisation facilitates interinstitutional co-operation, competition and comparison, which can enhance the quality of higher education by compelling institutions to meet or rise to international standards. In a globalised world, internationalisation is seen as an indispensable part of institutional recognition and branding, an essential attribute and asset in the intensifying competition for talented students, faculty, resources and reputational capital among universities within and among countries.

The manifestations and modalities of internationalisation are equally varied among regions. Student flows constitute a key dimension of internationalisation. This has become a huge global industry, which brings billions of dollars to universities and constitutes a major export industry for the major destination countries. In 2019, the US had 1.1 million students who generated US$42.4 billion. In Britain, in 2016, international students brought £20 billion to the British economy.

International student flows are characterised by uneven movements between and within regions, between sending and receiving regions and countries. Out of the 5,309,240 outbound students in 2017, Africa accounted for 549,713 (10.35 per cent), while there were only 226,091 inbound students (4.26 per cent); Asia accounted for the largest share of outbound international students (43.82 per cent) and North America and Europe accounted for the bulk of inbound international students (62.20 per cent).[3]

Since World War II there have been at least three dominant international models and three generations of internationalisation. The models include what can be called the European and derivative colonial institutional model, in the former European colonies of Latin America, Asia and Africa. In these postcolonial societies, higher education institutions are often replicas of those in the former imperial metropoles. Then two postwar models emerged: the Soviet Union model, which held sway in the socialist nations allied to the Soviet Union during the protracted era of the Cold War before the demise of the Soviet Union at the turn of the 1990s; and the United States model. The latter model is quite malleable and variously encapsulated in the preeminence of the research university, with prominence given to a liberal arts education or the primacy of market values. It manifests itself in the establishment of American-style institutions, the adoption of US-centred academic cultures and the performance of US-institutional identities.

As for the generations, internationalisation was characterised, first, by the mobility of people – students and faculty – which of course still persists. Second, there was the mobility of programmes and providers, which encompassed the creation of twinning, franchised, articulated/validated, joint/double award and online/distance programmes, and the formation of branch campuses and independent institutions abroad. The third was the establishment of global education hubs, which have mushroomed in several regions, especially western Asia, or the Middle East.

As the internationalisation of higher education has spread its tentacles, it has been accompanied by the expansion and diversification of global, regional, national and institutional actors. At the global level, the actors include higher education consortia, alliances and agencies, not to mention international NGOs and intergovernmental agencies, including those associated with the United Nations, from UNESCO to the World Bank.

Each region has also developed its own transregional actors. The most co-ordinated approach and process emerged in Europe, where higher education internationalisation through the Bologna Process became an integral part of the European unification project. Other regions, including Africa, have sought to replicate the European Union model with mixed results.

The International Association of Universities has conducted several global surveys on the internationalisation of higher education, which show divergent perceptions of the rationales and risks of internationalisation in different world regions. In its 2014 survey,[4] the most significant potential risk identified was the commodification of education, followed by unequal sharing of the benefits of internationalisation among partners and the growing gaps between higher education institutions within countries. In the 2019 survey,[5] the biggest risk was deemed to be the fact that internationalised opportunities were accessible only to students with financial resources, accompanied by the difficulties of assessing and recognising the quality of courses and programmes offered by foreign institutions and the excessive competition with other higher education institutions.

Clearly, international academic mobility, collaborations and cross-border provision remain decidedly unequal. In fact, in many ways, internationalisation has reinforced historic inequalities. The flows of people and programmes, institutions and infrastructures, epistemic perspectives and priorities, academic languages and literacies, research models and methodologies, between the global North and the global South, remain unequal and uneven. Global inequalities in knowledge production are reinforced by the allures and anxieties of rankings, which are at the centre of the growing chase for world-class university status.

The power of rankings lies in their material impact in influencing the flows of students, faculty and resources. The normalisation of rankings in institutional, national and global higher education discourses and expectations reflects three interlocking processes and projects. First, they are a product of globalisation and the transformation of higher education into a strategic knowledge-intensive industry for the knowledge economy and society. Second, rankings serve to establish hegemonic norms of excellence to influence, incentivise and change institutional behaviour. Third, they reflect and reinforce interinstitutional competition in an endless 'reputational' and 'positional' race.

The geographies and hierarchies of knowledge production and collaboration show some shifts, especially with the economic rise of Asia and the ascent of Asian universities in global rankings. Within Asia itself, the balance of power is shifting to China. The reshuffling can be seen in the 2020 World University Rankings by *The Times Higher Education.*[6] Overall, North America and Europe dominate, but Asia is climbing rapidly. Altogether, the US featured sixty universities in the top 200, Europe ninety-six, while Asia had twenty-three. The figures for the US and Europe were down from their previous levels, while they were up for Asia.

Africa's number of universities in the top 200 remained unchanged, at two: the University of Cape Town and the University of the Witwatersrand, Johannesburg. Altogether, Africa had seven universities in the top 500 and twenty-seven in the top 1,000. Not surprisingly, there have been strident calls for African universities not to participate in the 'biased' global rankings or to create African rankings that reflect continental realities and priorities. In September 2019, the Association of Arab Universities announced that it had 'agreed to embark on a process of classification of all Arab universities aimed at achieving consistency in the criteria used to assess institutions in global university rankings.'

A key feature of the internationalisation of global higher education post-World War II has been the expansion and strategic value placed on international research collaboration. Obviously, the motivations, dimensions and trends in international research collaboration vary and continue to change. One indicator of the growing practice of international collaboration is the increase in international co-authorship. More often than not, for academics in the global South, the flow of international collaboration is vertical towards the global North rather than horizontal in enhanced intraregional or South–South engagements.

International research collaboration has reproduced the uneven patterns of access to education and knowledge production evident in domestic settings. For example, there are pervasive and persistent gender and racial or ethnic disparities in international research collaborations. For Africa, the unusually high proportion of publications with international authors betrays the persistence of colonial and neocolonial intellectual dependence. The regional patterns of international co-authorship, in which Africa has the highest, are noted in Chapter 19.

Africa's Perpetual Struggle for Internationalisation and Indigenisation

While few African governments have developed specific policies on higher education internationalisation, the trek by African students and faculty to Europe, North America and increasingly Asia, continues to be valourised compared to intraregional mobility. In fact, as noted earlier, more African students and faculty flock to overseas institutions than the other way round. In addition, knowledge production in Africa is unusually prone to epistemic extraversion in which theoretical, methodological and analytical perspectives and preoccupations in the global North exercise undue influence on African scholars.

Other forms of institutional and intellectual dependence in African higher education persist and new ones are emerging. They include research funding, which disproportionately comes from foundations and international, intergovernmental and national agencies from the global North. In other world regions, research funding from business, government and local philanthropic organisations often plays a much bigger role.

Newer forms of internationalisation are also spreading, with the establishment of branch campuses, educational hubs and online education in some African countries, by universities – both non-profit and for-profit – from other parts of the world. Furthermore, African universities are increasingly aware of the potential marketing benefits of international rankings, although overall, as already noted, African universities do not feature as highly as universities from other world regions. More unsavoury trends are also growing, in the form of international predatory journals and conferences that often target academics in poorer institutions and countries.

However, since independence there has also been a strong drive to promote inter- and intraregional flows and co-operation among African universities. This manifests itself through university associations, such as the African Association of Universities (AAU), the Inter-University Council of East Africa (IUCEA) and the Southern African Regional Universities Association (SARUA). In 2018, the AAU established regional offices in North Africa and East Africa, in Cairo and Khartoum, respectively.

Additionally, there have been efforts to harmonise African higher education at continental and sub-regional levels spearheaded by the African Union (AU) and the regional economic communities. The AU launched its ambitious education vision as part of its Agenda 2063.[7] The vision encompasses a ten-year continental education strategy (2016–2025), TVET continental strategy, the Pan-African University with five campuses located in each of the continent's five regions, the Pan-African Institute for Education for Development, the African Union International Centre for Girls' and Women's Education, the Nyerere Scholarship and Academic Mobility Programme and the Harmonisation Strategy.

The Harmonisation Strategy seeks to promote co-operation in information exchange, development and maintenance of a continental framework for higher education qualifications, minimum standards in targeted qualifications, joint curriculum development and student mobility schemes. It also seeks to bridge the gap between disparate educational systems on the continent, facilitate joint curriculum development and institutional partnerships among African universities, ensure global competitiveness, enhance the recognition of academic qualifications and mobility of African students and academic staff across the continent and provide effective quality assurance mechanisms through the African Quality Rating Mechanism.

In 2017, the IUCEA and heads of state of the countries of the East African Community declared the establishment of the East African Common Education Area to facilitate the recognition of academic qualifications and the transfer of credits and co-operation among the region's higher education institutions, in terms of curriculum development and harmonisation of academic programmes, mobility schemes, training systems and research.

In reality, the boundaries between higher education internationalisation in Africa at global and regional levels are quite porous. The various regional university associations and harmonisation efforts are often funded and undertaken in collaboration with international and intergovernmental organisations and development agencies, such as UNESCO, the European Union and the World Bank. For example, by 2018 the World Bank had established forty-six centres of excellence in sixteen countries to 'increase quantity, quality and development relevance of post-graduate education in selected universities through regional specialisation'.[8]

The mobilisation of the African academic diaspora to engage African higher education institutions brings into sharp relief the complicated intersections of the global and regional internationalisation drives by African universities. The importance of the diaspora cannot be overemphasised, as noted in Chapter 10. We all know about the importance of diaspora remittances. For me, even more critical are the potential intellectual remittances, the enormous human and social capital the diaspora possesses. An example is the Carnegie African Diaspora Fellowship Program discussed in Chapter 10.

As noted earlier, a key priority in the Declaration and Action Plan from the First Higher Education Summit held in Dakar in March 2015 was the mobilisation of the diaspora by developing the 10/10 Programme. This envisaged sponsoring '1,000 scholars in the African diaspora across all disciplines every year, for 10 years, to African universities and colleges for collaboration in research, curriculum development and graduate student teaching and mentoring'.[9] To realise this goal, in 2019 we created the Consortium for African Diaspora Scholars Programs, which was registered as a limited liability company in Kenya and incorporated in New York as a 501(c) organisation.

The Dakar Summit called on African higher education institutions, governments and other stakeholders to promote 'mutually-beneficial internationalisation initiatives' that bridge the asymmetries and divides in the global knowledge system that accommodates all knowledges, to effectively address global challenges as articulated in national, regional and global visions such as the AU's Agenda 2063 and the UN's Sustainable Development Goals.

Conclusion

It is clear that internationalisation remains a site of struggle for African universities and scholars. For the continent, the challenge is to construct models and modalities of internationalisation that eschew the historic patterns of external institutional and intellectual dependency. These include: systems that bridge rather than exacerbate the yawning divides in the global education space; paradigms that promote knowledges that address the continent's and world's pressing problems and crises, including climate change, growing social inequalities, rising nationalist populisms and xenophobia and the massive economic and social disruptions of the Fourth Industrial Revolution; engagements that appropriately leverage the potential of information technologies for new internationalisation and effectively mobilise the African academic diaspora for mutual benefit.

This requires putting a premium on internationalisation at home, promoting interinstitutional and intellectual collaborations within and among African countries. At my own university, USIU-Africa, we are proud of the fact that 15 per cent of our students are international, from seventy-four countries, three-quarters of them from African countries. According to the African International Student Survey[10] conducted by Professor Chika Sehoole and Jenny J. Lee, covering seven countries, African students have strong preferences to study in other African countries.

Such regionalisation and domestication of internationalisation must be complemented and mediated, at the global level, by engagements with the African academic diaspora, from both the continent's new and historic diaspora communities around the world. In addition, this must be done by building robust linkages with universities and scholars in the global South. Such strategic and intentional drives are necessary to contain and transform the hierarchical and hegemonic patterns of internationalisation that have historically characterised internationalisation for African higher education institutions.

I would like to leave you with three questions to ponder:

1. How can African universities and academics construct comprehensive models of institutional, international and interdisciplinary collaboration within the continent and with other world regions that are mutually beneficial and productive rather than asymmetrical and inequitable?

2. How can African universities and academics ensure that the values of ethical integrity, intercultural competency, epistemic humility and reflexive deliberation characterise relations with universities and academics from other regions, especially in the global North?

3. What are the implications for internationalisation and research collaboration of the complex changes taking place in the global political economy, encompassing shifting hegemonies and hierarchies with the historic rise of China and the emerging economies, as well as the digitalisation of the economy and society brought by the Fourth Industrial Revolution?

Notes

1. Paul Tiyambe Zeleza, *The Transformation of Global Higher Education, 1945-2015.* New York: Palgrave Macmillan, 2016.
2. Ibid.
3. UNESCO, UIS, International student mobility in tertiary education. http://data.uis.unesco.org.
4. International Association of Universities, *Internationalization of Higher Education: Growing expectations, fundamental values,* 4th Global Survey, April 2014. https://iau-aiu.net/IMG/pdf/iau-4th-global-survey-executive-summary.pdf
5. International Association of Universities, *Internationalization of Higher Education: An Evolving Landscape, Locally and Globally,* 5th Global Survey.
6. Times Higher Education, 'World University Rankings 2020'. https://www.timeshighereducation.com/world-university-rankings/2020/world-ranking#!/page/0/length/25/sort_by/rank/sort_order/asc/cols/stats
7. African Union, *Agenda 2063: The Africa We Wan*t. https://au.int/en/documents/20141012/key-documents-agenda2063
8. The World Bank, 'World Bank Scales-Up Its Support for Regional Higher Education Centers for Excellence in Africa', 3 April 2019. https://www.worldbank.org/en/news/press-release/2019/04/03/world-bank-scales-up-its-support-for-regional-higher-education-centers-for-excellence-in-africa
9. Dakar Summit Declaration and Action Plan, First African Higher Education Summit on Revitalizing Higher Education for Africa's Future, March 10–12 2015, Dakar, Senegal. http://www.trustafrica.org/images/Executive%20SummaryFINAL.pdf
10. Chika Sehoole and Jenny Lee, 'African student flows – Challenging prevailing paradigms', *University World News,* 15 June 2018. https://www.universityworldnews.com/post.php?story=20180614114114977

Keynote address, 9th African Network for Internationalization of Education (ANIE) Conference, Kenya Institute of Curriculum Development, Nairobi, Kenya, 2 October 2019.

24

The Challenges and Opportunities of the Fourth Industrial Revolution for African Universities

Introduction

Like many of you, I try to keep up with trends in higher education, which are of course firmly latched to wider transformations in the global political economy, in all its bewildering complexities and contradictions, and tethered to particular national and local contexts. Of late one cannot avoid the infectious hopes, hysteria and hyperbole about the disruptive effect of the Fourth Industrial Revolution in every sector, including higher education. It was partly to make sense of the discourses and debates about this newfangled revolution that I chose this topic.

But I was also inspired by numerous conversations with colleagues in my capacity as Chair of the Board of Trustees of the Kenya Educational Network (KENET), Kenya's national research and education network that provides Internet connectivity and related services to enhance education and research in the country's educational and research institutions. Also, my university has ambitious plans to expand its programmes in STEM, the health sciences and the cinematic and creative arts, in which discussions about the rapid technological changes and their impact on our educational enterprise feature prominently.

I begin by briefly underlining the divergent perspectives on the complex, contradictory and rapidly changing connections between the Fourth Industrial Revolution and higher education. Then I seek to place them in the context of wider changes: first, in terms of global politics and economy; second, with reference to the changing nature of work; third, in the context of other key trends in higher education. Situating the Fourth Industrial Revolution in these varied and intersected changes and dynamics underscores a simple point – that it is part of a complex mosaic of profound transformations in the contemporary world that precede and will supersede it.

As a historian and social scientist, I am only too aware that technology is always historically and socially embedded; it is socially constructed as far as its creation, dissemination and consumption are socially marked. In short, technological changes, however momentous, produce and reproduce both old and new opportunity structures and trajectories, which are simultaneously uneven and unequal because the enduring social inscriptions of class, gender, race, nationality, ethnicity and other markers, as well as the stubborn geographies and hierarchies of the international division of labour, condition them.

The Fourth Industrial Revolution

As with any major social phenomenon and process, the Fourth Industrial Revolution has its detractors, cheerleaders and fence-sitters. The term often refers to the emergence of quantum computing, artificial intelligence, Internet of Things, machine learning, data analytics, Big Data, robotics, biotechnology, nanotechnology and the convergence of the digital, biological and physical domains of life. Critics dismiss the Fourth Industrial Revolution as a myth, arguing that it is not a revolution as such in so far as many innovations associated with it represent extensions of previous innovations. Some even find the euphoric discourses about it elitist, masculinist and racist. Some fear its destructive potential for jobs and livelihoods and privacy and freedom as surveillance capitalism spreads its tentacles.

To those who espouse its radical impact, the Fourth Industrial Revolution will profoundly transform all spheres of economic, social, cultural and political life. It is altering the interaction of humans with technology, leading to the emergence of what Yuval Noah Harari calls *Homo Deus,* who worships at the temple of dataism in the name of algorithms. More soberly, some welcome the Fourth Industrial Revolution for its leapfrogging opportunities for developing countries and marginalised communities. But even the sceptics seek to hedge their bets on the promises and perils of the much-hyped revolution by engaging with it.

In the education sector, universities are urged to help drive the Fourth Industrial Revolution by pushing the boundaries of their triple mission of teaching and learning, research and scholarship, public service and engagement. Much attention focuses on curriculum reform, the need to develop what one author calls 'future-readiness' curricula that prepare students holistically for the skills of both today and tomorrow; curricula that integrate the liberal arts and the sciences, digital literacy and intercultural literacy, technical competencies and ethical values; curricula that foster self-directed and personalised learning.

Because of the convergences of the Fourth Industrial Revolution, universities are exhorted to promote interdisciplinary and transdisciplinary teaching, research and innovation and to pursue new modes of internationalisation of knowledge production, collaboration and consumption.

Changes in the Global Political Economy

From Africa's vantage point, I would argue that there are three critical global forces to which we need to pay special attention. First, the world system is in the midst of a historic hegemonic shift. This is evident in the growing importance of Asia and the emerging economies, including Africa, and the impending closure of Euro-America's half a millennium of global dominance. Emblematic of this monumental transition is the mounting rivalry between a slumping United States and a rising China that is flexing its global muscles, not least through the Belt and Road Initiative.

The struggle between the two nations and their respective allies or spheres of influence marked the end of America's supremacy as the sole post-Cold War superpower. The outbreak of the trade war between the two in 2018 represented the first skirmishes of a bitter hegemonic rivalry that will probably engulf at least the first half of the twenty-first century. The question we have to ask ourselves is, how should Africa manage and position itself in this global hegemonic shift?

As noted in Chapter 7, this is the third such shift over the last 200 years. The first occurred between 1870 and 1914, following the rise of Germany and its rivalry with the world's first industrial power, Britain. For the world as a whole, this led to the 'New Imperialism' that culminated in World War I and, for Africa and Asia, in colonisation. The second hegemonic shift emerged out of the ashes of World War II with the rise of two superpowers, the Soviet Union and the United States. For the world, this led to the Cold War, and for Asia and Africa it facilitated decolonisation. Can Africa leverage the current shift to achieve its long-cherished but deferred dream of sustainable development?

As the highest concentration of collective intellectual prowess, African universities and researchers have a responsibility to promote comprehensive understanding of the stakes for Africa and inform policy options on how best to navigate the emerging treacherous quagmire of the new superpower rivalries, to maximise the possibilities and minimise the perils. More broadly, in so far as China's and Asia's rise are as much economic as they are epistemic, as evident in the exponential ascent of Asian universities in global rankings, the challenge and opportunity for our universities and knowledge production systems is how best to pluralise worldly engagements that simultaneously curtail the western stranglehold rooted in colonial and neocolonial histories of intellectual dependency without succumbing to the hegemonic ambitions of China and Asia.

Second, world demography is undergoing a major metamorphosis. On the one hand, this is evident in the ageing populations of many countries in the global North. China is also on the same demographic path, thanks to its ill-guided one-child policy imposed in 1979, which was abolished only in 2015. On the other, Africa is enjoying a population explosion. As noted in Chapter 22, 60 per cent of the African population is below the age of twenty-five. Africa is expected to have, on current trends, 1.70 billion people in 2030 (20 per cent of the world's population), rising to 2.53 billion (26 per cent) in 2050 and 4.5 billion (40 per cent) in 2100.

What are the developmental implications of Africa's demographic bulge and Africa's global position as it becomes the reservoir of the world's largest labour force? The role of educational institutions in this demographic equation is clear. Whether Africa's skyrocketing population is to be a demographic dividend or not will depend on the quality of education, skilling and employability of the youth. Hordes of hundreds of millions of ill-educated, unskilled and unemployable young people will turn the youth population surge into a demographic disaster, a Malthusian nightmare for African economies, polities and societies.

The third major transformative force centres on the impact of the Fourth Industrial Revolution. During the First Industrial Revolution of the mid-eighteenth century, Africa paid a huge price through the Atlantic slave trade that laid the foundations of the industrial economies of Euro-America. As the Second Industrial Revolution of the late nineteenth century rolled out, Africa was colonised. The Third Industrial Revolution that emerged in the second half of the twentieth century coincided with the tightening clutches on Africa of neocolonialism. What is and will be the nature of Africa's levels of participation in the Fourth Industrial Revolution – a player or a pawn, as in the other three revolutions?

The Future of Work

There is a rapidly growing academic literature and number of consultancy reports about the future of work. An informative summary can be found in a short monograph published by *The Chronicle of Higher Education*. In *The Future of Work: How Colleges Can Prepare Students for the Jobs Ahead*[1] it is argued that the digitalisation of the economy and social life spawned by the Fourth Industrial Revolution will continue transforming the nature of work as old industries are disrupted and new ones emerge. In the United States, it is projected that the fastest-growing fields will be in science, technology, engineering and health care, while employment in manufacturing will decline. This will enhance the importance of the soft skills of the liberal arts, such as oral and written communication, critical thinking and problem-solving, teamwork and collaboration and intercultural competency, combined with hard technical skills like coding.

In short, while it is difficult to predict the future of work, more jobs will increasingly require graduates who 'fully merge their training in hard skills with soft skills'[2] and are trained in both the liberal arts and STEM, with skills for complex human interactions and capacities for flexibility, adaptability, versatility and resilience. In a world of rapidly changing occupations, the hybridisation of skills, competencies and literacies together with lifelong learning will become assets. In a digitalised economy, routine tasks will be more prone to automation than highly skilled non-routine jobs. Successful universities will include those that impart academic and experiential learning to both traditional students and older students seeking retraining.

The need to strengthen interdisciplinary and experiential teaching and learning, career services centres and retraining programmes for older students on college campuses is likely to grow. So will partnerships between universities and employers as both seek to enhance students' employability skills and reduce the much-bemoaned mismatches between graduates and the labour market. The roles of career centres and services will need to expand in response to pressures for better integration of curricular programmes, co-curricular activities, community engagement and career preparedness and placement.

Some university leaders and faculty of course bristle at the vocationalisation of universities, insisting on the primacy of intellectual inquiry, learning for its own sake and student personal development. But the fraught calculus between academe and return on investment cannot be wished away for many students and parents. For students from poorer backgrounds, intellectual development and career preparedness both matter as university education may be their only shot at acquiring the social capital that richer students can acquire through other avenues.

Trends in Higher Education

Digital Disruptions

Clearly, digital disruptions constitute one of the key four interconnected trends in higher education that I seek to discuss. The other three include rising demands for public service and engagement, unbundling the degree, and escalating imperatives for lifelong learning. More and more, digitalisation affects every aspect of higher education, including research, teaching and institutional operations. Information technologies have affected research in various ways, including expanding opportunities for Big Science and increasing capacities for international collaboration. The latter is evident in the exponential growth in international co-authorship.

Also, the explosion of information has altered the role of libraries as repositories of print and audiovisual materials into nerve centres for digitised information communication, which raises the need for information literacy.

Moreover, academic publishing has been transformed by the acceleration and commercialisation of scholarly communication. The role of powerful academic publishing and database firms has greatly been strengthened. The Open Access movement is trying to counteract that.

Similarly far reaching is the impact of information technology on teaching and learning. Opportunities for technology-mediated forms of teaching and learning encompassing blended learning, flipped classrooms, adaptive and active learning and online education have grown. This has led to the emergence of a complex mélange of teaching and learning models, encompassing the face-to-face-teaching model without ICT enhancement, the ICT-enhanced face-to-face teaching model, the ICT-enhanced distance teaching model and the online teaching model.

Spurred by the student success movement arising out of growing public concerns about the quality of learning and the employability skills of graduates, 'the black box of college' – teaching and learning – has been opened, argues another recent monograph by *The Chronicle for Higher Education,* entitled *The Future of Learning: How colleges can transform the educational experience.*[3] The report notes:

> Some innovative colleges are deploying big data and predictive analytics, along with intrusive advising and guided pathways, to try to engineer a more effective educational experience. Experiments in revamping gateway courses, better connecting academic and extracurricular work and lowering textbook costs also hold promise to support more students through college.

For critics of surveillance capitalism, the arrival of Big Brother on university campuses is truly frightening in its Orwellian implications.

There are other teaching methods increasingly driven by artificial intelligence and technology, which include immersive technology, gaming and mobile learning, as well as MOOCs and the emergence of robot tutors. In some institutions, instructors who worship at the altar of innovation are also incorporating free, web-based content, online collaboration tools, simulation or educational games, lecture capture, e-books and in-class polling tools, as well as student smartphones and tablets, social media and e-portfolios, as teaching and learning tools.

Some of these instructional technologies make personalised learning for students increasingly possible. *The Chronicle* monograph argues that for these technologies and innovations, such as predictive analytics, to work it is essential to use the right data and algorithms, cultivate buy-in from those who work most closely with students, pair analytics with appropriate interventions and invest enough money. Managing these innovations entails confronting entrenched structural, financial and cultural barriers and 'requires investments in training and personnel'. For many under-resourced African universities with inadequate or dilapidated physical and electronic infrastructures, the digital revolution remains a pipe dream.

But such is the spread of smartphones and tablets among growing segments of African university students that they can no longer be effectively taught using the old pedagogical methods of the BBC generation – born before computers. After having catered to millennials, universities now have to accommodate Gen Z, the first generation of truly digital natives. Another study from *The Chronicle* entitled, *The New Generation of Students: How colleges can recruit, teach and serve Gen Z*,[4] argues that this 'is a generation accustomed to learning by toggling between the real and virtual worlds. ... They favor a mix of learning environments and activities led by a professor but with options to create their own blend of independent and group work and experiential opportunities.'

For Gen Z, knowledge is everywhere. 'They are accustomed to finding answers instantaneously on Google while doing homework or sitting at dinner. ... They are used to customization. And the instant communication of texting and status updates means they expect faster feedback from everyone, on everything.' For such students the instructor is no longer the sage on stage from whom hapless students passively imbibe information through lectures, but a facilitator or coach who engages students in active and adaptive learning. Their ideal instructor makes class interesting and involving, is enthusiastic about teaching, communicates clearly, understands students' challenges and issues and gives guidance and challenges students to do better as a student or as a person, among several attributes.

Teaching faculty to teach the digital generation, equipping faculty with digital competency, design thinking and curriculum curation, is increasingly imperative. The deployment of digital technologies and tools in institutional operations is expected to grow as universities seek to improve efficiencies and data-driven decision-making. As noted earlier, the explosion of data about almost everything that happens in higher education is leading to data mining and analytics becoming more important than ever. Activities that readily lend themselves to IT interventions include enrolment, advising and management of campus facilities. Similarly, institutions have to pay more attention to issues of data privacy and security.

Public Service Engagements

The second major trend centres on rising expectations for public engagement and service. This manifests itself in three ways. First, demands for mutually beneficial university–society relationships and for universities to have a social impact are increasing. As doubts grow about the value proposition of higher education, pressures will intensify for universities to demonstrate their contribution to the public good in contributing to national development and competitiveness, notwithstanding the prevailing neoliberal conceptions of higher education as a private good. On the other hand, universities' concerns about the escalating demands of society are also likely to grow. The intensification of global challenges, from climate change to socioeconomic inequality to geopolitical security, will demand more research and policy interventions by higher education institutions. A harbinger of things to come was the launch in 2019 by the *Times Higher Education*[5] of a new global ranking system, which assessed the social and economic impact of universities' innovations, policies and practices.

Second, the question of graduate employability will become more pressing for universities to address. As the commercialisation and commodification of learning persists and maybe even intensifies, demands on universities to demonstrate that their academic programmes prepare students for employability in terms of being ready to get or create gainful employment can only be expected to grow. Pressure will increase on both universities and employers to close the widely bemoaned gap between college and jobs, between graduate qualifications and the needs of the labour market.

Third, is the growth of public–private partnerships (PPPs). As financial and political pressures mount and higher education institutions seek to focus on their core academic functions of teaching and learning and generating research and scholarship, many universities have been outsourcing more and more the financing, design, building and maintenance of facilities and services, including student housing and food services, and monetising parking and energy. Emerging partnerships encompass enrolment and academic programme management, such as online programme expansion, skills training and student mentoring and career counselling.

Another *Chronicle* monograph, *The Outsourced University: How public–private partnerships can benefit your campus*,[6] traces the growth of PPPs. They take a variety of forms and duration. It is critical for institutions pursuing such partnerships to determine whether a 'project should be handled through a P3', to clearly 'articulate your objectives and measure your outputs', to 'be clear about the trade offs', 'bid competitively' and 'be clear in the contract'.

The growth of PPPs will lead to greater mobility between the public and private sectors and the academy as pressures grow for continuous skilling of students, graduates and employees in a world of rapidly changing jobs and occupations. This will be done through the growth of experiential learning, work-related learning and secondments.

Unbundling the Degree

The third major transformation that universities need to pay attention to centres on their core business as providers of degrees. This is the subject of another fascinating monograph in *The Chronicle entitled The Future of The Degree: How Colleges Can Survive the New Credential Economy.*[7] The study shows how the university degree evolved over time in the nineteenth and twentieth centuries to become a highly prized currency for the job market, a signal that one has acquired a certain level of education and skills.

As economies undergo 'transformative change, a degree based on a standard of time in a seat is no longer sufficient in an era where mastery is the key. As a result, we are living in a new period in the development of the degree, where different methods of measuring learning are materialising and so too are diverse and efficient packages of credentials based on data.'[8] In a digitalised economy where continuous reskilling becomes a constant, the college degree as a one-off certification of competence, as a badge certifying the acquisition of desirable social and cultural capital and as a convenient screening mechanism for employers, is less sustainable.

Clearly, as more employers focus on experience and skills in hiring and as the mismatch between graduates and employability persists or even intensifies, traditional degrees will increasingly become less dominant as a signal of job readiness and universities will lose their monopoly over certification as alternative credentialling systems emerge. As experiential learning becomes more important, the degree will increasingly need to embody three key elements. First, it will need to 'signify the duality of the learning experience, both inside and outside the classroom. Historically, credentials measured the learning that happened only inside the university, specifically seat time inside a classroom.'[9] Second, the 'credential should convey an integrated experience. … While students are unlikely to experience all of their learning for a credential on a single campus in the future, some entity will still need to help integrate and certify the entire package of courses, internships and badges throughout a person's lifetime.'[10] Third, credentials 'must operate with some common standard. … For new credentials to matter in the future, institutions will need to create a common language of exchange' beyond the current singular currency of an institutional degree.

The rise of predictive hiring to evaluate job candidates and people analytics in the search for talent will further weaken the primacy of the degree signal. Also disruptive is the fact that human knowledge, which used to take hundreds of years and, later, decades, to double, is now 'doubling every 13 months, on average and IBM predicts that in the next couple of years, with the expansion of the internet of things, information will double every 11 hours. That requires colleges and universities to broaden their definition of a degree and their credential offerings.'[11]

All these likely developments have serious implications for the current business model of higher education. Universities need:

> to rethink what higher education needs to be – not a specific one-time experience but a lifelong opportunity for learners to acquire skills useful thorough multiple careers. In many ways, the journey to acquire higher education will never end. From the age of 18 on, adults will need to step in and out of a higher-education system that will give them the credentials for experiences that will carry currency in the job market.[12]

In short, as lifelong careers recede and people engage in multiple careers, not just jobs, the quest for higher education will become continuous, no longer confined to the youth in the 18–24 age range. 'Rather than existing as a single document, credentials will be conveyed with portfolios of assets and data from learners demonstrating what they know.'[13] Increasing pressures for life for lifelong learning will lead to the unbundling of the degree into project-based degrees, hybrid baccalaureate and master's degrees, 'micro degrees' and badges. Students will increasingly stack their credentials of degrees and certificates 'to create a mosaic of experiences that they hope will set them apart in the job market'.[14]

As African educators, we must ask ourselves: How prepared are our universities for the emergence and proliferation of new credentialling systems? How are African universities effectively integrating curricular and co-curricular forms of learning, in person and online learning? How prepared and responsive are African universities to multigenerational learners, traditional and emerging degree configurations and certificates? What are the implications of the explosion of instructional information technologies for styles of student teaching and learning, the pedagogical roles of instructors and the dynamics of knowledge production, dissemination and consumption?

Lifelong Learning

The imperatives of the digitalised economy and society for continuous reskilling and upskilling entail lifelong and lifewide learning. The curricula and teaching for lifelong learning must be inclusive, innovative, intersectional and interdisciplinary. This entails identifying and developing the intersections of markets, places, people and programmes, and helping to illuminate the powerful intersections of learning, life and work. Universities need to develop more agile admission systems by smarter segmentation of prospective student markets (e.g., flexible admission by age group and academic programme). Some, such as the National University of Singapore, are exploring lifelong enrolment for students.

Lifelong learning involves developing and delivering personalised learning, not cohort learning; assessing competencies, not seat time, as most universities currently do. 'Competency-based education allows students to move at their own pace, showcasing what they know instead of simply sitting in a classroom for a specific time period.'[15] Lifelong learning requires encouraging enterprise education and an entrepreneurial spirit among students, instilling resilience among them, providing supportive environments for learning and personal development and placing greater emphasis on 'learning to learn' rather than rote learning of specific content.

As leaders and practitioners in higher education, we need to ask ourselves some of the following questions: How are African universities preparing for and going to manage lifelong learning? How can universities effectively provide competency-based education? How can African universities encourage entrepreneurial education without becoming glorified vocational institutions and maintain their role as sites of producing and disseminating critical scholarly knowledges for scientific progress and informed citizenship?

Conclusion

In conclusion, the Fourth Industrial Revolution is only one of many forces creating transformations in higher education. As such, we should assess its challenges and opportunities with a healthy dose of intellectual sobriety, neither dismissing it with Luddite ideological fervour nor investing it with the omniscience beloved by the techno-worshippers. In the end, the fate of technological change is not predetermined; it is always imbricated with human choices and agency.

At my university, USIU-Africa, we have long required all incoming students to take an information technology placement test as a way of promoting information literacy. We use an ICT instructional platform (Blackboard), embed ICT in all our institutional operations and we are increasingly using data analytics in our decision-making processes. We also have a robust range of ICT degree programmes and we are introducing new ones (BSc in Software Engineering, Data Science and Analytics, AI and Robotics, an MSc in Cybersecurity and a PhD in Information Science and Technology) and what we are calling USIU-Online.

Notes

1. The Chronicle of Higher Education, *The Future of Work: How Colleges Can Prepare Students for the Jobs Ahead*, Washington, DC, 2017.
2. Ibid
3. The Chronicle of Higher Education, *The Future of Learning: How Colleges can Transform the Educational Experience*, Washington, DC, 2018.
4. The Chronicle of Higher Education, *The New Generation of Students: How colleges can Recruit, Teach and Serve Gen Z,* Washington, DC, 2018.
5. Times Higher Education, Impact Rankings 2019. https://www.timeshighereducation.com/rankings/impact/2019/overall#!/page/0/length/25/sort_by/rank/sort_order/asc/cols/undefined
6. The Chronicle of Higher Education, *The Outsourced University: How Public–Private Partnerships can Benefit your Campus,* Washington, DC, 2019.
7. The Chronicle of Higher Education, *The Future of The Degree: How Colleges Can Survive the New Credential Economy,* Washington, DC, 2017.
8. Ibid.

9. Ibid.
10. Ibid.
11. Ibid.
12. Ibid.
13. Ibid.
14. Ibid.
15. Robert Mendenhall, 'What Is Competency-Based Education?', *HuffPost,* 11 November 2012. https:// www.huffingtonpost.com/dr-robert-mendenhall/competency-based-learning-_b_1855374.html

Plenary Address, Universities South Africa, First National Higher Education Conference, 'Reinventing SA's Universities for the Future', CSIR ICC, Pretoria, 4 October 2019.

25

Money Matters: The Financial Crises Facing Universities, from the USA to Kenya

In 2019, there were numerous conferences on the state of higher education in Africa and around the world, some of which I participated in and at which I even gave keynote addresses. From these conferences and the increasingly frantic higher education media, it was clear that the spectre of financial instability and unsustainability haunted many universities in the developed and developing countries alike, from the United States to Kenya. The challenges are of course mediated by local contexts embedded in levels of development and socioeconomic inequalities, prevailing political cultures and ideologies, institutional histories and capacities and a confluence of other forces.

Declining Outlook for American Universities

In the United States, the outlook for universities was largely negative in the 2010s. According to Moody's, in its 2019 higher education outlook:[1]

> Increasing expenses outpace constrained revenue for most universities and colleges ... owing to constrained tuition revenue growth, the main revenue stream for most universities and colleges. ... Colleges and universities will look to further control costs, which will lead to longer-term challenges related to programmatic and capital investment. For most colleges, rising labor costs, which are roughly 65 per cent–75 per cent of expenses, will remain the largest hurdle.

For 2020, the report stated, 'The outlook for the US higher education sector has been changed to stable from negative', underpinned by 'revenue growth in the 3 per cent–4 per cent range over the next year or so, driven mainly by larger, comprehensive universities'. It continued:

> Over the longer term, social risks will continue to transform the US higher education sector, with demographic changes presenting both challenges and opportunities. ... Governance will remain a key differentiator among higher

> education institutions. ... Those that are able to identify their strengths and weaknesses and take appropriate action where necessary will fare better than those that remain reactive.

A 2017 report by Ernst & Young[2] found that 800 institutions, largely concentrated among small universities and colleges excessively dependent on tuition fees, were facing the most serious risks. Some experts predicted that up to a quarter of American colleges would become extinct within a decade. Whether such predictions happen or not, the rate of closures has accelerated. Equally troubling is the staggering growth in student loan debt. In 2018, it reached US$1.5 trillion, encompassing 44.2 million borrowers. This was higher than credit card debt. In fact, student debt is the second-biggest source of household debt after mortgages in the United States.

The growth in student debt reflected changes in the financing model of American higher education fuelled by the neoliberal ideology unleashed by the Reagan Administration and followed by successive administrations. Increasingly regarded as a private rather than public good, state funding for education declined and student aid support shifted from grants to loans. Cash-strapped universities resorted to several strategies, including raising tuition and diversifying their revenue streams and on the expenditure side they embraced cost-cutting, especially on tenure-track (permanent) faculty employment, one of the largest expenses for universities.

Between 1980 and 2018, revenue from tuition grew by 213 per cent at public institutions and 129 per cent at private ones. This was higher than the growth in wages or the rate of inflation. Increasingly, public universities were becoming privatised as they depended less and less on state funding. Many of the flagship public universities were public in name only as they no longer relied on state support for the bulk of their funding, which in some cases came to less than a quarter.

For example, when I joined the University of Illinois at Urbana-Champaign as a faculty member and centre director in the 1995–1996 academic year, state appropriations comprised 38.65 per cent of the university's US$909,455,000 operating revenue. In the 2019 financial year, direct state appropriations had dropped to 7.48 per cent out of an operating budget of US$3.03 billion. Forty years earlier, in the 1979–1980 financial year, state revenues for the University of Illinois as a whole constituted 49.07 per cent and student fees a mere 5.47 per cent. Thirty years before I joined the university, in the 1965–1966 financial year, state appropriations made up 56.0 per cent of the budget and student fees 3.6 per cent.

In the meantime, students are becoming more indebted. Up to 70 per cent of American students currently graduate with debt. According to *Business Insider*,[3] the average student loan debt per graduating student who took out a loan reached US$29,800 in 2018. More than a hundred people owed over US$1 million compared to fourteen people in 2013! And more than three million people aged sixty and above owed over US$86 billion. The crippling burden of college tuition rose to the top of the political agenda in the Democratic Party's primaries for the 2020 US presidential election. As could be expected in such a racialised society, black graduates had more debt than their white counterparts.

For faculty, the proportion of tenure-track faculty declined precipitously while that of contingent faculty rose, reaching 73 per cent of all faculty in American colleges and universities in 2016, according to data from the American Association of University Professors.[4] The remuneration and working conditions of contingent faculty are often abysmal; they typically do not have benefits and some make less than the minimum wage. The academic media is full of heartbreaking stories about some contingent faculty subsisting on food stamps and making less than teenagers working in fast-food joints.

The expansion of the lumpen-professoriate of contingent faculty weakens the academy as a whole. It hurts students because these faculty are often hired by the hour, not given institutional support and tend not to participate in departmental affairs, all of which deprives students of robust faculty engagement. It also undermines all faculty by threatening the integrity of faculty work, limiting the distribution of faculty service responsibilities, creating hierarchies among faculty and eroding academic freedom, which vulnerable contingent faculty are hardly in a position to exercise.

The case of the US underscores the fact that financial challenges and their implications for students and faculty and the entire higher education enterprise are not confined to the global South. This should be a source of both solace and sobriety for African universities. Solace, because it shows that the challenges are not peculiar to African countries and higher education institutions. Sobriety, because we cannot import turnkey solutions from elsewhere. Rather, we must think strategically, smartly and systematically and devise solutions that will ensure financial stability and sustainability for our institutions.

Belt-Tightening for Kenyan Universities

In Kenya, it is not an exaggeration to say that the majority of the country's universities are virtually bankrupt. Many are unable to pay salaries on time, remit statutory obligations for health and pensions and provide adequate faculty, teaching and learning facilities, as well as student accommodation and support services. The Kenyan media is replete with stories about the billions of Kenyan shillings that public universities, including some of the largest and oldest ones, owe in statutory obligations and to their service providers.

The financial challenges facing most African universities, including those in Kenya, arise from the fact that they are primarily dependent on tuition fees. There is a mismatch between the rising demand for education, which is escalating because of the continent's youth bulge, and the ability of students to pay the full costs of a quality university education, as well as the absorptive capacity of institutions to provide student aid. As public funding per university student has generally declined, instructional costs have increased, and both the universities and students suffer, which is reflected in falling quality and standards.

It becomes a vicious cycle: poor-quality education undermines graduate employability, which burdens families and undermines their capacity to recover investments already made in education and to cover any future costs. This serves to reinforce questions about the value proposition of higher education. It helps to explain the extreme sensitivities about tuition increases among students and their parents or guardians. The fact of the matter is that notwithstanding the hype about Rising Africa/Africa Rising – one of the indicators of which is ostensibly the expansion of the middle classes – the majority of students in African universities are from lower-middle-income, working-class and peasant backgrounds.

Upper-middle-income and rich families tend to send their children abroad – to Europe, North America and the emerging economies of Asia, such as India, Malaysia and China – because they have little confidence in the quality of local universities. This is well articulated in a story in a local paper, the *Business Daily,* entitled 'Local universities are facing serious crisis of confidence'.[5] Those who vote with their wallets for their children's education abroad often include parents who were educated at the local universities, at least for their first degrees.

It becomes a double jeopardy for Kenyan and African universities: they are unable to attract students from their own countries as well as foreign students with the ability to pay for the full costs of high-quality university education. African universities are not serious players in the lucrative international student market. As noted in Chapter 23, out of the 5.09 million internationally mobile students in 2018, Africa accounted for a mere 4.39 per cent per cent of inbound students, but 10.26 per cent of outbound students.

The financial situation of universities in Kenya has been compounded by student demographics in terms of the number of students qualifying for university entry. Since 2016, when the Ministry of Education adopted stringent controls to curb cheating in national examinations, the pool of Kenya Certificate of Secondary Education (KCSE) students qualifying for university entrance has been historically low. In 2018, out of the 660,204 candidates who sat for KCSE examinations, only 90,755 (13.74 per cent) scored C+ and above, the minimum grade for university entry. In 2019, out of the 697,222 candidates 125,746 (18.05 per cent) got C+ and above.

The available capacity in the country's seventy-four universities in 2019 was 145,338, and in 2020 it was 193,878. Thus, the proportion of available capacity filled by qualified students from the 2018 and 2019 KCSE results was 62.44 per cent and 64.86 per cent, respectively. This was markedly down from the 2015 figures, before the clampdown on cheating. In that year, out of the 521,240 candidates who sat for the KCSE examinations, 32.52 per cent (or 169,492) got C+ and above. The reduced numbers resulted in fierce competition among the country's universities for the limited pool of qualified candidates, which affected their financial bottom line.

Financial constraints affect the ability of Kenyan universities to train, attract and retain qualified faculty. The core business of universities is teaching and learning, research and scholarship and public engagement and service. Recruitment and retention of top-rate academics is therefore imperative. Kenya suffers from acute shortages of faculty and the graduate student pipeline is severely limited. The yearly production of PhDs in Kenya is about 700, below the government target of 1,000.

Not surprisingly, only 34 per cent of faculty in Kenyan universities have terminal degrees. (My university, USIU-Africa, is an outlier with 76 per cent.) The Cabinet Secretary of Education was quoted in the *Daily Nation* on 8 May 2019 as saying that 'Less than 10pc of PhD holders are qualified'.[6] This was attributed to the prevalence of academic fraud, in which contract cheating is rampant. In fact, Kenya reportedly enjoys the dubious distinction of being a leading global centre of contract cheating.

Even more critical is the growing discrepancy between the growth in student enrolments and faculty. Between 2011 and 2018, while student enrolments increased fivefold, the number of academics teaching in Kenyan public universities grew by only 13 per cent. Consequently, faculty-student ratios rose, which in some public universities are close to 1:70. This has severely affected the quality of education and research productivity. In most universities, many of the often overworked and poorly paid faculty are forced into adjuncting and they rely on outmoded pedagogical practices and curricula. Moreover, student learning is frequently interrupted by employee strikes and student demonstrations.

The Harvests of Underinvestment

Higher education is critical to the development of the high-level human capital that is essential for economic growth and sustainable development. Two measures of the contribution of higher education are especially important. One is the employability of university graduates and the other is research productivity and impact. In the *African Economic Outlook 2020*,[7] the African Development Bank provided sobering reading on Africa's unpreparedness for the jobs of the future because of the low quality of its educational systems.

The problem cut across the educational ladder. In the words of the report: 'Many African countries have yet to catch up with the rest of the world in basic skills and education. … African students have lower average test scores than students in other world regions. Against global harmonised test scores ranging from 300 to 625, the average African student scored only 374 in 2017.'

It is universally acknowledged that human capital is a key driver of economic growth, but 'Human capital contributes less to labor productivity and economic growth in Africa than in other developing regions. This is due partly to the low quality of education, lack of complementary physical capital and widespread skill and education mismatches.'[8]

The report urged African governments, advice that applied to universities as well, to make strategic choices to build the workforce of the future. 'African countries will need to anticipate and build a flexible and productive workforce to meet future challenges. To strengthen worker employability, firm productivity and inclusive growth, African countries need a national strategy for education and skill development.' The report noted, 'A poorly skilled and educated labor force is typically the top constraint mentioned by global executives when considering manufacturing investments in Africa.'

Furthermore:

> Because 'soft skills' are likely to become increasingly important, education and training institutions should be encouraged to inculcate and reinforce positive values, starting with young children. These attributes include a strong work ethic, honesty, tolerance and respect for authority, punctuality and pursuit of excellence. These are the intangible characteristics of a high-quality workforce.

Massive investments are required for building educational infrastructure; in addition to soft skills, the development of critical future skills includes job-specific digital skills, job-neutral digital skills and ancillary skills related to manufacturing.

As noted in Chapter 22, reports on graduate employability in Kenya, as elsewhere across East Africa and the continent, show that there are glaring mismatches between what universities are producing and what economies need, resulting in high levels of graduate unemployment and underemployment. In fact, in much of Africa, university graduate unemployment and underemployment tend to be higher than for secondary school and vocational college graduates.

The conundrum African countries face is that they have low levels of tertiary enrolment, yet even the relatively small number of graduates have limited employability opportunities. In 2017, the gross enrolment ratio of Kenya stood at 11.7 per cent, which was below the African average of about 14 per cent, but above the sub-Saharan average of 9 per cent.

Essential employability qualities (EEQ) go beyond subject knowledge and technical competence. Acquisition of soft skills is paramount. These skills include communication, critical thinking, problem-solving, research and collaboration. And they go hand in hand with adaptability, ethics and professionalism. The cultivation of employability skills raises questions about curriculum design, assessment and teaching methods. It entails the intersection of the classroom, campus and community as learning spaces for a holistic educational experience.

The classroom requires a transforming pedagogy, adequate learning resources, curricular relevance, balance between theory and practice, passionate and enthusiastic teachers with high expectations and motivated students. The campus needs robust career services, extra-curricular activities, student engagement, employer involvement and innovation incubators. And the community contributes through the provision of internships and service-learning opportunities.

The second mission of universities, through which they make invaluable contributions to the economy and society, is knowledge production through research and scholarship. The low levels of research and development (R&D) among African countries are well known and were discussed in earlier chapters. Kenya spends about 0.8 per cent of its GDP on R&D,[9] which is among the highest on the continent. Compared to other African countries, the country's research output is also relatively high. In 2018, the rate for citeable documents per one million inhabitants was 565.1, higher than Ghana's 516.4 and Nigeria's 366.2, but far below South Africa's 4,233.5. Much of this research comes from the numerous research agencies and networks located in Kenya, and a few universities.

It is critical for African countries and universities to develop effective research policies, support and reward systems. Also critical is promoting modalities of research collaboration that are transformative in terms of interdisciplinarity, interprofessionalism and internationalisation. No less important is ensuring a productive balance between pure and applied research and addressing theoretical and analytical issues as well as pressing challenges as identified in national, regional and global agendas, such as Kenya's Vision 2030, East Africa's Vision 2050, the African Union's Agenda 2063 and the United Nation's Sustainable Development Goals.

In many of the developed and leading emerging economies, research grants constitute an important source of revenue for universities. It is also quite common for such institutions to have endowed professorships held by some of their most distinguished research faculty, which further brings additional resources and relieves the operational budget of significant employee costs. As far as I am aware, endowed professorships or chairs do not exist in most African universities. Also, research grants that not only bring administrative overheads, but also supplement faculty income, do not constitute a major source of institutional revenues.

Reframing Financial Models

Clearly, Kenyan and universities in other African countries need to develop more reliable and robust revenue streams. In a wide-ranging presentation at a conference convened by the World Bank and Kenya's Ministry of Education, held in Nairobi on 6 May 2019, Dr Jamil Salmi reminded his audience that there are five major funding sources for universities: government subventions, tuition fees, institutional income-generation activities, donations and loans. He noted that effective resource mobilisation requires promoting efficiency, responsiveness and innovation. This entails adhering to several key principles, such as alignment to national priorities, performance orientation, equity, objectivity and transparency, multiplicity of instruments, institutional autonomy and accountability.

Building on Salmi's observations, a World Bank Report published in August 2019, *Improving Higher Education Performance in Kenya: A Policy Report*,[10] argued that these principles could be realised by the Kenyan government through the introduction of:

> a combination of performance-based budget allocation mechanisms that would provide financial incentives for improved institutional results and better alignment with national policy goals. Policy makers may consider the following three types of innovative allocation mechanisms, separately or combined, to achieve this purpose: (a) funding formula, (b) performance contracts and (c) competitive grants.

The report proposed that the performance contracts and competitive funds should be open to both public and private universities.

> Rather than continuing to allocate annual budgets to the public universities on the basis of history ... [positive] experience in countries as diverse as Chile, China, Egypt, Indonesia and Tunisia has shown the ability of competitive funds to help improve quality and relevance, promote pedagogical innovations and foster better management, objectives that are difficult to achieve through funding formulas.

The African Development Bank's report quoted earlier[11] made some similar recommendations. Improving learning outcomes and skills development entails increasing spending per student across Africa, which remains the lowest in the world. Governments are encouraged to adopt performance-based financing and to improve aid targeting. In addition, they should facilitate philanthropic financing of private education, and develop the student loan market and effective costsharing mechanisms. Further, they ought to promote education-linked conditional cash transfers to girls and poor families and explore innovative finance options to channel more international private capital into education.

The report noted that the private sector underinvests in skills and urged it to complement government funding in promoting high-quality education and reduce the skills gaps they moan about so much. It urged the development of public–private partnerships that 'enable the government and the private sector to join in providing education infrastructure, products and services and in sharing costs and resources'. The report also challenged African schools and universities to 'mobilize funds through alumni associations. Dues and donations can be used to improve the school's facilities and curriculum and provide financial support to members of disadvantaged groups. Alumni associations could also be deployed to lobby governments for more effective education policies.'

As noted earlier, public support for higher education has been declining in many countries around the world. In my book, *The Transformation of Global Higher Education, 1945–2015*,[12] I note in a chapter on university financing around the world: 'Out of the 122 countries that had data on government expenditure on education in general as a share of GDP between 2000 and 2013, it rose in 83 countries and fell in 39 others. ... In terms of expenditure on tertiary education as a percentage of total government expenditure, between 2000 and 2013, it rose in 58 countries and fell in 34.' Digging deeper into the global data on expenditure on higher education, I show that:

> Out of the 95 countries for which data was available covering the 2000–2013 period, government expenditure on tertiary education as a percentage of its expenditure on education rose in 62 and fell in 33. ... Europe claimed the largest number of countries that experienced a rise (19) and Africa those that fell (12). ... The patterns in Asia and Latin America and the Caribbean fell in between those in the African and European regions.

Declines in public funding led to the development of cost-sharing. In my book, I identify five forms of cost-sharing.

> First, the introduction or imposition of sharp increases in tuition fees; second, establishment of dual-track tuition fees for different groups of students; third, the imposition of user-charges for services that were previously free or heavily subsidized; fourth, the reduction in the value of student loans, grants and other stipends; and fifth, the diminution in the size of the public sector and official encouragement of the expansion of tuition-dependent private institutions, both non-profit and for-profit.

Dual-track tuition fees were widely adopted in East Africa, pioneered by Makerere University. This is what came to be called 'parallel programmes' in Kenya, in which government-sponsored students were charged lower tuition fees and self-sponsored students paid much higher rates. In effect, the latter subsidised the former. This model collapsed from 2016 as the number of qualifying students in the KCSE examinations fell drastically and the market for self-sponsored students evaporated overnight. This is at the heart of the financial crisis that has engulfed Kenyan public universities since then.

Kenyan private universities have always been dependent on tuition charges, but in 2016 most of them opted to offset the declining numbers of students by accepting government-sponsored students when this option was made available to them for the first time. But this inadvertently ended up reinforcing their financial challenges, as the government student subventions barely covered a third of instructional costs per student and sometimes even less. Thus, they too fell into a spiral of severe financial instability. In fact, for some of them the situation became even worse than for public universities: none of their costs for employee salaries and capital expenditures were covered by the public exchequer.

Compounding the challenges for many students and universities is the absence of well-targeted and well-managed financial aid programmes at national and institutional levels. The World Bank report mentioned earlier[13] notes that student support from public funds needs to be better targeted to those who most need it. It shows that the disparity ratio in Kenya between households in the highest and lowest consumption quintiles is 49, 'meaning that a young Kenyan from the richest income group is 49 times more likely to access higher education than one from the lowest income group'.

In this context, the report stated:

> It is safe to assume, based on the experience of other countries with similar characteristics as Kenya, that a larger share of government subsidies goes to students from the richer family groups than from the lowest socioeconomic groups and that financing may still be a significant barrier for many needy students. The Kenyan situation is consistent with the extensive international literature showing that the cost of higher education is a deterrent for young people from low-income groups.

The report advised Kenya to consolidate existing bursary schemes under one single agency, reforming the tuition fee policy and strengthening the design and operation of the Higher Education Loans Board (HELB). A more effective tuition fee policy would entail:

> ... eliminating the present parallel fee system and move instead to a TFT [Targeted Free Tuition] scheme, following the example of South Africa. This would require shifting from a system of fee exemptions that benefit the most qualified students from an academic viewpoint to a system where the neediest students who qualify for higher education studies would not pay tuition fees.

For its part, HELB could be strengthened on three fronts:

> better targeting, (b) resource mobilization and (c) improved loan recovery. ... HELB could revisit the weights assigned to each indicator to refine the instrument and give priority to low-income students. It would also be important to discriminate more in terms of giving larger sums to the neediest students compared to middle-class students. With regard to resource mobilization ... HELB should focus on seeking alternate sources of funding by delegating fund management to local governments and private companies.

As for loan collection:

> ... no matter what type of student loan system operates in a country, it is doomed unless its collection mechanism is designed and operates in an effective manner. ... In the past few years, the Board has invested a lot to boost loan recovery, notably by tracing loan beneficiaries through employers and statutory bodies such as the KRA, the National Hospital Insurance Fund (NHIF) and the National Social Security Fund (NSSF). To further strengthen loan recovery, HELB could work on improving awareness among loan beneficiaries and their families, introduce a system of moral guarantors and invest in reliable ICT mechanisms to track graduates.

The report also advised that it is critical to build an income-contingent provision in loan repayment schemes. It stated:

> International experience shows that income-contingent loans, designed after the Australian and New Zealand model, tend to have higher repayment rates. Not only are they more efficient in terms of loan recovery through the national tax system, but they are also more equitable since graduates pay a fixed proportion of their income and are exempted from repaying whenever they are unemployed, or their income is below a predetermined ceiling.

Besides government subventions through student aid, it is also important for institutions to build student aid capacities from their own resources. At American universities, this often takes the form of differential pricing, in which well-resourced students pay the full listed price and more needy students pay a discounted price. The discount rate can be as much as 50 per cent, although a discount rate of more than 35 per cent can result in financial difficulties for the university if not backed by extensive additional institutional resources.

For example, the College Scorecard produced by the U.S. Department of Education,[14] which listed some key data on individual American colleges and universities, showed that the average tuition fee for such leading ivies as Harvard, Yale and Princeton was US$14,000, US$19,000 and US$10,000, respectively. In reality, in 2018–2019 the cost of attending Harvard, for tuition, fees, room and board, was US$67,340. Students from families earning below US$65,000 paid no tuition fees, those from families with incomes up to US$150,000 paid 0–10 per cent and there were proportional expectations from families with incomes above US$150,000.

Similar schemes were available at Yale, Princeton and many other rich American universities. These universities were able to offer them because of their huge endowments, which in 2018 stood at US$39.2 billion for Harvard (US$1.7 million per student), US$29.4 billion for Yale (US$2.3 million per student) and US$25.9 billion for Princeton (US$3.2 million per student). These endowments are of course simply unimaginable in Africa. In 2019, the University of Cape

Town, Africa's leading university, had an endowment of ZAR3.7 billion, equivalent to US$263.5 million, which would not even put it in the top 100 universities in the United States in terms of the size of endowments.[15]

Many African universities do not have their own institutional student aid programmes or fundraising capacities. Often times, student scholarships are from external donors and philanthropic organisations. At my university, which is a notable exception in some ways, we have a sizeable student aid programme covered by the university operational budget, which caters for hundreds of students every year. A feature of our student aid is a work–study programme. A few years ago, a group of students set up a scholarship fund called Educate Your Own that, at the time of writing, supported several dozen students.

Our internal efforts are supplemented by scholarships from external partners as well as loan schemes with various lending organisations. In July 2020, we signed a partnership with the Mastercard Foundation that would sponsor 1,000 students for ten years at a cost of $63.2 million.[16] However, these initiatives are not enough to meet the financial needs of all students from low-income backgrounds. This is evident by the fact that some students who undertake deferred payment plans are unable to fulfill their obligations and it takes the university years trying to recover the funds. Many others end up dropping out, which is a huge loss to them, their families, communities and society, as well as the university itself.

In Search of Philanthropists

As noted above, the third source of funding for universities comprises income-generating activities. To quote the World Bank report again:

> While the potential for resource mobilisation is much more limited in developing countries than in OECD nations, Kenyan universities could actively seek additional resources through donations, contract research, consultancies, continuing education and other fund-raising activities, as some of them have already done since the government started reducing university budgets in the mid-1990s.

But, the report warned,

> Not all sources of income have the same potential. Contrary to what is commonly assumed, technology transfer is not, on average, a highly beneficial activity from an income generation viewpoint. Even in the United States, which has a favorable policy framework for innovation and technology transfer, very few institutions hit the jackpot with path breaking innovations that can be successfully commercialised and bring in millions as revenue. At Harvard University, income from technology transfer licenses is equivalent to only 1 per cent of annual fund-raising receipts.

More important is undertaking productive activities. But, all too often, some of these activities may have little bearing on the university's core focus and expertise. Renting out facilities is popular; some universities have even established petrol stations and mortuaries! More lucrative are grants and contracts from consultancies that bring faculty expertise to bear. Above all, in the United States and other parts of the world with robust institutional fundraising cultures, alumni and corporations provide the most important income-generation sources.

Fundraising is grossly underdeveloped in most Kenyan and other African universities. As I noted in a keynote address on advancement in African universities at a forum of vice chancellors in Gaborone, Botswana, in May 2019, effective fundraising requires developing institutional capacities, cultures and commitments. Fundraising is a collective institutional enterprise that requires full commitment and participation of management, governing bodies and faculty.

African universities that are serious about advancement or fundraising must make the necessary investments in building their capacities in terms of databases, human capital, marketing and communications, mobilising and managing donors, and ability to run different types of activities, including the publication of annuals, offering major gifts and capital campaigns, etc. They also need to establish reward systems to incentivise those who attract philanthropic donations.

Typically, sophisticated fundraising operations require dozens and even hundreds of highly paid and specialised professionals, depending on the size of the institution. Institutional investment can raise up to a quarter of funds generated through fundraising. Fundraising professionals are sorely lacking in African universities. Advancement is a long-term project and process that takes many years and even decades to begin bearing fruit.

This is often not well understood among leaders and governing boards at many African universities. It is quite common, at universities with successful fundraising operations, for the governing boards to take the lead in working with the university management to mobilise donors, and, in their own personal philanthropy, through give or get. In capital campaigns, up to a third can be generated by the governing board.

Philanthropy in African universities is also affected by weak national cultures of institutional philanthropy. The culture of institutional advancement, too, is weak among alumni, the source of up to 70 per cent of external funds to universities in the United States and other countries with rich fundraising traditions. It is not unusual to hear alumni ask: 'Why give when we've already paid tuition when we were students?'

While the culture of giving is strong in many African societies, it tends to be limited to families and kinship networks. Public giving is largely confined to religious organisations. When it comes to education the tradition of giving has traditionally been stronger for the lower levels – primary and secondary schools (encompassing the construction and maintenance of schools in colonial and postcolonial Africa) – than higher education, because the latter was for so long dominated by the state. For higher education, giving is often confined to scholarships for family and relatives.

Some writers identify three types of philanthropy. One is horizontal philanthropy, which is largely peer-to-peer, focused on day-to-day subsistence and based on notions and expectations of solidarity, mutuality and reciprocity. It does not necessarily increase assets, although it can mutate into community foundations. The second is vertical philanthropy, in which the rich give to the poor, the powerful and wealthy to the needy. This encompasses organisations that depend on resources from members or raised from other sources and disburse funds to others. Finally, there are modern foundations, which first emerged in the US in the early twentieth century and are often established by wealthy individuals, families and corporations. American and other western foundations have dominated philanthropy in Africa. According to the report by the Council of Foundations, *The State of Global Giving by U.S. Foundations 2011–2015*,[17] international giving by American foundations rose from US$7.2 billion in 2011 to US$9.3 billion in 2015 and the average grant rose from US$200,900 to US$604,500. Health claimed the bulk (52.5 per cent) and education received only 7.9 per cent of the funds.

US foundations giving to Africa between 2002 and 2012 almost doubled from 135 to 248 grants. In dollar terms, the funding rose from US$289 million in 2002 to US$1.46 billion in 2012, given to thirty-six of the fifty-four African countries. From 2011 to 2015, sub-Saharan Africa led with US$9 billion (25.4 per cent of the total disbursed globally), followed by Asia and Pacific US$6.6 billion (18.7 per cent), Latin America and Mexico US$2.7 billion (7.7 per cent), western Europe US$2 billion (5.6 per cent), the Middle East and North Africa US$1.7 billion (4.7 per cent) and eastern Europe, Central Asia and Russia US$570.2 million (1.6 per cent).

An encouraging development in Africa in recent years has been the growth of African foundations. Often patterned on western foundations, they have been established by some of the continent's wealthiest individuals and largest companies. Thus, the exponential growth of high net worth individuals (HNWIs), those with net assets of more than US$1 million, has provided propitious grounds for the expansion of African institutional philanthropy.

According to the *World Wealth Report 2018*,[18] in 2017 the size of HNWIs in Africa reached 169,970 with a combined wealth of USUS$1.7 trillion (0.9 per cent out of the 18.1 million HNWIs globally and 2.4 per cent out of US$70.2 trillion global HNWI wealth). The leading HNWI regions were Asia-Pacific with 34.1 per cent and 30.1 per cent, North America 31.3 per cent and 28.2 per cent and Europe 7.3 per cent and 7.8 per cent, respectively.

Predictably, African foundations are heavily concentrated in South Africa, Nigeria and Egypt, Africa's three largest economies. Their current aggregate of giving is US$2 billion, typically in the US$20,000–US$25,000 range. They mostly focus on service delivery, poverty reduction and infrastructure support. Education is low on their list of priorities and higher education hardly features.

The 2018 World Bank report referred to above notes:

> With a few exceptions, fund raising has not been a major priority in all Kenyan public universities until now, on the assumption that resources are limited throughout the economy and that philanthropy is not part of the national culture. However, international experience shows that, even in resource-constrained countries, universities can find a few rich companies and individuals—locally and among members of the diaspora – that can be convinced to make financial contributions to universities if they are approached and presented with good reasons to support the universities.[19]

Until recently, fundraising among European universities was also underdeveloped. The World Bank report continued:

> Even though the economic conditions may be substantially different from those prevailing in Kenya, the fact that European universities are new to fund raising makes their experience relevant. The most important lesson is that success in fund raising is influenced by (a) the prestige and reputation of universities as proxies of their quality, (b) the existence of continuous relationships with different types of donors in the context of a solid fund-raising strategy and (c) the geopolitical context of the institution.

Clearly, there is a need for creating enabling conditions at the national level in terms of policy and legislation. As African governments increasingly recognise the important role philanthropy can play in fostering development, they are passing non-profit law that affects the philanthropic sector. In Kenya, this includes legislation applicable to public benefit organisations (PBOs), non-governmental organisations, companies limited by guarantee, including non-profit organisations (NPOs), societies and trusts. Tax laws make provisions for tax exemptions for PBOs and NPOs, deductibility of charitable donations and value-added taxes.

But, according to a Kenyan expert on the subject:

> The legal status of philanthropic institutions is imprecise and there are very few incentives for either corporate or individual giving. … Of particular concern is the fact that there is no legislative mechanism to distinguish between philanthropic institutions and other civil society organisations, or to distinguish among different kinds of philanthropic institutions. … For instance, corporate foundations and community foundations are in the same legal category despite their significant differences in goals, operations and governance. The process of claiming tax exemption deductions in Kenya is rigorous, burdensome and time-consuming for the donor.[20]

The Uncertain Seductions of Entrepreneurialism

The financial and other challenges facing contemporary higher education around the world require universities to become more nimble, adaptable and entrepreneurial, by carefully balancing the enduring mission of higher education and the emerging social, economic and technological demands and disruptions. They have to review regularly their value proposition and the organisation and delivery of their core functions of teaching and learning, research and scholarship and public service and engagement, as well as the provision of ancillary and essential operations and services.

In the *2019 Almanac of Higher Education published by The Chronicle of Higher Education,*[21] a sponsored essay notes:

> The pace of change in the world and workplace is accelerating and every industry, including higher education, is being disrupted. Disruption and change create new opportunities for entrepreneurship. Colleges and universities that cultivate a multidimensional entrepreneurial ecosystem can position themselves to thrive in a challenging and changing marketplace. … Entrepreneurial leaders are nimble, opportunity-driven, innovative, problem-solvers and growth-oriented.

The writer suggests five ways to develop an entrepreneurial university ecosystem. First, embracing experimentation, not being afraid to fail and learning from failure in a continuously iterative and action-oriented process. Second, creating a culture of inquisitiveness, innovative and critical thinking at all levels and normalising transformational thinking by rewarding entrepreneurial managers, employees and administrators. Third, encouraging collaboration internally by breaking down silos and through strategic partnerships externally. Fourth, creating powerful lifelong connections and a strong entrepreneurial ecosystem that will sustain institutions, stakeholders and society. Finally, developing the propensity to recognise opportunities by paying keen attention to market changes and demands for new forms of learning and skills in the economy and society.

Financing higher education is of concern to well-meaning governments, political leaders and university administrators and managers: how to provide high-quality teaching, learning and student support services in an era of tight and even declining resources, in addition to promoting the two other traditional missions of higher education, namely, research and scholarship, and public service and engagement. Now there is a fourth mission that is increasingly emphasised and which has its own financial constraints – developing universities as hubs of innovation and entrepreneurship.

Higher education institutions also have to increasingly navigate the digital disruptions of the Fourth Industrial Revolution, changing student demographics, escalating national, regional and global competition, growing demands for accountability and questions about the value proposition of university education from accreditation agencies, the general public, the students themselves and their parents. There are also governance challenges with the expansion and pluralisation of internal and external stakeholders in university affairs.

All these pressures are an integral part of the financial and structural crises facing universities. They demand clear and collective understanding, smart and strategic interventions, as well as creativity and imagination to turn the constellation of challenges to the flip side of opportunities. Universities are notoriously conservative institutions. Woodrow Wilson, who served as President of Princeton before becoming President of the United States, reportedly said, 'It is easier to change the location of a cemetery, than to change the school curriculum.'[22]

In other words, resistance to change in academia is deeply rooted. Alumni, for whom their college years are often imbued with wistfulness for their long-receded youth, often bolster it. Nostalgia is a powerful human emotion, especially in times of rapid and frightful changes, but it is no substitute for clarity of vision if universities are to survive let alone succeed in the twenty-first century, with its massive and unforgiving technological, economic, political, social, cultural and environmental disruptions and demands.

In short, the university of 2020 cannot be the university of 2010 or 2000, let alone of earlier decades. It must be a university prepared for 2030, 2040 and beyond, duly mindful and prepared for the unpredictability of the future. We must create institutional cultures and mindsets of nimbleness, creativity, continuous learning and improvement and data-driven decision-making.

Thus, lifelong learning is not simply an imperative for the successful students and graduates of the twenty-first century, but for the institutions of higher education themselves. Otherwise, some universities, especially the weaker ones and those in poorer countries, will join the long trail of historical dinosaurs and relics. Remember Blockbuster, the video rental giant that did not see streaming services coming and which Netflix cast into the dustbin of history; digital photography upended Kodak's glorious supremacy in the photographic film market; Amazon mauled bookstores and other stores in city centres and malls; and online platforms are destabilising taxi and hotel businesses.

Higher education cannot be an exception. Indeed, as I noted in the previous chapter, the disruptions in higher education are already underway. This is evident in the emergence of new modes of delivery for teaching, learning and assessment. Also, universities are losing their monopoly on credentialling. The unbundling of the degree is already underway with the rise of micro degrees, stackable credentials, joint undergraduate and graduate degrees and the imperatives of interdisciplinary and interprofessional teaching and learning and qualifications.

Employers will increasingly come to use predictive analytics to identify and hire talent. They will demand lifewide and lifelong portfolios combining the 4Cs of contemporary education: the curriculum (class learning), campus (co-curricular activities), community (experiential learning and engagement) and commerce (skills and mindset for employability).

Financial resources and effective financial management are essential to navigate these challenges, seize the opportunities and ensure institutional sustainability in a highly complex, competitive and unpredictable world. The question is, how prepared are African and Kenyan universities and their numerous stakeholders for the brave new world of twenty-first-century higher education?

Notes

1. Moody's, 'Research Announcement: Outlook for US higher education sector changed to stable from negative on steady revenue gains', 10 December 2019. https://www.moodys.com/research/Moodys-Outlook-for-US-higher-education-sector-changed-to-stable--PBM_1207036
2. EY-Parthenon, 'Public-private partnerships in higher education: what is right for your institution?', 2017. https://cdn.ey.com/echannel/parthenon/pdf/perspectives/EY-Parthenon-P3s-business-of-Highered.pdf
3. Hillary Hoffower, 'College is more expensive than it's ever been, and the 5 reasons why suggest it's only going to get worse', *Business Insider,* 26 June 2019. https://www.pulse.ng/bi/finance/college-is-more-expensive-than-its-ever-been-and-the-5-reasons-why-suggest-its-only/0y8g5ey
4. Association of American University Professors, 'Data Snapshot: Contingent Faculty in US Higher Ed', 2018. https://www.aaup.org/sites/default/files/10112018%20Data%20Snapshot%20Tenure.pdf
5. Ruthie Rono, 'Local Universities are facing serious crisis of confidence', *Business Daily,* 6 May 2019. https://www.businessdailyafrica.com/analysis/ideas/Local-universities-are-facing-crisis-of-confidence/4259414-5103274-9amivu/index.html
6. Wanzala Ouma, 'Magoha orders probe of local universities' PhDs amid quality concerns', *Daily Nation,* 7 May 2019. https://www.nation.co.ke/business/Magoha-orders-probe-of-local-universities-PhDs/1950106-5104986-hgvku2/index.html
7. African Development Bank Group, *African Economic Outlook 2020: Developing Africa's Workforce for the Future.* https://www.afdb.org/en/documents/african-economic-outlook-2020
8. Ibid.
9. World Bank, *Improving Higher Education Performance in Kenya: A Policy Report,* World Bank, Washington, DC., 2019. https://openknowledge.worldbank.org/handle/10986/32361
10. African Development Bank Group, *African Economic Outlook 2020: Developing Africa's Workforce for the Future.* https://www.afdb.org/en/documents/african-economic-outlook-2020

11. Paul Tiyambe Zeleza, *The Transformation of Global Higher Education,* 1945-2015, New York: Palgrave Macmillan, 2016.
12. World Bank, *Improving Higher Education Performance in Kenya: A Policy Report,* World Bank, Washington, DC., 2019. https://openknowledge.worldbank.org/handle/10986/32361
13. U.S. Department of Education, College Scorecard. https://collegescorecard.ed.gov
14. University of Cape Town, 2019 Annual Financial Statement, 88. http://www.uct.ac.za/sites/default/files/image_tool/images/431/finance/operations/statements/afs2019.pdf
15. Mastercard Foundation and USIU-Africa Partner to Expand Access to Higher Education in Africa https://mastercardfdn.org/mastercard-foundation-and-usiu-africa-partner-to-expand-access-to-higher-education-in-africa/
16. Council on Foundations, 'The State of Global Giving by U.S. Foundations 2011–2015'. https://www.cof.org/content/state-global-giving-us-foundations-2011-2015
17. World Wealth Report 2018. https://www.capgemini.com/service/world-wealth-report-2018/
18. World Bank, *Improving Higher Education Performance in Kenya: A Policy Report,* World Bank, Washington, DC., 2019. https://openknowledge.worldbank.org/handle/10986/32361
19. Faith Kisinga highlights from the Presentation on the Legal and Policy Framework for Giving in Kenya, presentation at the African Philanthropy Conference, The State of African Philanthropy: Setting the Agenda, University of the Witwatersrand, Johannesburg, 16–17 May 2019.
20. The Chronicle of Higher Education, *The Almanac of Higher Education 2019–2020.*
21. Peter DeWit, 'What's Easier to Change: Location of a Cemetery or Curriculum?' Education Week, 15 July 2016. http://blogs.edweek.org/edweek/finding_common_ground/2016/07/whats_easier_to_change_location_of_a_cemetery_or_curriculum.html

Paper first written February 2020
for a conference presentation.

Epilogue

In Memory of Two Intellectual Icons

Ali Mazrui: A Tribute to an Intellectual Griot

This tribute explores the intellectual legacy of Professor Ali Mazrui who died 12 October 2014, at the age of eighty-one. He was one of Africa's greatest intellectuals of the twentieth century and a prominent architect of postcolonial scholarship; an indefatigable voice for Africa's intellectual rebirth and empowerment. Mazrui's stature rests on several extraordinary achievements, three of which I single out.

First, there was his prodigious volume of scholarship. He published more than thirty books, hundreds of essays, commentaries and film documentaries. Second, the range, probity and impact of his intellectual analyses, interventions and debates was extraordinary. Mazrui embodied the life of the public intellectual par excellence. He was a towering intellectual who moved seamlessly between the classroom, conference circuit, popular media and corporate boardroom, to the corridors of political power. He relished intellectual debate and combat because he believed in the power of ideas as a dynamic force in human history. Third, his commitment to repositioning Africa's global standing and the place of African scholarship in global scholarship was unfaltering. He did this by unapologetically remapping and inserting Africa in global history, developments and discourses and through scholarship that was capacious in its interdisciplinarity, internationalism and interculturalism.

I first met Professor Mazrui in 1978 when he was a guest speaker at my MA class at the London School of Economics and Political Science. Over the years, I got to know him personally through my friendship with his nephew, Alamin Mazrui, as well as through our encounters at the annual meetings of the US African Studies Association and many other forums and contexts. My generation of African intellectuals admired his exceptional brilliance, infectious love of ideas and debate, passion for Africa's regeneration and generosity as a mentor. He was a man my generation of African academics admired, a scholar we sought to emulate.

His contributions to African studies were intellectual, ideological and institutional. Intellectually, against prevailing notions that sought to simplify and homogenise Africa, he insisted on the continent's diversities, complexities and contradictions of African histories and societies, of its multiple dimensions and trajectories. This was captured brilliantly in his BBC Reith Lectures, titled *The African Condition*, and most memorably in the 1986 television series and accompanying book, *Africa: A Triple Heritage,* in which he built on Edward Blyden and Kwame Nkrumah's ideas that Africa represented a complex confluence of three civilisational forces: the indigenous, Islamic and western.

His trenchant critiques of Eurocentrism remained a permanent feature of his work. A methodological subversion of Eurocentric historiography was most evident in two books: *Nationalism and New States in Africa: From About 1935 to the Present*, published in 1984, and Vol. 8 of the UNESCO *General History of Africa,* which he edited and was published in 1993. In both books, decolonisation and contemporary African history were dated to 1935, not 1945, to the Italian invasion of Ethiopia rather than from the end of the Second World War.

His attack on the authoritarian propensities of nationalism, the assault on democratic aspirations and ideals of what has come to be called the 'first independence' by the African postcolonial leaders was perceptively captured in a series of his early books on post-colonial African politics. They include two books he published in 1967, On *Heroes and Uhuru-Worship: Essays on Independent Africa* and *Towards a Pax Africana: A Study of Ideology and Ambition.*

Another major intellectual contribution centred on his work on Pan-Africanism, to which he brought his multilayered analytical perspective. He distinguished between five versions of Pan-Africanism: transatlantic, continental, sub-Saharan, Pan-Arab and global. He underscored the complex interconnections between them as an essential part of understanding African liberation movements and ideologies. This also allowed him to complicate conventional conceptions of Pan-Africanism and advance the notion of 'Afrabia' that challenged imperial constructs of Africa and the Middle East.

Mazrui's historically and culturally expansive and more accurate understanding of Pan-Africanism reflected and reinforced a broader conception of African diasporas that is evident in his later work, including *The African Diaspora: African Origins and New World Identitie*s that he co-edited in 1999.

Equally remarkable is Mazrui's work on the globalisation of Africa. He believed passionately that Africa was a global civilisation, that it was central, not peripheral, to the development of world history, both as a victim and a player. This is powerfully articulated in a series of publications including his 1990 book, *Cultural Forces in World Politics* and *Africa and other Civilisations: Conquest and Counter-Conquest* and *The Collected Essays of Ali A. Mazrui,* published in 2002.

Mazrui's ideological contributions to African scholarship and politics are similarly broad and remarkable. He was the epitome of liberal thought. He engaged in spirited attacks on both the rigidities of Marxism and African socialism. This was evident at the famous May 1970 debate with Walter Rodney, the Guyanese Marxist scholar-activist, at Makerere University's Main Hall.

Mazrui's relocation from Idi Amin's Uganda to the United States in the early 1970s refocused and sharpened his scholarship into an expansive humanism. His work was increasingly marked by a deep concern and commitment to human rights, agency and freedom. He wrote copiously on struggles for social justice for marginalised communities based on race, gender and religion. He became a fierce critic of postcolonial tyrannies, apartheid and racial oppression in the diaspora and of women's exploitation, Islamic fundamentalist intolerance and the Euro-American demonisation of Muslims.

The eclectic works of Mazrui from the late 1970s to the time of his death reflect a mind increasingly agitated by oppression in all its forms, scholarship animated by moral passion and fearlessness, an abiding faith in the indomitability of human agency. He ruffled many feathers among western intellectuals, some of whom had lauded him while he was in Uganda as a paragon of liberalism. The National Endowment for the Humanities withdrew its name from the credits of his acclaimed television series.

He entered the fray of the fraught debate for reparations against slavery when he was appointed to the Eminent Persons Group by the OAU on the subject. In 2002 he published *Black Reparations in the Era of Globalization.* His commitment to gender was articulated in a series of interventions both intellectual and political. Writing on the African Renaissance, he argued that it needed three major revolutions, in skills, values and gender relations. Thus, he saw women's emancipation and empowerment as an ethical, cultural, political and economic necessity, as a developmental and democratic imperative.

Mazrui's scholarship also increasingly focused on the ferocious debates about trends in Islam and the rising Islamophobic post-Cold War West looking for a new eternal enemy to feed the insatiable hate machine of the military industrial complex. This is reflected in a series of publications including *Islam: Between Globalization & Counterterrorism, published in 2006,* and the co-edited collection *Islam in Africa's Experience,* published in 2008.

As for his institutional contributions, space only allows the listing of a few highlights. He was instrumental in the development of the field of African political science beginning at Makerere University, where he became the first African professor of Political Science. The topics he dealt with helped to set the terms of debate in the field of African politics and Africa's international relations. Moreover, he mentored generations of African students.

Mazrui was also an influential figure in the development of the field of African and African American Studies, first as Director of the Center for Afro-American and African Studies at the University of Michigan, from 1978 to 1981. Later, when he relocated to Binghamton University, he served as Director of the Institute of Global Cultural Studies. It is also important to mention that he was elected President of the US African Studies Association (1978–1979).

In addition to his role as an institutional builder of African, African American and global studies, he left an indelible legacy on the development of African higher education, both as a scholar and as an academic leader. His prodigious scholarship on African universities and intellectuals include two books. The first was *Political Values and the Educated Class in Africa*, published in 1978, on the problematic colonial legacies of African universities and ambiguous identities of the educated class. The second, *The Power of Babel: Language and Governance in the African Experience,* published in 1998, on the disempowering effects of the dominance of European languages in African scholarly knowledge production and governance

He also held a series of administrative and consultative positions. They included Chancellor of Jomo Kenyatta University of Agriculture and Technology; member of the Pan-African Advisory Council to the United Nations International Children's Fund; Vice-President, World Congress of Black Intellectuals; member of the United Nations Commission on Transnational Corporations; member of the World Bank's Council of African Advisors; and Vice-President, International African Institute.

For me, Professor Mazrui was one of Africa's most important intellectual griots, a fierce guardian of African memory and dignity, a seer of our present condition, who fervently believed in our future possibilities. He was a giant of the first postcolonial generation of African scholars to whom my generation and the generations coming after us owe tremendous debt and gratitude for giving us the permission to think big, critically and confidently about our history and humanity in the past, present and future.

Presentation at the Symposium on the Life and Legacy of Ali Mazrui, 15–16 July 2016, organised by Twaweza Communications and the University of Binghamton, Institute of Global Cultural Studies.

Thandika Mkandawire: In Memory of an Intellectual Giant

Thandika Mkandawire, the towering Pan-African Malawian-Swedish public intellectual, died on 27 March 2020. The world of social thought, as Samir Amin, another departed luminary, called it, is so much poorer that he has left us, but so much richer that he lived for eight decades enlightening the world with his prodigious mind. Through his copious writings, engagements in numerous forums and teaching in various universities he provoked and animated minds and imaginations for generations across Africa, the diaspora and world at large. His extraordinary intellectual insights and incisive and surgical critiques of conventional, sometimes celebrated and often cynical analyses of development and the African condition, to use a beloved phrase of the late Ali Mazrui, the iconic man of letters, were truly inspiring.

Thandika, as we all fondly called him, has joined our illustrious intellectual ancestors, whose eternal wisdom we must cherish and embrace in the continuing struggle for the epistemic, existential and economic emancipation of our beloved continent.

When I think of Thandika, many images come to me: of the luminous beauty and brilliance of his mind; his passion for rigour and impatience with lazy thinking; his bountiful joy of living; his love of music and the arts; his boundless faith in Africa and his equal dismissal of Afro-pessimism and Afro-euphoria; his devotion to Pan-Africanism and the diaspora; his deep sense of globalism; his lifelong and unromantic commitment to progressive causes; his generosity in mentoring younger African scholars; his exemplary leadership of the Council for the Development of Social Science Research in Africa (CODESRIA) and the United Nations Research Institute for Social Development (UNRISD). And his remarkable modelling of the life of a principled public intellectual.

He was simply one of the most brilliant people I have ever known in my life. As my wife observed on several occasions, Thandika was the only person she witnessed who I was so enthralled by that I could sit and listen to for hours! To be in his company was to marvel at the power of the human mind for extraordinary insights and the joys of living, for he was a bundle of infectious joviality, humour and wit. The breadth and depth of his intellectual passions and unwavering faith in Africa's historic and humanistic agency and possibilities was dazzling.

I had known Thandika years before I met him in person. I had heard of the fiery Malawian intellectual who as a young journalist had been at the forefront of the nationalist struggle. Like many of us born before independence, his personal biography encompassed the migrant labour political economy of southern Africa: he was born in Zimbabwe and grew up in Zambia and Malawi. And like many smart and ambitious young people of his generation in the early 1960s, he trekked to the United States for higher education, as there was no university in Malawi at the time. He did not return to Malawi until 1994, after spending thirty-two years in exile, following the installation of a new democratic government.

He was a student in the United States in the 1960s at the height of the Civil Rights movement, and as an activist he immediately saw the intricate connections between the nationalist and civil rights movements in Africa and the diaspora. This nurtured his profound respect and appreciation of African-American society, culture and contributions, which was a bedrock of his Pan-Africanism in the tradition of Kwame Nkrumah and others. Also, like many activists of his generation, the trajectory of his life was upended by the political crisis in Malawi, known as the 'Cabinet Crisis', that erupted a few months after independence in 1964.

The octogenarian, conservative and authoritarian Malawi leader, Dr Hastings Kamuzu Banda, fell out with his radical younger ministers who preferred democratic politics and more progressive development policies. They were forced to escape into exile. Thandika was suspected of sympathising with the 'rebels' as Banda's regime vilified them and his passport was revoked. Thus began his long personal sojourn into exile and the diaspora and professional trajectory from journalism into academia. His exile began while he was in Ecuador on a project and, unable to return to the USA, he was given asylum in Sweden.

His experiences in Latin America and Sweden globalised his intellectual horizons and reinforced his proclivities towards comparative political economy, a distinctive hallmark of his scholarship. They also reshaped his interests in economics, pulling him away from its dominant neoclassical paradigms and preoccupations and anchoring him in the great questions of development and developmental states, areas in which he made his signature intellectual and policy contributions.

Thandika also immersed himself in the great debates of the 1960s and 1970s, centred on Marxism, dependency and underdevelopment, African socialism and the struggles for new international orders, from economics to information.

The intellectual ferment of the period prepared him well to participate in African debates about the state, democracy and development when he joined the newly established Institute for Development Studies at the University of Zimbabwe, in the early 1980s, in the immediate euphoric aftermath of Zimbabwe's liberation victory. In 1985, he became the head of CODESRIA as Executive Secretary.

He joined CODESRIA in the midst of the draconian anti-developmentalist assaults of the Structural Adjustment Programmes (SAPs). These were imposed on hapless and often complicit authoritarian African states by the international financial institutions, who were working at the behest of the market fundamentalist ideology of neoliberalism propagated by conservative governments in Washington, London, Berlin, Ottawa and Tokyo.

Through his own comparative scholarship on regional economic histories, development paths and the patrimonial state in Africa and other world regions, especially Asia, as well as national and multinational projects commissioned by CODESRIA, he led the progressive African intellectual community in mounting vigorous critiques of SAPs. Moreover, his monumental work offered alternatives rooted in the historical realities of African economies and societies, the aspirations of African peoples and the capacities of reconstructed African democratic developmental states.

In the late 1980s, when the gendarmes of neoliberalism and apologists of Africa's bankrupt one-party states were railing against democracy, or watching struggles for the 'second independence' with indifference or suspicion, Thandika unapologetically called for democracy as a fundamental political right and economic necessity for Africa. He was particularly concerned about the devastation wrought on African capacities to produce knowledge through the willful dismantling of African universities and research capacities.

At a conference of vice chancellors in Harare in 1986, the World Bank infamously declared that Africa did not need universities. Mendacious studies were produced to show that rates of return were higher for primary education than for tertiary education. Rocked by protests against tyranny and the austerities of SAPs that had dissolved the post-independence social contract of state-led developmentalism, African governments were only too willing to wreck African universities and devalue academic labour.

Under Thandika, CODESRIA valiantly sought to protect, promote and project an autonomous space for African intellectual development, for vibrant knowledge production. That is how I finally met him in person. In 1989, CODESRIA established the Reflections on Development Fellowship. I was one of about a dozen African scholars to win the scholarship. My project was on 'African Economic History in the Nineteenth and Twentieth Centuries'. This resulted in the 1993 publication of *A Modern Economic History of Africa. Volume 1: The Nineteenth Century*, which went on to win the prestigious Noma Award for publishing in Africa. Some regard this as my most important book.

Thus, I am deeply indebted to Thandika and CODESRIA, as are many other African scholars who experienced the devastation of African universities during the continent's 'lost decades' of the 1980s and 1990s, for ensuring our intellectual support, networking, sanity and productivity. This is at the heart of the outpouring of tributes by African scholars for Thandika since his passing. He was not only one of the most important African intellectuals of the late twentieth and early twenty-first centuries, he was also an architect of an African intellectual community during one of the bleakest periods in the history of the African knowledge enterprise. His intellectual and institutional legacies are mutually reinforcing and transcendental.

In August 1990, the recipients of the Reflections on Development Fellowship met for nearly two weeks at the Rockefeller Conference and Study Center, in Bellagio, Italy. I had not experienced an intellectual indaba like that before. Thandika dazzled the fellows, who included several prominent African scholars, with his incisive comments and erudition, legendary humour and striking joyousness. Meeting him at Bellagio left a lasting impression on me. His brilliance was accompanied by his uncanny ability to put very complex thoughts in such a pithy way, rendering an idea so obvious that one wondered why one had not thought about it that way before.

Thandika was one of those rare people who effectively combined institutional leadership and intellectual productivity. This was the praxis of his reflexive life, in which administrative challenges inspired academic work. While at CODESRIA, he pioneered and produced important studies on structural adjustment, development and African universities and intellectuals. In 1987, he edited the groundbreaking collection, *The State and Agriculture in Africa;* in 1995, he edited the comprehensive collection on structural adjustment, *Between Liberalisation and Oppression*; in 1999 he co-authored *Our Continent, Our Future.*

After he joined UNRISD, he continued working on his old intellectual preoccupations as he embraced new ones, as reflected in his journal articles and book monographs. The latter include the co-authored *African Voices on Structural Adjustmen*t (2002) and the edited *African Intellectuals: Rethinking Politics, Language, Gender and Development* (2005). Soon after joining UNRISD, which he led from 1998 to 2009, he launched a programme on social policy that increasingly reflected his growing research interests. His journal articles included, 'Thinking about developmental states in Africa', *Cambridge Journal of Economics,* 25, 3 (2001); 'Disempowering New Democracies and the Persistence of Poverty' (UNRISD, 2006); 'Maladjusted African Economies and Globalization' (UNRISD, 2005); '"Good governance": the itinerary of an idea', *Development in Practice,* 17 (4–5) (2007); 'Transformative Social Policy and Innovation in Developing Countries', *European Journal of Development Research 19* (2007); 'From the national question to the social question', *Transformation*

Critical Perspectives on Southern Africa (2009); 'Institutional monocropping and monotasking in Africa' (UNRISD, 2009); 'On Tax Efforts and Colonial Heritage in Africa', *The Journal of Development Studies,* 46:10 (2010); 'Aid, Accountability and Democracy in Africa', Social Research 77, 4 (2010); and 'How the New Poverty Agenda Neglected Social and Employment Policies in Africa,' *Journal of Human Development and Capabilities,* 11:1 (2010).

In 2009, he was appointed at the London School of Economics as the inaugural Chair in African Development. This gave him space to expand his intellectual wings and produce some of his most iconic and encyclopedic work, as evident in the titles of some of his papers. They include 'Running While Others Walk: Knowledge and the Challenge of Africa's Development' (Inaugural Lecture London School of Economics, 2011); 'Welfare Regimes and Economic Development: Bridging the Conceptual Gap' (in *Overcoming the Persistence of Inequality and Poverty,* edited by Valpy FitzGerald and Rosemary Thorp (2011); 'Aid: From Adjustment Back to Development', SSRN (2013); 'Social Policy and the Challenges of the Post-Adjustment Era' in Eva Paus, ed., *Getting Development Right* (2013); 'Findings and Implications: The Role of Development Cooperation','in Yoichi Mine et al., eds., *Preventing Violent Conflict in Africa: Inequalities, Perceptions and Institutions* (2013); 'Neopatrimonialism and the Political Economy of Economic Performance in Africa: Critical Reflections,' *World Politics* 67, 3 (2015); and 'Colonial legacies and social welfare regimes in Africa: An empirical exercise' (UNRISD, 2016). He also published monographs including the co-authored *Learning from the South Korean Developmental Success* (2014) and a collection of lectures he gave at the University of Ghana, *Africa Beyond Recovery* (2015).

Following my encounter with Thandika at Bellagio, our personal and professional paths crossed many times over the next thirty years. The encounters are too numerous to recount. Those that stand out include CODESRIA's conference on Academic Freedom, held in November 1990, at which 'The Kampala Declaration on Intellectual Freedom and Social Responsibility' was issued; and numerous CODESRIA conferences, workshops and general assemblies, including the one in 1995 where I served as a rapporteur. These forums were truly invigorating for a young scholar meeting the doyens of African intelligentsia. Like many of those in my generation, I matured intellectually under the tutelage of CODESRIA and Thandika.

In return, when I relocated to the United States in 1995 from Canada, I invited Thandika or played a role in his invitation to conferences in the US. This included the 25th Anniversary Celebration of the Center for African Studies at the University of Illinois in 1995, where I served as director of the centre, and the 1996 US African Studies Association meeting where he gave the Bashorun M.K.O. Abiola Distinguished Lecture. The lecture, later published in the *African*

Studies Review entitled 'The Social Sciences in Africa: Breaking Local Barriers and Negotiating International Presence', was a veritable tour de force. It brilliantly traced the development of social science knowledge production on Africa and offered a searing critique of Africanist exclusionary intellectual practices.

Later, when Thandika was head of UNRISD, he invited me to join the nine-member Gender Advisory Group to work on a report on the implementation of the United Nations Fourth World Women's Conference held in Beijing in 1995. Out of this conference came the report, *Gender Equality: Striving for Justice in an Unequal World*, published in 2005 to coincide with the tenth anniversary of the Beijing conference. In return, I also invited Thandika to contribute to my own edited collections, including *The Encyclopedia of Twentieth Century African History*, to which he contributed a fine essay on African intellectuals.

Our personal encounters were even more frequent and deeply gratifying. In the 1990s, I used to go to Dakar frequently, sometimes several times a year. On many occasions, Thandika hosted me or took me out to sample the incredible culinary delights and vibrant music scene of Dakar nightlife. I recall one night going to a club where Youssou N'Dour was playing. It was an indescribable treat. In his customary insightful and pithy way, he made me understand the social vibrancy of Dakar. In contrast to the apartheid cities of southern Africa from which we were alienated in the townships, Dakar is an old city whose residential patterns and social geography are deeply embedded in the rhythms of local culture.

Another memorable encounter was Christmas in the early 2000s, when our two families and close friends spent the entire day at Lake Malawi. As usual, he regaled us with jokes interspersed with acute observations on Malawian history, society, economy and politics. In December 2019, he and his dear wife, Kaarina Klint, were in Nairobi. What had been planned as a luncheon evolved into an engagement that lasted until dinner and late into the night. We had not seen each other for several years, although we had been in touch, so there was so much to cover. We excitedly discussed his forthcoming eightieth birthday celebration and the possibility of him joining our university as a Visiting Distinguished Professor.

It turned out to be our last meeting. But what a special day it was. Thandika was his usual self, affable, hilariously funny and of course he made brilliant observations about African and global developments. Thank you Thandika for the privilege of knowing you and your beautiful mind. You will always be a shining intellectual light for your generation, my generation and generations to come of committed, progressive African, diaspora and global academics, researchers, thinkers and activists.

First written 1 April 2020

References

Abramowitz, M. J. 'Democracy in Crisis: Freedom in the World 2018', Freedom House, 2018. https:// freedomhouse.org/sites/default/files/FH_FITW_Report_2018_Final_SinglePage.pdf.

Adams, Tim '"Now is the time': London's Black Lives Matter rally looks like a turning point', *Guardian*, 7 June 2020. https://www.theguardian.com/us-news/2020/jun/06/now-is-the-time-londons-black-lives-matter-rally-looks-like-a-turning-point

Ade Ajayi, J. F., The Continuity of African Institutions under Colonialism, in T. O. Ranger (ed), *Emerging Themes of African History: Proceedings of the International Congress of African Historians held at University College, Dar es Salaam, October 1965*. London: Heinemann, 1968: 189–200.

Adichie, Chimamanda Ngozi, 'The Danger of a Single Story,' TEDGlobal 2009. https://www.ted.com/talks/chimamanda_adichie_the_danger_of_a_single_story

AfrAsia Bank, *The AfrAsia Bank Africa Wealth Report 2018*. https://www.afrasiabank.com/media/3205/africa-wealth-report-2018.pdf.

African Development Bank, *Jobs for Youth in Africa: Catalyzing youth opportunity across Africa*, March 2016. https://www.afdb.org/fileadmin/uploads/afdb/Images/high_5s/Job_youth_Africa_Job_youth_Africa.pdf

———. *African Economic Outlook 2020: Developing Africa's Workforce for the Future*. https://www.afdb.org/en/documents/african-economic-outlook-2020

———. *African Economic Outlook—Supplement*, 7 July 2020. https://www.afdb.org/en/documents/african-economic-outlook-2020-supplement

African Union, *Agenda 2063: The Africa We Want*. https://au.int/en/documents/20141012/key-documents-agenda2063

Alessandrini, Anthony, 'Their Fight Is Our Fight: Occupy Wall Street, the Arab Spring, and New Modes of Solidarity Today', *Is This What Democracy Looks Like?* https://what-democracy-looks-like.org/their-fight-is-our-fight/

Alexander, Michelle, *The New Jim Crow: Mass Incarceration in the Age of Colorblindness*, New York: The New Press, 2020.

———. 'America, This Is your Chance', *The New York Times*, 8 June 2020. https://www.nytimes.com/2020/06/08/opinion/george-floyd-protests-race.html?referringSource=articleShare

Allen, Chris and Dunst, Charles, 'COVID-19: Africa and the African Union', London School of Economics. http://www.lse.ac.uk/international-relations/centres-and-units/global-south-unit/COVID-19-regional-responses/Africa-and-COVID-19

———. 'COVID-19: Latin America and the Caribbean and MERCOSUR and CARICOM', London School of Economics. http://www.lse.ac.uk/international-relations/centres-and-units/global-south-unit/COVID-19-regional-responses/Latin-America-and-COVID-19

Allen, Danielle, 'We seek reforms to policing. But something deeper needs repair', *The Washington Post*, 11 June 2020. https://www.washingtonpost.com/opinions/2020/06/11/we-seek-reforms-policing-something-even-deeper-needs-repair/

Allen, John, 'A Moment of National Shame and Peril – and Hope', *Foreign Affairs*, 3 June 2020. https://foreignpolicy.com/2020/06/03/trump-military-george-floyd-protests/

Altman, Steven A., 'Will COVID-19 have a Lasting Impact on Globalization?' *Harvard Business Review*, 20 May 2020. https://hbr.org/2020/05/will-COVID-19-have-a-lasting-impact-on-globalization

Amadiume, Ifi, *Male Daughters, Female Husbands: Gender and Sex in an African Society*, London: Zed Press, 1987.

Anderson, Charles W. 'Youth, the "Arab Spring", and Social Movements', *Review of Middle East Studies*, (2013) 47(2), 150–156.

Aoun, Joseph E., *Robot-Proof: Higher Education in the Era of Artificial Intelligence*, Cambridge, MA: MIT Press, 2017.

Appiah, Kwame Anthony, *The Lies That Bind: Rethinking Identity*, New York: Liveright Publishing, 2018.

Applebaum, Anne 'The Coronavirus Called America's bluff', *The Atlantic*, 15 March 2020. https://www.theatlantic.com/ideas/archive/2020/03/coronavirus-showed-america-wasnt-task/608023/

Asian Development Bank, 'ADB Announces $6.5 billion Initial Response to COVID-19 Pandemic', 18 March 2020. https://www.adb.org/news/adb-announces-6-5-billion-initial-response-COVID-19-pandemic

Association of American University Professors, 'Data Snapshot: Contingent Faculty in US Higher Ed', 2018. https://www.aaup.org/sites/default/files/10112018%20Data%20Snapshot%20Tenure.pdf

Attah, Ayesha Harruna, *The Hundred Wells of Salaga*, New York: Other Press, 2019.

Austin, Allan D., *African Muslims in Antebellum America: Transatlantic Stories and Spiritual Studies,* New York: Garland Publishing, 1984.

Axelrod, David, 'I thought I understood issues of race. I was wrong', *The Washington Post,* 12 June 2020. https://www.washingtonpost.com/opinions/i-thought-i-understood-issues-of-race-i-was-wrong/2020/06/12/a18d18ae-ac0d-11ea-9063-e69bd6520940_story.html

Balko, Radley 'There's overwhelming evidence that the criminal justice system is racist. Here's the proof', *The Washington Post,* 10 June 2020. https://www.washingtonpost.com/graphics/2020/opinions/systemic-racism-police-evidence-criminal-justice-system/?no_nav=true&p9w22b2p=b2p22p9w00098&tid=a_classic-iphone

Baradaran, Mehrsa, *The Color of Money: Black Banks and the Racial Wealth Gap,* Cambridge, MA.: Belknap Press, 2019.

Beckles Hilary McD, *Britain's Black Debt: Reparations for Caribbean Slavery and Native Genocide*, Kingston, Jamaica: University Press of the West Indies, 2013.

Bennett, Catherine, 'As statues of slave traders are torn down their heirs sit untouched in the Lords', *Guardian*, 14 June 2020. https://www.theguardian.com/commentisfree/2020/jun/14/as-statues-of-slave-traders-are-torn-down-their-heirs-sit-untouched-in-the-lords

Berger, Stefan and Nehring, Holger, *The History of Social Movements in Global Perspective*, New York: Palgrave Macmillan, 2017.

Blow, Charles, 'The Civil Rights Act of 2020', *The New York Times*, 10 June 2020. https://www.nytimes.com/2020/06/10/opinion/police-brutality-protests-legislation.html?referringSource=articleShare

Blyden, Edward, *A Vindication of the African Race: Being a Brief Examination of the Arguments in Favor of African Inferiority*, Monrovia, 1857.

———. *The Negro in Ancient History*, Mansfield Centre, Connecticut: Martino Fine Books, 2020 [1869].

———. *Christianity, Islam and the Negro Race*, Mansfield Centre, Connecticut: Martino Fine Books, 2016 [1887].

Botsman, Rachel, *Who Can You Trust?: How Technology Brought Us Together and Why It Might Drive Us Apart*, New York: Public Affairs, 2017.

British Council, *Universities, Employability and Inclusive Development: Repositioning Higher Education in Ghana, Nigeria, Kenya and South Africa*, 2016. https://ereadiness.kenet.or.ke/sites/default/files/ctools/Graduate%20employability%20final%20report.pdf

Business Roundtable, 'Business Roundtable Redefines the Purpose of a Corporation to Promote "An Economy That Serves All Americans"', 19 August 2019. https://www.businessroundtable.org/business-roundtable-redefines-the-purpose-of-a-corporation-to-promote-an-economy-that-serves-all-americans

Cambridge History of Africa, Cambridge: Cambridge University Press, 1975–1986.

Capgemini, *World Wealth Report 2019*. https://worldwealthreport.com/wp-content/uploads/sites/7/2019/07/World-Wealth-Report-2019-1.pdf.

Casselman, Ben and Tankersley, Jim, 'Economics, Dominated by White Men, is Roiled by Black Lives Matter', *The New York Times*, 10 June 2020. https://www.nytimes.com/2020/06/10/business/economy/white-economists-black-lives-matter.html?referringSource=articleShare

Cave, Damien and May, Tiffany, 'World Feared China Over Coronavirus. Now the Tables Are Turned', *The New York Times*, 19 March 2020. https://www.nytimes.com/2020/03/19/world/asia/coronavirus-china-united-states.html?referringSource=articleShare

Cavna, Michael, 'George Floyd's death has inspired powerful protest art: "I needed to have another way of seeing him"', *The Washington Post*, 11 June 2020. https://www.washingtonpost.com/arts-entertainment/2020/06/11/protest-art-black-lives-matter/

Chiuta, Wongani, 'Chief Justice reports to ACB attempt to bribe judges in Malawi election case', *Nyasa Times*, 12 January 2020. https://www.nyasatimes.com/chief-justice-reports-to-acb-attempt-to-bribe-judges-in-malawi-election-case/

Chua, Amy, *Political Tribes: Group Instinct and the Fate of Nations*, New York: Penguin Books, 2018.

Coates, Ta-Nehisi, 'The Case for Reparations', *The Atlantic*, June 2014. https://www.theatlantic.com/magazine/archive/2014/06/the-case-for-reparations/361631/

———. 'My President was Black', *The Atlantic*, January/February Issue, 2017. https://www.theatlantic.com/magazine/archive/2017/01/my-president-was-black/508793/

———. 'The First White President', *The Atlantic*, October 2017 Issue. https://www.theatlantic.com/magazine/archive/2017/10/the-first-white-president-ta-nehisi-coates/537909/

Cohen, Stanley, *States of Denial: Knowing about Atrocities and Suffering*, Cambridge, UK: Polity Press, 2001.

Cohn, Nate and Quealy, Kevin 'How Public Opinion Has Moved on Black Lives Matter', *The New York Times*, 10 June 2020. https://www.nytimes.com/interactive/2020/06/10/upshot/black-lives-matter-attitudes.html

Credit Suisse, *Global Wealth Report 2018*, 2018. https://www.credit-suisse.com/media/assets/corporate/docs/publications/research-institute/global-wealth-report-2018-en.pdf

Crenshaw, Kimberlé, 'The Urgency of Intersectionality', TEDWomen 2016. https://www.ted.com/talks/kimberle_crenshaw_the_urgency_of_intersectionality/discussion

Cuncic, Arlin, 'How to Cope with Loneliness during the Coronavirus Pandemic', *verywellmind*, 27 March 2020. https://www.verywellmind.com/how-to-cope-with-loneliness-during-coronavirus-4799661

Curtin, Philip, *The Atlantic Slave Trade: A Census*, Madison, Wisc: University of Wisconsin Press, 1969.

———. 'The Ghettoization of African History', *The Chronicle of Higher Education*, 3 March 1995.

Council on Foundations, 'The State of Global Giving by U.S. Foundations 2011–2015'. https://www.cof.org/content/state-global-giving-us-foundations-2011-2015

Dakar Summit Declaration and Action Plan, First African Higher Education Summit on Revitalizing Higher Education for Africa's Future, 10–12 March 2015, Dakar, Senegal. http://www.trustafrica.org/images/Executive%20SummaryFINAL.pdf

Dawson, Michael, 'Racial Capitalism and Democratic Crisis', *items: Insights from the Social Sciences,* 4 December 2018.

Developing Employability Educator Site, https://developingemployability.edu.au/about/

DeWit, Peter 'What's Easier to Change: Location of a Cemetery or Curriculum?' *Education Week*, 15 July 2016. http://blogs.edweek.org/edweek/finding_common_ground/2016/07/whats_easier_to_change_location_of_a_cemetery_or_curriculum.html

Diouf, Sylviane, *Dreams of Africa in Alabama: The Slave Ship* Clotilda *and the Story of the Last Africans Brought to America*, Oxford: Oxford University Press, 2007.

Dubois, W.E.B., *The World and Africa: Inquiry Into the Part Which Africa Has Played in World History*, New York: International Publishers Co., Inc, 1979 [1947].

Ducharme, Jamie, 'COVID-19 is Making America's Loneliness Epidemic Even Worse', *Time*, 8 May 2020. https://time.com/5833681/loneliness-COVID-19/

EarthPowernews, 'Africa: bigger than you think! Greenland: much smaller'. http://www.earthpowernews.com/africa-bigger-than-you-think/

Edge Foundation, *Employers' perceptions of the employability skills of new graduates*, London: Edge Foundation, 2011. https://www.educationandemployers.org/wp-content/uploads/2014/06/employability_skills_as_pdf_-_final_online_version.pdf

Edmondson, Katie and Fandos, Nicholas, 'G.O.P. Scrambles to Respond to Demands for Police Overhaul', *The New York Times,* 9 June 2020. https://www.nytimes.com/2020/06/09/us/politics/republicans-police-reform.html?referringSource=articleShare

Edugyan, Esi, *Washington Black*, New York: Knopf Doubleday Publishing, 2018.
Ellis, Lindsay, 'For Colleges, Protests Over Racism May Put Everything On The Line', *The Chronicle of Higher Education*, 12 June 2020. https://www.chronicle.com/article/For-Colleges-Protests-Over/248979
Epstein, Helen, 'Kenya: The Election & the Cover-Up', *The New York Review of Books*, 30 August 2017. https://www.nybooks.com/daily/2017/08/30/kenya-the-election-and-the-cover-up/
Equiano, Olaudah, *The Interesting Narrative of the Life of Olaudah Equiano, or Gustavus Vassa, The African: Written by Himself*, Mineola, New York: Dover Publications, 1999 [1789].
European Union Commission, General Data Protection Regulation, 2016. https://eur-lex.europa.eu/legal-content/EN/TXT/PDF/?uri=CELEX:02016R0679-20160504&from=EN
EY-Parthenon, 'Public-private partnerships in higher education: what is right for your institution?', 2017. https://cdn.ey.com/echannel/parthenon/pdf/perspectives/EY-Parthenon-P3s-business-of-Highered.pdf
Fabris, Casey, 'College Students Think They're Ready for the Work Force. Employers Aren't so Sure', *The Chronicle for Higher Education*, 20 January 2015. https://www.chronicle.com/article/College-Students-Think/151289
Fang, Marina, 'How Asian Americans are Reckoning with Anti-blackness in their Families', *Huffpost*, 6 June 2020. https://www.huffpost.com/entry/anti-blackness-asian-americans_n_5ed87ca8c5b6ea15610b5774
Fanon, Frantz, *The Wretched of the Earth*, Harmondsworth: Penguin, 1963.
FAO, 'Q&A: COVID-19 pandemic – Impact on Food and Agriculture'. http://www.fao.org/2019-ncov/q-and-a/impact-on-food-and-agriculture/en/
Fernandez, Paige, 'Defunding the Police Isn't Punishment – It Will Actually Make Us Safer, *Cosmopolitan*, 4 June 2020. https://www.cosmopolitan.com/politics/a32757152/defund-police-black-lives-matter/
Fontaine, Richard 'Globalization Will Look Very Different After the Coronavirus Pandemic', *Foreign Policy*, 17 April 2020. https://foreignpolicy.com/2020/04/17/globalization-trade-war-after-coronavirus-pandemic/
Frey, William H., 'New Projections Point to a Minority Majority Nation in 2044', *Brookings*, 12 December 2014. https://www.brookings.edu/blog/the-avenue/2014/12/12/new-projections-point-to-a-majority-minority-nation-in-2044/
Friedman, Uri, 'We Were Warned', *The Atlantic*, 18 March 2020. https://www.theatlantic.com/politics/archive/2020/03/pandemic-coronavirus-united-states-trump-cdc/608215/
Fukuyama, Francis, *The End of History and the Last Man*, New York: Free Press, 2006.
Gallup, 'Many Business Leaders Doubt Colleges Prepare Students', February 2014. https://news.gallup.com/poll/167630/business-leaders-doubt-colleges-prepare-students.aspx
Gambino, Christine P. *et al.*, *The Foreign-Born Population from Africa*, U.S. Census, 1 October 2012. https://www.census.gov/content/census/en/library/publications/2014/acs/acsbr12-16.html
Gates, Henry Louis Jr, 'Ending the Slavery Blame-Game', *The New York Times*, 22 April 2010. https://www.nytimes.com/2010/04/23/opinion/23gates.html

Gelante, Riyanti *et al.*, 'The ASEAN's Response to COVID-19: A policy science analysis', https://www.researchgate.net/profile/Jonatan_Lassa1/publication/341309394_The_ASEAN%27s_Responses_to_COVID-19_A_Policy_Sciences_Analysis/links/5ed084c9299bf1c67d26f4ef/The-ASEANs-Responses-to-COVID-19-A-Policy-Sciences-Analysis.pdf?origin=publication_detail

Gelles, David, 'Corporate America Has Failed Black America', *The New York Times*, 6 June 2020. https://www.nytimes.com/2020/06/06/business/corporate-america-has-failed-black-america.html?referringSource=articleShare

Gilroy, Paul, *The Black Atlantic: Modernity and Double Consciousness*, Cambridge, MA: Harvard University Press, 1993.

Gomez, Jim, 'ASEA Ministers Endorse New COVID-19 Fund', *The Diplomat*, 10 April 2020. https://thediplomat.com/2020/04/asean-ministers-endorse-new-COVID-19-response-fund/

Goodman, Peter S., Thomas, Katie, Wee, Sui-Lee and Gettleman, Jeffrey, 'A New Front for Nationalism: The Global Battle Against a Virus', *The New York Times*, 10 April 2020. https://www.nytimes.com/2020/04/10/business/coronavirus-vaccine-nationalism.html?referringSource=articleShare

Gotlieb, Lori, 'Dear Therapist's Guide to Staying Sane During a Pandemic', *The Atlantic*, 17 March 2020.

Graff, Garret M., 'What Americans Are Now Doing is Beautiful', *The Atlantic*, 19 March 2020. https://www.theatlantic.com/ideas/archive/2020/03/inspiring-galvanizing-beautiful-spirit-2020/608308/

Grasgreen, Allie, 'Ready or Not', *Inside Higher Ed*, 26 February 2014. https://www.insidehighered.com/news/2014/02/26/provosts-business-leaders-disagree-graduates-career-readiness

Guardian, '"This ends today": over 300 stage figures call out "anti-blackness" of US theatre', 9 June 2020. https://www.theguardian.com/stage/2020/jun/09/us-theater-racism-called-out-open-letter?CMP=Share_iOSApp_Other

———. 'Black people are more than four times likely to die from Covid-10 than white people', 7 May 2020. https://www.theguardian.com/world/2020/may/07/black-people-four-times-more-likely-to-die-from-COVID-19-ons-finds?CMP=Share_iOSApp_Other

Guesmi, Haythem, 'The Gentrification of African Studies', *Africa is a Country*, 22 December 2018. https://africasacountry.com/2018/12/ the-gentrification-of-african-studies.

Gurung, Prabal, 'It's time for Asian Amerians to shed the "Model Minority" myth and stand for George Floyd', *The Washington Post*, 5 June 2020. https://www.washingtonpost.com/nation/2020/06/05/prabal-gurung-its-time-asian-americans-shed-model-minority-myth-stand-george-floyd/

Gyasi, Yaa, *Homegoing*, New York: Knopf Doubleday Publishing, 2016.

Hansberry, William Leo, *Africa & Africans as Seen by Classical Writers*, Washington, DC: Howard University Press, 1977.

Harari, Yuval Noah, *Homo Deus: A Brief History of Tomorrow*, New York: HarperCollins, 2017.

Harmon, Amy *et al.*, 'From Cosmetics to NASCAR, Calls for Racial Justice Are Spreading', *The New York Times*, 9 June 2020. https://www.nytimes.com/2020/06/13/us/george-floyd-racism-america.html?referringSource=articleShare

Hegel, G.W.F., *The Philosophy of History*, J. Sibree (transl.), Introduction C.J. Friedrich, New York: Dover Publications, 1956.

Helmore, Edward, 'Can Anna Wintour survive fashion's reckoning with racism?', *Guardian*, 13 June 2020. https://www.theguardian.com/fashion/2020/jun/13/anna-wintour-vogue-diversity-racism-debate

Hernandez, Arelis R. and Wilson, Scott, 'Black police chiefs express anger and dismay as they try to change their departments from within', *The Washington Post*, 7 June 2020. https://www.washingtonpost.com/national/protests-black-police-chiefs/2020/06/06/120770dc-a738-11ea-b473-04905b1af82b_story.html

Hobsbawm, Eric, *Nations and Nationalism since 1780: Programme, Myth, Reality*, Cambridge UK: Cambridge University Press, 1990.

Hoffower, Hillary, 'College is more expensive than it's ever been, and the 5 reasons why suggest it's only going to get worse', *Business Insider*, 26 June 2019. https://www.pulse.ng/bi/finance/college-is-more-expensive-than-its-ever-been-and-the-5-reasons-why-suggest-its-only/0y8g5ey

Ilcheong, Yi and Mkandawire, Thankdika, *Learning from the South Korean Developmental Success: Effective Developmental Cooperation and Synergistic Institutions and Policies*, London: Palgrave Macmillan, 2014.

ILO Monitor, *World Employment Social Outlook Trends 2018*, Geneva: International Labour Organization, 2018. http://www.ilo.org/wcmsp5/groups/public/--dgreports/---dcomm/-publ/documents/publication/wcms_615594.pdf

———. *World Employment Social Outlook Trends 2019*, Geneva: International Labour Organization, 2019. https://www.ilo.org/wcmsp5/groups/public/-dgreports/-dcomm/--publ/documents/publication/wcms_670542.pdf

———. *COVID-19 and the world of work*, 5th ed, 27 May 2020. https://www.ilo.org/wcmsp5/groups/public/@dgreports/@dcomm/documents/briefingnote/wcms_749399.pdf

Inikori, Joseph, *Africans and the Industrial Revolution in England: A Study in International Trade and Economic Development*, Cambridge, UK: Cambridge University Press, 2002.

International Association of Universities, *Internationalization of Higher Education: Growing expectations, fundamental values*, IAU 4th Global Survey, April 2014. https://iau-aiu.net/IMG/pdf/iau-4th-global-survey-executive-summary.pdf

———. *Internationalization of Higher Education: An Evolving Landscape, Locally and Globally*, IAU 5th Global Survey, 2018. https://www.iau-aiu.net/IMG/pdf/iau_5th_global_survey_executive_summary.pdf

International Monetary Fund, IMF DataMapper, 2018. https://www.imf.org/external/datamapper/NGDP_RPCH@WEO/OEMDC/ADVEC/WEOWORLD

———. 'Coronavirus economic planning: Hoping for the best, prepared for the worst', 12 March 2020. https://blogs.imf.org/2020/03/12/coronavirus-economic-planning-hoping-for-the-best-prepared-for-the-worst/

———. *June 2020 World Economic Outlook Update*. https://www.imf.org/-/media/Files/Publications/WEO/2020/Update/June/English/WEOENG202006.ashx?la=en

International Panel on Climate Change (IPCC), Sixth Assessment Report, https://www.ipcc.ch/assessment-report/ar6/

Inter-Parliamentary Union, Women in National Parliaments. http://archive.ipu.org/wmn-e/classif.htm

International Renewable Energy Agency, *Global Landscape of Renewable Energy Finance 2018*. https://irena.org/-/media/Files/IRENA/Agency/Publication/2018/Jan/IRENA_Global_landscape_RE_finance_2018.pdf

Jacques, Martin 'This decade belonged to China. So will the next one', *Guardian*, 31 December 2019. https://www.theguardian.com/commentisfree/2019/dec/31/decade-china-west-china-ascent?CMP=Share_iOSApp_Other

Jakes, Lara and Wong, Edward, 'U.S. Diplomats Struggle to Defend Democracy Abroad Amid Crises at Home', *The New York Times*, 8 June 2020. https://www.nytimes.com/2020/06/06/us/politics/protests-diplomats-coronavirus.html?referringSource=articleShare

Jamieson, Dave, The Labor Movement Faces a Reckoning over Police Unions, *Huffpost*, 6 June 2020. https://www.huffpost.com/entry/the-labor-movement-faces-a-reckoning-over-police-unions_n_5eda9958c5b640424ef70cd2

Johnson, Samuel, *The History of the Yorubas from the Earliest Times to the Beginning of the British Protectorate*, London: Forgotten Books, 2012 [1921].

Joseph, Peniel E., 'Protests in the wake of MLK's assassination and George Floyd's death show what hasn't – and has – changed since 1968', *The Washington Post*, 6 June 2020. https://www.washingtonpost.com/nation/2020/06/06/protests-wake-mlks-assassination-george-floyds-death-show-what-hasnt-has-changed-since-1968

Kagwanja, Peter, 'New revolutionary Xi expands Africa's strategic ties with China', *Daily Nation*, 24 March 2018. https://www.nation.co.ke/oped/opinion/Xi-Jinping-expands-Africa-s-strategic-ties-with-China/440808-4356182-bpbcgpz/index.html

Kayser-Bril, Nicolas, 'Africa is not a country', *Guardian*, 24 January 2014. https://www.theguardian.com/world/2014/jan/24/africa-clinton

Keith, Tamara and Gharib, Malaka, 'A Timeline of Coronavirus Comments From President Trump And WHO', *National Public Radio*, 15 April 2020. https://www.npr.org/sections/goatsandsoda/2020/04/15/835011346/a-timeline-of-coronavirus-comments-from-president-trump-and-who

Kim, Seun Min and Wagner, John, 'Senate GOP unveils the bill that would discourage, but not ban, tactics such as chokeholds and no-knock warrants', *The Washington Post*, 17 June 2020. https://www.washingtonpost.com/powerpost/senate-republicans-to-unveil-competing-police-reform-bill/2020/06/17/39ae8304-b085-11ea-856d-5054296735e5_story.html

Kirkpatrick, David D., Apuzzo, Matt and Gebrekidan, Selam, 'Europe Saint Was Pandemic Ready. Pride was its Downfall', *The New York Times,* 20 July 2020. https://www.nytimes.com/2020/07/20/world/europe/coronavirus-mistakes-france-uk-italy.html?referringSource=articleShare

Kiwuwa, David, 'Why China's removal of term limits is a gift to African despots', *The Conversation*, 8 March 2018. https://theconversation.com/why-chinas-removal-of-term-limits-is-a-gift-to-african-despots-92746

Koren, Marina, 'Social Distancing Could Change Our Relationship With FaceTime', *The Atlantic*, 14 March 2020. https://www.theatlantic.com/science/archive/2020/03/social-distancing-coronavirus-videochat-facetime/608038/

Lafi, Nora, The 'Arab Spring' in Global Perspective: Social Movements, Changing Contexts and Political Transitions in the Arab World (2010–2014), in Berger S., Nehring H. (eds), *The History of Social Movements in Global Perspective*, London: Palgrave Macmillan, 2017.

Lagarde, Christine, 'Our response to the coronavirus emergency,' ECB blog, 19 March 2020. https://www.ecb.europa.eu/press/blog/date/2020/html/ecb.blog200319~11f421e25e.en.html

Laremont, Ricardo Rene and Kalouche, Fouad, *Africa and other Civilisations: Conquest and Counter-Conquest, The Collected Essays of Ali A. Mazrui*, Trenton, NJ and Asmara, Eritrea: Africa World Press, 2002.

Laurent, Claire, *FEMICIDE: The Killing of Women and Girls Around the World*, Academic Council on the United Nations System (ACUNS) Vienna Liaison Office, 2013. https://acuns.org/wp-content/uploads/2013/05/Claire-Laurent.pdf.

Leary, Alex and Peterson, Kristina, 'Trump Prods Police with Executive Order', *The Wall Street Journal*, 16 June 2020. https://www.wsj.com/articles/trump-signs-policing-executive-order-11592325988

Lee, Benjamin '"This ends today": over 300 stage figures call out "anti-blackness" of U.S. theater', *The Guardian*, 9 June 2020. https://www.theguardian.com/stage/2020/jun/09/us-theater-racism-called-out-open-letter?CMP=Share_iOSApp_Other

Levitsky, Steven and Ziblatt, Daniel, *How Democracies Die*, New York: Broadway Books, 2018.

Leung, Sandra, 'It's finally time for business to address racism. Here's how.' *The Washington Post*, 10 June 2020. https://www.washingtonpost.com/opinions/2020/06/10/its-time-businesses-finally-address-racism-heres-how/

Lorenz, Taylor, 'Upper East Side Mom Group Implodes Over Accusations of Racism and Censorship', *The New York Times*, 9 June 2020.

Louw-Vaudran, Liesl and Diatta, Mohamed, 'How Have Africa's Regions Fared in Tackling COVID-19?' Institute for Security Studies, 8 July 2020. https://allafrica.com/stories/202007110122.html

Mandela, Nelson, *Long Walk to Freedom*, New York: Little Brown & Co., 1994.

———. Statement from the dock at the opening of the defence case in the Rivonia Trial, 20 April 1964. http://db.nelsonmandela.org/speeches/pub_view.asp?pg=item&ItemID=NMS010&txtstr=prepared%20to%20die

Maske, Mark and Kilgore, Adam, 'What made Roger Goodell Say "Black Lives Matter" and where it leaves the NFL', 7 June 2020. https://www.washingtonpost.com/sports/2020/06/06/roger-goodell-black-lives-matter/

Mastercard Foundation and USIU-Africa Partner to Expand Access to Higher Education in Africa, 14 July 2020. https://mastercardfdn.org/mastercard-foundation-and-usiu-africa-partner-to-expand-access-to-higher-education-in-africa/

Mazrui, Ali *Political Values and the Educated Class in Africa*, London: Heinemann Educational Books, 1978.

———. *The African Condition: A Political Diagnosis*, BBC Reith Lectures, London and New York: Heinemann Educational Books and Cambridge University Press, 1984.

———. (writer and narrator), *The Africans: A Triple Heritage* (film documentary), British Broadcasting Corporation, New York and London: Little Brown and Co. and BBC, 1986.

———. *Cultural Forces in World Politics*, London and Portsmouth: James Currey and Heinemann,1990.

———. *On Heroes and Uhuru-Worship: Essays on Independent Africa*, London: Longman, 1967.

———. *Towards a Pax Africana: A Study of Ideology and Ambition*, London and Chicago: Weidenfeld & Nicolson and University of Chicago Press, 1967.

Mazrui, Ali, Dikirr, Patrick, Ostergard, Robert Jr, Toler, Michael and Macharia, Paul, *Islam in Africa's Experience*, New Delhi: Sterling Paperbacks, 2008.

Mazrui, Ali and Mazrui, Alamin, *The Power of Babel: Language and Governance in the African Experience*, Oxford and Chicago: James Currey and University of Chicago Press, 1998.

———. *Black Reparations in the Era of Globalization,* Binghamton: The Institute of Global Cultural Studies, 2002.

Mazrui, Ali, Kafrawi, Shalahudin, Mazrui, Alamin and Sebuharara, Ruzima (eds), *Islam: Between Globalization & Counter-terrorism*, Trenton, NJ and Asmara, Eritrea: Africa World Press, 2006.

Mazrui, Ali and Tidy, Michael, *Nationalism and New States in Africa: From About 1935 to the Present,* London: Heinemann Educational Books, 1984.

Mbue, Imbolo, *Behold the Dreamers*, New York: Penguin Random House, 2016.

McEwan, Ian, 'Brexit, the most pointless, masochistic ambition in our country's history, is done', *Guardian*, 2 January 2020. https://www.theguardian.com/politics/2020/feb/01/brexit-pointless-masochistic-ambition-history-done?CMP=Share_iOSApp_O

McKaiser, Eusebius, 'We know from South Africa that toppling statues is no answer – but it's a start', *Guardian,* 9 June 2020. https://www.theguardian.com/commentisfree/2020/jun/09/south-africa-toppling-statues-racist-cecil-rhodes-cape-town?CMP=Share_iOSApp_Other

McTague, Tom, 'The Coronavirus Brings Political Perspective', *The Atlantic*, 11 March 2020. https://www.theatlantic.com/international/archive/2020/03/coronavirus-COVID19-brexit-united-kingdom-politics/607687/

Mendenhall, Robert, 'What Is Competency-Based Education?', *HuffPost*, 11 November 2012. https://www.huffingtonpost.com/dr-robert-mendenhall/competency-based-learning-_b_1855374.html

Meredith, Martin *Mandela: A Biography*, London: Simon & Schuster, 2010.

Mishra, Pankaj, *Age of Anger: A History of the Present*, New York: Farrah, Straus and Giroux, 2017.

Mkandawire, Thandika (ed), *Between Liberalisation and Oppression: The Politics of Structural Adjustment in Africa*, Dakar: CODESRIA Books, 1995.

———. 'The Social Sciences in Africa: Breaking Local Barriers and Negotiating International Presence. The Bashorun M. K. O. Abiola Distinguished Lecture Presented to the 1996 African Studies Association Annual Meeting', *African Studies Review* 40, 2 (1997): 15-36.

———. 'Thinking about developmental states in Africa', *Cambridge Journal of Economics*, 25, 3 (2001)

———. *African Intellectuals: Rethinking Politics, Language, Gender and Development*, London: Zed Books, 2005.

———. *Gender Equality: Striving for Justice in an Unequal World*, Geneva: UNRISD/UN Publications, 2005. http://www.unrisd.org/80256B3C005BCCF9/search/1FF4AC64C1894EAAC1256FA3005E7201

———. 'Maladjusted African Economies and Globalization', *Africa Development* 30, 1–2 (2005); also UNRISD, 2005. http://www.unrisd.org/unrisd/website/document.nsf/(httpPublications)/CA8763580CBBB2CEC125704A004BA535?OpenDocument

———. 'Disempowering New Democracies and the Persistence of Poverty', Geneva: UNRISD/UN Publications, 2006. http://unrisd.org/80256B3C005BCCF9/(httpAuxPages)/660234231C9D6710C125717800248890/$file/mkand-pp-dghr.pdf

———. '"Good governance": the itinerary of an idea,' *Development in Practice*, 17, 4–5 (2007).

———. 'Transformative Social Policy and Innovation in Developing Countries', *European Journal of Development Research* 19, 1 (2007).

———. 'From the national question to the social question', *Transformation: Critical Perspectives on Southern Africa,* 69 (2009).

———. 'Institutional monocropping and monotasking in Africa', in Oman, Akbar, Botchwey, Kwesi, Stein, Howard and Stieglitz, Joseph (eds), *Good Growth and Governance in Africa: Rethinking Development Strategies*, Geneva: UNRISD/UN Publications, 2009.

———. 'On Tax Efforts and Colonial Heritage in Africa', *The Journal of Development Studies*, 46, 10 (2010).

———. 'Aid, Accountability and Democracy in Africa', *Social Research* 77, 4 (2010).

———. 'How the New Poverty Agenda Neglected Social and Employment Policies in Africa,' *Journal of Human Development and Capabilities*, 11, 1 (2010).

———. 'Running While Others Walk: Knowledge and the Challenge of Africa's Development', Inaugural Lecture London School of Economics, *Africa Development,* 36, 2 (2011).

———. 'Welfare Regimes and Economic Development: Bridging the Conceptual Gap', in FitzGerald, Valpy, Heyer, Judith and Thorp, Rosemary (eds), *Overcoming the Persistence of Inequality and Poverty*, New York: Palgrave Macmillan, 2011.

———. 'Aid: From Adjustment Back to Development', 21 June 2013, SSRN. https://papers.ssrn.com/sol3/papers.cfm?abstract_id=2283199

———. 'Findings and Implications: The Role of Development Cooperation', in Mine, Yoichi, Stewart, Frances, Fukuda-Parr, Sakiko and Mkandawire, Thandika (eds), *Preventing Violent Conflict in Africa: Inequalities, Perceptions and Institutions*, London: Palgrave Macmillan, 2013.

———. 'Social Policy and the Challenges of the Post-Adjustment Era', in Paus, Eva (ed), *Getting Development Right: Structural Transformation, Inclusion and Sustainability in the Post-Crisis Era*, New York: Palgrave Macmillan, 2013.

———. 'Neopatrimonialism and the Political Economy of Economic Performance in Africa: Critical Reflections,' *World Politics* 67, 3 (2015).

———. 'Colonial legacies and social welfare regimes in Africa: An empirical exercise', Working Paper 2016–4, Geneva: UNRISD/UN Publications, 2016.

Mkandawire, Thandika and Bourenane, Naceur (eds), *The State and Agriculture in Africa*, Dakar: CODESRIA Books, 1987.

Mkandawire, Thandika and Soludo, Charles (eds), *Our Continent, Our Future: African Perspectives on Structural Adjustment*, Dakar: CODESRIA Books, 1999.

———. *African Voices on Structural Adjustment: A Companion to Our Continent, Our Future*, Dakar and Asmara, Eritrea: CODESRIA and Africa World Press, Inc., 2002.

Moody's, 'Research Announcement: Outlook for US higher education sector changed to stable from negative on steady revenue gains', 10 December 2019. https://www.moodys.com/research/Moodys-Outlook-for-US-higher-education-sector-changed-to-stable--PBM_1207036

Moore, Peter, 'Overwhelming opposition to reparations for slavery and Jim Crow', 2 June 2014. https://today.yougov.com/topics/politics/articles-reports/2014/06/02/reparations

Mounk, Yascha, *The People vs. Democracy: Why Our Freedom is in Danger and How to Save It*, Cambridge, MA: Harvard University Press, 2018.

Moyo, Dambisa, *Edge of Chaos: Why Democracy is Failing to Deliver Economic Growth – and How to Fix It*, New York: Basic Books, 2018.

Myers Stephen Lee and Rubin, Allysa J., 'Its Coronavirus Cases Dwindling, China Turns Focus Outward', *The New York Times*, 18 March 2020. https://www.nytimes.com/2020/03/18/world/asia/coronavirus-china-aid.html?referringSource=articleShare

Nairn, Tom, *The Breakup of Britain: Crisis and Neo-nationalism*, London: Verso, 1977.

Nesbitt, F. Njubi, 'African Intellectuals in the Belly of the Beast: Migration, Identity, and the Politics of Exile', *African Issues*, 30, 1 (2002): 70-75.

Nganga, Gilbert, 'Unprepared Graduates are Raising Our Costs', *University World News*, 20 June 2018. https://www.universityworldnews.com/post.php?story=20180620145937689

Ngetich, Jacob, '20 Western Envoys Welcome Supreme Court Ruling', *The Standard*, 2 September 2017. https://www.standardmedia.co.ke/kenya/article/2001253340/20-western-envoys-welcome-supreme-court-ruling-call-for-fair-election

Nkolokosa, Chem'bwana, 'Mutharika files court response to discredit evidence of Chilima, Chakwera in polls case: 'Petitioners fail to prove alleged irregularities', *Nyasa Times*, 22 July 2019. https://www.nyasatimes.com/mutharika-files-court-response-to-discredit-evidence-of-chilima-chakwera-in-polls-case-petitioners-fail-to-prove-alleged-irregularities/

Nkrumah, Kwame, *Consciencism: Philosophy and Ideology for Decolonization*, New York: Monthly Review Press, 1964.

Nyasa Times, 'Chilima & Chakwera Vs Mutharika & EC – Final Judgment', 3 February 2020. https://www.nyasatimes.com/chilima-chakwera-vs-mutharika-ec-final-judgment/

OECD Economic Outlook, Volume 2020, Issue 1. https://read.oecd-ilibrary.org/economics/oecd-economic-outlook/volume-2020/issue-1_0d1d1e2e-en#page41

Okpewho, Isidore, Davies, Carol Boyce and Mazrui, Ali (eds), *The African Diaspora: African Origins and New World Identities*, 1999.

Olusoga, David, 'Britain is not America. But we too are disfigured by deep and pervasive racism', *Guardian,* 7 June 2020. https://www.theguardian.com/commentisfree/2020/jun/07/britain-is-not-america-but-we-too-are-disfigured-by-deep-and-pervasive-racism

Ombuor, Joe, 'Kenya third party in the world and first in Africa to annul a presidential election', *The Standard*, 2 September 2017. https://www.standardmedia.co.ke/article/2001253337/kenya-third-country-in-the-world-and-first-in-africa-to-annul-a-presidential-election#

Ombuor, Rael and Schemm, Paul, 'Kenya's Supreme Court annuls presidential election result for irregularities, orders new vote', *The Washington Post*, 1 September 2020. https://www.washingtonpost.com/world/kenya-supreme-court-cancels-presidential-election-result-for-irregularities-orders-new-election/2017/09/01/ceee81d6-8ef4-11e7-84c0-02cc069f2c37_story.h

Oreh, Adaeze a, 'Impact of COVID-19 loneliness on mental health', *Punch*, 26 May 2020. https://www.msn.com/en-xl/news/other/impact-of-COVID-19-loneliness-on-mental-health/ar-BB14AmnM

Orthofer, Anna 'Wealth Inequality in South Africa: Evidence from survey and tax data', REDI3x3 Working Paper 15, June 2020. http://www.redi3x3.org/sites/default/files/Orthofer%202016%20REDI3x3%20Working%20Paper%2015%20-%20Wealth%20inequality.pdf

Osei-Opare, Nana, 'Around the World the U.S. is seen as a symbol of anti-black racism', *The Washington Post,* 5 June 2020. https://www.washingtonpost.com/outlook/2020/06/05/around-world-us-has-long-been-symbol-anti-black-racism/

Ouma, Wanzala, 'Magoha orders probe of local universities' PhDs amid quality concerns', *Daily Nation*, 7 May 2019. https://www.nation.co.ke/business/Magoha-orders-probe-of-local-universities-PhDs/1950106-5104986-hgvku2/index.html

Overbye, Dennis 'For a Day, Scientists Pause Science to Confront Racism', *The New York Times*, 10 June 2020. https://www.nytimes.com/2020/06/10/science/science-diversity-racism-protests.html?referringSource=articleShare

Owino, Peres (director), *Bound: Africans vs African Americans* (motion picture), Los Angeles: Quiver, 2015.

Oxfam, *Wealth: Having It All and Wanting More*, Oxford: Oxfam GB, 2015. https://oxfamilibrary.openrepository.com/bitstream/handle/10546/338125/ib-wealth-having-all-wanting-more-190115-en.pdf;jsessionid=3632B6E6986C434FADD0C61E506D145F?sequence=8

———. *An Economy for the 99%*, Oxford: Oxfam GB, 2017. https://oi-files-d8-prod.s3.eu-west-2.amazonaws.com/s3fs-public/file_attachments/bp-economy-for-99-percent-160117-summ-en.pdf

———. *Time to Care*, Oxford: Oxfam GB, 2019. https://oxfamilibrary.openrepository.com/bitstream/handle/10546/620928/bp-time-to-care-inequality-200120-en.pdf

Oyewùmí, Oyèrónké, *The Invention of Women: Making an African Sense of Western Gender Discourses*, Minneapolis: University of Minnesota Press, 1997.

Patterson, Orlando, *Slavery and Social Death: A Comparative Study*, Cambridge, MA.: Harvard University Press, 2018.

Pazzanese Christina, 'After the protest … what next?', *The Harvard Gazette,* 11 June 2020. https://news.harvard.edu/gazette/story/2020/06/harvard-experts-discuss-how-to-effect-lasting-change/

Peck, Emily, 'Why the U.S. Needs to do Reparations Now', *Huffpost,* 8 June 2020. https://www.huffpost.com/entry/us-needs-reparations-black-americans_n_5ede5dfbc5b6fb8854dd8d00

Piketty, Thomas, *Capital in the Twenty-First Century*, Cambridge, MA: Harvard University Press, 2014.

POLITICO Magazine, 'Coronavirus Will Change the World Permanently. Here's How', 19 March 2020. https://www.politico.com/news/magazine/2020/03/19/coronavirus-effect-economy-life-society-analysis-COVID-135579

———. 'It Really is Different this Time', 4 June 2020. https://www.politico.com/news/magazine/2020/06/04/protest-different-299050

———. 'White America is Reckoning with Racism. It could reshape America', 9 June 2020. https://www.politico.com/news/2020/06/09/white-voters-2020-biden-304804

Pullman Bailey, Sarah, 'Southern Baptist president wants to retire famed gavel named for slave owner', *The Washington Post,* 11 June 2020. https://www.washingtonpost.com/religion/2020/06/10/southern-baptist-gavel-greear/

Putnam, Lara, Chenoweth, Erica and Pressman, Jeremy, 'The Floyd protests are the broadest in U.S. history—and are spreading to white, small-town America', *The Washington Post*, 6 June 2020. https://www.washingtonpost.com/politics/2020/06/06/floyd-protests-are-broadest-us-history-are-spreading-white-small-town-america/

Quick, Jonathan D., 'What we can learn from the 20th century's deadliest pandemic', *The Wall Street Journal*, 6 March 2020. https://www.wsj.com/amp/articles/what-we-can-learn-from-the-20th-centurys-deadliest-pandemic-11583510468

Robinson, Randall, *The Debt: What America Owes to Blacks*, New York: Dutton, 2001.

Rodney, Walter, *How Europe Underdeveloped Africa*, Washington, DC: Howard University Press, 1981 [1972].

Rono, Ruthie, 'Local Universities are facing serious crisis of confidence', *Business Daily*, 6 May 2019. https://www.businessdailyafrica.com/analysis/ideas/Local-universities-are-facing-crisis-of-confidence/4259414-5103274-9amivu/index.html

Rose, Gideon, *The Fourth Industrial Revolution: A Davos Reader*, Council on Foreign Relations, 2016.

Rosenbaum, Eric, 'Millions of Americans only $400 away from financial hardship. Here's why', *CNBC*, 23 May 2019. https://www.cnbc.com/2019/05/23/millions-of-americans-are-only-400-away-from-financial-hardship.html

Rostow, Walt Whitman. *The Stages of Economic Growth: A Non-Communist Manifesto*. Cambridge: Cambridge University Press, 1960.

Rozsa, Lori, Janes, Chelsea, Weiner Rachel and Achenbach, Joel, 'The battle over masks in a pandemic: An all-American story', *The Washington Post*, 19 June 2020. https://www.washingtonpost.com/health/the-battle-over-masks-in-a-pandemic-an-all-american-story/2020/06/19/3ad25564-b245-11ea-8f56-63f38c990077_story.html

Said, Edward, *Orientalism*, New York: Random House, 1979.

Sampson, Anthony *Mandela: The Authorised Biography*, New York: HarperCollins, 1999.

Sayej, Naja, '"It's a big turning point': Is this the end of racist monuments in America?' *Guardian*, 9 June 2020. https://www.theguardian.com/artanddesign/2020/jun/09/america-racist-monuments-civil-war-confederate?CMP=Share_iOSApp_Other

Scheidel, Walter, *The Great Leveler: Violence and the History of Inequality from the Stone Age to the Twenty-First Century*, Princeton, NJ: Princeton University Press, 2017.

Sehoole, Chika and Lee, Jenny, 'African student flows-Challenging prevailing paradigms', *University World News*, 15 June 2018. https://www.universityworldnews.com/post.php?story=20180614114114977

Specia, Megan, 'Top U.K Brands Urge #Solidaritea With Anti-Racism Protests', *The New York Times*, 18 June 2020. https://www.nytimes.com/2020/06/09/world/europe/yorkshire-tea-pg-tips-black-lives-matter.html

Steinberger, Michael 'What is the stockmarket even for any more?' *The New York Times*, 29 April 2020. https://www.nytimes.com/interactive/2020/05/26/magazine/stock-market-coronavirus-pandemic.html

Sullivan, Patricia, 'Thousands gathered across city to protest death of George Floyd', *The Washington Post*, 7 June 2020. https://www.washingtonpost.com/dc-md-va/2020/06/06/dc-protests-saturday-george-floyd/

Taylor, Alan, 'Images From a Worldwide Protest Movement', *The Atlantic*, 8 June 2020. https://www.theatlantic.com/photo/2020/06/images-worldwide-protest-movement/612811/

The Chronicle of Higher Education, *The Future of Work: How Colleges Can Prepare Students for the Jobs Ahead*, Washington, DC, 2017.

———. *The Future of The Degree: How Colleges Can Survive the New Credential Economy*, Washington, DC, 2017.

———. *The Future of Learning: How Colleges can Transform the Educational Experience*, Washington, DC, 2018.

———. *The New Generation of Students: How colleges can Recruit, Teach and Serve Gen Z*, Washington, DC, 2018.

———. *The Outsourced University: How Public–Private Partnerships can Benefit your Campus*, Washington, DC, 2019.

———. *The Almanac of Higher Education 2019–2020*. https://www.chronicle.com/package/the-almanac-of-higher-education-2019-20/

The Economist, 'Hopeless Africa', 11 May 2000. https://www.economist.com/leaders/2000/05/11/hopeless-africa.

———. 'Inequality Illusions', 30 November 2019.

———. 'Chinese Technology: From the people who brought you fireworks …', 4 January 2020.

———. 'Closed', 21 March 2020.

———. 'Fighting the Slump', 21 March 2020.

———. 'American protests turn jubilant', 11 June 2020. https://www.economist.com/united-states/2020/06/11/americas-protests-turn-jubilant

———. 'Bosses say they want to tackle racial injustice', 11 June 2020. https://www.economist.com/business/2020/06/11/bosses-say-they-want-to-tackle-racial-injustice

———. 'The power of protest and the legacy of George Floyd', 13 June 2020. https://www.economist.com/weeklyedition/2020-06-13

The Economist Intelligence Unit, 'Free speech under attack', Democracy Index 2017. http:// www.eiu.com/Handlers/WhitepaperHandler.ashx?fi=Democracy_Index_2017.pdf&mode= wp&campaignid=DemocracyIndex2017

The New York Times, 'The Real Suspense in Kenya', 13 August 2017. https://www.nytimes.com/2017/08/13/opinion/the-real-suspense-in-kenya.html

———. 'Sharpton Delivers Eulogy', 9 June 2020. https://www.nytimes.com/2020/06/09/us/george-floyd-funeral-protests.html?referringSource=articleShare

The New York Times Magazine, 'Why we Published The 1619 Project', 20 December 2019. https://www.nytimes.com/interactive/2019/12/20/magazine/1619-intro.html

'The Voices of the Loneliness Epidemic', *In Time We Trust*, 10 March 2020. http://www.rachidakiki.com/the-voices-of-the-loneliness-epidemic/

The Wall Street Journal, 'Trump prods police with executive order', 16 June 2020. https://www.wsj.com/articles/trump-signs-policing-executive-order-11592325988

The Washington Post, 'How COVID-19 is a perfect storm for black Americans', 26 April 2020. https://www.washingtonpost.com/opinions/2020/04/26/we-must-address-social-determinants-affecting-black-community-defeat-COVID-19/

Thorpe, Vanessa, 'Censoring old films and TV shows misses the point, say BAME leaders', *Guardian*, 13 June 2020. https://www.theguardian.com/world/2020/jun/13/censoring-old-films-and-tv-shows-misses-the-point-say-bame-leaders

Thompson, Alex, 'White America is reckoning with racism. It could reshape 2020', *POLITICO Magazine*, 9 June 2020. https://www.politico.com/news/2020/06/09/white-voters-2020-biden-304804

Times Higher Education, 'Best universities for graduate jobs: Global University Employability Ranking 2019'. https://www.timeshighereducation.com/student/best-universities/best-universities-graduate-jobs-global-university-employability-ranking.

———. Impact Rankings 2019. https://www.timeshighereducation.com/rankings/impact/2019/overall#!/page/0/length/25/sort_by/rank/sort_order/asc/cols/undefined

———. 'World University Rankings 2020'. https://www.timeshighereducation.com/world-university-rankings/2020/world-ranking#!/page/0/length/25/sort_by/rank/sort_order/asc/cols/stats

Tisdall, Simon, 'Trump uses force as a first resort. And now the firepower is aimed at his own people', *Guardian,* 7 June 2020. https://www.theguardian.com/commentisfree/2020/jun/07/trump-firepower-aimed-at-own-people-george-floyd?CMP=Share_iOSApp_Other

Tracy, Marc, 'Top Editor of Philadelphia Inquirer Resigns after "Buildings Matter" Headline', *The New York Times*, 9 June 2020. https://www.nytimes.com/2020/06/06/business/media/editor-philadephia-inquirer-resigns.htm

Trent, Sydney, 'Young Asians and Latinos push their parents to acknowledge racism amid protests', *The Washington Post*, 22 June 2020. https://www.washingtonpost.com/local/young-asians-and-latinos-push-their-parents-to-acknowledge-racism-amid-protests

The World Association of Cooperative and Work-Integrated Education (WACE). https://waceinc.org/

UN, Policy Brief: COVID-19 and the Need for Action on Mental Health, 20 May 2020. https://www.un.org/sites/un2.un.org/files/un_policy_brief-COVID_and_mental_health_final.pdf

UN, *World Population Prospects: Key findings and advance tables*, 2017 Revision. https://population.un.org/wpp/publications/Files/WPP2017_KeyFindings.pdf

United Nations Development Program, *Human Development Report 2019*, New York: UNDP, 2019. http://hdr.undp.org/sites/default/files/hdr2019.pdf

UNCTAD, *How COVID-19 is changing the world: A statistical perspective*, Committee for the Coordination of Statistical Activities, 2020. https://unstats.un.org/unsd/ccsa/documents/COVID19-report-ccsa.pdf

United Nations Department of Economic and Social Affairs, 'Greta Thunberg tells world leaders "You are failing us", as nations announce fresh climate action', September 2019. https://www.un.org/development/desa/youth/news/2019/09/greta-thunberg/

UNESCO, 'Distance learning strategies in response to COVID-19 school closures'. https://unesdoc.unesco.org/ark:/48223/pf0000373305

———. *General History of Africa*, London: Heinemann, 1981–1993.

———. 'Global monitoring of school closures caused by COVID-19'. https://en.unesco.org/COVID19/educationresponse

———. 'Health & nutrition during home learning'. https://unesdoc.unesco.org/ark:/48223/pf0000373277

———. 'Nurturing the social and emotional wellbeing of children and young people during crises'. https://unesdoc.unesco.org/ark:/48223/pf0000373271

———. 'Supporting teachers and educational personnel during times of crisis'. https://unesdoc.unesco.org/ark:/48223/pf0000373338

———. 'Unlocking the potential of family and intergenerational learning'. https://unesdoc.unesco.org/ark:/48223/pf0000373512

UNESCO, UIS, International student mobility in tertiary education. http://data.uis.unesco.org.

UNIDO, 'Coronavirus: the economic impact', 10 July 2020. https://www.unido.org/stories/coronavirus-economic-impact-10-july-2020

UNRISD, *Gender Equality: Striving for Justice in an Unequal World*, Geneva: United Nations Research Institute for Social Development, 2005. http://www.unrisd.org/80256B3C005BCCF9/search/1FF4AC64C1894EAAC1256FA3005E7201

University of Cape Town, 2019 Annual Financial Statement, 88. http://www.uct.ac.za/sites/default/files/image_tool/images/431/finance/operations/statements/afs2019.pdf

U.S. Department of Education, College Scorecard. https://collegescorecard.ed.gov

Vaitilingam, Romesh, 'How economists view the policy response to the COVID-19 so far', London School of Economics, 31 March 2020. https://blogs.lse.ac.uk/businessreview/2020/03/31/how-economists-view-the-policy-response-to-the-COVID-19-crisis-so-far/

Villarosa, Linda, '"A Terrible Price": The Deadly Racial Disparities of COVID-19 in America', *The New York Times,* 29 April 2020. https://www.nytimes.com/2020/04/29/magazine/racial-disparities-COVID-19.html?referringSource=articleShare

Wafula, Paul, 'Over one million rendered jobless in Kenya as COVID-19 takes toll on businesses', *The East African*, 5 June 2020. https://www.theeastafrican.co.ke/business/COVID19-Over-a-million-rendered-jobless-in-Kenya/2560-5571598-format-xhtml-13v1usc/index.html

Walkman, Paul, 'Why Donald Trump is standing up for the Confederacy', *The Washington Post,* 11 June 2020. https://www.washingtonpost.com/opinions/2020/06/11/why-donald-trump-is-standing-up-confederacy/

Weiwei, Zhang, 'How China Elects their political Leaders', *Vanguard*, 7 April 2018. https://www.vanguardngr.com/2018/04/china-elects-political-leaders-prof-zhang-weiwei/

Wilder, Craig Steven, *Ebony & Ivy: Race, Slavery and the Troubled History of America's Universities*, New York: Bloomsbury Publishing, 2013.

World Bank, World Development Indicators database. https://data.worldbank.org/indicator/NY.GDP.MKTP.PP.CD

———. *The Changing Wealth of Nations 2018: Building a Sustainable Future*, Washington, DC: The World Bank, 2018.

———. *Leveraging Economic Migration for Development*, World Bank Board Briefing Paper, Washington, DC: World Bank Group, 2019. https://www.knomad.org/sites/default/files/2019-08/World%20Bank%20Board%20Briefing%20Paper-LEVERAGING%20ECONOMIC%20MIGRATION%20FOR%20DEVELOPMENT_0.pdf

———. 'World Bank Scales-Up Its Support for Regional Higher Education Centers for Excellence in Africa', 3 April 2019. https://www.worldbank.org/en/news/press-release/2019/04/03/world-bank-scales-up-its-support-for-regional-higher-education-centers-for-excellence-in-africa

———. 'The World Bank in South Africa', 10 October 2019. https://www.worldbank.org/en/country/southafrica/overview

———. *Improving Higher Education Performance in Kenya: A Policy Report*, World Bank, Washington, DC, 2019. https://openknowledge.worldbank.org/handle/10986/32361

———. 'World Bank Group Increases COVID-19 Response to $14 Billion To Help Sustain Economies, Protect Jobs,' 17 March 2020. https://www.worldbank.org/en/news/press-release/2020/03/17/world-bank-group-increases-COVID-19-response-to-14-billion-to-help-sustain-economies-protect-jobs

———. *June 2020 Global Economic Prospects*, Washington, DC: World Bank, 2020. https://openknowledge.worldbank.org/bitstream/handle/10986/33748/9781464815539.pdf

World Economic Forum, 'Most people see COVID-19 as an economic crisis first, health risk second, survey finds', 18 March 2020. https://www.weforum.org/agenda/2020/03/COVID-19-public-perception-economic-health-crisis-coronavirus-pandemic-ipsos/

World Health Organization, 'Coronavirus disease (COVID-19) advice for the public.' https://www.who.int/emergencies/diseases/novel-coronavirus-2019/advice-for-public

———. 'New WHO estimates: Up to 190 000 people could die of COVID-19 in Africa if not controlled', 7 May 2020. https://www.afro.who.int/news/new-who-estimates-190-000-people-could-die-COVID-19-africa-if-not-controlled

———. 'COVID-19 could deepen food insecurity, malnutrition in Africa', 14 May 2020. https://who-africa.africa-newsroom.com/press/coronavirus-africa-COVID19-could-deepen-food-insecurity-malnutrition-in-africa

———. Coronavirus Disease (COVID-19) Dashboard 18 July 2020. https://COVID19.who.int

World Higher Education Database. https://www.iau-aiu.net/World-Higher-Education-Database-WHED

World Population Review, 'Countries That Allow Dual Citizenship 2020'. https://worldpopulationreview.com/country-rankings/countries-that-allow-dual-citizenship

World Wealth Report 2018. https://www.capgemini.com/service/world-wealth-report-2018/

Yahr, Emily, 'Lady Antebellum changes to Lady A, is "regretful and embarrassed" about the name's association with slavery era', *The Washington Post*, 11 June 2020. https://www.washingtonpost.com/arts-entertainment/2020/06/11/lady-antebellum-change-name-lady-a/

Yglesias, Mathew, 'The Great Awokening', *Vox*, 1 April 2020. https://www.vox.com/2019/3/22/18259865/great-awokening-white-liberals-race-polling-trump-2020?referringSource=articleShare

Younge, Gary 'What Black America means to Europe', *Guardian,* 11 June 2020. https://www.theguardian.com/world/2020/jun/11/what-black-america-means-to-europe-protests-racism-george-floyd?CMP=Share_iOSApp_Other

Zeleza, Paul Tiyambe, 'The Political Economy of British Colonial Development and Welfare in Africa', *Transafrican Journal of History* 14 (1985): 139-161.

———. *A Modern Economic History of Africa*, Dakar: CODESRIA Books, 1993.

———. *The Joys of Exile*, Toronto: House of Anansi Press, 1994.

———. 'The Perpetual Solitudes and Crises of African Studies in the United States Today', *Africa Today* 44, 2 (1997): 193-210.

———. *Manufacturing African Studies and Crises*. Dakar: CODESRIA Book Series, 1997.

———. 'The Past and Futures of African Studies and Area Studies', *Ufahamu* XXV, 2 (1999).

———. The Academic Diaspora and Knowledge Production in and on Africa: what Role for CODESRIA?, in Mkandawire Thandika (ed), *African Intellectuals: Rethinking Politics, Language, Gender and Development*, Dakar and London: CODESRIA Books and Zed Books, 2005.

——— (ed). *The Study of Africa, Volume 1: Disciplinary and Interdisciplinary Encounters*. Dakar: CODESRIA Book Series, 2006.

——— (ed). *The Study of Africa, Volume 2: Global and Transnational Engagements*. Dakar: CODESRIA Book Series, 2006.

———. The African Academic Diaspora: The Struggle for a Global Epistemic Presence, in Paul Tiyambe Zeleza (ed), *The Study of Africa Volume 2: Global and Transnational Engagements*, Dakar: CODESRIA Book Series, 2006, 86–111.

———. 'Angelina Jolie Discovers Africa', *Africa Resource*, 7 July 2006. https://www.africaresource.com/essays-a-reviews/essays-a-discussions/144-angelina-jolie-discovers-africa

———. 'Holding a Nation Hostage to a Bankrupt Political Class', *Pambazuka*, 4 January 2008. https://www.pambazuka.org/global-south/holding-nation-hostage-bankrupt-political-class

———. 'The Challenges of Studying the African Diasporas', *African Sociological Review* 12, 2 (2008): 4–21.

———. 'The Fall of Thabo Mbeki: Whither South Africa?' 20 September 2008. http://www.zeleza.com/blogging/u-s-affairs/fall-thabo-mbeki-whither-south-africa

———. *Barack Obama and African Diasporas: Dialogues and Dissensions*, Athens OH and Oxford UK: Ohio University Press and Ayebia, 2009.

———. 'What Happened to the African Renaissance? The Challenges of Development in the Twenty-First Century', *Comparative Studies of South Asia, Africa and the Middle East* 29, 2 (2009): 155–170.

———. 'Africa and Its Diasporas: Remembering South America', *Research in African Literatures* 40, 4 (2009): 142–164.

———. Diaspora Dialogues: Engagements between Africa and Its Diasporas, in Isidore Okpewho and Nkiru Nzegwu (eds), *The New African Diaspora: Assessing the Pains and Gains of Exile*, Bloomington and Indianapolis: Indiana University Press, 2009, 31–60.

———. 'African Diasporas: Towards a Global History', *African Studies Review* 53, 1 (2010): 1–19.

———. 'Reconceptualising African Diasporas: Notes from an Historian', *Transforming Anthropology* 18, 1 (2010): 74–78.

———. 'From African Studies and African American Studies to Africana Studies in the United States', *Afrika Focus* 24, 2 (2011): 15.

———. *In Search of African Diasporas: Testimonies and Encounters*. Durham, NC: Carolina Academic Press, 2012.

———. The Role of African Diasporas in Reconstruction, in Veney, Cassandra R. and Simpson, Dick (eds), *African Democracy and Development: Challenges for Post-Conflict African Nations*, Lanham, MD: Lexington Books, 2012: 185–218.

———. *Engagements between African Diaspora Academics in the U.S. and Canada and African Institutions of Higher Education: Perspectives from North America and Africa*. Report for Carnegie Corporation of New York, January 3, 2013. https://p.widencdn.net/af4g73/Engagements- between-African-Diaspora-Academics-and-Africa--Final-Report-2- for-distribution.

———. *Africa's Resurgence: Domestic, Global and Diaspora Transformations*, Los Angeles: TSEHAI Publishers, 2014.

———. The African Diaspora's Role in Forging US-Africa Relations, in Veney, Cassandra R (ed), *U.S.–Africa Relations from Clinton to Obama*, Lanham, MD: Lexington, 2014, 169–200.

———. Framing Paper, First African Higher Education Summit, Dakar, Senegal, March 2015. http://www.trustafrica.org/en/publications-trust/books-and-ebooks?download=410:african-higher-education-summit-revitalising-for-african-s-future

———. *The Transformation of Global Higher Education, 1945–2015*, New York: Palgrave Macmillan, 2016.

———. 'The Decolonization of African Knowledges', 9th Africa Day Lecture, University of the Free State, Bloemfontein, South Africa, 24 May 2017.

———. 'Positioning Universities as Engines of Innovation for Sustainable Development and Transformation', paper presented at the 2nd Biennial Conference on the State of Higher Education in Kenya, Commission for University Education, 30 October–2 November 2018, Nairobi, Kenya.

———. 'Leveraging Africa's Global Diasporas for the Continent's Development', paper presented at conference on Contribution of the Diaspora to Sustainable Blue Economy for National Development and International Solidarity, University of Nairobi, 26 November 2018.

———. 'Africa's persistent struggles for development and democracy in a multipolar world', *Canadian Journal of African Studies* 53, 1 (2019): 1–16.

———. 'The Fourth Industrial Revolution and African Universities', *The Elephant*, 17 October 2019. https://www.theelephant.info/ideas/2019/10/17/gen-z-the-fourth-industrial-revolution-and-african-universities/

Zeleza, Paul Tiyambe, and Adebayo Olukoshi, *African Universities in the 21st Century. Volume 1: Liberalization and Internationalization*. Dakar and Pretoria: CODESRIA Book Series and Unisa Press, 2004.

Zeleza, Paul Tiyambe and Adebayo Olukoshi, *African Universities in the 21st Century, Volume 2: Knowledge and Society*. Dakar and Pretoria: CODESRIA Book Series and Unisa Press, 2004.

Zeleza, Paul Tiyambe and Veney, Cassandra R., African Diasporas, Immigration and the Obama Administration, in Sharma, Dinesh and Gielen, Uwe P. (eds), *The Global Obama: Crossroads of Leadership in the 21st Century*, New York and London: Routledge, 2013: 99–114.

Index

H

I

J

Q

R

W

X

Y

Z

Lightning Source UK Ltd.
Milton Keynes UK
UKHW012032300121
377954UK00007B/121

9 782869 789975